Business and the State in

Developing Countries

A volume in the series

Cornell Studies in Political Economy

EDITED BY PETER J. KATZENSTEIN

A full list of titles in the series appears at the end of the book.

Business and the State in Developing Countries

Edited by

SYLVIA MAXFIELD AND
BEN ROSS SCHNEIDER

CORNELL UNIVERSITY PRESS

Ithaca and London

First published 1997 by Cornell University Press.
First printing, Cornell Paperbacks, 1997.

Library of Congress Cataloging-in-Publication Data

Business and the state in developing countries / edited by Sylvia
    Maxfield and Ben Ross Schneider.
        p.   cm. — (Cornell studies in political economy)
    Includes bibliographical references and index.
        ISBN 0-8014-3371-1 (alk. paper). — ISBN 0-8014-8406-5 (pbk. :
    alk. paper)
        1. Industrial policy—Developing countries.   2. Business and
    politics—Developing countries.   3. Developing countries—Economic
    policy.   I. Maxfield, Sylvia.   II. Schneider, Ben Ross.
    III. Series.
    HD3616.D452B87   1997   97-3385

Printed in the United States of America

Cornell University Press strives to utilize environmentally responsible suppliers and materials to the fullest extent possible in the publishing of its books. Such materials include vegetable-based, low-VOC inks and acid-free papers that are also either recycled, totally chlorine-free, or partly composed of nonwood fibers.

Cloth printing   10 9 8 7 6 5 4 3 2 1
Paperback printing   10 9 8 7 6 5 4 3 2 1

For our children
Max, Kate, and Zoë
Andy and Amelia

Contents

Contributors

JESSE BIDDLE teaches sociology at Pennsylvania State University.

RICHARD F. DONER is Associate Professor of Political Science at Emory University.

FRANCISCO DURAND is Assistant Professor of Political Science at the University of Texas in San Antonio.

PETER EVANS is Professor of Sociology at the University of California, Berkeley.

KARL FIELDS is Associate Professor of Political Science at the University of Puget Sound.

STEPHAN HAGGARD is Professor in the Graduate School of International Relations and Pacific Studies at the University of California, San Diego.

SYLVIA MAXFIELD is Associate Professor of Political Science at Yale University.

VEDAT MILOR was Assistant Professor of Sociology at Brown University and is currently studying law at Stanford University.

ANSIL RAMSAY is Professor of Government at St. Lawrence University.

BEN ROSS SCHNEIDER is Associate Professor of Political Science at Northwestern University.

MICHAEL SHAFER is Associate Professor of Political Science and Director of the Rutgers Citizenship and Service Education Program at Rutgers University.

EDUARDO SILVA is Assistant Professor of Political Science and a Fellow of the Center for International Studies at the University of Missouri, St. Louis.

ROSEMARY THORP is Professor of Economics at Oxford University.

Preface

This project was born of the multiple problems we found in the existing research and theory on relations between elite bureaucrats and capitalists. While an increasing number of scholars had identified this nexus as crucial to a variety of economic and political outcomes, the general and comparative work left much undone. Furthermore, existing arguments were so imbued with the suspicions of economists and Americanists that the question whether anything positive could come of close relations between business and the state rarely arose. Yet the question did come up with increasing frequency in the conclusions of dispersed empirical analyses of development in Asia and Latin America. Unfortunately, however, even studies that pointed to the benefits of collaboration rarely engaged one another.

This book began as an attempt to start a dialogue across disciplines and regional specializations. Ben Schneider drafted an initial agenda for discussion and began canvassing for potential participants. Sylvia Maxfield soon joined to help organize the first workshop, at Princeton University, in October 1993. We identified a small group of scholars who were already conducting research on business-state relations and invited them to relate that research to a common agenda and broaden their coverage of countries. Since the first meeting, the parallel projects of the participants proceeded; and books by Richard F. Doner and Ansil Ramsay, Peter Evans, Karl Fields, Michael Shafer, and Eduardo Silva have appeared or are on their way to publication. At a minimum, what distinguishes their contributions to this volume is the consistent engagement of a common theoretical agenda as well as sustained debate with the sometimes divergent perspectives taken by other contributors.

The debates at the first workshop, as well as the subsequent evolution of the project, were greatly enhanced and enlivened by the comments of Caren Addis, Alice Amsden, Eva Bellin, Kent Calder, Jeffry Frieden, Gary Gereffi, Robert Gilpin, Robert Kaufman, Atul Kohli, Ziya Önis, Adam Przeworski, Dani Rodrik, Helen Shapiro, John Waterbury, and Carol Wise. Stephan Haggard and Michael Shafer came to that meeting as discussants, but we later persuaded them to develop their contributions into chapters. Gregory Felker assisted ably with logistics and, with Katrina Burgess, drafted rapporteurs' reports. We thank the International Studies Program at Princeton University, sponsored by Title VI of the U.S. Department of Education, for funding this meeting. Sylvia Maxfield organized the second workshop, at Yale University, in December 1994. We are grateful to the Yale Provost's Office, and Arline McCord in particular, for allocating money from the Kempf Fund to support the Yale meeting. Kathleen Rosetti's keen administrative skills eased the job of organizing it. Thanks also to discussants and commentators at the meeting: James McGuire, James Mahon, David Cameron, and Walter Molano.

The Center for International and Comparative Studies (CICS) at Northwestern University provided the home base for the final stages of this project. We are grateful to CICS and its director, Bruce Cumings, for financial and administrative support and to Christina van Wijnbergen for her invaluable assistance in putting together the final manuscript. Roger Haydon went well beyond the call of editorial duty in his long and unflagging association with this project. He came to our first meeting and ever since has been a steady source of advice, encouragement, good humor, and suggestions.

SYLVIA MAXFIELD

New Haven, Connecticut

BEN ROSS SCHNEIDER

Evanston, Illinois

PART I

CONCEPTS AND ARGUMENTS

CHAPTER ONE

Business, the State, and Economic Performance in Developing Countries

BEN ROSS SCHNEIDER
AND SYLVIA MAXFIELD

In July 1995 the Brazilian tax authorities uncovered a scam in the government's International Trade System (SISCOMEX): a government official, who assumed the name of the Japanese actor Toshiro Mifune, logged phantom exports into the system's computer using the passwords of retired employees. The firms credited with these fictitious exports then received very real tax rebates.[1] What is remarkable about the story is not the apparent nonchalance of the perpetrators but how common such stories are in Brazil and many other developing countries. The general presumption is that when business and the state have close congenial relations, democratic ideals, economic efficiency, and social welfare will suffer. How can poorly paid officials defend the common weal when they come into close, lasting contact with capitalists who have keen appreciation of self-interest, flexible scruples, and vast resources? And if bureaucrats (not to mention contribution-dependent politicians) who mete out subsidies can be bought, why would rational capitalists invest in anything else?

Several strands of social science analysis, mostly from the perspectives of rational and public choice, elaborate on this common suspicion. According to Mancur Olson (1982), capitalists and their allies tend to

We are grateful to Richard Doner, Stephan Haggard, Blanca Heredia, Kenneth Shadlen, Jennifer Mansbridge, Kathleen Thelen, Michael Wallerstein, Jeffrey Winters, and many of the project participants for comments on previous drafts. Ben Schneider thanks the Center for International and Comparative Studies at Northwestern University for financial support and Sarah Hughes and Christina van Wijnbergen for research assistance.

[1] *Correio Brasilense,* 19 July 1995, pp. 1, 5, via e-mail.

3

form "distributional coalitions" that pressure the government to divert resources to them and away from their most efficient and socially optimal use. Olson's arguments draw on Anne Krueger's (1974) influential analysis of rent seeking, which spells out in greater detail the extent of economic dissipation caused by close relations between business and government. Rent-Seekers are wasteful because they both squander rents captured and invest more resources in pursuit of them. Jagdish Bhagwati (1982) developed a more precise if less felicitous taxonomy of "directly unproductive profit-seeking" (DUP) activities, which include tariff evasion, premium seeking, revenue seeking, and tariff seeking.[2] Whatever the terms, the consensus is that rents are irresistible. So potent is the temptation that Dennis Mueller postulated "the iron law" of rent seeking: "wherever a rent is to be found, a rent seeker will be there trying to get it" (1989: 241).

Given the wide circulation of such theories (discussed further in Chapter 2) as well as numerous journalistic accounts of corruption, "iron triangles," and pervasive venality in dealings between business and government, it is not surprising that scholars have devoted much attention to proposals to reduce the dangers in the relationship between business and the state. Diagnoses of rent seeking lead directly to prescriptions for market-oriented reform. If the problem is government provision of rents, then eliminating rents would allow business to concentrate its efforts on market competition and allocative efficiency. These motivations were strong in the Washington consensus on neoliberal reform in the developing world, especially Latin America, in the 1980s (see J. Williamson 1990).

Even if the trend toward freer markets persists, it is unwise to conclude that the problems of business-government relations are resolved. Market-oriented reforms have eliminated some points of potential collusion between business and government, but they have not eliminated contact altogether. For one thing the process of reform itself has created new rents—for example, in the privatization of state firms. More important, the road to markets is easier to negotiate if business actively cooperates. In both Mexico and Chile, as Schneider and Eduardo Silva show in their chapters, isolated reformers were initially less effective than their successors, who sought business input and cooperation. Moreover, once

---

[2] In this volume *subsidies* and *rents* are understood in the political sense: any policy-induced gain beyond what would be expected from a competitive market. Subsidies include any gain from grants, regulations, licenses, protection, tax incentives, or other government measures whether or not they involve direct transfers from government to business. Rent seeking is any unproductive activity designed to get subsidies from government. For more recent developments in the study of rent seeking, see Reynolds 1992, Alexeev and Leitzel 1991, other issues of *Public Choice*, and the compendium of articles in Tollison and Congleton 1995.

4

reformed, these economies offered newly unbound capitalists opportunities to abuse their market powers. Market failures in natural monopolies, finance, and public utilities clearly signaled the need for government regulations and bureaucrats to administer them (see, for example, Martin 1988). At a minimum, regulation entails monitoring and enforcement costs that in turn depend on the quality of relations between business and government. In practice, then, the issue is not whether business and government will have more or less close relations but how best to manage these relations.

In theory, and against the iron law of rent seeking, an eclectic group of institutionalists have argued that good, growth-enhancing relations between business and government elites are possible. The next section of this chapter draws on this literature to develop further the positive case that collaboration between business and the state can contribute to development. Nevertheless, the institutionalist case is typically cast at such an aggregate level it is difficult to specify the causal mechanisms. Precisely what in the relationship leads capitalists to be more efficient than they would otherwise be? Understanding these causal mechanisms requires going beyond existing institutionalist formulations. Our goal is to disaggregate various facets of the relationship in order to specify their impact on various aspects of economic performance, such as policy implementation, exporting, and investment. Ironically, choice theories and microeconomic analysis contribute a great deal to this disaggregation and consequent elaboration of the institutionalist position.

The next section answers the question *how* a collaborative relationship can enhance performance but doesn't tell us *when* the relationship is more likely to be collaborative than collusive. A relationship that enhances economic performance is probably not in equilibrium because it is subject to strong corrupting temptations. Therefore, the following section analyzes the conditions that keep benign collaboration from degenerating into collusion. An insulated, meritocratic bureaucracy is a first bulwark against corruption. But such bureaucracies are scarce in the cases covered in this book and in the developing world as a whole. In their absence, self-policing business associations as well as encompassing firms and associations reduce, ex ante, the likelihood that collaborative relations will degenerate into collusion and rent seeking. In the final section the analysis moves further up the causal chain to consider the threats and vulnerabilities that encourage state and business elites to invest in cooperation and in institutions that diminish incentives for "opportunism with guile." These threats differ across actors; business usually responds to economic competition and state actors to political threats to their survival.

5

Unpacking Collaboration

In the past decade institutionalist analyses of development have often concluded that relations between business and government account for a large part of the variation in economic performance.[3] Alice Amsden, for example, concludes her pathbreaking study of Korea with the general conclusion that "the more reciprocity that characterizes state-firm relations . . . , the higher the speed of economic growth" (1989: 146). Nearly all states in developing countries hand out subsidies; what distinguishes high-growth countries is that their governments exact improved firm performance in exchange for subsidies. Such reciprocity is in turn premised on state capacity to monitor firms and punish noncompliance as well as business willingness to provide information and abide by sanctions.

According to Peter Evans, "embedded autonomy"—where bureaucrats have close ties to business yet are still able to formulate and act on preferences autonomously—"is the key to the developmental state's effectiveness" and the factor that best explains divergent patterns of industrial transformation (1989: 574). Embedded autonomy depends on "an apparently contradictory combination of Weberian bureaucratic insulation with intense immersion in the surrounding social structure" (16). As Evans highlights in his chapter in this book, neither autonomy nor embeddedness alone is effective; it is the combination that accelerates development.

In Southeast Asia, Richard Doner has found "differences in the relations between governments and business to be the most important explanation of cross-national variation in sectoral bargaining performance" (1991: 4–5). In Latin America, Rosemary Thorp concludes that economic policy was consistently more effective in Colombia than in Peru in large part because the relationship between the state and the private sector in Colombia was "characterized by greater mutual confidence and respect" (1991: 195).[4] In these major studies of development, the dependent vari-

---

[3] This approach is common in research on industrial countries (Katzenstein 1978). In the 1980s, interest in European corporatism kept the focus on relations between state and business. By the 1990s, this interest had evolved into an analysis of governance, which focused heavily on institutional intermediation between business and government (see especially Hollingsworth et al. 1994). In the study of Japan, controversy has been greater between statists such as Chalmers Johnson (1982) and anti-statists such as David Friedman (1988). Other scholars take a more ecumenical view that both business and the state, and good relations between them, are indispensable to a full explanation of Japan's economic success (Okimoto 1989; Samuels 1987; Sabel 1994). For a recent review of the literature on developed countries and an argument that state-society relations account for variations in competitiveness, see Hart 1992.

[4] A large literature in the 1970s and 1980s on business-state relations in Latin America analyzed multinational corporations (MNCs). For one of the last works in this literature and a review of previous work, see Bennett and Sharp 1985. Many studies argued that states

6

able changes from growth to state effectiveness to bargaining performance, but in each case the authors conclude that relations between business and the state had a decisive impact on economic outcomes.

Studies by these and other scholars concluded that collaboration is associated with rapid development, but they did not explain the precise causal connections between collaboration and economic performance. Many things transpire in meetings, phone conversations, or handshakes between bureaucrats and capitalists. What exactly changes subsequent behavior on either or both sides? Moreover, the dependent variable of development is so aggregate and depends on so many other factors that it is very difficult to isolate the contribution of collaboration between business and government. The solution for furthering the research is to disaggregate collaborative relations between bureaucratic and business elites and assess the impact of separate features of these relations on specific aspects of economic performance, which in turn have consequences for overall growth.

The rest of this section focuses on information exchange, reciprocity, credibility, and trust and discusses how these features contribute to better policies that are flexibly adjusted and encourage businesses to make productive use of government assistance rather than squandering it and investing in seeking more. Economic policies, even those designed according to the best available theories, can fail for a variety of reasons. Foremost among these reasons are incomplete information in policy formulation, ineffective implementation (for example, when private agents choose not to comply), and negative side effects (when policies induce rent seeking and corruption). This range of dependent variables of economic performance can also be expressed in terms of costs. Effective policies can entail high information costs, monitoring costs, uncertainty costs, and rent-seeking costs. As we discuss in greater detail later in this chapter, features of close communicative relations between bureaucrats and capitalists, such as credibility or reciprocity, reduce one or several of these costs. Moreover, these features interact and generally reinforce one another. The first step, however, is to distinguish these various aspects of business-state relations analytically and then isolate their impacts on policy-making and economic performance.

Information

An increased flow of accurate, reliable information between business and the government is the first potential benefit of close relations. This

could negotiate better deals with MNCs, but most shared the view that close relations would generally not promote long-term social welfare.

exchange depends on the technical capacity within the state to compile and analyze data and on the willingness, mostly of business, to share it. Basic data collection is precarious in most developing countries; so when a great deal of information flows easily from business to state actors, it can significantly improve the information base that officials use to evaluate policy options. Most policies aim to provoke some change in the behavior of private economic agents; therefore, the more accurately that policymakers can predict the responses of these agents, the more likely it is that the policy will have the desired effect. Policies that fit industrial and economic reality will be more credible. Information flows are central to Evans's concept of embedded autonomy, for embeddedness allows state actors to "secure full information" (1992: 158). In his discussion of India, Evans highlights the lack of policy networks that would allow officials "to collect and disseminate information" (174). Moreover, the "Indian state cannot count on the private sector . . . as a source of information about what kind of industrial policy will 'fly' " (1995: 69). Mexico's negotiations over the North American Fair Trade Agreement (NAFTA), discussed in Schneider's chapter in this book, illustrate the value of this form of information exchange: Government negotiators with no previous experience in trade policy relied on private exporters to bring them up to speed on practical issues in trade with the United States.

The timely flow of accurate and relevant information in the opposite direction, from state to business, can enhance performance on the business side. If the state provides information on sectoral markets, export opportunities (as Michael Shafer notes in the case of the Korean Trade Promotion Corporation [KOTRA]), labor market conditions, and other issues that affect investment planning, then this planning can be more precise and efficient. Such information can, of course, be disseminated without close interaction between business and government, but closer interaction allows officials to target recipients to ensure that the right information gets to the right managers. Other crucial information flows, both formal and informal, shape expectations about government intentions and enhance the credibility of government policies by giving investors signals about political commitments to particular courses of action. In his chapter, Karl Fields argues that a tight relationship between business associations and government officials can serve this sort of "transmission belt" function.[5]

---

[5] A more recent and visible illustration of the effects of information flows on credibility came in the wake of the 1994 peso crisis. The Mexican government, pressured by the U.S. Treasury, agreed to make announcements (posted on the Internet) on its international currency reserves every week rather than every three months (as it had done before the crisis). Such information on reserves is indispensable to the credibility of any government commitment on exchange rates.

Of course, the exchange of information between business and state actors is complicated by information asymmetries and incentives on both sides to manipulate the exchange strategically. Government officials have strong political incentives to control information. In 1994, Rubens Ricúpero, then finance minister of Brazil, had the misfortune to admit to such manipulation while under the mistaken impression that the microphones had been turned off. In the second month of the Real Plan to reduce inflation (on which Cardoso based his ultimately successful presidential campaign) Ricúpero said he had "no scruples" about manipulating information: "What is good we publicize; what is bad we hide."[6] In his chapter, Shafer highlights the importance of business sectors in determining initial asymmetries. Specifically, light manufacturing uses simple technologies, so state actors do not have to rely on business for information and expertise. As we discuss later, the *incentives* to exploit such information asymmetries depend heavily on how information influences the distribution of government benefits.

Business associations are often crucial conduits for the exchange of information in both directions (as analyzed in the chapters on Korea, Taiwan, and Mexico). Associations can aggregate data before passing it on to government and at the same time reduce firms' incentives to bias information on their individual performance. Moreover, states have ways to control information in associations that they lack in firms. Fields documents the enormous direct control that states in Korea and Taiwan have over associations, including personnel recruitment and appointment, which enhances the state's capacity to gather accurate data on firms.

Transparency provides another mechanism to remove information from the hands of those who might manipulate it. Transparency is a passive form of information exchange, distinct because the availability of information as much as the information itself affects behavior. Although scarce in developing countries, transparency in government decision making, through dissemination of decision rules and criteria, can reduce political uncertainty for investors. Moreover, transparency in the distribution of rents, as in opening closed bids for utility concessions in a public forum, nips rent-seeking temptations in the bud. If capitalists know that unproductive rent seekers will be exposed, then they will not worry about the potential competitive disadvantage of not seeking rents. In the private sector, transparency in business operations can reduce greatly the costs of government monitoring. If firms know that information on their behavior is readily available, then they will be more likely to behave as if government investigators were watching them closely.

---

[6] *Latin American Regional Report: Brazil,* 22 September 1994, p. 1. See Cukierman and Meltzer 1986 for a formal theoretical treatment.

Reciprocity

Once state actors possess relatively unbiased information, their next issue is whether they can act to sanction subsidy recipients who do not use the subsidies as they were intended. The free exchange of information is regularly enlisted in the pursuit of private gain at the expense of the public good. In economic theory rational investors will respond to subsidies; the hard part is to keep them from shirking or worse. For Amsden, reciprocity "means that in direct exchange for subsidies, the state exacts certain performance standards from firms" (1989: 146). Hence, state actors must have the capacity and autonomy to require improved performance in return for subsidies.

Some governments require subsidy recipients to promise to do something to promote development but then lack the capacity to follow up (as Jesse Biddle and Vedat Milor discuss in respect to Turkey). In order to enforce reciprocity, government officials need to know that firms receiving subsidies are doing something in return. But if subsidies are contingent on performance, then firms have a strong incentive to distort information on performance. Performance targets that are clear and measurable reduce opportunities to manipulate information. Toshiro Mifune scams notwithstanding, export performance is easier to measure, more transparent, and harder to distort than policy goals such as technological development or increases in productivity. Perhaps it is not trade per se that has a positive impact on growth but trade in countries with interventionist states. That is, free trade itself is less important than the ease of monitoring export performance in countries where reciprocity is essential to the success of industrial policies.

Finally, some governments make reciprocal agreements and monitor compliance but lack the ability to discipline or punish subsidy abusers. If the state does not discipline miscreants, then its demands for reciprocity lose credibility. In principle, disciplining should not be too costly because punishing only a few firms signals government intentions and establishes credibility. Park's Law on Illicit Wealth Accumulation is one of the more notorious examples of discipline (see Fields in this book; Amsden 1989; E. M. Kim 1988). But when firms are big and politically influential and governments are weak, both common situations in developing countries, then even simple signals can be too costly. When governments make it a policy to bail out troubled firms, as in Brazil and Mexico in the 1970s and early 1980s (or in savings and loan firms in the United States), they invite abuse.

Credibility

Government credibility, which reduces a major source of political uncertainty, is another calming influence on business anxieties over whether state actors will manipulate information. Many economic policies have problems of time or dynamic inconsistency because governments have incentives to promise rewards before investors commit; then to change policies once they have committed (Hillier and Malcomson 1984; Rodrik 1989). For example, governments often offer lengthy tax holidays for businesses that invest in particular activities, regions, or sectors. Once the firms have invested, however, government policymakers, particularly the incoming appointees of new governments, have incentives to cancel the holidays. Capitalists consequently have reason to discount the value of the incentives and withhold investment unless officials can make credible long-term commitments.

When policies are reasonably sound, credibility has mostly positive consequences for economic performance. For example, political uncertainty has a high cost in terms of postponed or foregone private investment (Cukierman 1980; Pindyck 1993). In one forceful argument, Aymo Brunetti and Beatrice Weder go so far as to claim "that problems of credibility constitute the major obstacle to a better growth performance of many LDCs" (1994: 27). States in developing countries have come increasingly to rely on private economic agents to execute the changes that policymakers want. Credibility in this context means that capitalists believe what state actors say and then act accordingly. For Evans this execution is a key aspect of embeddedness because it allows officials to "count on the private sector for effective implementation" (1992: 158). Enacting policies that lack credibility can be worse than doing nothing at all. Of course, credible governments can enact wrongheaded policies; other aspects of collaboration such as information exchange can increase the probability of detection and correction.

The credibility of a policy measure depends on numerous factors, including the type of policy, the flows of information discussed earlier, the reputations of officials associated with the measure, the degree of institutionalization of the rules and agencies involved, and the political backing of the government adopting the policy. For some economists the key is to eliminate government discretion through strong constitutions, democratic checks and balances, and the rule of law (see Cukierman and Meltzer 1986; Brunetti and Weder 1994). But in many policies intended to promote economic transformation, discretion is likely to continue to be the rule. Here, interactions between business and government, especially repeated interactions that generate trust, can have a positive impact on credibility that is independent from the characteristics of the policy or implementing agency.

To the extent that credibility depends on tying the hands of policy-makers, it constrains another benefit, flexibility, which is also associated with close relations between business and state elites. For Evans, embed-dedness further provides "institutionalized channels for the continual negotiation and renegotiation of goals and policies" (Evans 1992: 164). Such flexibility is often noted as a factor in successful implementation of economic policy (see Stallings and Brock 1993; World Bank 1993a). Too much flexibility, however, creates problems of a different sort in business-state relations. According to some economists, if the government is a willing negotiator, its responsiveness undermines its credibility (Rodrik and Zeckhauser 1988). To create an appropriate balance, policymakers must adjust policies in ways necessary to respond to new conditions without giving investors the impression that they are abandoning the policy itself. Information exchange, transparency, and trust can all permit state actors to be both flexible and credible.

Trust

Effective collaboration between capitalists and officials implies exten-sive mutual dependence or vulnerability. Bureaucrats depend on man-agers to implement policies, and capitalists depend on bureaucrats to ensure the profitability of investments made in furthering these policies. Credibility and trust are both crucial in managing this mutual depen-dence. Credible is an adjective applied to particular policies; trust char-acterizes a more enduring and multifaceted relationship.[7] Policies can be credible whether or not trust exists, depending on immediate factors such as political support for the government or policy design; but prior trust makes all policies and statements more credible (see Rodrik 1989). More generally, a relationship of trust subsumes most features discussed so far: credibility, transparency, and reciprocity.

Economists have long extolled the positive effects of trust on economic performance, especially on reducing transaction costs. In principle, trust is "extremely efficient and makes the whole economy work better" (Arrow 1974: 23). In poor countries the lack of trust between economic agents can inhibit all types of beneficial exchanges and retard overall develop-

---

[7] Oliver Williamson cites Gambetta's definition of trust as fairly consensual: Trust "is a particular level of the subjective probability with which an agent assesses that another agent or group of agents will perform a particular action. . . . When we say we trust someone . . . we implicitly mean that the probability that he will perform an action that is beneficial . . . is high enough for us to consider engaging in some form of cooperation with him" (1993: 463). See Gambetta 1988 and Coleman 1990.

ment (Leff 1986: 2 and passim). In industrial countries, trust is an elixir for many economic woes, and overall "high trust systems" are more competitive (Soskice 1991; Lorenz 1993; Fukuyama 1995).[8] Societies where trusting is common are said to have large stocks of "social capital," which, when marshalled into service with other forms of capital, are a boon for the economy (Putnam 1993a, 1993b; see also Coleman 1988).

Much of this literature on trust and social capital is too aggregate to use in analyzing relations between elite bureaucrats and capitalists. The studies in this book do not delve into the enduring cultures of the elites they examine nor the national stock of social capital. Trust in business-government relations is a more specific, calculated, contingent phenomenon where protagonists on each side expect those on the other not to betray them.[9] In this book such circumscribed trust emerges in societies such as Mexico, Colombia, and Turkey, which do not usually rank high on national comparisons of trust and social capital.

Trust between business and government elites can reduce transaction and monitoring costs, diminish uncertainty, lengthen time horizons, and thereby increase investment (and policy fulfillment generally) above normal levels. Capitalists commit themselves and their resources beyond what they would in response to material incentives in any particular policy because they know that, if the going gets tough, the state will stick by them. Thorp's description of Colombia is worth quoting at length because it appears to apply to trust in other developing countries. She characterizes business trust of government officials in Colombia as "widespread confidence that the web of friendships and contacts is such that interests will be sensibly looked after. Thus with regard to an import control policy, for example, there is trust that the system will be 'reasonably' operated. This does not mean that some abstract and neutral system will arbitrate, but that reasonable common sense and practicality will prevail" (1991: 197–98).

Trust can shore up wobbly property rights. Pervasive discretionary state intervention weakens property rights and exacerbates political uncertainty. (At the same time it can reduce market uncertainty.)[10] The impo-

---

[8] Moreover, trust helped declining industries in Pennsylvania adjust (Sabel 1992), and trust infuses successful subcontracting practices in Japan (Smitka 1991). See also Hardin 1993, who reviews other studies on the benefits of trust.

[9] Oliver Williamson (1993) distinguishes between calculative trust, where individuals trust one another because of some expected gain, and societal trust, where individuals trust one another because the institutional environment enforces relations of trust. The trust we examine in this book is closest to calculative trust. The distinction between calculative and societal trust corresponds to the distinction made in Chapter 2 between strategic and embedded networks.

[10] On political sources of uncertainty, see Barzelay 1986, Przeworski and Wallerstein 1988, and Stewart and Venieris 1985.

sition of import quotas, for example, shifts investor attention from international markets to the officials who distribute the quotas. Subsequent changes in subsidies and policies can be tantamount to confiscation. Government instability or influential bureaucrats with doubts about capitalism exacerbate political uncertainty and can thereby reduce private investment and increase the risk premium in expected return (and hence raise the social cost of private investment). In contrast, trust between officials and industrialists can reduce political uncertainty and increase the flow of long-term, low-cost investment. In this sense, informal trust substitutes for formal property rights.

Of all the aspects of business-government interaction discussed in this section, trust provides the greatest benefits to various aspects of economic performance and generally improves other aspects of the relationship. Trust increases the voluntary exchange of information, makes reciprocity more likely even without active monitoring and disciplining, and generally reduces uncertainty and increases credibility on all sides. Trust, of course, is also the feature that is most costly and time-consuming to construct and easiest to destroy. Most state and business elites, especially in developing countries, face relative distrust and hence must work on other, more immediately tractable aspects of the relationship. Even when it exists, trust is problematic because it is a neutral instrument that can be used effectively to promote any kind of activity, from corruption through export expansion.

Trust, in the narrow sense used here, depends on friendships, contacts, and common sense and thus is sensitive to changes in personnel. Trust between bureaucrats and capitalists depends first on the length of their interaction, both past and expected.[11] When individual bureaucrats and industrialists interact over long periods of time and expect to continue doing so, they become predictable to one another, and the cost of defection increases. In addition, the movement of retiring bureaucrats to private firms enhances trust when it strengthens personal ties between bureaucrats and the new managers, reduces monitoring costs, and gives sitting bureaucrats incentives not to betray future employers (see Schneider 1993a). In sum, calculative or instrumental trust does not

[11] Chapter 2 continues the analysis of trust within networks. See O. Williamson 1993 for a recent review. Soskice notes that there are no high-trust systems where relations between economic agents are short term (1991: 49). Additional factors that enhance trust in other relations include common socialization and multifaceted interaction, where, for example, defection in business can be punished by exile from the extended family (Leff 1986). These factors do not seem to be universally important, although they may be in cases such as Japan and France, where university and career socialization are strong (see Taira and Wada 1987 on Japan). In Chapter 5, Fields highlights the strength of regional and school ties in Taiwan and especially Korea.

depend on diffuse cultural or social norms; rather, the cost of opportunism in long-term relations becomes prohibitive. Over time, however, norms of trust and reciprocity can assume an aura of a moral economy of capital. (On moral economy within business groups, see Granovetter 1994.)

Despite the overall skepticism in much of the literature on business-state relations, this section has identified aspects of the relationship that can, in principle, enhance performance by both government and business. Moreover, the methodological disencounter between skeptical choice theorists and optimistic institutionalists has not helped advance the analysis of more beneficial relations. Unpacking the relationship shows that in fact arguments on the potential benefits of collaboration can be drawn from microeconomic and game theoretic analyses that go beyond the conventional wisdom of venal bureaucrats and rent-seeking capitalists. Identifying ways in which the interaction can be positive does not mean that all or even most interactions are likely to be so. Most of the rest of the volume is devoted to specifying how and when business-government relations contribute to, rather than detract from, development. The next section summarizes these arguments.

THE CONDITIONS FOR COLLABORATION

What sustains the collaborative advantage that some countries or sectors have over others?[12] What keeps collaborative government-business relations from degenerating into the unproductive exchange of favors for bribes? The chapters in this book identify several key characteristics of the state and of business organization that mitigate the tendency for government-business relations to degenerate into unproductive, rent-seeking activity. The studies first confirm the traditional argument that collusion and corruption are less likely where bureaucracies are more insulated and Weberian (by which Evans means bureaucracies characterized by meritocratic recruitment and promotion, career service, and reasonable pay and prestige). The contributions to this volume also examine cases where officials in non- or unevenly Weberian bureaucracies (the dominant type in the developing world) interacted closely with capitalists without succumbing to unproductive collusion. In some cases other features of the state (a hard budget constraint, for example) kept rent seeking in check. In others, collective business action, or developmental associations,

---

[12] The term *collaborative advantage* is from Saxenian 1994.

worked to minimize incentives for "directly unproductive profit-seeking" (DUP) activity.

State Characteristics

In the now conventional view of state intervention in development, the insulation of policymakers from societal pressures is essential for success. Evans and other contributors to this book focus on the importance of a career civil service, a Weberian bureaucracy, and the resulting coherence of the state. As Biddle and Milor note, in a bureaucracy with "'Weberian' characteristics . . . individual business agents have little opportunity to rent-seek successfully because bureaucrats' self-interest is firmly anchored to institutional goals and not easily diverted toward private ends." Evans writes that "certain states are able to bind the behavior of individual incumbents to the pursuit of common goals. They are coherent bureaucracies in the Weberian sense of the term." When the state is a coherent corporate body rather than a collection "of individual maximizers masquerading as organizations in pursuit of the common good . . . dense ties with the business community can become vehicles for the construction of joint public-private projects in pursuit of economic transformation."

Fields's chapter illustrates the extent to which Korean and Taiwanese bureaucracies approximate the Weberian ideal. He notes that after Park Chong Hee seized power in Korea in 1961, he staffed the "economic bureaucracy with talented personnel bound in a Weberian sense by a shared confidence in their own skills and their national mission." In restoring the Weberian bureaucracy Park drew on a long Korean (and Japanese and Chinese) Confucian tradition of meritocratic civil service. Fields argues that Taiwanese leaders in the 1970s consciously tried to emulate the bureaucracy that Park had built in Korea. Moreover, he notes that ethnic divisions between officials from the Chinese mainland and Taiwanese capitalists enhanced the state's insulation (in ways not dependent on Weberian features of the bureaucracy) but also made it more difficult to embed officials.

A Weberian bureacracy (especially expertise, meritocratic promotion, and long tenure in office) enhances most of the features of a collaborative relationship discussed in the previous section. The expertise of Weberian bureaucrats enhances their ability to collect and possess information and monitor firm behavior. Promotion by merit criteria is the key feature that insulates bureaucrats from pressures and hence allows them to exact reciprocity and make credible longer-term commitments. The linchpin in theories of rent seeking is that capitalists invest in lobbying only if they perceive a reasonable probability of success. If meritocratic procedures for promotion insulate bureaucrats from lobbying, then the probabilities fall, and rent seeking ceases to be a profitable alternative to productive investment (see Tollison and Congleton 1995).[13]

Other findings in this book highlight the features of bureaucracy that embed rather than insulate. Evans and others emphasize that the key for business-state collaboration is insulation, not isolation. To extend the weather metaphor, embedded officials can be individually rather than institutionally insulated; they can foray outside the state with good coats rather than huddle inside insulated structures. Some features of bureaucratic careers make officials more autonomous and less easily pressured and corrupted. Other features embed them, especially incentives that reward bureaucrats who seek out close ties to business rather than hide behind a desk in a ministry.[14] Moreover, long tenure in a Weberian bureaucracy permits extended interaction with business and allows personal trust and networks to develop. In Taiwan, KMT (Guomindang) leaders were preoccupied with maintaining strict state autonomy, yet business and government elites nonetheless found intriguing ways to promote embeddedness. In one instance described by Fields, bureaucrats and businessmen used the pretext of a shared lunar birth month to build social networks. In the context of a non-Weberian bureaucracy, Rosemary Thorp and Francisco Durand argue that pervasive movement in and out of the Colombian bureaucracy was instrumental in creating the networks that embedded state officials.

Business associations provide other means to construct dense networks between business and state officials. In Taiwan the government appointed ex-government officials of unquestioned loyalty to run compulsory business associations. Similarly, in Korea businesses hire retiring officers and officials to staff their associations. In both countries the associations serve as valuable and reliable sources of information for state officials. Here, and in the case of Turkish ready-wear clothing, the presence of ex-officials seems to make the associations extensions of the public sphere: the association leaders are extensions (*handmaiden* is the term Fields uses to describe Taiwanese associations) of the economic bureaucracy rather than representatives of the private sector. These cases of business associations' being run by ex-officials make it clear that we need to think of "capture" as potentially working in either direction, depending on the

---

[13] Moreover, Weber emphasized that the long-term rewards of a civil service career needed to be well known and predictable. This feature bears emphasis in a discussion of business-state relations, where the short-term material temptations can be huge. Here, for example, patterns of movement from public employment to well-paid positions in the private sector at the end of a successful public career may ease the short-term pressures and make the cumulative rewards of a career in bureaucracy very high.

[14] For an interesting example, see Leonard's 1977 analysis of agricultural extension in Kenya. See also Schneider 1993a.

force of different incentives in the career trajectories of the officials involved.

Weberian bureaucracy is the exception rather than the rule in developing countries. Nonetheless, the cases examined in this book provide examples of positive government-business interaction in the absence of a merit-based, politically insulated bureaucracy. In Chile, for example, administrative reforms in the 1970s and 1980s moved the bureaucracy in a Weberian direction; nevertheless, Silva highlights other features of the bureaucracy. Low porosity, another term for insulation, freed officials from particularistic pressures (although in Chile it was enforced through dictatorship rather than Weberian procedures). Silva also emphasizes the impact of hierarchy or unity in command on the coherence of economic policy, which is crucial in establishing credibility, especially for economy-wide reforms. Finally, technocrats and technocratic discourse were important, although less for autonomy than for embeddedness. In other words, Silva argues that, a common technocratic language facilitated communication between business and government and helped to embed new officials, even from a potentially threatening center-left government, in business networks.[15]

Doner and Ansil Ramsay highlight two other state characteristics that inhibit unproductive government-business interaction when, as in Thailand, the bureaucracy is politicized and porous. First, when rival government factions compete for clients among the business community by giving out favors (licenses, subsidies, tax breaks), their value is rapidly competed away. This competitive clientelism reduced barriers to entry; and because rents gained were generally temporary, Doner and Ramsay conclude that "recipients had to limit inefficient investments in anticipation of market competition." Second, a hard budget constraint imposed by the Thai central bank and the Finance Ministry limited the potential damage that clientelism could cause. Elsewhere the costs of clientelism, even where competitive, tend to exceed government resources in ways that are inflationary and detrimental to the economy as a whole. But if other political and institutional forces keep spending within fiscal balance, then the typical disruptions characteristic of unbridled clientelism can be avoided.[16]

---

[15] Katzenstein, citing Harold Wilensky, emphasizes the importance of shared technical expertise in facilitating "social partnership" across deep ideological divides in small corporatist countries of Europe (1985b: 88).

[16] Doner and Ramsay found in the Thai case that the hard budget constraint was the result of fears on the part of political leaders in the late nineteenth and early twentieth centuries concerning capital flight. As such, it provides a revealing example of the interaction over time of the positive force of business-as-capital to restrain business-as-network (discussed further in Chapter 2).

Most of the countries examined in this book were governed by authoritarian regimes for most of the period analyzed, so political regime was not a central causal factor in explaining variation among the cases. Logically (and empirically in some of the cases) democracy affects most of the conditions for sustaining collaborative relations, especially by bringing labor and politicians back into the picture. Labor was conspicuously absent in most of the empirical chapters largely because labor in most developing countries has been weak, disorganized, and repressed. Democratization and socioeconomic modernization have changed the political position of labor and have two major implications for business-state relations. First, the changing strength and strategy of organized labor will likely alter business strategies for collective action. In Brazil Schneider documents the novel role played by labor when the metalworkers' union coaxed business and the state to sit down to discuss long-term sectoral development in the automobile industry. These sectoral negotiations changed business associations (especially relations among upstream and downstream associations) at the same time they recast business relations with government and labor.[17] To the extent that the state in developing countries withdraws as the primary arbiter of industrial relations and business associations begin to bargain collectively, labor relations will have stronger influences on business organization and by extension business-government relations.

Second, what happens to collaboration between business and government when labor is included in the negotiations? At a minimum, relations become more complex, more formal, and more involved with distributional issues. In this sense, incorporating labor leaders may make close business-government collaboration less likely. But they may also help actors on the state side inhibit collusion and rent seeking. Labor representatives will likely have a keen appreciation for exacting reciprocity from business, especially if they, too, are making concessions to business, and will therefore be willing to invest in monitoring. Evans concludes his chapter along these lines, arguing that unless embedded autonomy becomes more inclusive it is likely to become "self-limiting and ultimately self-defeating."

Democracy squeezes elected politicians into all sorts of previously exclusive relations between bureaucrats and capitalists. The issue for bureau-

---

[17] This experience echos findings in research on industrial countries that document how labor affected business-state relations by encouraging collective action by business. In a comparison of the organization of construction firms in Britain and Germany, Wyn Grant and Wolfgang Streeck conclude that differences in industrial relations go "a long way in explaining the variation" in business association (1985: 166). In his analysis of the coal industry in the United States, Bowman (1989) also attributes to labor a major impetus to collective action by capitalists.

cratic insulation then shifts from the relationship between business and executive bureaucracy to a triangular relationship where the key is the insulation of the bureaucracy from politicians. Insulation from politicians is more problematic for bureaucrats because politicians, who cannot be easily and institutionally insulated from the particularistic pressures of business, have legitimate influence over the bureaucracy. Career incentives for bureaucrats can be partially shielded from temptations for corruption; however, incentives for politicians cannot because careers in elected office depend heavily on campaign contributions from business. Thus, in cases where insulated bureaucracies existed under authoritarian regimes, democratization has increased political pressures on bureaucrats. And where Weberian bureaucracies did not exist before democratization, they are not easy to build. Historically, most insulated, embedded Weberian bureaucracies emerged under authoritarian auspices. Authoritarianism is not so much necessary as it is functional, yet the probabilities of reform in some democracies are low (see Geddes 1990).

The dependent variable in this book is economic performance. The ways in which close ties between unelected bureaucrats and business elites affect the distribution of power and democratic governance are key issues for further research. The analysis in this book could contribute to this agenda for political research on two interrelated issues.[18] First, how does the variable organization of business across countries affect the articulation of business demands and collective power? Issues of distributional coalitions, encompassing associations, and rent seeking are all core concerns for democratic governance. More generally, if capital indeed votes twice, once directly in its political influence and once indirectly in its investment decisions, then political leaders have incentives to fashion government relations with business organizations (business voice in Albert Hirschman's terms) that restrain business as capital (exit). Second, in major theories the consolidation of democracy depends on what democracy delivers, especially in policies designed to reduce inequality and poverty. (See Haggard and Kaufman 1995 for a full recent treatment.) To the extent that good relations between business and government contribute to policy effectiveness generally, they enhance governability and democratic governance, to mention only two key concerns in recent debates on democratization. More specifically, some of the ways in which business-state collaboration has enhanced economic performance might also be harnessed to improving social welfare.

In sum, from the state side of the relationship, a Weberian bureaucracy is the best defense against the tendency for close government-business

---

[18] For general discussions of democracy and business-state relations, see Katzenstein 1984, Cohen and Rogers 1992, and Doner and Schneider 1994.

relations to degenerate into rent seeking. The virtues of Weberian bureaucracy are one of the few points of consensus among students of development. Yet for performance-enhancing relations with business, bureaucrats also need to maintain close contact with business, and career incentives to embed themselves are key. Short of a Weberian bureaucracy, some other features of the state, such as hard budget constraints, also reduced the overall drain of rent seeking. In other instances, officials in non-Weberian states can delegate the administration of policy to associations that, for reasons analyzed in the next section, are better able than the delegating bureaucracies to restrain DUP activities by their members.

Collective Business Action

Colombian coffee producers, textile manufacturers in Turkey and Thailand, and Mexican retailers participated in organizations that distributed benefits and exacted productive use of them by the recipients. What makes some associations like these developmental (in Charles Sabel's terms) while others devote themselves to rent seeking?[19] The answers in the empirical studies in this book are "encompassingness" and business associations capable of monitoring performance and ensuring compliance.

Mancur Olson noted in his original theory, although only briefly and skeptically, that strong, encompassing associations inhibit the pursuit by firms or sectoral associations of particularistic benefits. Encompassing, multisectoral associations are more likely to press for policies that promote growth throughout the economy rather than favor particular sectors at the expense of others (Olson 1982: 48–53). The reform experiences analyzed in the chapters by Silva and Schneider confirm these hypotheses on the benefits of encompassingness. In Chile the contrast between interactions between particular firms and government in the failures of the 1970s and the interactions between encompassing associations and the government in successful reforms in the 1980s is especially stark. Concerning Mexico, Schneider argues that encompassing peak associations helped to overcome severe obstacles to collective action in the struggle against inflation by promoting simultaneous price moderation across sectors.

---

[19] Our use of the term *developmental association* is broader than Sabel's and is defined mostly by the negative characteristic of not engaging in DUP activities. As such, it includes cases of private-interest governance through associations that aggregate interests or administer routine regulations as well as Sabel's more restricted notion of associations that promote learning and transformation among members of the associations. Nevertheless, most of the examples in the empirical studies in this book seem to fit Sabel's restrictive definition (see 1994: 149).

Although the idea has been neglected by Olson, findings in this book suggest that encompassingness *in firms* has similar beneficial effects to those that Olson predicted for associations. Thai bankers, managers of Taiwanese conglomerates, and Colombian coffee producers, for example, endorsed broader definitions of what was good for their respective economies because their business holdings were diverse and their company interests therefore more encompassing. Fields argues that Taiwanese conglomerates resisted sectorally based collective action (along the lines of Olsonian distributional coalitions). Doner and Ramsay place considerable weight on the multisectoral agglomerations typical of Thai business and on the role of banks in creating large, diverse, but collectively organized business networks.[20]

When encompassing firms also include agriculture, they may mitigate the disruptive effects of a strong landowning elite on relations between industry and the state. In many historical analyses, land reform and the absence of a strong landed elite in Japan, Korea, Taiwan, and Thailand facilitated the subsequent emergence of collaborative relations between industry and the state. Conversely, agricultural oligarchies in the Philippines and Peru, as discussed in the chapters by Doner and Ramsay and Thorp and Durand, were obstacles to performance-enhancing relations between business and the state. Why does a strong agricultural elite inhibit collaboration? One hypothesis is that such elites establish close, exclusive relations with the state that inhibit the rise of a developmental state and by extension impede close relations with industry.[21]

Short of eliminating the agricultural elite through radical land reforms (as in East Asia), the Colombian experience suggests that, if the agricultural elite is regionally dispersed, economically diversified, and formally organized, then it may not hinder more collaborative ties between industry and the state. Thorp and Durand's comparative analysis of Colombia and Peru highlights the way that collective action and encompassingness can inhibit particularistic rent seeking. The Colombian coffee association (FNC) encompassed producers, merchants, and financiers and provided collective warehousing, marketing, and financing to both large and small coffee producers from all over Colombia. The strength of the association, the major selective benefits it provided, and the multisectoral and geographic diversity of businesses it represented limited the extent of corruption and particularistic rent seeking in its relations with government. Other sectors of the business community did not engage in collective

---

[20] Chapter 2 considers additional benefits derived from conglomeration. Similarly, research on MNCs shows that they tend to be less protectionist than firms without international subsidiaries because they are more geographically encompassing (see Maxfield and Nolt 1990, Milner 1988, and Winters 1996).

[21] See Cardoso and Falleto 1979 and Evans 1987 and Shafer 1994 more recently.

action or establish such encompassing business associations, which helps account for the numerous examples of particularistic, unproductive exchange in government-business relations in other sectors in Colombia and more generally in Peru.

Nonencompassing sectoral associations were sometimes developmental because they provided selective and public benefits in ways that enhanced economic performance. These associations might participate in distributional coalitions in order to channel resources to their sectors, as Olson would expect, but they then used these resources productively. In these cases the analysis of rent seeking, monitoring, and reciprocity shifts from the relationship *between* the state and associations to the relationship *within* associations. If the association distributes subsidies, then how does the association stop individual members from seeking them for unproductive purposes? One answer, derived from the Colombian experience, is to insulate the staff and the leaders of the association. Meritocratic norms within the bureaucracy of the FNC seemed to substitute in part for the generalized lack of Weberian characteristics in the state as a whole and contributed to insulating FNC leaders and by extension economic policymakers in the government.

Monitoring member use of selective benefits is essential to the success of developmental associations. Where defection is costly to all members, investing in monitoring makes sense (as discussed further in the following section). Even in the absence of insulated staffs and leaders, transparency, as several chapters note, makes monitoring easier, cheaper, and less vulnerable to distortion. For example, Doner and Ramsay argue that the tightly knit business community of ethnic Chinese in Thailand increased transparency. This in turn lowered costs of detection. They write: "[Because] ethnic kinship and status/identity . . . transmit cheap signals of reputation and trustworthiness . . . entrepreneurs can . . . thus economize on the need to investigate" their colleagues.[22]

Biddle and Milor show that cross-sectoral variation in the extent to which close government-business relations decay into rent seeking depends in part on the strength of the sectoral association. The Turkish bureaucracy they describe is far from the Weberian ideal, yet there are still positive examples of government-business relations. In the auto sector, although a business association exists, the large auto firms bypass

---

[22] Developmental associations must then be able to act on the results of their monitoring and penalize violators. The empirical chapters lack extensive evidence on cases of punishment, yet the credible and costly threat of expulsion does seem to exist. Presumably, the higher the costs of free riding to other members of the association, the more likely members are to develop strong peer pressure for norms of cooperative behavior. For Sabel, it is exactly this kind of transformation of interests and identities that defines developmental associations (1994: 149–50).

the organization and deal in a private, particularistic way with government officials. Lack of transparency, Biddle and Milor argue, is both cause and consequence of the weakness of the auto sector business association. Major firms in the sector do not know what subsidies other firms receive and presume their rival's success results as much from rent-seeking skills as entrepreneurial talents, so each firm feels compelled to engage in rent seeking. In the absence of transparency regarding business actions, itself due partly to the weakness of the Association of Automotive Manufacturers, "the major players in the auto industry assume that their rivals have managed to obtain maximum benefits with minimum performance obligations. This gives them every incentive to bad-mouth their rivals and engage in costly and inefficient rent seeking."

The situation is very different in the Turkish ready-wear sector. The Turkish Clothing Manufacturers Association brokers access to production incentives that the association ties to firm performance. Members who contemplate circumventing the association to seek particularistic benefits have to weigh the likelihood and costs of losing membership in the association against the likely benefits from private relations with government officials. High transparency within the association increases the likelihood that cheating will be detected. In this case, the costs of defection (particularistic, rent-seeking behavior) and the likelihood of detection are the crucial factors preventing close government-business relations from degenerating into DUP activities. In sum, according to Biddle and Milor, business associations shape the likelihood that close government-business collaboration will slip into rent seeking in two ways. First, the more important the selective benefits provided by the association, the more leverage it has to keep its members from engaging in particularistic behavior. Second, to the extent that business associations increase transparency, they increase the likelihood that particularistic behavior will be detected.

Subsidiaries of multinational firms complicate relations between business and government. The chapters on Colombia, Korea, Thailand, and Turkey all emphasize the absence of multinational corporations (MNCs) in countries or sectors where government collaborated effectively with business. Thorp and Durand in particular argue that the Peruvian state did not intervene much in the economy because MNCs provided essential infrastructure and business did not organize formally because a handful of MNC representatives functioned as an executive committee for big business. MNCs obviated the need to develop close working relations between the state and business. They rarely manufacture a wide range of products, are generally not integrated into encompassing business conglomerates (although they create specific alliances through joint ventures), and usually keep a low profile in business associations. Moreover, expatriate managers of multinational firms circulate rapidly in and out of the country and are not embedded in either the local elite generally or in specific state-business networks. Nevertheless, the embeddedness of MNCs is variable as illustrated by the case of the Brazilian automobile industry. In this case MNC subsidiaries approximate domestic firms: Top managers are Brazilian, the firms participate actively in business associations, and production is geared primarily to the domestic market.

In sum, the chapters in this book identify several ways to inhibit temptations for rent seeking when relations between government and business elites are close. On the state side, the key factors are traditional Weberian features of bureaucracy combined with career incentives to embed the bureaucracy in dense networks with business. On the business side, the key factors are features of business organization, either encompassingness or the organizational capacity of associations to monitor and sanction the behavior of their members. The initial discussion of the costs associated with free riding in developmental associations leads to the next set of questions and to the next link further up the causal chain. Given that Weberian bureaucracies and developmental associations are costly to construct and maintain, what incentives do state and business elites have to invest in them?

COLLABORATING TO SURVIVE

If states or associations discipline business, then who or what disciplines these states and associations (see Amsden 1989). Weberian bureaucracies or agencies cannot survive without political protection (see Schneider 1991b), and developmental associations require ongoing infusions of political resources from both state and business actors. Why would state and economic elites invest scarce political capital in collaborative relations? The general answer that emerges from the studies in this book is that the elites feel threatened.[23] These studies permit greater precision in specifying the causal mechanisms at work between threats and cooperation. First, threats—or, more important, perceived threats—affected actors in different ways. Sometimes these threats were greatest on the business side from competitors in the same product markets. In other cases,

[23] The positive impact of economic and political vulnerability on cooperation has been a theme in a wide variety of arguments. It was a keystone in Katzenstein's arguments on the emergence of corporatism: "since the 1930s the small European states have experienced in economic openness and international vulnerability at least a partial substitute for the 'moral equivalent of war.' . . . cooperative politics has been one consequence" (1985b: 208). Arendt Lijphart concluded that "in all of the consociational democracies the cartel of elites was either initiated or greatly strengthened during periods of international crisis" (cited in Katzenstein 1985b: 34).

especially for state actors, the economic threats had major political consequences, as in Mexican stabilization programs in the 1980s or geopolitical concerns in the frontline states of East Asia. Second, threats often
affected only some groups and facilitated cooperation in societies such as
Colombia, Brazil, Mexico, and Turkey that are not characterized by consensual politics or large stocks of social capital. Third, as Peter Katzenstein has argued (and Thorp and Durand also do in this book),
cooperative responses to threats are not inevitable but highly contingent.
They depend heavily on historical sequences, political strategies and
resources, institution building, and path dependence.

Vulnerability to international competition provides one incentive to
cooperate to survive. For example, Ronald Rogowski countered Olson's
theory of debilitating distributional coalitions and posited that, "to the
extent that a country's factor endowments require it to trade, . . . its coalitions will seek efficiency and quality rather than a bigger share" except
where the country's exports were "the simplest primary products . . .
subject to little variation in quality and hence to little improvement"
(1988: 317).[24] In some cases in this book, the perceived threats came from
international markets and Rogowski's "quality export dependence." In
the case of coffee and textiles, the threat was to small exporters who
lacked independent means to market their products and enforce
minimum quality standards on all producers. In the automobile industry
in Brazil all actors had an incentive to collaborate because the perceived
cost of not doing so would be to sit by and watch the sector be overrun
by imports.

The empirical chapters reveal a diverse set of developmental associations that responded successfully to this sort of economic vulnerability.
What did rice merchants and associations of Chinese businessmen in
Thailand, Colombian coffee growers, and Turkish ready-wear manufacturers have in common? At a fundamental level these associations (1) distributed major selective benefits (usually first granted to the association
by the state); (2) stood to suffer greatly if members free rode; (3) monitored their members (usually aided by transparent procedures within the
association); and (4) had the ability to impose sanctions on members, few
of whom could survive without the association. In such associations, the
logic of collective action is considerably more complex and centripetal
than the usual Olsonian logic: The selective benefits provide an initial
reason to join, but the high cost of defection by others makes members

---

[24] Rogowski drew several illustrations from developed countries but unfortunately did not
elaborate on the causal mechanisms that would drive the argument or apply it to developing countries. Also lacking is a threshold for "simplest export products." Many agricultural
products would seem to fall into this category, but in this book quality concerns were paramount for Thai rice and Colombian coffee producers.

invest in monitoring and agree to abide by severe sanctions. The importance of selective benefits is well known (although their origin in the state is often neglected), and the previous section considered some of the internal features of developmental associations that allowed them to monitor and sanction. The key issue here is to isolate vulnerabilities that ratchet up the costs of defection.

What is relatively neglected in conventional analyses of collective action is a full consideration of the costs of free riding or defecting from the cooperative game (but see Ostrom 1990). In the conventional calculation of these costs, some members contribute a disproportionate share of the resources required for collective action yet share equally in the benefits. In the developmental associations discussed in this book, however, cooperating members stood to lose much more from defection than just disproportionate investment in collective action. Therefore, member firms had incentives to invest more in making sure the association could monitor and punish than the usual logic of collective action would lead one to expect.

High barriers to exit was one factor that increased the costs of defection associated with the development associations examined in this book. In sectors such as rice, coffee, and textiles, the barriers to entry were low; yet strong associations emerged nonetheless, partly because barriers to exit were high. High barriers made these sectors especially vulnerable to political and economic changes (see Frieden 1991). Extending his arguments on exit and voice, Hirschman has noted that Colombian coffee producers had few opportunities to exit because of the high investment sunk into coffee bushes and hence greater incentives to amplify their voices. In contrast, Argentine wheat producers could easily stop growing from one harvest to the next and could thus rely on exit to signal their preferences (1971: 12).

Another factor that makes these associations especially developmental is a "bad apple" syndrome that gives members strong incentives to agree to monitoring and severe punishment in the case of transgression. These incentives are especially visible in the case of small producers who export commodities and cannot compete in export markets without a good sectoral reputation as well as a common marketing infrastructure. International coffee marketing depends on consistent good quality; the Colombian coffee association delivered this for producers by effectively monitoring and enforcing quality standards. Doner and Ramsay find that associations provided similar benefits for Thai rice producers.

In the abstract, the costs free riding to other members of the association vary greatly according to the nature of the collective benefit: typical collective goods, common pool resources, or reputation. Conceived graphically, the curve derived from plotting numbers of free riders against costs borne by remaining members have quite different slopes. With a typical collective good such as a common warehouse, the cost of each free rider is simply a small increase in payments by other members to maintain the collective good. With this kind of collective good the cost curve rises fairly slowly. In the case of common pool resources analyzed by Ostrom (1990), such as meadows and fishing grounds, this cost curve may rise slowly with the first few defectors but then kink upward as further defection or poaching severely depletes the common pool resources. In the case of collective reputation, the upward kink in the curve comes earlier (after only a few free riders) and is very steep thereafter. In cases of common pool or reputational resources, members have strong incentives to stop the first defector.

Some threats to business were more political yet similarly encouraged collective action. In Turkish textiles, the fear was that abuse of government subsidies would lead the government to discontinue them. Concerning Thailand, Doner and Ramsay argue that political uncertainties on the part of the minority Chinese business community facilitated collective action and in some instances effective private-interest governance. An intriguing hypothesis that emerges from the Thai case is that ethnically based business associations are more likely to refrain from rent seeking because they are politically vulnerable, have multiple monitoring mechanisms (through ethnic networks), and wield costly sanctions because exclusion would be socially and economically disastrous to any member (see also Leff 1986).

High collective costs due to free riding hardly guarantee an adequate collective response, a situation commonly lamented in the literature on the tragedy of the commons. A full assessment of the origins of developmental associations is beyond the scope of this chapter, but it is worth highlighting that collective action was rarely spontaneous despite the strength of centripetal incentives (see also Chapter 2). In Michael Taylor's terms, these associations are characterized by a high predisposition (due to political and economic vulnerability) to an internal solution to the problems of collective action combined with, or triggered by, an external solution (1990: 224–25).

The most common source of external solutions for developmental associations was, directly or indirectly, the state.[25] For example, in Latin America, particularly in Brazil and Mexico, the state forced business into elaborate corporatist structures. In addition, government attacks on property rights in Mexico encouraged further collective action by business in

---

[25] See Chapter 2 (and Bowman 1989) for further review. The Japanese state actively promoted business associations (Miyamoto 1988). Schneiberg and Hollingsworth (1991) argue that the incentive to organize is economic but the form of organization and its success depend primarily on the state.

the 1970s and 1980s. Fields clearly documents state initiative and continuing control in business associations in Taiwan and Korea. In other instances, state actors have reduced obstacles to collective action by ceding the distribution of significant selective benefits to associations. This was the case in Turkey, with the export incentives distributed by the textile association; in Colombia, where the FNC controlled the revenues from an earmarked tax; and in Thailand, where business associations distributed export quotas.

On the state side, vulnerability is also crucial to explaining why government officials pursue collaboration with business and refrain from defecting. Here, the economic threats that matter are those that affect political survival. These threats seem to have a similar impact in encouraging cooperation and restraining temptations to defect or renege on the part of state actors. In some of the cases in this book, the perceived threats were constant and encouraged state actors to build enduring patterns of collaboration with business. In the frontline countries of Asia, communism was the threat that motivated political leaders to seek out cooperation with business in order to promote the growth that would help consolidate capitalism (see Evans 1987; Woo 1991). Concerning Colombia, Thorp and Durand argue that the long-term dominance of coffee in total exports contributed to a shared sense of vulnerability and overall like-mindedness that greatly facilitated cooperation between government and business. In Peru, in contrast, the diversity of exports impeded the emergence of any comparable sense of mutual vulnerability among business and state elites.

In other cases the political threats were more immediate and led political leaders to construct ad hoc arrangements for cooperation. Silva argues that in Chile, after the opposition mobilized in the early 1980s, leaders in the Pinochet government arranged for more systematic consultation with business associations in part to keep business from joining the opposition movement. Similar concerns prompted leaders of the new democratic government to consult extensively with business in order to ensure a smooth transition (see also Boylan 1996). Schneider claims that in Mexico, at the end of de la Madrid's term, capital flight was a major threat to the government's stabilization policies and hence to the PRI (Institutional Revolutionary Party) in an election year. These fears gave government leaders strong incentives to invest in concertation with business in the anti-inflation pact of 1988.

Beyond encouraging state actors to cooperate, political threats can further facilitate collaboration by making government commitments more credible. As we discussed earlier, most policies suffer from an inherent lack of credibility because of problems with time inconsistency. But when government elites seek business cooperation because they feel threatened, their policies may be more credible. When the threat is apparent to business participants as well, they know to which political pressures government officials are responding. Such threats make governments more transparent and in this sense help authoritarian regimes resemble more inherently transparent democracies.

In sum, the research in this book suggests that the key conditions for sustaining benign collaboration include embedded Weberian bureaucracy or, in its absence, competitive clientelism, hard budget constraints, and encompassing and developmental associations. Market and political threats, in turn, provide state and business elites with strong incentives to invest in maintaining these favorable conditions. These conditions and threats do not rule out corruption and collusion, but for individual bureaucrats or capitalists they systematically increase the costs of (or reduce the benefits of) collusion while raising the benefits of collaboration (or the costs of defection from cooperation).

Policy Implications

In any particular historical instance, business-state collaboration has resulted from a particular mix of ingredients such as political or economic vulnerability and long-existing practices such as bureaucratic recruitment through examination. Thus, collaboration has rarely been the unique result of deliberate state action, nor has a single recipe for collaboration emerged from the case studies (see Kaufman et al. 1994: 405). Nonetheless, policymakers looking at the near term might ask which of the conditions discussed in this chapter are most susceptible to simple, low-cost manipulation. The chapters in this book were not designed to generate policy recommendations; yet they can, if the implications are drawn out fully, provide several provisional answers.

The first set of implications is sobering for enthusiasts of business-government collaboration. More determinist versions of sectoral analysis leave little room for independent action by state officials. Sectors themselves (by virtue of their structural rigidities) or in combination with overwhelming collective political action on their behalf can derail contrary adjustment policies. Moreover, state actors are likely to have expertise and interests tied to dominant sectors and hence be less likely even to conceive of independent courses of action. If sectoral distributions of economic activity set the range of possible forms of interaction between business and government, then state actors have little impact in the short run. Nevertheless, the sectoral analyses in the chapters by Shafer and Thorp and Durand end with considerably less determinism. Over the long run, state actors can promote a diversity of sectors as in Korea, which enlarges their freedom of maneuver; and they can promote more encompassing forms of associations as in Colombia.[26]

Sectoral and institutional approaches emphasize the long historical evolution of many of the conditions favorable to collaboration, which raises further doubts about the efficacy of short-run measures. Political leaders in most developing countries, especially those with new democracies and non-Weberian bureaucracies, have short time horizons that make some of the conclusions of our studies less interesting, given immediate concerns of governing. Easing sectoral constraints; creating Weberian bureaucracies; building strong, encompassing associations; and institutionalizing hard budget constraints are costly endeavors that require decades if not generations. Moreover, the brief empirical considerations of ineffective forms of interaction in Peru, the Philippines, and Venezuela make it hard to imagine short-term solutions that would lead quickly to more productive collaboration in these or other cases of longstanding relations of antagonism or corruption. But even some of the short-term measures considered in this book can have positive consequences down the road for insulating bureaucracies or nudging associations in more developmental directions. Virtuous cycles, such as those identified by Thorp and Durand, often begin with fairly simple policies even though the long-term, virtuous consequences are rarely fully appreciated by the protagonists at the time the policies are adopted. A final reason for pessimism results from the mismatch of the incomplete information available to state actors and the complexity of conditions for collaboration. If collaboration results from rare and peculiar combinations of variably organized agents reacting to distinct, sometimes ephemeral, vulnerabilities, then the complexity may be too much to handle for most policymakers in developing countries, who operate under severe resource and time constraints. In sum, the studies in this book give ample grounds for skepticism regarding policies to promote collaboration.

Notwithstanding these cautions several types of state action seem more likely than others to induce more positive relations. For instance, in the absence of widespread administrative reform, authority to interact with capitalists can be delegated to the most Weberian agencies in the economic bureaucracy. Moreover, by exercising greater selectivity and dis-

---

[26] These two chapters come to somewhat contradictory conclusions on the benefits of sectoral diversification. For Thorp and Durand, the Peruvian experience demonstrates the pitfalls of export diversity and Colombia the benefits of export concentration. In contrast, Shafer argues that it was diversity (a textile sector counter to heavy industry) that permitted adjustment in the 1980s in Korea. In Shafer's overall framework, export concentration in low/low sectors is not problematic. Thorp and Durand might add the qualifier that export concentration is beneficial only if adequate public and private institutions exist to manage the vulnerability.

cretion, the range and number of industrial policies and subsidies might be adjusted to the range of more Weberian agencies in the state.[27] One of the notable aspects of many experiences of neoliberal reform was the few bureaucrats needed to dismantle the state. Moreover, bureaucratic personnel, even for rather complex policies, can be kept to a minimum, as the experience of Japan's Ministry of International Trade and Industry shows (C. Johnson 1982).[28]

One of the more intriguing policy options is to harness the self-interest of business to the task of effective administration of subsidies. If such administration can be delegated to developmental associations with strong incentives to monitor and sanction, then policymakers can bypass an unreliable bureaucracy.[29] Of course, policymakers often depend on clientelist bureaucracies to further their political careers, so the incentive to delegate and forego their discretion may be weak.

What if associations do not exist? One of the consistent conclusions of the studies in this book is that state action can be effective in resolving obstacles to collective action and creating strong business associations. But encouraging collective action when the bureaucracy is not Weberian is risky unless business managers feel vulnerable (as, say, most small exporters do). A key task for policymakers is to identify vulnerable sectors where capitalists perceive the costs of free riding to be high. Otherwise, like Dr. Frankenstein, officials may be better off doing nothing than failing in efforts to create sufficiently developmental associations that instead turn on their creators, much strengthened, to seek rents. In the effort to rein in the associations they promote, state actors, especially in unevenly Weberian states, may find essential allies among representatives of organized labor or other non-elite groups (see Evans's chapter). These groups, especially if they are relatively encompassing, have stronger incentives to inhibit rent seeking and sometimes built in monitoring capacities.

In many developing countries the problem is less the lack of strong associations and more the existence of strong but narrow particularistic trade associations. State action is essential to harness these sectoral associations into encompassing peak associations (because in Olson's analysis of collective action, the spontaneous formation of peak associations is hardly likely). State actors can use a range of instruments, from legal fiat (in cases of state corporatism) to strong economic and political incentives

---

[27] See Evans 1995 for a general defense of selective state intervention.

[28] The instances of successful circumscribed collaboration in Turkey, Brazil, Colombia, and Thailand do not give rise to optimism about a natural evolution to less circumscribed forms of collaboration. For one thing, the business interlocutors were sometimes fairly narrow sectoral associations. And as Thorp and Durand emphasize, the interests (and vulnerabilities) driving one form of collaboration may not extend to other areas.

[29] On the benefits of such delegation, see Streeck and Schmitter 1985 and Sabel 1992, 1994.

(in instances of societal corporatism), to strengthen peak associations. At the level of the firm, as discussed further in Chapter 2, state action has also been decisive in prodding big business to become more diversified and hence encompassing. Making business more encompassing in either peak associations or conglomerates is likely to be more costly than attempting to create developmental associations in particular sectors, but it is also less risky because encompassing associations of business have built-in mechanisms to inhibit particularistic rent seeking.

In sum, officials can attempt to improve conditions for collaboration on the margin by judicious delegation of policy implementation to Weberian agencies and by helping to overcome obstacles to collective action in potentially developmental or encompassing associations. Nonetheless, optimal circumstances for collaboration are rare, and inaction is likely to remain a strong contender among policy options. Because the convergence of appropriate forms of bureaucratic capability, collective business action, and shared anxiety is so infrequent, discretion seems to be one of the better parts of valor in policies designed to promote collaboration between business and the state.

ORGANIZATION OF THE BOOK

Chapter 2 completes our review of the current state of theorizing on relations between business and the state. Haggard, Maxfield, and Schneider analyze varying conceptions of business—capital, sector, firm, association, and network—and spell out causal hypotheses on the nature of ties between business and the state associated with each level of analysis. Much of the muddle in theorizing about business-state relations is the result of confusion among these five conceptions of business. Our review of the current literature further explores the generally dim view that authors take of close relations between business and government. Our chapter counters with examples of more positive hypotheses.

Chapters 3 through 10 present empirical analyses of nearly a dozen developing countries. The methodological starting point for this project was that the causes and consequences of collaboration between business and the state are best analyzed through in-depth, often historical comparison among a small number of cases. With a few notable exceptions, existing analyses of business-state relations, especially those using historical and institutional methods, are confined to single countries.[30] In contrast, most of the chapters in this book examine several countries to

---

[30] Exceptions include Evans 1995, Doner 1991, Garrido 1988, MacIntyre 1994, and Bartell and Payne 1994.

33

broaden the base of comparison. A few use different dimensions for comparison. Biddle and Milor compare sectors in Turkey; Silva and Shafer both concentrate on comparisons over time and across regimes in Chile and Korea, respectively. All the empirical chapters contrast better and worse forms of business-state interaction in order to specify the consequences of the interaction for economic performance and the conditions under which the better forms are likely to emerge.

The design of this project attempted to maximize geographic variation while concentrating substantive attention on one admittedly broad feature of developing capitalist economies: the relationship between business and state elites. The chapters cover many of the major middle-income countries of Latin America and East Asia, where the private sector is relatively well developed. We decided to exclude other African, Asian, and post-Communist countries in order to reduce the range of variation in the development of the private sector.

Although most chapters compare various kinds of states, we have grouped the empirical chapters according to whether they focus predominantly on strong or weak states, defined by the existence of a Weberian bureaucracy. The empirical chapters begin with a set of stronger states. In Chapter 3 Evans cuts into the analysis of business-state relations from the state side and emphasizes the importance of its internal structure to the evolution of the state's relationship with business. States without Weberian bureaucracies (defined by meritocratic recruitment and promotion as well as rewarding career ladders) will have difficulty resisting predation by business. But the relationship is dynamic, Evans argues, and even states with Weberian bureaucracies face challenges over time as business grows and develops close ties with international capital.

In Chapter 4 Shafer presents a sectoral theory of development. In one sense this theory represents the latest in statist analysis because Shafer argues that the keys to successful adjustment are the relative and absolute capacities of the state. States lacking such capacities will be unable to overcome opposition from business in order to promote adjustment and growth. Shafer adds nuance to the one-sided statist vision. For him, state capacity is itself partly a function of sectoral development. Moreover, the partial adjustment in Korea in the 1980s illustrated the dependence of state elites on private-sector allies in order to overcome opposition from other segments of business. In Chapter 5 Fields examines the same paragons of state capacity, Korea and Taiwan. He, too, emphasizes the role of Weberian bureaucracy and dictatorship in structuring the private sector according to the ideologies of political leaders in each country. He also demonstrates, however, that these states were hardly acting in isolation and that their success in promoting economic transformation depended in large measure on the dense networks and continuous inter-action that linked state elites with business.

Among Latin American countries, the autonomy and capacity of states in Mexico and Chile may approximate most closely that of states in East Asian NICs (newly industrializing countries), although more as the result of authoritarianism than of state structure and Weberian bureaucracy. But autonomy and capacity were not enough to consolidate market-oriented reform. Chapters 6 and 7 by Silva and Schneider add a greater appreci-ation of the role of collaboration between business and government in the process of their market-oriented reforms. In both cases, concertation and consultation between state actors and business leaders produced better economic results than previous, unsuccessful attempts to reform by fiat. These results in Latin America provide an essential control on the analysis of Korea and Taiwan, where it is difficult to separate the causal contributions of authoritarian rule, Weberian bureaucracy, and embed-ded autonomy to economic performance. These cross-regional compar-isons lend support to arguments that authoritarianism alone does not have much weight in explaining divergent development patterns in East Asia and Latin America.

Chapters 7 through 10 focus largely on weaker, non-Weberian states. The analyses of Colombia, Thailand, Turkey, and Brazil offer surprising findings of performance-enhancing collaboration between business and the state despite the absence of insulated Weberian bureaucracies. These countries are representative of the majority of middle-income developing countries, where states are unevenly Weberian and economic perfor-mance lags behind that of countries with classic developmental states. The chapters find unusual instances, in some periods or some sectors, where business-state collaboration overcame limitations in the public or private sectors to enhance economic performance. In Brazil, union leaders and state actors coaxed the auto producers into collective action and a sec-toral agreement that reduced prices, taxes, and layoffs while spurring record-breaking production. In their discussion of Colombia, Thorp and Durand argue that the coffee confederation mediated relations with the state in ways that aided performance in the sector as well as in the economy as a whole. In Thailand, clientelism permeated a non-Weberian bureaucracy yet without crippling the economy. According to Doner and Ramsay, a hard budget constraint and competitive clientelism coupled with collective action in the private sector had synergistic effects for the Thai economy. Finally, Biddle and Milor examine a curious sectoral asso-ciation in ready-wear clothing in Turkey that was very effective in distrib-uting government subsidies and monitoring firm compliance in ways the state could not.

35

CHAPTER TWO

Theories of Business and Business-State Relations

STEPHAN HAGGARD, SYLVIA MAXFIELD,
AND BEN ROSS SCHNEIDER

Despite an explosion of empirical work on business-government relations, research on the topic remains theoretically diffuse. Some of the difficulty stems from contending views of the state and how political influence is exercised. Yet a substantial part of the problem resides in competing and sometimes contradictory ways in which business is theorized. In vernacular English, the term can mean anything from a particular legal entity to the sum of all economic activity outside the household. This conceptual muddle is no less apparent in the social sciences. Our chapter is organized around a typology of five theoretical approaches to the political economy of business-state relations. These approaches differ primarily in how they conceptualize the private sector: as capital, sector, firm, association, or network. Yet all emphasize the fact that market outcomes, investment, and growth are heavily influenced by the relationship between governments and private sectors.

We begin with the most aggregate and homogeneous level: business as a factor of production or as capital. Models in this vein focus on the structural constraints posed by private control of physical and financial assets and capital mobility. What are the political consequences of the fact that most investment decisions in a capitalist economy are made by private actors responding to both market signals and expectations about the future course of government action?

We are grateful to David Cameron, Edward Gibson, Mark Granovetter, James McGuire, William Munro, Meredith Woo-Cumings, Jeffrey Winters, and the book's contributors for comments on previous versions.

The business-as-capital research program does not typically draw distinctions among different types of economic activity. A less homogeneous view can be found in a growing literature on how the distribution of economic activity and different sectoral interests affect politics, policy, and growth. In sectoral analyses, characteristics of economic activity such as factor intensity, asset specificity, and the degree of industrial concentration appear to shape business preferences, the capacity for collective action, and therefore policy outcomes. States are constrained not by private control of investment resources per se but by the contending interests of different sectors.

A third approach examines the political consequences of corporate organization. In this business-as-firm approach, characteristics of corporate structure, including size, internal organization, ownership, and patterns of financing, seem to affect both business preferences and the leverage that firms have vis-à-vis government actors. Two organizational dimensions are especially important in developing countries: the relative size of major firms and the extent of diversification within particular firms or groups.

These three approaches generally take a structural view of business influence but pay little attention to either the political organization of business or the institutions that mediate business interests. If the political interaction between the state and private actors is modeled at all, it tends to take a spare, game-theoretic form. In contrast, the dominant empirical approach to the study of business in both the advanced industrial states and the Third World adopts a more instrumental approach, focusing on how business associations and interest groups aggregate, reconcile, and intermediate business interests. The business-as-association approach seeks to understand not only how associations affect the expression of business preferences through lobbying but also how they influence policy implementation—for example, through private-interest governance, where business associations assume governmental functions.

At the final level of disaggregation is a more sociological conception of business as individual managers and owners. According to this perspective, interaction with government comes not through formal institutional channels but through networks of personal relationships and the occupancy of overlapping roles that may blur the distinction between the government and private actors.

In the following sections, we review these alternative conceptions in more detail, tracing their intellectual parentage, outlining fundamental theoretical assumptions, and linking them to the overall concern of the chapters in the book: the effects of government-business relations on economic performance in developing countries. Our review seeks to be comprehensive in covering the range of alternative approaches to the study

37

of business yet selective in concentrating on scholarship that explicitly examines the relationship between the state and the private sector.[1] Of course, conceptions of the state also vary substantially, and different conceptions of business are likely to be associated with different conceptions of the state.[2] Other chapters, however, especially the contribution by Peter Evans, analyze the state at greater length; and reviews of alternative conceptions of the state are available elsewhere (Evans et al. 1985; Carnoy 1984; Evans 1995).

BUSINESS AS CAPITAL: CONSTRAINING THE STATE

Private-sector actors need not be organized nor engaging in explicit lobbying efforts in order to influence government behavior. One important body of literature models business as capital and examines the constraining effects of uncoordinated private-investment decisions on government decision making. Lindblom (1984) presents the closed-economy version of this approach in its simplest form.[3] Because the level of investment determines economic growth, government decision making in a mixed economy is always constrained by anticipated private reactions. In effect, capital votes twice: once through the organized pressure it can bring to bear on the political process, again through its investment decisions.

This insight has recently been extended to consider the openness of national economies to capital movements. A seminal contribution in this vein is Albert Hirschman's "Exit, Voice, and the State," in which he outlines the role of "movable property and its exit" as a restraint on the government's freedom of maneuver (1978: 96). Although free capital movements can restrain despotic and predatory rule, they can also undermine the government's ability to "introduce some taxation that would curb excessive privileges of the rich or some social reforms designed to distribute the fruits of economic growth more equitably" (100).

Hirschman's view has even greater resonance to day, given the dramatic increase in international financial integration. As national barriers to financial movements fall, international capital flows pressure governments through the foreign exchange and financial markets. Macroeco-

---

[1] For example, we omit vast literatures on networks and corporate organization that neglect the state.

[2] For the most part we use the terms *business-state* and *business-government relations* interchangeably. In more specific usages we follow the convention of viewing governments as the more temporary collections of top political leaders and states as the more permanent personnel and bureaucracy of the public sector.

[3] See Winters 1994, 1996; Cohen 1996; and Haggard, Maxfield, and Lee 1993 for full reviews of the literature on business as capital.

nomic and exchange-rate policy are the points of greatest vulnerability (Mundell 1963, 1968; Fleming 1962). Countries choosing to pursue macroeconomic policies that are more expansionary than those of their trade and investment partners face the risk of capital outflows, downward pressure on the exchange rate, and the subsequent necessity to adjust through fiscal and monetary tightening. Foreknowledge of this sequence of events serves to constrain government policy.

Pressure for convergence is also evident in policies regulating financial markets. Several new studies of both developed and developing countries find that the internationalization of financial markets generates strong pressures on governments to abandon regulatory controls (Rosenbluth 1989; Goodman and Pauly 1993; Haggard and Maxfield 1996). Maxfield (1995) extends the convergence hypothesis to the choice of institutions, arguing that increased capital mobility helps explain the global trend toward granting central banks greater independence.

Beyond this emerging consensus that capital mobility constrains macroeconomic policy and the regulation of financial markets, debate continues on how far capital mobility forces convergence in other policy areas. A number of studies conclude that capital mobility limits what governments can do across a range of policies and that it has put particular pressure on social democratic governments. Kurzer (1993), for example, argues that corporatism has been eroded in four small, open, European economies by increased capital mobility; Schwartz (1994) concludes that it has contributed to the erosion of the welfare state in Australia, Denmark, New Zealand, and Sweden.[4] The unraveling of Mitterrand's Socialist program in France in the early 1980s is frequently cited as a victim of growing financial integration in Europe (Loriaux 1991).

The need to appeal to foreign investors and creditors and to deter capital flight has also been invoked as an explanation for the near universal trend toward economic liberalization and deregulation in the developing world.[5] The former president of Citibank, Walter Wriston, made the claim bluntly with respect to Latin America: "Not only are governments losing control over money, but this newly free money . . . is asserting its control over them, disciplining irresponsible policies" (Wriston 1992: 66, cited in Mahon 1994). Maxfield (1990) and Winters (1996) trace changes in the orthodoxy of Mexican and Indonesian economic policy respectively to the loosening and tightening of balance-of-payments constraints. Schneider's chapter in this book argues that Mexico pursued a more radical reform course than Brazil did due to a deeper investment

[4] See Andrews 1994 for a general argument that capital mobility is a structural feature of the international system that forces interest-maximizing states to compete for capital.

[5] See, for example, Haggard 1995 and Haggard and Maxfield 1996.

crisis and more extensive capital flight. As the Mexican crisis of 1994–95 demonstrates, the resurgence of flows of portfolio capital to developing countries has by no means alleviated the risks of volatility; interestingly, the Mexican government's response has been to accelerate rather than retreat from the liberalization process.

Although international capital mobility constitutes a constraint, not all countries are equally vulnerable to it (Cohen 1996). Governments' vulnerability depends on inherent characteristics of different international financial assets, the degree of effective control exercised over the capital account, and the country's dependence on foreign investment; the last variable, in turn, is a function of the current account position and the domestic savings/investment balance. Even though external constraints have been salient in most developing countries (Stallings 1992), the export-oriented countries of East Asia have generally avoided serious balance-of-payments constraints through a combination of aggressive promotion of exports and, until recently, aggressive capital controls. A large internal market (as in India or Brazil) or the presence of an exportable natural resource (oil in Indonesia and Mexico in the 1970s) can either increase bargaining power vis-à-vis foreign capital or alleviate external constraints, at least temporarily.

But the constraining impact of capital mobility is also mediated by the domestic political and institutional context. In studies of Europe, Garrett and Lange (1991) and Kitschelt (1994) have explicitly argued against the convergence hypothesis by showing that national economic policies continue to reflect partisan differences despite increasing capital mobility. It is worth underlining the theoretical reasoning behind this finding because it points to the importance of institutional relationships between business and government in determining the nature of government policy.

The typical theoretical model of state-capital relations assumes that liquid asset holders seek to maximize profits and favor strong property rights, low taxation, and favorable regulation. Governments also seek to maximize growth or returns to particular constituencies, but in a mixed economy this means reaching compromises with the private sector; in his important book *Capitalism and Social Democracy* (1985), Adam Przeworski shows that this is no less true for social democratic governments. It is also the case, however, that governments face coalitional and electoral constraints that make it attractive to favor consumption over investment, tax capital or regulate business activities, and even renege on past commitments.

If business and government are able to cooperate and reach stable compromises, the restraining effects of private control over investment decisions and capital movements can be mitigated. One problem in reaching such understandings is that each player is uncertain about the other's future behavior. If government makes concessions with respect to taxation, regulation, or wages, investors may not respond. Conversely, private agents may fear that political calculations will prevent the government from keeping its commitments to sustain a profitable business environment.

In such settings, the credibility of the two sides is a critical factor in determining economic outcomes, and much attention has been given to understanding how such credibility is established (see Chapter 1). One strand of thinking, explored by economists, examines the role of signaling. Committed governments can reassure private investors by taking policy stances that demonstrate their credibility even if that stance cuts against short-run political interests (Rodrik 1989). Political scientists, in contrast, have focused greater attention on how institutional arrangements constitute solutions to commitment problems. Basic political institutions, including constitutional government itself (Olson 1993; North and Weingast 1989), have been interpreted as solutions to the problem of credible commitments; and other analysts have explored variables such as the nature of the party system (Alesina 1994; Haggard and Kaufman 1995) or the relative strength of labor (Alvarez, Garrett, and Lange 1991).

Nevertheless, the institutional structure of business-government relations also plays a role. For example, research on corporatism, social pacts, and concertation argue that such institutions provide a forum for negotiation between representatives of business, government, and labor that can resolve the strategic dilemma of government-business cooperation. By creating opportunities for repeated interactions, such institutions lengthen time horizons and create trust.

Although few chapters in this book focus directly on the structural constraints posed by business as capital, virtually all provide evidence on the institutional mechanisms that enhance trust and credibility and reduce political uncertainty in investor calculations. Schneider's chapter documents how concertation in Brazil and Mexico helped build investor confidence and coordinate expectations about government policies. Silva's analysis of reform in Chile is particularly interesting in this regard because it shows how regular consultation and negotiation between business and government can blunt the negative effects of tax increases initiated by a reformist government of the center-left (see Wallerstein and Przeworski 1995).

Any discussion of business-government relations must bear in mind the structural power of capital and remember that business need not be organized to exercise influence. But the business-as-capital approach also has important defects. One that we have just noted is the inattention to institutions that affect the nature of state-capital relations; we return to this question later in a discussion of business associations. A second is the emphasis on the common interests of capital vis-à-vis the state. Although capitalists may share common interests in the protection of property rights and a favorable business climate, they can also have divergent interests when it comes to particular public policies. These differences typically derive from the sectoral location of different private-sector actors.

BUSINESS AS SECTOR: STRUCTURAL SOURCES OF DIVERGENT BUSINESS INTERESTS

Peter Gourevitch was among the first political scientists to predict economic policy on the basis of sectoral differences. In *Politics in Hard Times* (1986), he asked how different countries responded to similar external economic shocks. The answer, he argued, had to do with characteristics of the country's leading economic sectors, including their international competitiveness, vulnerability to fluctuations in demand, and labor intensity. Gourevitch argued that different production profiles gave rise to different sectoral coalitions, which in turn determined which of five broad types of policy options a country would follow at any given time, ranging from classical liberalism to planning and neomercantilism.[6]

This logic—from sectorally determined interests, to coalition formation, to conflict and influence over public-policy outcomes—has been at the heart of a significant strand of recent theoretical and empirical work on the political economy of economic policy. In this literature, the private sector, or business, does not have homogenous preferences; rather, economic policy is understood as the resultant of a vector of divergent and often contending business interests.

The central debates have focused on how sectoral interests should be conceptualized. In *Commerce and Coalitions* (1989), Ronald Rogowski argues that the dominant cleavages in an economy run along factoral lines and are determined by a country's resource endowment and exposure to trade. Working with a three-factor model (land, labor, capital) and assuming factor mobility, Rogowski draws on standard (Stolper-Samuelson) trade theory to note that abundant factors in an economy

---

[6] In a study of the New Deal, Ferguson (1984) argued similarly that the core business interest at the heart of the Roosevelt coalition was from capital-intensive sectors that stood to gain from freer trade. Along with internationally oriented commercial and investment banks, these industries supported the Democrats' free-trade policy until international economic changes in the 1960s and 1970s forced the coalition apart and contributed to the gradual weakening of the Democrats' hegemony. See Ferguson 1995 for further elaboration of this approach to U.S. politics.

gain from trade while scarce factors lose. He suggests four ideal patterns of social, class, and policy conflict that follow from these divergent interests and explores them against evidence from a variety of national settings since the early 1800s.

Like those who follow the business-as-capital approach, Rogowski assumes that capital has homogenous preferences; coalitions and conflicts occur between factors of production. Yet as Jeffry Frieden (1991) has pointed out (mirroring a long line of work on endogenous tariff theory [Nelson 1988]), the Stolper-Samuelson assumptions about factor mobility that undergird Rogowski's approach are usually less warranted than the assumption that some factors are immobile in the face of changes in relative prices. This is particularly true in developing countries. In his work on Latin America, Frieden argues that the more specific or dedicated the assets, the greater the costs of policy adjustments and the greater the incentive to lobby against them. The sectoral distribution of economic activity thus becomes an important variable in determining the range of government economic policies likely to find a positive reception from business and labor in leading sectors.[7] In Brazil, Mexico, and Venezuela, capital goods and consumer-durables industries with highly specific assets emerged or thrived during the borrowing boom of the 1970s. Yet these same sectors also posed stiff opposition to economic reform efforts in the 1980s.

Once the shift is made from the traditional factors of the Stolper-Samuelson world to a model of asset specificity, the range of sectoral characteristics that might be salient for understanding business preferences broadens. For example, Milner (1988) takes a theoretical tack similar to Frieden's, beginning with the assumption that business interests drive economic policy. For Milner, however, the distinguishing feature of different sectors is not asset specificity but dependence on trade and the degree of multinationalization. She argues that firms facing severe import competition may nonetheless remain internationalist if they are also exporters, dependent on imports, or have extensive foreign operations. Milner uses this observation to explain the puzzle of why U.S. trade policy in the 1970s and 1980s remained more internationalist than would be expected given declining U.S. hegemony and rising import competition.

Sectoral approaches to politics face two analytic problems. First,

---

[7] In other work Frieden is among the few scholars who are trying to adapt a sectoral approach to policy choices beyond trade and adjustment. Still assuming relatively low mobility of factors between sectors, he examines how increasing capital mobility will affect sector preferences over exchange rate and monetary policy. Frieden argues that growing capital mobility will hinder choice and implementation of sectoral-oriented policies unless policymakers adopt flexible exchange rates. Government policymakers will increasingly have to choose between exchange-rate control and sectoral targeting.

common sectoral interests do not necessarily generate collective action. Since Olson's pioneering work on the topic, the puzzle is to explain why collective action problems are overcome. Yet even if collective action problems are overcome, there is a second question: How are sectoral interests translated into policy outcomes? The implicit model of politics in most sectoral approaches is one of rent seeking, lobbying, or "vulgar" pluralism in which policy favors are exchanged on the political market for various forms of support; institutional mediations are of limited significance. In his work on Latin America, Frieden places somewhat more emphasis on the organizational capacity of business-led coalitions; but neither Frieden, Rogowski, nor Milner discuss how the institutions of government, such as the electoral system or rules governing campaign contributions, might shape government responses to societal pressures. Indeed, they are united in discounting the intervening role of institutions.[8]

Recent sectoral analysis by Michael Shafer, including his contribution to this book, offers ingenious solutions to both of these analytic problems: the origins of collective action and the vulnerability of states to pressures from organized sectors. Shafer argues that sectoral characteristics are a determinant not only of firms' preferences but also of their capacity for collective action: The lower the economies of scale in a sector, the simpler the technology and skill-level used; and the lower the capital required for entry, the lower the capacity for collective action. On the state side, states are not merely passive registers for sectoral preferences. Some states develop relative and absolute capacities to counter sectoral preferences. But state capacities are themselves in part the result of earlier stages of sectoral development. In effect, Shafer endogenizes both the propensity to collective action and state capacity in a sectoral framework.

In the empirical studies as well as in the conclusion to Shafer's chapter, we find some surprising divergence from the cretical expectitions. Thorp and Durand, Doner and Ramsay, and Biddle and Milor all find collective action in sectors characterized by low barriers to entry, small scale (and hence relatively large numbers), and high vulnerability to market fluctuations. In the Colombian case discussed by Thorp and Durand, the nature of small-scale coffee production has created strong incentives for coordination and led producers to organize and seek state assistance. Doner and Ramsay have also found collective action in labor-intensive, small-scale textile production. Biddle and Milor contrast collective action and business-government relations in the auto, glass, and textile sectors in

---

[8] Ferguson (1995) and Gourevitch (1986) are more historical and eclectic in their method and partly for this reason bring in supply-side factors such as the nature of government institutions and potentially autonomous preferences.

Turkey. In the auto and glass sectors there are few producers, but sectoral associations are weak because firms can secure particularistic rents from the government on their own and have no interest in collective action. In textiles, however, small-scale producers have a strong association that both lobbies the government and performs governmental functions such as monitoring the use of export and investment subsidies.

When we probe the question of why small businesses are able to overcome collective action problems, we often find the visible hands of state actors and political entrepreneurs (see Chapter 1). Doner and Ramsay, in particular, show that political competition in the Thai state facilitated business organization while simultaneously limiting the possibilities of rent seeking through clientelism; a sectoral approach remains incomplete without complementary analysis of both the state and the actual patterns of business organization. Before turning to the role of these business associations in more detail, however, it is important to examine some crucial political consequences of the organization of private enterprise in developing countries.

BUSINESS AS FIRM: SIZE, HORIZONTAL DIVERSIFICATION, AND PATTERNS OF FINANCING

One of the striking yet understudied phenomena of late, late development is the dominance of the private sector by a handful of diversified business groups. Third World industrialization in the twentieth century produced firms in most developing countries that are large compared to the economy as a whole and relatively diversified when compared to those in advanced industrial countries at comparable levels of development.[9] Such conglomerates typically pursue a dizzying array of activities: As Fields shows in this book, the chaebol in Korea are involved in a range of related and unrelated manufacturing activities, service industries, land development, and (more recently) finance. Korean chaebol are the most extreme examples, but the overwhelming importance of a relatively small number of large groups is a theme also echoed in the chapters on Turkey, Mexico, and Chile.[10]

Concentration (large firm size) and conglomeration (multisectoral

---

[9] The classic reference is Leff 1978. Amsden and Hikino 1994 provide the most comprehensive review. See Steers et al. 1989 and Amsden 1989 on Korea; Durand 1994 on Peru; and Schvarzer 1994 on Argentina. For contrast, see Fligstein 1990 on the history of conglomeration in the United States.

[10] A looser group structure can be seen as a further extension of the conglomerate form of organization: a group of related firms held together through interlocking directorates, holding companies, cross-financing, and often continued family ownership (see Granovetter 1994).

diversification) are often associated but should in fact be distinguished because their causes and consequences for business-government relations differ. There are several sources of concentration. In the twentieth century, technological change has usually served to increase the minimum efficient scale of production. Moreover, as technology is more easily transferred, firm or group size increases due to economies of scope (see Amsden 1989). Government policy also frequently serves consciously or unconsciously to encourage greater concentration. Leff (1978) has argued that in developing countries firms merge and affiliate in order to gain greater leverage vis-à-vis a sometimes threatening state. Military dictators in Korea and Brazil have made corporate concentration an explicit goal of industrial policy, in part in the belief that such concentration is required to achieve international competitiveness.

The obvious implication of concentration for relations between business and the state is the power that large firms are likely to wield from their sheer weight in aggregate economic activity. A high degree of concentration can also enhance the capacity of firms to overcome collective action problems by reducing their numbers (although with the reservations that Biddle and Milor outline in the Turkish case). When big business in the United States rivaled the federal government in size, Teddy Roosevelt remarked that J. P. Morgan treated him more as a competitor than as the head of state. Biddle and Milor document that Turkish bureaucrats feared the political wrath of big business if they were to monitor the use of subsidies more aggressively, let alone attempt to discipline miscreant corporations. Fields shows that the chaebol came to wield substantial power over government policy in Korea by the 1980s. In Taiwan, however, concerns about business influence were a major reason why the Nationalist Party (Kuomintang, or KMT) controlled the financial sector and sought to keep private firms small (Cheng 1993).

Patterns of corporate or group financing can mute or amplify the effects of large size.[11] Generally, we might expect firms with high ratios of debt to equity to be more attentive to government directives if the state controls credit allocation; this was the case in the 1960s and 1970s in Korea, where the chaebol were "in technical bankruptcy at any give time" (Cumings 1984: 31; see Woo 1991).[12] But the effects of high levels of indebtedness on the power of business may be U-shaped. Particularly under conditions of high concentration, high levels of indebtedness shift the balance of power toward the firms, even giving them the power to blackmail the government. Continuing to provide preferential finance

---

[11] See Haggard and Maxfield 1993 for a general discussion.

[12] Debt/equity ratios vary significantly crossnationally. In 1975, ratios in the United States averaged 0.9, in Germany 2.1, in Korea 3.4, and in Japan 4.9 (Jones 1987: 158).

led to further concentration in Korea, but efforts to wean the chaebol from cheap credit threatened business and bank failures (E. Kim 1988; Choi 1993).

Both economic and political factors are also at work in the tendency toward conglomeration and diversification (see Granovetter 1994). Amsden (1989) and Amsden and Hikino (1994) emphasize economies of scope and the advantages that conglomeration creates with respect to technological borrowing. If a firm develops the capacity to absorb new technologies, negotiate the appropriate licensing agreements, and construct new plants in one industry, then it has an advantage (economies of scope) in other types of manufacturing. On the political side, analyses of the Korean chaebol, including Fields's analysis in this book, again stress the role of industrial policy. The Korean government extended finance to a shifting set of industrial activities, thus encouraging existing firms to enter to secure preferential credit even when it may not have otherwise been economically efficient to do so.

A potential negative implication of conglomeration is that it creates a number of monitoring and regulatory problems for government because intrafirm relations are opaque. Hutchcroft (1993) and Hastings (1993) show for the Philippines and Chile respectively that groups including banks were subject to substantial corruption. Group owners were capable of exploiting both depositors and the central bank (as lender of last resort) to channel the resources of group-owned banks into speculative investments or related companies.

On the positive side, the multisectoral organization of conglomerates means that they are not wedded as strongly to particular sectors, rents, or distributional coalitions and can therefore adapt with less friction to changing sectoral priorities. Leff argues that the group structure provides a "mechanism for capital mobility between activities," functions like a capital market, and relieves the government of responsibility for micromanaging industrial policy (1978: 672–73). In effect, conglomerates increase factor mobility; by contrast, firms with all their eggs in one sector are more likely to oppose shifts in policy priorities.

The existence of diversified conglomerates thus raises a frontal challenge to variants of sectoral analysis that assume that firms are constrained by the specificity of assets. Rather, the conglomerate form cuts across a variety of different types of activities: traded and nontraded goods, import-substituting and export-oriented activities, manufacturing, services, and land development. A conglomerate's preferences may therefore be conflicted or ambiguous; if so, it may be a less forceful voice for particular industrial or adjustment policies than one might assume.

Surprisingly, given usual assumptions about oligopoly, multisectoral conglomerates may also serve to promote rather than retard competition.

47

Despite high levels of overall industrial concentration, multisectoral groups in Japan and Korea compete among themselves across a range of markets.[13] Amsden argues that Korean groups have an interest in competing because of a desire to maintain overall parity with other groups (1989: 130, 149–53); competition for government finance acts as an additional spur. Such a competitive outcome is possible is precisely because economies of scope render most markets contestable. Large conglomerates can consider entry even into activities where technological or financial barriers to entry are high; this is particularly true when the government is willing to provide support. Although conglomerates may increase the difficulty of monitoring business, when conglomerates compete for subsidies, they may provide information otherwise unavailable to officials. Competing conglomerates can expose laggard subsidy recipients either directly by ratting on them or indirectly by outperforming them.[14]

In sum, the size, financing, and diversification of big business in developing countries can have important implications for relations between government and business.[15] To date, we still know more about why and how firms became large, diversified, and indebted than about how these characteristics affect their economic and particularly political behavior; clearly, the political economy of the diversified group is central to future research on business-government relations in developing countries.

BUSINESS ASSOCIATIONS: COLLECTIVE ACTION AND SELF-GOVERNANCE

We have argued that the business-as-capital and sectoral approaches pay little attention to issues of political organization. The chapters by

---

[13] An econometric study of French industry by Encaoua and Jacquemin (1982: 25–26, 42–48) supports these arguments, showing that diversified groups were less likely than unlinked firms to exploit market power in individual markets.

[14] Ha-Joon Chang ([1990?]: 27) argues that "the fact that the chaebols as conglomerates are potentially able to move into any line of business . . . makes it difficult for a particular chaebol to keep a particular industry as its fiefdom. Unless it remains reasonably efficient, other chaebols can easily persuade the state that they can do a better job and get the state support in the next round of capacity expansion."

[15] A full analysis of firm-level variables would also need to assess several additional ownership issues. First, family ownership is still the norm in developing countries (see Schvarzer 1994 on Argentina; Bresser Pereira 1974 on Brazil; Steers et al. 1989 on Korea; Durand 1994 on Peru). Little work, however, has been done on the effects of family ownership on relations between business and the state. Second, as we mentioned in Chapter 1, foreign ownership affects relations, as documented in a large literature on MNCs. Third, variations in the role of stock markets and equity financing, over time and across countries, probably influence relations between firms and governments (see Zysman 1983; Haggard et al. 1993).

Silva, Doner and Ramsay, Biddle and Milor, Thorp and Durand, and Schneider, however, all highlight the role of business associations in mediating relations between government officials and capitalists. In contrast to the literature on rent seeking, these studies underline the fact that business organization can *enhance* economic performance. First, business associations can maximize the positive effects of government-business collaboration by limiting the pursuit of particularistic benefits. Second, associations can promote collective self-governance of business, or private-interest governance, that can be equally if not more efficient and effective than direct state intervention or regulation.

Many studies from the business-as-sector school share with the pluralist tradition the premise that common economic position dictates both interests and propensity to collective action.[16] Mancur Olson's work (1965, 1982) accepted the first proposition but strongly challenged the second. Common interests do not necessarily lead to effective organization or concerted political action because of the free-rider problem. Interest groups often remain latent. Olson's work generated puzzles of its own: If collective action is so difficult, why is it so pervasive? And more important for comparative analysis, why does it appear to be more dense in some places and on certain issues than on others?

One of Olson's answers was small numbers. Concentration facilitates organization, and at least certain segments of business are likely to enjoy advantages in this regard when compared with other social actors.[17] Smaller numbers of firms, especially large firms, can monitor each other and either sanction free riders or absorb the costs of organization. As we have already noted, however, the relationship between size and business organization may not be linear. Where business is highly concentrated, economic ministers and capitalists controlling a large proportion of gross domestic product (GDP) can all sit at the same dinner table. Thorp and Durand note how Peru's tiny oligarchy dispensed with formal organizations and dealt directly with the government. Schneider considers the case of the thirty or so members of the Mexican Council of Businessmen, who control a significant share of GDP and lunch together every month. At such extreme levels of concentration, organization is easy; but interaction with the government is likely to take a highly personal form, and

---

[16] As Moe states succinctly, a common premise in the pluralist tradition is that "groups arise on the basis of common interests, that they are maintained through member support of group policies, and that group policies are an expression of underlying common interests" (1980: 2; see also Anderson 1977).

[17] Such propositions are central to Shafer's formulation of the sectoral approach in Chapter 4 and to Offe and Wiesenthal's (1980) class approach.

capitalists may prefer informal coordination in order to avoid public scrutiny.[18]

Nevertheless, Olson's arguments remain fundamentally pluralist in their neglect of the state as a determinant of patterns of business association. (See Skocpol 1985 for a review.) State actions strongly influence collective action in several ways, both intended and unintended. State intervention in the economy influences the incentives to organize. The central argument of Krueger's classic piece on rent seeking (1974) was not that organized interests created rents but that government intervention and the existence of rents produced rent seekers. The more the state intervenes in the economy, the greater the incentive of business to mobilize politically to influence that intervention.

In addition, business organization tends to be isomorphic with government organization (Skocpol 1985; Nordlinger 1981: 190; see also Lodge 1989; Verdier 1994). The greater the centralization of decision-making authority in the government, the more likely it is that business associations will be centralized. In the United States, by contrast, authority is fragmented by the division of powers and federalism; business is similarly fragmented in its organization. Finally, perceived threats from the government have often had lasting organizational consequences for business. In Latin America, spurts of business organization, including the formation of peak associations, appear to be correlated with government actions that changed labor relations (as in Brazil and Mexico in the 1930s) or threatened property rights through direct expropriation (as in Mexico in the 1970s or Peru in the 1980s).

More deliberately, governments often play a role in overcoming collective-action problems by organizing business directly. Schmitter (1974) drew a distinction between societal corporatism that was rooted in independent interest-group association and state corporatism, in which government actors directly organized and controlled social interests. In many Latin American countries, as well as in Korea and Taiwan, the government has determined which associations can form and made membership and dues compulsory. But even where corporatism is societal rather than state, states have sometimes transferred administrative functions to business associations, thereby creating private-interest government (Streeck and Schmitter 1985). The assumption of these functions has greatly strengthened societal associations by expanding the selective benefits they can offer and raising the costs of entry to competing associations.

---

[18] Streeck (1991) argues more generally that capitalists have an interest in weak associations (that permit members maximum discretion) despite their greater capacity for collective action.

The consequences of business organization for both government-business relations and economic policy and performance are disputed. One pattern of thinking follows a long line of skeptics since Adam Smith who are profoundly distrustful of any form of business association: Whenever capitalists organize and meet with government officials, consumers and taxpayers should hold on to their purses. This tradition has continued in the literature on rent seeking and on what Olson calls distributive coalitions. Business organization is habitually aimed at securing rents and as a result drags on efficiency and growth.

But this pessimistic perspective has several obvious limitations. Empirically, associations do not always seek rents; much depends on the nature of the policy status quo.[19] In a heavily regulated economy or one suffering from substantial policy distortions, segments of business become important lobbyists for rent-reducing reform (see Haggard 1995). Moreover, as Olson himself admits, and as we have seen with reference to corporate organization, the preferences of associations are partly a function of their scope. Encompassing, multisectoral organizations are more likely to champion policies conducive to economy-wide efficiency rather than narrow ones that represent particular sectors (Olson 1982: 48–53). In essence, an encompassing organization gives business leaders a more statelike perspective (see Nordlinger 1981: 35).[20]

As we discussed in Chapter 1, the chapters in this book offer several arguments about the benefits of capitalist collective action for business-government relations and consequently the economy. Concertation is perhaps the clearest example of the advantage of close relations between business associations and the government. In Europe, especially in the smaller countries, corporatist bargaining that includes labor has been effective in stabilizing prices, output, and employment (see Katzenstein 1984, 1985b; Garrett and Lange 1991). European-style corporatism is typically based on formal consultative mechanisms and requires sticks and carrots from not only government but also peak associations of business capable of enforcing agreements among their members. The absence of peak organizations has been blamed for the lack of effective concertation in a number of developing countries, including Brazil and Turkey (Öniş

[19] Work by Milner (1988), for example, has chronicled the rise of antiprotectionist forces in the formulation of American trade policy, and Gary Becker (1983) has made the more general point that competition among interest groups can act as a check on rent seeking.

[20] As Thorp and Durand show, formal appearances of encompassingness can be misleading. The multisectoral peak association in Venezuela was not as encompassing as it appeared because it could not reconcile conflicting interests of its members. The interests of the Colombian coffee federation, in contrast, were not as narrow as they appeared: Because of the diversified holdings of its leaders, the federation approximated a multisectoral peak association.

and Webb 1994; Haggard and Kaufman 1995, chap. 10; more generally, Streeck and Schmitter 1985: 11).

Nonetheless, the chapters by Silva, Schneider, and Thorp and Durand highlight the positive contribution of concertation in Latin America to the process of economic reform, even if such concertation was only informal and partial. In the second round of reform in Chile (1983–89), officials consulted systematically with leaders of business associations, although Silva argues that the combination of peak associations and a "tight, hierarchical state structure" reduced particularism and made for productive government-business collaboration. In Mexico and Brazil business associations met with officials to negotiate and accelerate transitions to more open economies and more competitive industries. Thorp and Durand argue that Colombia's elite and centralized coffee-producer association facilitated collaboration with government; access to government through the business association contributed to private investment and overall growth because it helped build business trust and confidence in government.

The delegation of certain functions to business associations can also enhance business-government relations and economic performance. For example, Streeck and Schmitter (1985) have argued that business associations may be able to administer certain state functions, including the details of policy implementation, more efficiently than bureaucratic agencies can (see also Anderson 1977). Katzenstein argues similarly that encompassing peak associations in Austria and Switzerland unburden democracy by resolving disputes internally rather than foisting them on the government. This interest intermediation is politically efficient because "political conflicts within the business community [do] not immobilize the public agenda and government machinery" (1984: 197).

The chapters in this book offer several concrete examples of benign self-governance. Biddle and Milor document a remarkable association in the Turkish textile industry that was able to monitor firm use of government subsidies and enforce reciprocity, even where the government itself was weak. An essential component of this success was transparency within the association; individual firms did not bypass the association to seek particular gains because they knew they would be found out. Biddle and Milor argue that the textile industry enjoyed greater success and used government subsidies more wisely than other Turkish industries did. In Colombia the government helped coffee producers organize, gave the association control of an export tax, and ceded it responsibility for developing the sector by investing in infrastructure, marketing, and research. Doner and Ramsay find several instances where businesses in Thailand attempted to regulate themselves, especially in export sectors. Finally, Schneider notes the capacity of the Mexican retailers' association to monitor and enforce the price agreements contained in the anti-inflation pacts of the late 1980s. In all cases some impetus from the government was crucial to the establishment of private-interest governance: formal concertation in Mexico, export incentives in Turkey, government assistance in organizing in Colombia, and a generalized uncertainty about government intentions in Thailand.

The analysis of business associations is an obvious point of entry into the study of business-government relations; but it, too, has a number of significant pitfalls. We have already noted how an instrumental conception of business-government relations can miss the structural constraints that the private sector places on the state. Yet the business-as-association approach can also overlook the importance of informal networks that provide alternative mechanisms for aggregating interests and interacting with state officials. Schmitter's exhaustive study (1971) of business associations in Brazil, for example, concluded candidly that both their members and government officials regularly ignored them; in practice, the crucial business-government relations were personal and informal. All the empirical chapters offer examples of close, informal, personalized ties between capitalists and bureaucrats. We now turn to this final conception of business.

BUSINESS AS NETWORK: SOCIAL CONSTRUCTIONS OF TRUST AND COLLABORATION

In his influential analysis of the power elite, C. Wright Mills (1956) argues that the business networks he studied were maintained through interlocking board memberships, leading to a system in which a relatively small number of individuals exercised inordinate economic power. He also argues that the relatively small number of individuals in the United States who occupied top positions of corporate leadership maintained close relations to political leaders through intermarriage, clubs, and other social ties. Business influence over government came not through distant lobbying but through a shared world view, informal personal networks, and overlapping roles. Subsequent power elite studies have invested substantial energy in documenting the existence of such closed networks, including thorough posipographic analysis and careful attention to biographical detail.[21] In general, however, they are more interested in issues of personal power, status, and stratification than in

---

[21] Domhoff (1970, 1978) furthered Mills's research agenda in the United States. Useem (1984) contributed from a somewhat different angle. Zeitlin and Ratcliff (1988) conducted similar work on Chile (see also Silva, forthcoming).

documenting the policy and economic consequences that they presumed would result.

In the 1970s, students of American politics generated a plethora of concepts and metaphors for understanding the policy consequences of relations among business lobbies, legislators, and bureaucrats: iron triangles, policy whirlpools, subgovernments, policy and issue networks, and "the hollow core" (Heinz et al. 1993; see Berry 1989 for a review). Although the major goal of this research was typically to illuminate the input side of politics, the implications for policy, including economic policy, were typically negative. A cousin of the rent-seeking approach, this line of analysis usually emphasized how collusion among politicians, interested bureaus, and organized constituencies permitted policies that favored narrow interests over the common good.

In developing countries, the political analysis of networks has focused more on clientelism: personalized, multifaceted, unequal, exchange relations. The concept of clientelism has been elastic enough to encompass both social interactions, such as those between landlord and tenant, and the political exchanges that evolved within bureaucracies and parties or between politicians and government officials and their clients. But clientelism has also nearly always carried a negative connotation, bad for politics because it distorts democratic principles, bad for economics because it diverts public resources from more productive uses. The clientelistic networks surrounding Marcos, Somoza, and Mobutu were taken as archetypes: dense yet especially effective at corruption and pillage.

As with the analysis of associations, however, expectations about the consequences of networks are not uniformly negative. It has long been recognized that formal organizations and institutional hierarchies are interlaced with informal networks that strongly affect their performance. Drawing on a tradition that dates to the early work of Karl Polanyi, observers have also increasingly recognized that market transactions are embedded in such networks as well. In a recent review, Powell and Smith-Doerr (1994) identify dozens of different types of network analysis in economic sociology alone. It is possible, however, to distinguish two basic conceptions of network: embedded and strategic.

Embedded networks are natural, generalized, and preexisting, as in extended family, regional, or ethnic networks. (For a recent example, see Putnam 1993a). In the radical view, such networks form a kind of primal social fabric in which all other forms of social, economic, and political interaction are embedded.[22] In contrast, strategic networks are artificial creations—narrower, instrumental forms of cooperation established to

[22] See Granovetter 1985 for an analysis of what he calls oversocialized conceptions of embeddedness.

achieve some specific goal. Common examples include research on technology sharing, marketing agreements, and subcontracting. (See, for example, Smitka 1991 and Sabel 1992.)

A major shortcoming of most network analysis in economic sociology is the neglect, sometimes intentional, of the state (for example, Gerlach 1992). States are not central to the creation of embedded networks; on the contrary, governments are embedded in them (Putnam 1993a). The driving force behind strategic networks is the effort of individuals and firms to manage their contracting relations; again, state actors are typically excluded from the analysis.

Peter Evans (1995) has led the effort to bring the state back into sociological research on networks. His notion of embedded autonomy encompasses both the networks linking bureaucrats and capitalists (thus "embedded") as well as the internal organizational characteristics of the bureaucracy that give it independence. His main analytic target is conceptions of state autonomy that overemphasize the insulation of state actors. He admits that without state autonomy, "embeddedness will degenerate into a super-cartel, aimed like all cartels, at protecting is members" (58). Nonetheless, he argues that the capacity of the state can be strengthened when officials are "embedded in a concrete set of social ties that bind the state to society and provide institutionalized channels" for continual interaction (59). Empirically, such networks among capitalists and bureaucrats are strengthened when bureaucrats and managers have relatively stable tenure and work for the same companies or ministries for long periods of time and when the circulation of personnel between the public and private sectors is widespread (Evans 1995; Thorp 1991).

Game theorists have argued that trust and cooperation can emerge where interaction is repeated, information on participants is abundant, relations are multifaceted, and participants do not discount the future too much. These factors have received particular attention in the analysis of embedded networks in which reciprocity constitutes a generalized norm of behavior. Dense networks and norms of trust and generalized reciprocity constitute what Putnam (1993a) calls social capital; where such capital exists, those participating in the networks minimize on transactions costs and thus get more out of scarce resources than do agents operating in an environment in which social capital is scarce. Game theorists also emphasize that relations of trust and reciprocity are difficult to maintain without mechanisms for monitoring compliance and sanctioning. To the extent that networks are based on frequent and crosscutting interactions, they also provide such enforcement mechanisms.

In this positive light, networks (what Biddle and Milor call growth-oriented networks) can enhance all the functions introduced in Chapter 1. Networks can promote the two-way flow of information between government and private sector, which in turn enhances policy design and subsequent adjustment. To the extent that networks build reciprocity and trust, they benefit the economic policy process by lowering transactions costs between government and business and minimizing the likelihood of policy stalemates. Networks are also beneficial to the extent that they increase transparency because this raises the costs of individual rent seeking.

Research on East Asia, particularly Japan, offers the dominant example of how enduring networks between businesspeople and bureaucrats can have beneficial effects. Ties among graduates of elite universities (Tokyo University and four others) create the natural foundation for dense, embedded, private-public networks that facilitate the policy-making process (Taira and Wada 1987). Over time, individual bureaucrats spend years interacting with the same managers in the sectors they regulate (C. Johnson 1982). Moreover, hundreds of top bureaucrats retire every year into top positions in business or into the Diet in a process known as *amakudari*, or descent from heaven (C. Johnson 1974; Calder 1989). *Amakudari*, in essence, extends a preexisting network within a bureaucracy (which itself is often built on preexisting school ties) beyond the state into the private sector. Taira and Wada conclude that these networks create a Todai-Yakkai-Zaikai complex (Tokyo University-bureaucracy-organized business) and that "the personal networks and contacts of public officials and private business leaders render the formal structural distinction of government and business almost meaningless" (1987: 264; see also C. Johnson 1982).

Still lacking is more comparative and empirically based assessments specifying when such business-state networks thrive and make positive contributions to growth in developing countries. Several chapters in this book contribute to the task; a recurrent theme is the extent to which networks are open, transparent, or competitive as opposed to closed and monopolistic. Doner and Ramsay emphasize that uncertainty and competition among and within networks keeps them from ossifying into rent-seeking coalitions. Clientelistic networks between Thai officials and Chinese businesses were competitive because barriers to entry were low; the internal factionalization of government guaranteed that a dissatisfied client could find a different patron. Other networks within the Chinese business community further enhanced information exchange and transparency. These networks were embedded and dense and in themselves reduced transactions costs and enhanced self-governance. Nevertheless, Doner and Ramsay also argue that the negative consequences of patron-client networks are bounded by independent economic officials capable of imposing a hard budget constraint on the demands emanating from competing factions.

56

Silva (and, to a lesser extent, Biddle and Milor) also compare good and bad networks and argue that formal structures, transparency, and visibility are all key to maintaining the beneficial consequences of government-business networks. In Chile, the contrast between the closed networks, and the negative consequences thereof, in the first period of reform (through 1983) and the more open networks in the second period (1983–88) are especially telling because other major political and economic variables were constant.

Network analysis provides a new and potentially powerful entry point into the study of business-government relations. It lends itself to detailed empirical work, including quantitative analysis: Data on interlocking directorates, school and other social ties, marriages, and so forth can be used to generate complex network maps. But research on the *form* that networks take is more advanced than research on the nature and consequences of the interactions through them and the consequences that are likely to result. An important analytic ambiguity still remains: The line between those networks that enhance efficiency and those that provide the opportunity for public goods to be appropriated for private ends remains thin and poorly understood. Where state actors belong to Weberian bureaucracies, the opportunities are greater for generating growth-oriented networks. But the empirical studies in this book of Colombia, Turkey, and Thailand document growth-oriented networks despite their non-Weberian bureaucracies; here other factors such as transparency and ethnic cleavages have detered more collusive behavior by network participants.

In each of the previous sections, we highlighted scholarship identified with different conceptions of business and tried to do no more than the necessary Procrustean violence in our categorizing. Of course, for most specific outcomes some synthesis of approaches is required to do justice to the complexity of business-government interactions.[23] The empirical studies in this book employ a mix of different conceptions depending on the peculiarities of the case and the aspect of economic performance explored. For other scholars, complexity is the point of departure. For instance, Hollingsworth and his colleagues argue that "markets, hierarchies, states, networks, and associations represent distinctive modes of governance" that are all present in varying combinations in any given economy or economic activity (1994: 8). They conclude that the primary research task should be "to determine the relative importance of the

---

[23] The literature on relations between governments and MNCs in developing countries ranges across the five levels of analysis, although often without the explicit distinctions we advocate here. See Moran 1974, Evans 1979, D. Becker 1983, and Bennett and Sharp 1985.

various modes of governance in different contexts, to describe how they are articulated with one another, and to assess the extent and direction of change in regimes over time" (8; see also Kitschelt 1991).

To some extent, this book shares that synthetic goal. By describing a variety of regimes of business-government relations, the following chapters map changing structural and organizational patterns over time in a number of important middle-income developing countries. But the governance literature has not been especially rich in simple, general hypotheses on the impact of varying forms of business-state relations on economic performance. Here, contending theories associated with each of the five conceptions offer clearer causal arguments that orient the rest of this book.

If there is a modal view among social scientists about the effects of business influence on economic policy and performance, it is a negative one. Thinking among economists has been almost totally dominated by models of rent seeking in which distributive coalitions (whether sectors, individual firms, business associations, or networks) have the effect of distorting allocative efficiency by lobbying for intervention. Much writing by sociologists and political scientists is hardly less crude. Sociological work following in the power-elite tradition continues to emphasize how corporate assets are deployed to maintain social hierarchy. Although pluralists argue that business power may be offset by countervailing organization such as the environmental movement or public-interest lobbies, most political scientists concede that business occupies a privileged political position in any capitalist economy, which it will use to its particular advantage.

Despite this generalized skepticism, some work in each of the five perspectives explored here suggests conditions under which business-state collaboration can enhance economic performance. Whether capital's power to invest and flee is seen as good or bad depends largely on normative priors: For conservatives, it constitutes a restraint on a potentially predatory state; for reformists, it limits the government's freedom of maneuver. All would agree, however, on the calming influence of stable rules, trust, transparency, and government credibility in restraining capital flight and encouraging private investment. Clearly, the political relationship between business and government is an important variable in this regard and one that goes beyond the business-as-capital approach.

Sectoral analysis offers several hypotheses that are germane to a political theory of economic growth. In a static sense, performance is likely to be superior where the political system provides strong representation of those sectors that are representative of the country's underlying comparative advantage. Understanding the conditions under which this is likely demands much closer scrutiny of the institutions of government than is

58

usually offered in sectoral analyses. More generally, the government's freedom of maneuver vis-à-vis the private sector is likely to be greater where leading production sectors have low barriers to entry and low economies of scale, are labor-intensive, and are vulnerable to market fluctuations.

Conversely, as the business-as-firm literature also emphasizes, a high degree of industrial concentration constitutes a powerful constraint on the government. For a number of reasons, such concentration is likely to imply high business leverage vis-à-vis government. Not only does a high degree of concentration ease coordination problems in the private sector and increase the potential for blackmail, but it is also likely to tie the state to the interests of a limited range of economic activities. We have noted, however, that this tendency might be partly offset by the existence of multisectoral economic groups.

The conclusions about business associations are more complex. Following Mancur Olson, we have noted that encompassing organizations can mitigate centrifugal sectoral pressures. Such organizations are essential for the strategy of macroeconomic management through corporatism or concertation. The organizational weakness of social groups in most developing countries means that concertation is likely to be more ad hoc, sporadic and crisis-driven rather than an ongoing feature of government policy-making. Nonetheless, experiences in Mexico and Chile suggest that concertation may be a large part of solutions to some specific economic problems.

Even in the absence of overarching peak associations, more narrow sectoral associations can still be developmental in the ways they promote competitiveness in the sector and distribute public resources for productive ends. Moreover, they are capable of providing government officials with information—albeit always potentially biased—about market conditions and policy needs. The well-known dangers of sectoral associations center on government capture and the fear that such associations will become little more than Olson's distributive coalitions. The availability of rents from government will condition the political activities of associations; however, certain features of the organizations themselves, including barriers to entry and transparency, are likely to mitigate their tendency to seek rents and increase their capacity for productive self-governance.

The business-as-network perspective emphasizes that repeated interaction and multiple ties that reinforce personal connections can build trust between state actors and their private-sector counterparts, in effect reducing political and policy transactions costs. But this still may constitute a bad from the perspective of coherent policy; other conditions are required to keep such networks honest. As we analyzed in Chapter 1, one such condition has to do with the government itself. Structures and practices internal to the state are important for determining business-state relations in all conceptions for business, but they are perhaps most important in determining the consequences of close networks because few other internal features of networks are especially significant in determining whether they are benign or malign. An appropriate balance between insulation from business and engagement with it is crucial for combining the capacity to monitor and discipline powerful social actors while also extracting cooperation and information from them. In Chapter 3, Peter Evans examines these issues at greater length.

PART II

BUSINESS ORGANIZATION, FIRM STRUCTURE, AND STRONG STATES

CHAPTER THREE

State Structures, Government-Business Relations, and Economic Transformation

PETER EVANS

Any analysis of government-business collaboration must be grounded in a vision of economic transformation. From the newly industrializing countries (NICs) of East Asia to the "basket cases" of the sub-Sahara, enhanced welfare depends on growth, and growth requires transformation. Throughout the Third World, achieving sustained growth has meant first complementing agriculture with industrial capacity and then moving from simple, low value-added manufacturing to more sophisticated, higher-return kinds of industrial activities.[1] Transformation depends in turn on business. In the contemporary world, citizens of all countries depend on capital to provide them with the means of becoming more productive participants in the global economy.

Analyses of government-business collaboration that focus on rent seeking and corruption are grounded on the assumption that business's contribution to transformation can be taken for granted as long as economic decisions are not tainted by politics. In fact, the problem is more complicated. Politics aside, business has a dual character as an economic actor. On the one hand, it is engaged in a search for profit. On the other hand, it is the source of productivity-enhancing investments.[2] Unfortu-

---

[1] Eventually, of course, it must also mean finding a way to participate in high-return activities involving the global production of services; but for Third World countries this remains a challenge still to be faced.

[2] Most contemporary analyses of the political relation between business, conceived abstractly as capital, ignore this duality. They stress the quest for short-run profit and therefore focus on the struggle of business as capital to avoid whatever encumbrances the state might place in the way of unfettered profit seeking. Unfortunately, these analyses are generally mute on the question whether profit seeking coincides with enhancement of local

nately, in a world of increasing returns, path dependence, and multiple equilibria, there is no guarantee that the two coincide.[3] The search for profit does not necessarily give workers a chance to produce more and improve their standards of living. Speculation and the pursuit of financial rents are often more attractive than investing in assets that will only produce a return in the long run. Business is risk averse and transformation involves exploring unknown economic territory.

Schumpeter's "gale of creative destruction" may be essential to the workings of capitalism, but from the point of view of individual businesses, avoiding the risks of competition is always the order of the day. Avoiding the gale of creative destruction may mean looking for easy rents that do not involve long-term investments. Leaving aside the question of politically generated rents, many attractive routes to profit do not enhance the productive opportunities open to a country's citizenry. Such routes may involve staying with activities in which major costs have already been sunk and successful routines already established. They may involve constructing oligopolistic cartels or redoubts of monopoly power. Or they may involve fleeing to environments that are more developed and predictable. All of these strategies separate the pursuit of profit from productivity-enhancing investments that will produce higher living standards for the citizens of the countries we are interested in here.

Keeping the profit-seeking face of capital connected to its transformative face is the essence of preserving the economically progressive potential of market societies, but it is not an easy task. Whether the pursuit for profit can be successfully connected to economic transformation within a given country or region depends on the character of the business community. Part of that character is the commitment of the business community to different sectors of production. In any epoch, some sectors of the global economy produce higher returns than others. Some sectors are dead ends, while others are, in the words of Albert Hirschman (1977: 96), "multidimensional conspiracies in favor of development." If business has placed its bets on dead-end sectors and is determined to defend its sunk costs, there will be no transformation.

As Haggard, Maxfield, and Schneider point out in Chapter 2, the potential for transformation also depends on business's capacity for collective action. Without minimal standards of trust and reciprocity, even routine business activities are impossible. Unless formal norms and informal practice combine to ensure that commitments are kept, investment

---

productivity, thus leaving unexplored the implications of the state's relations with business for the realization of capital's transformative potential. Compare the discussion by Haggard, Maxfield, and Schneider in Chapter 2.

[3] See, for example, Arthur 1990, Krugman 1990, and Romer 1994.

makes no sense. Exploring new activities or pioneering new sectors requires more. New sectors are not built by individual firms. Increasingly, they depend—Silicon Valley–style—on complementary combinations of many firms. Innovative investments depend on confidence that inputs will be available, buyers ready, and complementary goods forthcoming. The capacity for collective action depends in turn on concrete organizational characteristics. Trust and reciprocity are built around continually iterated patterns of interaction. Formal organizations such as firms and business associations institutionalize the normative bases of collective action. Informal ties and networks accomplish the same thing in different ways.

In all of the interrelated facets of business that either make transformation possible or put it out of reach, the state is deeply implicated. The structure of the state and the character of the capital that operates within its territory are inextricably linked and mutually determined. Disorganized states lead to disorganized business communities and vice versa. Investors flounder in the absence of coherent public policy. Without an organized business community, even an organized state cannot promote structural change. Coherent public policy helps organize the business community. Being able to work with a business community that is organized in the pursuit of long-term economic growth promotes competence and vision in the public sector. Changes on either side of the public-private boundary are reflected on the other side. As Haggard, Maxfield, and Schneider said in Chapter 2, there is a strong tendency toward isomorphism in the organization of business and government.

My own way of cutting into these complex interdependencies is to start with the state and work from there to business. Starting with the structure of the business community may be equally fruitful. We live, however, in an ideological climate that systematically attempts to obscure the state's possible contribution to economic transformation. Making an extra effort to delve into the ideologically unpopular sequence in which the structure of the state shapes the character of business in such a way as to enhance possibilities of transformation is therefore crucial to achieving a more balanced understanding of how business and the state interact.

Starting points should not be confused with causal claims. It would be a terrible error to turn the state into the necessary and sufficient deus ex machina that determines all outcomes. Even if states were unitary actors, which they clearly are not, they would not be able to shape growth as they choose. The extent to which states can promote transformation depends on the character of the business community with which they have to work. If states succeed in changing the character of the business community, that changed character must in turn have an impact on the state. The state and business reshape each other in reciprocal iteration.

My strategy for exploring the effects of state structure and policy on the business community is straightforward. Four propositions, which I will sketch in the remainder of this introduction, underlie my argument. In subsequent sections, I will flesh out the argument as a whole, adding some illustrative empirical detail and drawing on some of the other chapters in this book as well as on my own research.[4]

1. Government-business relations cannot be interpreted without first specifying the internal structure of the state. Several simply defined variations in how states are structured internally are the starting point for this argument. Certain states are able to bind the behavior of individual incumbents to the pursuit of common goals. They are coherent bureaucracies in the Weberian sense of the term.[5] Other state apparatuses are not Weberian bureaucracies at all. They are collections of individual maximizers masquerading as organizations in pursuit of the common good. Depending on the internal structure of the state, similar business-government networks have different implications. When the state apparatus has the corporate coherence necessary to pursue collective goals, dense ties with the business community can become vehicles for the construction of joint public-private projects in pursuit of economic transformation. Corporate coherence plus dense ties leads to "embedded autonomy," which lies at the structural heart of economically successful "developmental states" (Evans 1995: 50). In the context of a state apparatus that is a collection of individual maximizers, dense ties create the negation of joint projects, an incoherent form of clientelism not only incapable of supporting long-term investment but actively predatory in relation to the rest of society. When the state lacks the capacity to monitor and discipline individual incumbents, every relationship between a state official and a businessperson is another opportunity to generate rents for the individuals involved at the expense society at large.[6]

2. The character of the business community can be reshaped by state policy. As the previous discussion suggests, variations in internal state structure not only affect the character of government/business ties but also shape the nature of the business community itself. Having a public counterpart that is organized and predictable makes it much more likely that the business community moves from merchant-capital strategies of "buying cheap and selling dear" to a more developmentally desirable Schumpeterian strategy of confronting risk and making long-term investments. Left to their

---

[4] In terms of my own research I draw principally on *Embedded Autonomy: States and Industrial Transformation* (1995).

[5] See ibid.: 29–30, 48–49, as well as the following discussion.

[6] As several of the chapters in this book illustrate, many Third World states lie somewhere between the incoherent despotism of the predatory state and the relative efficacy of the developmental state. In such intermediate states, the consequences of state structure for business organization is likely to vary across sectors and administrations (compare Evans 1995: 60).

own devices, most businesses gravitate toward activities that have low risk and maximize short-run returns. Sustained economic growth requires a longer-run perspective and less risk aversion than most entrepreneurs can afford, particularly in developing economies. Embedded autonomy provides the structural basis for pursuit of a joint public-private project of economic transformation in which the state lowers risks and enables individual businesses to pursue a more Schumpeterian program of entrepreneurship. The distribution of business activities across sectors can also be affected in the same way. Given a modicum of internal coherence and effective ties to the business community—that is, some approximation, at least at the sectoral level, of embedded autonomy—the state can play a role in encouraging entrepreneurial exploration of new sectors. New strategies and new sectors add up to a transformation of the country's entrepreneurial resources.

3. *When state policies succeed in reshaping the business community, they are likely to undercut the very patterns of government-business relations that made the policies effective to begin with.* Government-business relations must be seen as iterative. If embedded autonomy fosters a more economically powerful business community, the state then has a different interlocutor to deal with. If state policy succeeds in promoting a new sector, the same is true at the sectoral level. Business-government relations in succeeding periods will change to reflect the new character of the business community. Previously effective state structures may be undermined. As local economic groups grow and gain economic stature, the tutelage of the developmental state is less appreciated. Instead of requiring the state as an intermediary in order to bargain with transnational capital, local entrepreneurs can attract transnational allies on their own. New global alliances replace old ties to the state. The increasing power and wider options of local capital weaken business support for sustaining a Weberian bureaucracy and increase the likelihood that connectedness will degenerate into capture.

4. *As government-business relations evolve, a more encompassing set of state-society networks that includes institutionalized ties between the state and other social groups may provide a better means of sustaining future transformation.* As business becomes more powerful and less tolerant of the autonomy of Weberian bureaucracies, government-business ties are more likely to mean capture rather than joint projects. Some counterweight is needed to keep public-private networks oriented toward collective goals rather than particularistic rent seeking. Building institutionalized ties with groups other than business is a politically difficult but logically plausible countervailing strategy. Institutionalizing a more encompassing set of state-society ties may be the only way to keep embedded autonomy from losing its developmental effectiveness.

These four propositions—or, more accurately, subthemes—have a single heuristic purpose: to highlight crucial components of the overall claim that starting with the state, working outward to the changing character of business, and then returning to the consequences of change for the state is a useful way of understanding possibilities for economic transformation. The discussions that follow do not claim to provide comprehensive empirical tests. Rather, they illustrate and elaborate the argument, leaving it available as a potential lens for the interpretation of other case material and therefore more open to refinement and reconstruction.

BUREAUCRATS AND PREDATORS

If all state actions were aimed at maximizing the general welfare, analyzing government-business relations would be much simpler. If we could count on state actors to "implement the logic of capital," as structural Marxist theories (such as Poulantzas 1973) argued they did, analysis would be simpler still. The theoretical premise of modern neo-utilitarians also offers a seductively simplifying assumption: States are simply collections of individual maximizers, each intent on using his or her official power to gain wealth and informal power.[7] In reality, states are neither universally benign nor universally malignant. They vary. Understanding the variation in state structures is the first step in understanding why dense ties between policymakers and businesspeople sometimes produce growth but sometimes only spoils.

While states are not necessarily benign, they do, as institutions, tend to have a more encompassing definition of their interests than private actors do. As Guillermo O'Donnell pointed out some time ago (1978, 1979), even relatively malevolent states are constrained by the fact that the state is identified as the defender of the "national interest." If officeholders behave as individual maximizers (which neo-utilitarian models suggest they should) rather than as agents of the state as institution, the constraint no longer applies. Predation is only a pejorative term for individually maximizing rational behavior. The first divide among state structures is therefore between those in which the interests of individual incumbents are allowed free rein and those in which individual incumbents are successfully constrained to behave as members of a larger collectivity with a more encompassing set of interests.

States in which incumbency is viewed as an opportunity for individual maximization are almost inevitably predatory. They become, like Zaire,

---

[7] For a discussion of neo-utilitarian approaches see ibid.: 22–25.

states where "everything is for sale, everything is bought. . . . In this traffic, holding any slice of public power constitutes a veritable exchange instrument, convertible into illicit acquisition of money or other goods."[8] The state's monopoly on the organized use of force combined with the unbridled acquisitiveness of state officials turns the citizenry into prey. Whatever surplus the society produces is siphoned off by those who share official power; even the simplest collective goods such as roads and schools are left unprovided. Any incentive to make long-term investments in productive assets disappears, and economic decline follows.

For the state to be something other than a predator, something other than a simple logic of individual rent seeking must prevail among officeholders. But how can an aggregation of officeholders be transformed into a collectivity capable of carrying out a common project? The best answer still seems to be the one offered several generations ago by Max Weber. Weber (1968) saw bureaucracy not as the synonym for inefficient rigidity that it has become in contemporary perception but as a specific kind of coherent organizational entity in which pursuing collective goals becomes the best way to maximize individual self-interest.

Bureaucracy in the Weberian sense requires a demanding combination of characteristics. Being a Weberian bureaucrat means renouncing immediate possibilities for income and informal power in order to retain the rewards accruing to members of the organization over the long run. For this to happen, membership of the organization must be seen as a distinctive, valued status, and the prospect of long-run rewards must be clear.[9] Construction of a Weberian bureaucracy begins with a meritocratic system of recruitment. If being someone's nephew is the best way to get a job, then kinship is the distinctive status that is reinforced, not membership in the employing organization. In addition, of course, nephews unable to get jobs on their own are less likely to have any relevant competence than meritocratically selected recruits are, however arcane the means of assessing "merit." Patterns of promotion are as important as patterns of recruitment. Finally, the overall combination of rewards to the career must be commensurate with those available to people of comparable qualifications in other walks of life. If prestige and security are higher, then salaries can be lower; but if the overall combination of incentives is inferior, the bureaucracy is likely be inferior as well.

Having a real bureaucratic organization in the public sector makes it much more likely that private entrepreneurs will turn to investments in productive assets as the central thrust of their search for profit. A meri-

---

[8] The quotation is from Joseph Mobutu Sese Seko, cited in Lemarchand 1979: 248.
[9] Biddle and Milor point out in Chapter 10 that networks can sometimes develop similar properties.

tocratically selected set of individuals, capable of concerted corporate action, whose horizons extend over the length of their careers, is the best guarantee of the competent provision of productivity-enhancing collective goods. Among these collective goods, the single most important is a predictable set of rules. The sine qua non of long-term investment is predictability, and bureaucratic organizations are uniquely designed for the universalistic application of stable sets of rules. Bureaucracy's predictable rules and cohesive pursuit of common goals are not only important to individual businesses but also crucial in helping business as a whole overcome its inherent collective-action problems. Whether the problem is eliminating excess capacity in a mature sector or putting together a critical mass of firms to initiate a new growth pole, the existence of a stable bureaucracy with encompassing interests is a big advantage.

If the potential advantages of Weberian bureaucracy are obvious, its scarcity is equally evident. The equation of *government agency* and *bureaucracy* is all too often false, especially in the Third World. Public careers are unrewarding; bureaus are stuffed with nephews; public jobs are way stations on the path to more rewarding private-sector opportunities; every bureaucrat must look out for him or herself. Such state organizations are not Weberian bureaucracies at all but exactly the kind of aggregations of rent-seeking individuals that neoliberals rightly rail against. The point is not that states are usually Weberian bureaucracies; rather, insofar as state structures approximate the ideal typical characteristics of the Weberian bureaucracy, they are more likely to provide the counterparts that will enable business to realize its potential as a transformative agent.

Of course, even when cohesive, coherent state structures do exist, they need close and continuous connection to a broad set of private firms in order to make a real contribution to economic transformation. Bureaucratic capacity will always be inadequate to produce transformation on its own. No conceivable formal organization could successfully deal with all the innumerable intricacies involved in promoting economic transformation. The state needs business first of all as a source of decentralized intelligence about what is possible. Even more important, any transformative project that the state might contrive must in the end be implemented largely by private capitalists. In short, the state needs business as much as business needs the state.

The necessity of connectedness is obvious; but connectedness, like business itself, has a dual potential. Biddle and Milor capture the duality nicely by dividing business-government connectedness into growth-oriented and rent-seeking networks. Growth-oriented networks are instruments for the pursuit of collective goals, while rent-seeking networks are vehicles for allowing capital to avoid the risks of transformation in favor of directly unproductive means of securing profits. There are various ways of trying to keep networks from being dominated by rent seeking; but as Biddle and Milor also point out, the best way of increasing the probability that networks will be growth-oriented is to have the public side of the network anchored in a Weberian bureaucracy.

The basic argument is quite simple. The goal is to make sure that the search for profit remains connected to business's potential for transformation. Close connections between business and government can be a means of achieving this goal, but their effectiveness depends primarily on the character of the state itself. Without a state apparatus whose internal structure allows it to exact compliance to growth-oriented norms, networks become the problem rather than the solution. What is required is not just embeddedness but embedded autonomy. Efforts to vindicate this argument with systematically collected empirical evidence covering a range of developing countries have only recently begun.[10] Nevertheless, there is already a wealth of case studies and partial comparisons whose findings generally support the idea that a coherent, cohesive state bureaucracy joined to business in an institutionalized way provides an exceptionally effective basis for economic transformation.

As this book's introductory chapters have already pointed out, and the chapters by Fields and Shafer will underline, the East Asian NICs offer the best empirical grist for the theoretical mill connecting state structures, government-business relations, and superior economic performance. Once analysts began to probe the origins of East Asia's miraculous industrialization, it was hard to ignore the formidable bureaucratic infrastructures that pervaded the region. Chalmers Johnson's characterization of Japan's ministry of International Trade and Industry (MITI) as "without doubt the greatest concentration of brainpower in Japan" drew attention to an aspect of East Asian industrialization that soon became part of standard accounts (1982: 26). Subsequent analysts (such as Okimoto 1989; Samuels 1987; Calder 1993) felt that Johnson neglected other crucial elements in Japan's success, but they still agreed that the "powerful, talented and prestige-laden economic bureaucracy" that Johnson had so vividly described was a crucial part of the story (1982: 26).

Turning to Korea and Taiwan, scholars such as Alice Amsden and Robert Wade found equally compelling approximations of Weberian bureaucracies. Here again there were exam systems, with histories going back hundreds of years, that were as selective as the one Johnson had described in Japan. His description of a society in which "official agencies

---

[10] James Rauch and I have gathered systematically comparable data on variations in the structure of economic bureaucracies across a set of 35 developing countries. Preliminary analysis of these data indicates a strong statistical confirmation of the Weberian hypothesis, but a great deal of further analysis is required before the results can be presented with real confidence.

attract the most talented graduates of the best universities in the country and positions of higher level official in these ministries have been and still are the most prestigious in the country" found clear echoes in the NICs (1982: 20).

Even the World Bank eventually joined the chorus. While carefully avoiding any endorsement of state intervention at the sectoral level, the World Bank acknowledged the importance of East Asia's cohesive, well-trained, well-paid state bureaucracy. The bank's *East Asian Miracles* report (1993a: 176–77) points out that high-performing East Asian economies (in contrast to the Philippines, for example) have all made conscious efforts to provide their bureaucrats with wages comparable to those in the private sector, noting the contrast between Singapore (where bureaucratic salaries are 110 percent of wages in comparable private-sector positions) and Somalia (where they are 11 percent). The report also notes that the efforts of developmental states to gain the cooperation of big business would be "hamstrung without an efficient and reputable civil service" (1993a: 187).[11]

Most of the strength of the global correlation between Weberianism and growth is accounted for by the strong Weberian character of the successful East Asian region and the predominance of states that are the antithesis of Weberianism in the decaying nations of sub-Saharan Africa. In other regions, such as Latin America, states are more than simple aggregations of individual maximizers but still far from approximating the Weberian ideal type. Nonetheless, a close examination of variation both among intermediate cases and within states of all types reconfirms the important role of Weberianism.

Research in intermediate states such as Brazil has shown that, even when the state bureaucracy as a whole is a badly fractured sea of clientelism, it can still be characterized by certain "pockets of efficiency" that both approximate the Weberian model and contribute to transformative growth (see Schneider 1991b and especially Geddes 1986). Doner and Ramsay make the same point with regard to Thailand. While they note in Chapter 9 that "the Thai bureaucracy has generally earned strong marks compared to its LDC counterparts," they emphasis that there is vast variation across different state agencies. On the one hand, the core agencies that deal with monetary and fiscal policy (the Bank of Thailand, the Ministry of Finance, the Bureau of the Budget) are highly cohesive and pro-

---

[11] The reader should be aware that the effort to be succinct has left the discussion here overstated and one-sided. The Weberian model is an ideal type, while actual state apparatuses have all the flaws and failings of empirical cases. Examples of corruption, inefficiency, nepotism, and favoritism are not hard to find in East Asian bureaucracies. Such deformities are simply more successfully contained than those in less well developed bureaucracies.

fessional. Correspondingly, Thailand has traditionally enjoyed effective management of fiscal and macroeconomic policy. Sectoral ministries (such as the Ministry of Industry), on the other hand, are much more Latin American in their organizational style, which is one reason why Doner and Ramsay are doubtful that Thailand will be able to accomplish the kind of industrial upgrading that has been the hallmark of growth in East Asia.

Even East Asia contains good examples of intrastate variations supporting the Weberian hypothesis. Okimoto, for example, makes the point that the Japanese bureaucracy has always included agencies such as the Ministry of Agriculture that are "pockets of conspicuous inefficiency" (1989: 4). Consistently, while Japanese industrial growth achieved "miraculous" proportions in the 1960s and 1970s, Japanese agriculture was conspicuous in its lack of transformative growth and predatory relationship with the rest of Japanese society.

Overall, the impressionistic empirical support for the importance of Weberian state structures is surprisingly powerful and certainly warrants collection of more systematic evidence. Comparative evidence also supports the idea that coherent state structures need connectedness to business.

The extreme case against insulated bureaucracies that try to promote economic change on their own is obvious. If bureaucracy were sufficient in itself, state socialism would not have suffered the economic humiliation that it did in the Soviet Union. High-performance bureaucracies, such as those in East Asia, depend on the combination of embeddedness and autonomy rather than simply bureaucratic prowess. Post-Johnson analysis of Japan has emphasized the extent to which effective strategies of transformation emerge "from the complexity and stability of [the state's] interaction with market players" (Samuels 1987: 262). Japanese industrial policy depends fundamentally on the maze of ties that connect ministries and major industrialists. Deliberation councils, which join bureaucrats and businesspeople in rounds of data gathering and policy formation around an ongoing series of specific issues, are only one example of the "administrative web" (World Bank 1993a: 181). Okimoto (1989) and Wade (1990) both emphasize the central role that visits to factories and on-site discussions with corporate personnel play in the life of a bureaucrat in MITI or IDB (Industrial Development Bureau). Karl Fields offers a variety of additional examples in Chapter 5.

Other examples complement the Soviet-East Asia contrast. India, for example, had the benefit of a formidable Weberian bureaucracy.[12] What

[12] The Indian Administrative Service was built on a tradition that stretched back at least to the Mughal Empire. In its colonial incarnation it provided "the steel frame of empire,"

separates its bureaucracy from more industrially effective East Asian counterparts was less its internal structure than the underdevelopment of its
institutionalized relations with business. India lacked the kind of
state/private-sector networks that allowed industry experts from within
state agencies, such as Japan's MITI or Taiwan's IDB, to deliver a combination of information dissemination, consensus building, and tutelage to
the private sector.

In Chapter 6 Eduardo Silva offers a nice, small-scale example of the disadvantages of having a coherent but isolated state apparatus. According
to Silva, the Pinochet regime, one of the most autonomous in any region,
found its technocrats' implementation of economic policy littered with a
growing series of disasters during the first decade of its rule, largely
because it disdained to develop systematic ties with business. Only after it
combined autonomy with embeddedness did its economic record begin
to improve.

What these illustrations underline is that successful collaboration is not
a question of choice between either having cohesive, insulated bureaucracies or having close connections with the private sector. The former is
the foundation that makes the latter work. Without a sufficiently cohesive
administrative structure, connectedness turns the bureaucracy into an
instrument for private gain; but given a sufficiently coherent, cohesive
state apparatus, connectedness ceases to be synonymous with capture.
Internal bureaucratic coherence is an essential precondition for the
state's effective participation in external networks. MITI's autonomy was
what allowed it to address the collective-action problems of private capital,
helping capital as a whole to reach solutions that it would have had a hard
time attaining on its own. If MITI was not able to formulate goals or count
on its officials to devote themselves to implementing them, it would have
had little to offer the private sector.

In short, either autonomy without embeddedness or embeddedness
without autonomy are likely to produce perverse results. Without autonomy, embeddedness becomes capture. Without embeddedness, joint
projects that engage the energy and intelligence of business cannot be
constructed. The state's contribution to transformation depends on combining the two. All of this reinforces the basic message of the first proposition: Government-business relations cannot be interpreted without first
specifying the internal structure of the state. The consequences of
government-business ties depend fundamentally on the character of the
state's internal organization. A dense network of ties between business

---

serving as a model not just for other colonial administrations but also for England's own
civil service (Taub 1969: 3). While its traditions and esprit de corps have eroded seriously
in recent years, its entry examinations are still as competitive as its East Asian counterparts.

and a cohesive, Weberian state will have completely different consequences from a dense network connecting business with a set of officeholders who are an unconstrained aggregation of individual maximizers.
But a question still remains: Can even the most effective and connected
state expect to be able to move business into new kinds of activities,
thereby changing the character of a country's entrepreneurial resources?

LEGACIES AND MIDWIFERY

Breaking into new sectors and investing in the continuing improvement
of productive capacity necessary to stay competitive in a globalized
economy is a daunting business for local capitalists in developing countries.[13] Even transnational firms are intensely conscious of the risks
involved in pursuing such activities on unfamiliar turf. The structural
capacities implied by embedded autonomy give the state the potential to
make a difference. Promotional policies—including signaling, regulation,
and temporary sheltering from the full rigors of the global economy—
can encourage business to explore new sectors. Variations of these
policies can be applied to sectors that have been established but need to
keep investing and changing. Thus, the degree to which capital is concentrated in more challenging, technologically complex sectors depends
in part on state policies and the effectiveness of government-business
relations.[14]

Nevertheless, social structural starting points do matter. Any project of
transformation must begin with a set of property holders who can envis-
age some prospect of realizing their quest for profit through investments
in new, productivity-enhancing assets. Without some entrepreneurial
resources to work with, even the most clever, deftly administered set of
policies cannot bear fruit. A state without at least a nascent business class

---

[13] My use of the term *legacies* in the heading of this section is inspired by Collier and
Collier 1991, although I use it here in a slightly different way.

[14] Some analysts, like Shafer in Chapter 4, prefer to focus on the reverse causal sequence.
Instead of looking at how institutional structures affect possibilities for sectoral specializations, they look at how past sectoral specializations have shaped existing institutional structures. Obviously, existing institutions reflect, among other things, past patterns of economic
activity; but an approach that gives causal priority to sectoral specializations has its own problems. As Hirschman (1977) and later Jeffrey Paige (1987) have pointed out, even a simple
agricultural specialization, such as exporting coffee, can be based on quite different forms
of production in different settings, forms which then have different institutional and political consequences. Specifying the institutional consequences of particular sector specializations becomes even harder when manufacturing and services are involved. My own position
follows that of Biddle and Milor (Chapter 10), who "disagree with approaches that endogenize business's likelihood to organize collectively by reducing it to industry- or sectoral-
specific factors."

will suffer the disadvantages of insufficient embeddedness despite its best efforts to build connections. Conversely, the members of a mature business class, which already enjoys economic power and political clout, are unlikely to see why they should abandon individual strategies of profit seeking to engage in a joint transformative project. In this case, it will take an exceptional level of autonomy for the state to avoid seeing its agencies and officeholders turned into instruments for private rent seeking. Sometimes the two problems are combined. Entrepreneurial groups potentially able to contribute to transformative projects are absent, but the state confronts an entrenched class of traditional property holders anxious to use political connections as a source of rents.

In the Third World, politically powerful property holders are typically not industrialists but landholders who have little interest in transformative projects of any kind. Brazil is a good example, illustrating how the legacy of a powerful class of landholders can persist despite substantial industrialization. From the colonial period on, the Brazilian state was inextricably embedded in networks of rural oligarchic power. While industrialization modernized these relations, they were by no means erased. As Hagopian (1986, 1994), has carefully documented, the traditional exchange in which landowning families delivered political support in return for the fruits of state patronage became tighter rather than looser as industrialization proceeded in Brazilian states such as Minas Gerais. The expansion of the state's economic role led descendants of Minas Gerais's old governing families to rely increasingly on access to state resources as their principal source of power and wealth. Efforts at transformation were undercut and diverted by this perverse legacy.

Social structural legacies shape prospects for transformation in other regions as well. Doner and Ramsay's comparison of Thailand and the Philippines in this book offers a good example. In Thailand, the absence of a landed aristocracy diminished the dangers of embeddedness. Furthermore, as in the case of Taiwan, ethnic divisions left the business elite politically dependent, increasing the state's autonomy. The Philippines, in contrast, faced an even more debilitating version of Brazil's problems. A tightly knit traditional landholding class, combined with the ambivalent traditions of an Americanized colonial bureaucracy, loaded the dice in favor of capture and corruption.

In contrast, as many observers have noted, East Asia after World War II has enjoyed a felicitous set of social structural legacies. (Compare the chapters by Fields and Shafer in this book.) During and after the war, exogenous influences ranging from the Americans to the Communists freed these states from the burden of traditional agrarian elites. The historical depth of bureaucratic tradition provided a foundation for the construction of a cohesive state apparatus.[15] The undercapitalization and relative disorganization of nascent industrial groups made it less likely that connectedness would turn into capture. In short, in the aftermath of World War II the region became fertile ground for a project based on a combination of embeddedness and autonomy.

Inherited legacies can create institutional potential, but the potential must still be realized through an intricate and uncertain process of purposive change. In the East Asian case, the potential for change contained in post–World War II business-government relations was far from apparent at the beginning of the period. As Wade (1990) points out forcefully, the immediate postwar period found countries such as Korea and Taiwan miserably poor, with populations relying primarily on agriculture to earn their livings. Taiwan was warned by its American advisors that textile production was well outside the boundaries of its comparative advantage. Korea was, in Shafer's words (see Chapter 4), "an exporter of duck feathers and seaweed." Even in Japan, the formidably industrial organization that would emerge in the 1960s and 1970s was only dimly foreshadowed at the beginning of the 1950s.

In all of these cases, a generation's worth of change in the structure, strategy, and sectoral focus of local business communities had to occur before hindsight could reveal the potential of post–World War II institutions. Over the course of the three or four decades after the war, robust, coherent state apparatuses supported the emergence of, highly organized, dynamic business sectors. State policies rewarded firms that were able to carve out new global markets or provide the inputs that exporters needed in order to compete abroad. The existence of a predictable public interlocutor facilitated private collective action. State support helped turn tiny disorganized firms into major corporate actors. First in Japan, then in Korea and Taiwan, internationally competitive industrial classes were created where they had not existed before.

As Shafer's chapter makes clear, the transformation of East Asian business classes was not simply a shift in sectoral orientation but a change in the scale and scope of business organization and the character of entrepreneurship. Firms began to rely less on cheap labor, seeking their comparative advantage instead in the prowess of their production engineering (Amsden 1989) and the ability of their research and development teams to come closer to globally defined technological frontiers. Nonetheless, sectoral shifts were also part of the process. Moving into more challeng-

[15] Learning to make use of this inheritance was, of course, not quite as simple as my shorthand implies. See Shafer (Chapter 4) and Fields (Chapter 5) on the contrast between the Rhee and Park regimes. Likewise, the contrast between the KMT bureaucracy on the mainland and its renaissance on the island is central to the story of the state's role.

ing sectors was part of moving toward higher-value-added, higher-return strategies of production.

In all of this, the state played the role of midwife.[16] While new sectors were occasionally pioneered directly by the state, even the most entre-preneurially oriented bureaucrats were aware that inducing private capital to enter new sectors, push their technological capacities forward, and develop the organizational skills necessary to deal with rapidly chang-ing markets was the only effective way to build a new sector.[17] Part of the state's contribution was the simple Hamiltonian ploy of providing a pro-tective greenhouse in which new sectors could emerge. This temporary sheltering was combined, however, with a variety of other strategies. State agencies weighed in at the bargaining table to help local firms extract technological collaboration from transnational firms. Selective state financing made risky industrial ventures more attractive. State R&D orga-nizations helped establish technological foundations that the private sector could build on, sometimes even generating new products that could be farmed out to local firms. At the same time, the state mediated precompetitive joint research projects that brought major firms together in pursuit of breakthroughs. In the end, this eclectic combination of state efforts was largely successful in facilitating the emergence of new sectors and bringing forth a new kind of business class.

No where is midwifery better illustrated than in the emergence of East Asia as a world center of advanced electronics production. Kenneth Flamm (1987, 1988) and Marie Anchordoguy (1988) have documented the process nicely in the case of the Japanese computer industry. Starting in the early 1960, when Japanese computer companies were considered mosquitoes in relation to the American elephant, IBM MITI engaged in a multifaceted campaign to create local computer production.[18] Before there was sufficient commercial interest to stimulate private R&D, gov-ernment laboratories took the lead in generating local technological capacity. Controls on imports and foreign investment helped convince local business that it would not be wiped out if it tried to enter more advanced areas of electronics production. Then the carrot of access to the domestic market was used to persuade IBM to share its technology with a select set of Japanese firms. In order ensure that local producers would have a market, government procurement was heavily biased in favor of local suppliers. Even more imaginatively, a joint public-private financing organization was set up to ensure that potential purchasers of

[16] For a discussion of midwifery as a form of state involvement, see Evans 1995: 80–81.

[17] Examples of state pioneering include steel in Korea and semiconductor wafer fabrica-tion in Taiwan.

[18] The comparison is Sabashi Shigeru's, head of MITI's Heavy Industries Bureau in the early 1960s (see Anchordoguy 1988: 515).

locally produced computers were not deterred by cash-flow problems. Once local firms got started, a series of MITI-sponsored research programs stimulated and focused their R&D activities.

By the beginning of the 1980s Japan had a computer industry that was second only to the U.S. industry. This achievement was the product of private investment, but multifaceted government involvement was pivotal in getting business to take on a challenge that would have seemed hopelessly risky to any individual firm when the process began. State policy helped change the sectoral composition and technological capabilities of the private sector. Consequently, the state had a very different business community to work with at the beginning of the 1980s from the one it had at the end of the 1950s.

In Korea and Taiwan, a similar process was repeated with a lag. The overall scope of changes in the capacity and organization of local business communities was even more dramatic. In Korea, the same set of targeted loans at below-market rates that were applied to the "heavy and chemical industry" (see Shafer's chapter) also drew selected firms into the production of more advanced electronics goods during the 1970s. At the same time, KIET (Korean Institute of Electronics Technology; later KETRI [Korean Electrotechnology and Telecommunications Research Institute], then ETRI [Electronics and Telecommunications Research Institute]) played the same role that government laboratories had played in Japan, starting research and pilot industrial production before there was sufficient commercial incentive to draw local firms into the act. In the case of semiconductors, for example, KIET developed a pilot line that was later sold off to the private sector. Once private sector semiconductor production had gotten started, ETRI helped organize a series of DRAM dynamic random access memory projects that drew major firms into concurrent efforts to break through new technological barriers in memory-chip production.[19] Taiwan's Electronics Research Service Organization (ERSO) not only developed products and spun them off to the private sector but even spun off firms. In the case of semiconductors, Taiwan found itself at a disadvantage because its less concentrated industrial structure left it without firms with deep enough pockets to risk the billions of dollars necessary to get into wafer fabrication (see Chapter 5). Direct state investment in new wafer fabrication was the answer. Transnational corporations (TNCs) were drawn in as joint-venture partners, and a crucial lacuna in Taiwan's electronics sector was filled.[20]

By the mid-1990s, Korea's Samsung had outstripped NEC, Hitachi, and Toshiba to become the world's largest producer of merchant memory

[19] See Ernst and O'Connor 1992 and Evans 1995: chap. 7.
[20] See Wade 1990; Ernst and O'Connor 1992.

chips; and Korea's semiconductor industry was in a league well beyond that of the industrial countries of Western Europe. Taiwan had become a power in the personal computer industry and was using its new wafer fabrication capacity to provide its myriad small electronics firms with the specialized chips they needed in order to stay at the frontier of information-technology production. Once again, a new sector had been created that was only vaguely foreshadowed in the entrepreneurial resources of a generation earlier. The new industrial order had been generated primarily by private investments, but midwifery on the part of the state had been central to transforming the business class.

When embedded autonomy characterizes state-business relations as a whole, midwifery is much easier; but even more problematic state apparatuses can sometimes succeed in generating something like embedded autonomy at the sectoral level. Brazil offers a number of excellent examples. Autos (see Shapiro 1994) and petrochemicals (Evans 1979, 1982, 1986) illustrate, in different ways, how cohesive, competent, state organizations can act as midwife for investments in new sectors, reshaping the local business community in the process. The range of sectors that can be affected by even imperfect approximations of embedded autonomy is nicely illustrated by the emergence of Brazil's information-technology sector.

In Brazil, as in East Asia, midwifery played a central role in creating a local information-technology sector. Faced at the beginning of the 1970s with no local producers and a market completely dominated by foreign subsidiaries, a group of Brazilian technocrats persuaded the military regime to allow them to use exchange controls as a means of setting up a protected "greenhouse" at the lower end of the computer market in which local firms could be grown. By the end of the 1980s, a multibillion-dollar local industry with hundreds of locally owned firms employed tens of thousands of professionals and sold billions of dollars worth of hardware.[21] The state was successful in drawing the country's largest financial groups, some of which had little prior involvement in any kind of industrial entrepreneurship, into this exceptionally demanding sector.[22]

For a variety of reasons, ranging from the character of the local industrial establishment to Brazil's quite different relation to the global economy and the flawed nature of the state apparatus itself, the outcome

---

[21] None of this is to deny that Brazil's nascent informatics sector had serious problems. Dividing 1 percent of the global market among hundreds of local firms made it very difficult for any individual firm to achieve sufficient scale. Being largely cut off from international supplier networks made the problem worse. Local hardware products were expensive (although prices did fall), and with a few exceptions firms were unable to export. These performance problems must be balanced against the potential of the strong human and institutional infrastructure that was created in a surprisingly brief period of time.

[22] See Evans 1995: chaps. 5–7 for a better sense of the twists and turns of this process.

of Brazil's midwifery in the information-technology sector was not nearly as robust as Korea's. Nevertheless, construction (from almost nothing) of a local information-technology sector over the course of a fifteen-year period provided a striking illustration of the fact that local entrepreneurial classes can be reshaped as a consequence of state action, even in the most challenging industrial sectors.

All of this supports my second proposition: The character of the business community can be reshaped by state policy. Inherited institutional configurations and sectoral specializations facilitate or impede possibilities for future transformation, but there is always room for maneuver and unexpected outcomes. States do not create business classes, but neither do they have to live with what they inherit. Existing business communities can be drawn into joint projects and reshaped by their participation in them. In cases such as Brazil, where both the internal character of the state apparatus and the nature of its ties to business are flawed, reshaping is likely to be partial and limited to particular sectors. In cases such as Korea, where embedded autonomy prevails, state policies have been instrumental in dramatically reshaping the overall character of the business community. The question then becomes, What are the consequences of such changes for the future character of government-business relations? Are they self-reinforcing, or do they generate new contradictions that will have to be overcome in order to sustain past dynamism?

THE PITFALLS OF SUCCESS

Successful execution of a project of transformation must change the character of government-business relations. What is less obvious is the expected content of those changes. One might expect that participation in a successfully executed joint project of transformation would make the business community more beholden to the state, more willing to accept future constraint and direction. The historical record suggests that the outcome is not so straightforward. Korea offers the best illustration.

As Shafer's chapter in this book documents, the increasing organizational capacity and economic power of Korean business during the 1980s tended to undermine embedded autonomy rather than strengthen it. By the beginning of the 1990s Korean firms were full-fledged participants in the international economy, not only selling abroad but investing abroad and forming strategic alliances with transnational corporations. Firms that had been dependent on the state to channel foreign loans in their direction in the early 1970s could go after such loans directly at the end of the 1980s (compare Woo 1991).

The new structural position of business was reflected in turn in the nature of the ties between business and government. The World Bank notes that in the Korea of the late 1980s and early 1990s "relations between government and business have become more distant and meetings less frequent" (1993a: 183). Structure and interaction has been, in turn, reflected in ideology. The election campaign of Chung Ju Yung in 1992 was emblematic of the shift. Chung's Hyundai empire was archetypal of the chaebol that had been built in the nurturing environment of state support and subsidy. It was a prime beneficiary of President Park's efforts at deepening Korea's industrial base, and the state was fundamentally involved in the company's shifting production profile. Yet Chung's campaign slogan, rather than reflecting past relations, was typically American: "Get government out of business."

The shifting position of business does more than change government-business relations. It has a potential effect on the internal coherence of the state as well. Rising opportunities in the private sector threatened the material base of the distinctive status of the state bureaucracy by magnifying the gap between private and public salaries (see Evans 1995: 233). The new ideological climate, which increasingly denied the bureaucrats' contribution to Korea's growth, diminished the intangible rewards to participation in the state apparatus at the same time that structural change diminished the material rewards. In short, the internal structure of Korea's developmental state seems in danger of being eroded by the very economic growth that the state was so effective in promoting.

Overall, Korea offers an excellent illustration of my third proposition: When state policies succeed in reshaping the business community, they are likely to undercut the patterns of government-business relations that made the policies effective to begin with. Marx believed that the bourgeoisie's economic success created its own "gravediggers." Similarly, developmental states may create the gravediggers of embedded autonomy in the form of a more economically and politically powerful, more internationally oriented business class. New connections with international allies and greater prominence of direct investments in overseas markets diminish interest in nationalist economic policies and leave business less convinced of the need for overcoming collective-action problems at the local level. Greater economic and political power means that the business community is not only less easily engaged in a joint project of local transformation but less willing to tolerate the level of state autonomy necessary to balance high levels of connectedness. With a more powerful business community and a less cohesive and coherent state, connectedness risks becoming capture, and growth-oriented networks threaten to deteriorate into "rent-seeking networks" (compare Biddle and Milor, Chapter 10 in this book).

It would be absurd to predict an immediate deterioration in the dynamism that has been constructed over the course of a generation. The entrepreneurial system that has been put into place is likely to continue to perform for some time to come. My argument here is not that "the sky is falling on the developmental state" but only that ability of government-business relations to stimulate productivity-enhancing investment over the long run has been vitiated. Nevertheless, if the kind of embedded autonomy that has worked in the past has been undermined by the very social and political changes that it helped to bring about, a new question is raised: How might state-society ties be restructured in such a way as to preserve embedded autonomy (i.e. the balance of autonomy and connectedness) despite the new power and international orientation of the business community?

RESTRUCTURING EMBEDDED AUTONOMY

Any theory of how embedded autonomy might be reconstructed must be speculative, but there are good reasons to speculate. The kind of business-government relations that characterized East Asian developmental states grew out of a particular set of historical circumstances in which the traumatic social dislocations caused by a world war played a central role. Obviously, other countries trying to achieve the same balance of autonomy and embeddedness cannot replicate the same process. Because exogenous geopolitical change is unlikely to provide the structural foundations for embedded autonomy elsewhere, thinking about how the balance of embeddedness and autonomy might be recaptured is more likely to be relevant to other developing countries than is historical analysis of its initial emergence.

The central issue in recapturing embedded autonomy is clear. The heart of the problem is finding a way to counterbalance the weight of a more powerful business community so that embeddedness is less likely to degenerate into capture. At least one logical possibility presents itself. Extending the institutionalized connectedness that characterizes government-business relations under East Asian–style embedded autonomy to include a broader range of societal groups could potentially solidify the state's position and contribute to prospects for economic transformation.

Comparative evidence suggests that including additional actors whose interests partially conflict with those of business in the institutionalized network that bind state and society could strengthen the institutionalized character of business-government relations. Inclusion of groups with diverse and partially conflicting interests in public-private networks creates, as Biddle and Milor point out, strong pressures for transparency. Austria in the 1970s, as described by Peter Katzenstein (1984, 1985b), offers an excellent illustration. Because business and labor are both organized in powerfully centralized ways, translating the interests of capital and labor into policies requires a set of formal state institutions, such as the joint commission, in which capital, labor, and representatives of the state can resolve conflicts.

A more encompassing form of embedded autonomy also has the effect of legitimating the state's contribution to joint projects, in the eyes not just of the newly included groups but also of business. If government and business are the only political players, the state can only defend its claims to be an actor in its own right during unusual periods of business weakness (as in postwar East Asia). If other social actors are empowered, business needs a state capable of reconciling conflicting definitions of the shared project, not just in principal but in the day-to-day practice through which economic plans are constructed and implemented. Once groups other than business are included in the same kind of dense networks that characterize business-government relations in the developmental state, private economic strategies can no longer be forged independently of the state, and collaboration becomes indispensable.

The traditional objection to developing institutionalized ties to labor and other subordinate groups is that they will become a dreaded "distributional coalition." In contemporary internationalized capitalist economies, this specter is almost certainly a false one. The likelihood of labor's mounting a successful rent-seeking campaign are slim. The fact that labor has a direct interest in binding capital's search for profit to productivity-enhancing investments is much more relevant to the likely consequences of a more encompassing embeddedness. As Przeworski has argued elegantly in *Capitalism and Social Democracy*, the best overall deal for labor in a capitalist economy is precisely the same deal that forms the core of the joint government-business transformative projects. To be willing to eschew disruptive militancy, labor needs credible institutionalized assurances that profits will be invested in ways that will enhance productivity (and therefore increase labor's take in the long run). In this sense, then, labor is a natural ally in joint public-private transformative projects.

There are, of course, serious political difficulties entailed in making the transition to a more encompassing embeddedness. If we take Korea as an illustration, the problems are evident. Resistance from business would be intense. Nor is labor, the most organized segment of the subordinate population, likely to consider building ties to the state an attractive strategy.

The industrial transformation in which the developmental state played a key role unquestionably benefited Korean workers. Despite a repressive system of labor control, Korean workers experienced a rise in real wages during the 1970s and 1980s that was among the most rapid in the world. Rising wages flowed from a combination of higher productivity; moreover, increasing scale of manufacturing establishments, combined with rising skill levels and value added per worker, gave workers greater bargaining leverage. Nevertheless, the developmental state did not get credit from workers for rising wages or their increasing bargaining clout, and with good reason. Workers were excluded from the kinds of public-private networks that connected government and business. The state presented itself to them primarily as a powerful repressive apparatus. As Shafer documents, Korea's industrial transformation has corroded the state's relation to labor even more than the state's relation to capital. Labor is more likely to want to dismantle the developmental state than build connections to it.

Overcoming the political obstacles to a more encompassing form of embedded autonomy is no mean task, but this does not diminish the potential advantages of successful restructuring. The historical precedents are stronger than contemporary rhetoric would lead us to believe. On the one hand, arrangements that closely resemble encompassing embeddedness have provided the basis for a half-century of successful transformative growth in the social democracies of Northwestern Europe. On the other hand, there are at least scattered Third World examples to suggest that the increased political participation of labor can help push government-business relations toward higher levels of institutionalization and a greater orientation toward transformation.

There are even some interesting examples in this book that support the encompassing embeddedness hypothesis. Schneider's story of the leaders of Brazil's powerful metallurgy union coming back from a trip to Detroit with the conclusion that the state would have to force Brazil's transnational auto assemblers to modernization is an excellent case in point. An even more unlikely example is provided by Silva's chapter on Chile. Silva points out that the popular mobilization in 1982–83 was a significant element in shifting the regime away from its economically ineffectual reliance on idiosyncratic personal ties between individual technocrats and selected businesses in the direction of an institutionalized model that was much more successful in terms of transformation. The transformative success of the elected post-Pinochet regime is also grist for the argument that making embeddedness more encompassing can improve economic performance.

All of this circumstantial evidence supports my fourth proposition: As government-business relations evolve, a more encompassing set of state-society networks that includes institutionalized ties between the state and other social groups may provide a better means of sustaining future transformation. This proposition is clearly the most speculative of the four and undeniably requires additional support before it can be put forward with real confidence, but it certainly deserves further exploration.

Prospects for Transformation

Hopefully, this more detailed exposition of the four propositions with which I began the chapter has contributed to unpacking the conditions of successful government-business collaboration. I have argued that the possibility of transformative collaboration depends fundamentally on the character of the state apparatus. Linking a state apparatus that lacks cohesive coherence to business can only result in capture and corruption. To keep embeddedness from slipping into capture requires a high degree of internal corporate coherence, best ensured by some approximation of Weberian bureaucratic structures. To emphasize this point is not to deny that social structural legacies are also critical. Embedded autonomy can help create a complementary set of private interlocutors, but even the most competent and organized state cannot turn an entrenched set of traditional landholders into a farsighted, entrepreneurial industrial bourgeoisie.

Despite its emphasis on the importance of social structural legacies, the argument developed in this chapter may seem too optimistic. It certainly has more room for agency than do arguments that see possibilities for government-business relations as determined by the logic of globalized markets. It also has more room than do arguments in which both policy and development are determined by a technoeconomic sectoral logic. The opportunities for agency in my argument should not, however, be exaggerated. Not only do institutional and social structural legacies confine possibilities for action, but any transformative success carries with it a new set of even more challenging problems. In fact, my argument suggests that in the long run successful government-business collaboration requires fundamental political restructuring.

In my argument, agency on the part of the state, and with it the leverage necessary channel the quest for profit in the direction of productivity-enhancing investment, is inevitably undercut by the increased economic and political power of business that must inevitably flow from successful transformation. Escaping this limitation depends on institutionalizing a more politically inclusive set of ties between state and society. Other chapters in this volume (such as Thorp and Durand's Chapter 8 and Silva's Chapter 6) make the point that effective collaboration between government and business is not sufficient to ensure that broader issues of societal welfare will be addressed. My argument goes further. I am arguing that even the ability of government-business collaboration to produce transformative growth depends in the long run on the institutionalization of state-society ties that include subordinate groups.

Embedded autonomy, like any other institutional structure, must be reconstructed as economic transformation proceeds. Helping to foster a more powerful business class generates problems as well as solutions. In a highly internationalized economy such as ours, increases in the economic (and consequently political) power of the business class are likely to result in a diminished sense of mutual interdependence with the state, making it harder to construct joint projects. Industrial success makes the unconstrained pursuit of profit seem more legitimate and any form of state-imposed constraint less acceptable. Possibilities for future collaboration are undercut by past achievements. Precisely because of these contradictions, government-business collaboration does not in itself offer a permanent recipe for transformation. Unless the rest of the society is eventually included, narrowly constructed embeddedness is self-limiting and ultimately self-defeating.

CHAPTER FOUR

The Political Economy of Sectors and Sectoral Change: Korea Then and Now

MICHAEL SHAFER

The Republic of Korea is a model of success that has been held up to other Third World countries as an example. Academic analysts often explain this success by referring to Korea's developmentalist state, top-down government-business relations, and export-led growth strategy; policy analysts often recommend that states wishing to emulate Korea's economic success should also emulate the politics and policies of "Korea, Inc." But what makes Korea a marvelous case study is the extent of the changes it has experienced as well as their often unexpected character. In the past thirty-five years, Korea has not only gone from poor to rich; its government has also gone from being the despair of its American advisers, to a model of étatist success, to a fledgling democracy struggling to manage popular demands and maintain control of economic policy in the face of the growing independence and power of big business and labor.

In other words, what makes Korea a marvelous case study is how well it lends itself to an examination of the two major analytic questions of this book: How can we best theorize the political economy of business-state relations? (or what does *business* mean in the contect of understanding how business-state relations shape development?) and What sort of business-state relationship is best for economic development; how, why, and when does it arise; and by what mechanism does it work? Specifically, Korea allows us to pose the critical questions of variation: What explains the varying capacity of states to set and implement economic policy, and what explains the nature and direction of change in this capacity over time?

In this chapter, I take up these questions using a sectoral analysis of the Korean state's changing capacity to restructure the economy—that is, its ability to reallocate resources and reorient economic activity to reduce the risks and increase the gains from international engagement. Or as Thorp and Durand put it in their chapter on Colombia, Peru, and Venezuela, I want to explain how the changing character of the Korean export economy has shaped its "capacity to negotiate structural change"; for what matters for development are less the good times than "the periods when change has to be negotiated if reasonable progress is to be secured and sectoral shifts are needed."

I first consider the question of how best to theorize business-state relations. Specifically, I establish the need for sectoral approaches and the limits of those now available. Second, I explore the character of current explanations of business-state relations and, in particular, their inability to move beyond descriptive categorization. I then offer a new variety of sectoral analysis intended to correct the limits of existing sectoral arguments identified in Chapter 2 and many of the other explanations of business-state relations sketched there. While less elegant than the models of Ronald Rogowski (1989) and Jeffry Frieden (1991), my approach confronts the two key problems with existing sectoral arguments: their inability to account for the differential capacity of sectoral actors for collective action or the differential capacity of state institutions to set and implement policy. By the same token, it refines existing explanations of business-state relations by permitting us to answer not only the question "What sustains the collaborative advantage that some states or sectors seem to have over others?" but also "How, why, and when does such collaborative advantage arise?" Having set the stage, I then compare and contrast Korea in the 1960s and the 1980s to test my claims and explore the political consequences of the sectoral shift in the Korean economy effected by state-led restructuring in the 1970s. I conclude with a mini-case comparison of Korea and Taiwan and a reanalysis of Thorp and Durand's discussion of Columbian coffee as a way to explore the limits of sectoral analysis.

SETTING UP SECTORAL ANALYSIS

In real estate everything boils down to location, location, location. In social science everything boils down to specification, specification, specification. Here is where the argument for sectoral analysis in general begins and, more specifically, for a new variant of it. In this section, I do two things. First, I argue for a business-as-sector rather than a business-as-capital approach to theorizing business-state relations in order to correct the overgeneralization of the latter with better specification. Second, I argue for sectoral analysis as an essential addition to existing descriptions of the proper character and workings of business-state relations, again in order to correct the overgeneralization of the latter.

In a world of rapidly falling barriers to trade and capital mobility, the exit option of business as capital clearly contrains governments' capacity to set and implement economic policy. But as Haggard, Maxfield, and Schneider note in Chapter 2, such generic explanations offer no leverage when the questions involve how to explain the wide variation in (1) the actual preferences of specific segments of the business community in a given country; (2) the institutional capacity of states to ignore, resist, or channel pressures from business; and (3) the balance of power in government-business relations at any given time or over time. One promising corrective to the overgeneralization typical of business-as-capital models is to specify the interests and policy preferences of businesspeople according to their location in the domestic political economy and the nature of their assets—that is, to define *business* in government-business relations as "business as sector."

Sectoral analysis has a long lineage, but its most influential recent proponents are Rogowski (1989) and Frieden (1991). Rogowski asserts that the critical economic—and therefore political—cleavages in society follow factoral lines. Politicizing Stolper-Samuelson, he argues that, as changing exposure to trade changes the relative abundance or scarcity of a country's factors, holders of abundant factors will prevail politically while holders of scarce factors will lose. Rogowski assumes frictionless *factor* mobility and therefore frictionless *political* adjustment to changing trade exposure. Frieden rejects frictionless factor mobility in favor of a model that begins from the assumption of *differential* mobility in the face of changing international market exposure. Thus, according to Frieden, actors' policy preferences and predilections for political action will be determined by how specific (*im*mobile) their assets are. Nevertheless, Frieden rejoins Rogowski in assuming the unproblematic translation of the most motivated actors' policy preferences into political reality.

Rogowski's and Frieden's versions of sectoral analysis share problematic similarities. Both focus on economic preferences and preference formation, but neither engages the politics of how, or whether, preferences become policy. Consequently, both do well explaining variation in the preferences of specific segments of business in a country. But neither explains the variation in the institutional capacity of states vis-à-vis actors with strong preferences or why the balance of power between government and business, and the actual course of policy, often diverges from what might be deduced from private actors' preferences alone. In other words, although Rogowski and Frieden differentiate among private actors according to their preferences, they assume no differences in actors' capacity for collective action to realize those preferences. Likewise, because both assume a frictionless translation of private actors' preferences into policy, neither seeks to explain how differing political institutions and the interests of state actors may decide whether private actors realize their preferences and may even shape those preferences.

In this chapter, I offer an alternative sectoral analysis that addresses the limits of existing sectoral approaches, permits us to correct all three problems with business-as-capital approaches, and goes further. Specifically, I offer an argument that provides a sectoral explanation of private actors' preferences, their capacity for collective action in pursuit of those preferences, the autonomy and institutional capacity of the governments they confront, and the balance of power between government and business.[1]

At issue in this book is not just the question of the best theoretical approach for understanding business-state relations but also the questions of what sort of business-state relations are most productive of development and how, why, and when these relations arise. Considerable attention is paid to the "what" question in the chapters by Schneider and Maxfield and Evans. But no systematic answers emerge to the "how, why, and when" questions; indeed, considerable evidence offered by Biddle and Milor, Doner and Ramsay, and Thorp and Durand seems to contradict even the answer given to the "what" question.

In Chapter 1 Schneider and Maxfield offer a tour d'horizon of the available arguments about the character of business-state relations. They show the need for something broader than the prevailing pessimistic iron law of rent seeking and offer a "positive case that collaboration between business and the state can contribute to development." The key to collaboration that promotes growth is the existence of a meritocratic, technically competent bureaucracy possessing the information required to act wisely and to monitor firms' compliance with policy, as well as the autonomy, capacity, and credibility to implement it. As Evans notes in Chapter 3, when states possess such a bureaucracy, they "can become vehicles for the construction of joint public-private projects in pursuit of economic transformation."

But these claims about Weberian bureaucracies have limits. Even if we accept Schneider and Maxfield's contention that "a Weberian bureaucracy is the best defense against the tendency for close government-business relations to degenerate into rent seeking," we must still ask why, how, and when such bureaucracies arise where they do. Specifically, if we wish to move beyond a descriptive categorization (Weberian bureaucracy equals

---

[1] For a more complete version of the argument, see Shafer 1994, especially chap. 2.

developmental, no Weberian bureaucracy equals rent seeking), then we must also move beyond ad hoc historicist and circumstantial explanations of the origins of such bureaucracies to grounded, causal arguments. Empirically, we must also ask how true this claim is, and here the evidence presented in this book is mixed. Korea and Taiwan, of course, both possess developmentalist bureaucracies and are models of economic success. As the chapters by Biddle and Milor, Doner and Ramsay, and Thorp and Durand make clear, however, while Turkey, Thailand, and Colombia do not boast Weberian bureaucracies, all have done quite well nonetheless. Finally, this sort of analysis also risks obscuring important but prosaic questions such as. What is the structure of the bureaucracy, where does this structure come from, and what implications does it have for how it performs its functions now and in the face of change?

Here I argue with Thorp and Durand that sectoral analysis can help us better specify the conditions under which effective bureaucracies can arise; explain the actual pattern and character of business-state relations; understand apparently anomalous findings—for example, Colombia; and even predict the specific structure of states' bureaucracies as well as their likely ability to respond to new demands. Thus, as Thorp and Durand argue, "different sectors' need for governance of different kinds [has] consequences for institutional development and therefore in due course for policy styles, coherence, and efficiency." Moreover, once these sectorally determined bureaucracies are established, "path dependency is important, particularly because the institutions responding to the needs of a period of export expansion may or may not be helpful where the issue becomes one of structural change."

A NEW VARIETY OF SECTORAL ANALYSIS

Let me start by defining the terms of my argument. *Sector* refers to a type of economic activity (mining, industrial plantation-crop production, peasant cash-crop production, or light manufacturing) comprising an enduring, coherent whole defined by distinctive combinations of four variables—capital intensity, economies of scale, production flexibility and asset/factor flexibility—which produce equally distinctive state structures and capabilities, external and internal distributions of power, and sets of societal actors. Because the economic variables covary across sectors, we can imagine a continuum stretching between two polar types: high/high sectors (mining, industrial plantation-crop production) marked by high capital intensity, high-scale economies, and high production and asset/factor inflexibility; and low/low sectors (light manufacturing, peasant cash-crop production) marked by the opposite. We can also

imagine a parallel continuum stretching between polar types of the resulting high/high and low/low political economies.

Capital intensity refers to the capital costs of start-up, production,
research and development, inventory, and distribution and is a proxy for
other critical characteristics such as fixed costs, technical complexity,
management professionalism, and work-force skill levels. Similarly, the
extent of *scale economies*—the extent to which efficiency demands large-
scale production—may affect production, research, marketing, distribution, and financing and is a proxy for the size and geographical
concentration of facilities; the size, concentration, and stability of the
work force, and the extent of specialized infrastructure required. Finally,
capital intensity and the extent of economies of scale account for the divi-
sibility of production (its openness to participation), the sector specificity
of assets, and the barriers to exit from the sector.

Production flexibility expresses a sector's degree of short-run market vulnerability and therefore the severity of the shocks that market shifts
deliver to firms and the state.[2] It is composed of three elements reflecting the extent of capital intensity and scale economies: the size of fixed
costs, which determines whether production decisions respond to market
conditions or are driven by debt service requirements; the size of firms'
investment in the work force; and the sensitivity of firms' physical plant
to shutdown, which rises with capital intensity and economies of scale.

Asset/factor flexibility determines the long-term difficulty of reallocating
resources and therefore the (in)tractability of restructuring. It reflects five
dimensions of sector specificity. The greater a sector's capital intensity and
scale economies, (1) the larger, more geographically concentrated, and
more specialized are its facilities and equipment; (2) the more concentrated and sector specific are the necessary infrastructures (power grids,
railroads); and (3) the more specialized is the production technology. On
the human side, the greater a sector's capital intensity and economies of
scale, (4) the greater the concentration of skilled workers in stable, homogeneous communities that owe their existence to the sector they serve
and (5) the more specialized management is, reflecting the greater need
for specialized management organizations, training, and corporate cultures. Finally, each element of asset/factor flexibility is reflected—
inverted, as in a mirror—in the development of other sectors: The greater
a sector's size, concentration, and specialization, the less developed other
sectors are.

Restructuring refers to state-led efforts to reallocate resources and reori-

---

[2] Production flexibility, asset/factor flexibility, and, more generally, the resulting effort
to specify the (in)tractability of the restructuring project are my effort to specify and oper-
ationalize the amorphous notion of vulnerability, identified in Chapter 1 as an important
cause of the rise of developmentalist bureaucracies.

ent economic activity by altering the sectoral composition of the economy to reduce a country's vulnerability to the risks associated with its leading export sector or seize greater or safer opportunities presented in other sectors. Restructuring thus has economic and political aspects and involves firms and the state. Firms in different sectors face different competitive pressures, possess different growth and exit options, wield different amounts of political clout, and therefore have different adjustment problems. The different sector-specific adjustment problems facing a country's firms set the restructuring project confronting the state. Restructuring, therefore, varies in nature and extent—from state aid for firms that are trading up within a sector to efforts by the state to shift the sectoral base of the economy—and in difficulty, depending on the nature of firms' adjustment problems.

Equally important are three terms that describe state capacity. *Autonomy* is the extent to which leaders can insulate themselves from societal pressures and autonomously define national tasks. Autonomy is not enough, however; states must also be able to act. But while autonomy is always relative, state capacity is both absolute and relative. *Absolute capacity* is the extent to which the state has the authority and means to extract and deploy resources. *Relative capacity* is the balance of state resources and institutional capacity, augmented by those of its allies, and the resources and capacity for collective action of the actors it confronts. Over time, its relative capacity varies as a function of changes in its absolute capacity in relation to changes in the abilities of its opponents and allies.

In brief, then, the developmental prospects of a state depend on the leading sector through which it is tied to the international economy. Sectoral attributes result in distinct international market structures, each of which rewards different kinds of actors, offers different opportunities and risks, and demands a different strategy. They also shape firms' ability to pursue the required strategies and states' capacity to help. Market structure and the prospects for successful pursuit of the strategies they demand outline the characteristic crises that states in a sector face and the restructuring project they must undertake.

States' actual ability to restructure depends on the tractability of their restructuring project and the domestic political economy of the leading sector. Sectoral attributes set the difficulty of the restructuring project; its implications for the state and sectoral actors; and the location, nature, and intensity of support or opposition. They also result in distinct patterns of state institutional capabilities and of interest groups with sectorally determined interests and collective action capabilities.[3] These

---

[3] As Thorp and Durand note in Chapter 8, sectoral analysis includes at its core an analysis of "the institutional consequences of different sectoral characteristics."

interact to produce distinct patterns of state autonomy and relative capacity. Sectoral analysis thus explains how different sectors affect the relative autonomy and capacity of the state vis-à-vis leading sector actors and the size and political weight of other actors with which the state can ally itself to raise its autonomy and capacity relative to leading sector elites as it seeks to restructure.

Intersectoral differences explain the patterned variation in states' development trajectories and capacity for adjustment. By providing an explanatory common ground, sectoral analysis also highlights the unique features of individual countries that account for intrasectoral variation—that is, for variation among countries with similar sectoral bases. Further, in a given case at a given time, sectoral analysis explains the interests of state and social elites, the relative autonomy of the former from the latter, and their relative capacities. Over time, it allows us to trace the recursive relationship between state action, the changing sectoral composition of the economy, and its implications for future state action.

This final observation is the starting point for the Korean case study that follows, for Korea offers a natural experiment for testing it. In the 1960s Korea's economy fit the light manufacturing ideal type; in the 1970s Korean leaders used their autonomy and capacity to shift the sectoral base of the economy to high/high heavy manufacturing. The results were startling. Having thrived in the 1960s despite intense international competition, Korea now faces tougher challenges abroad and an entirely new situation at home. For despite continued institutional growth, the state's relative capacity to manage the economy has declined because of the increased capacity of business and labor for collective action, resulting from altered sectoral circumstances.

I offer the following propositions. If read from top to bottom, they describe the low/low and high/high sectoral ideal types against which we will compare Korea in the 1960s and 1980s; if read from left to right, they describe the change we ought to find.

Low/Low Sectors   High/High Sectors

International Market Structure and Restructuring

Low/Low Sectors	High/High Sectors
Low/low sectors display low barriers to entry and highly competitive markets. MNCs play a minor role at the production stage, and market-conforming strategies are key to survival. Profit margins are thin; but Third World firms can compete on an equal footing with any player in the market, and their governments	High/high sectors display high barriers to entry, oligopolistic markets prone to boom and bust, and sharp shifts in market power up and downstream. They are dominated by MNCs able to collude in oligopoly management or pursue. individual risk management strategies National firms are disadvantaged in

can aid them. Restructuring thus entails deepening and diversification, not radical change.

the pursuit of either strategy, their governments cannot aid them, and thus they and their countries suffer the violence of market volatility. States must shift sectors.

The (In)tractability of the Restructuring Project

Low/low sector firms' production flexibility means that they can meet market downturns. Their capacity for evasive action reduces the pressures put on the state and the damage done to revenues. Asset/factor flexibility born of the general-purpose nature of public and private investments minimizes barriers to exit, gives leading sector actors incentives to switch rather than fight, and cuts the burden on the state.

High/high sector firms' production inflexibility means that they respond badly to market signals. Downturns devastate firms, lead to intense pressure for state aid, and gut government revenues. But asset/factor inflexibility born of big investments in sector-specific facilities, infrastructure, work-force training, and so on raise barriers to exit, incite leading sector actors to fight restructuring, and force the state to build something new from nothing.

Absolute Capacity

States with low/low sectors face myriad tiny, geographically dispersed firms. They develop flexible, deeply penetrating tax authorities to extract revenue from these tiny, only marginally profitable firms and flexible, general-purpose agencies to monitor, regulate, and promote the diverse activities of firms across the country. These institutions lend themselves easily to restructuring.

States with high/high sectors face a few, large, leading sector firms. They develop specialized tax authorities to tap the huge, concentrated revenue streams these sectors produce and specialized agencies to monitor, regulate, and promote the activities of these few critical firms. They do not build institutions to tax, monitor, regulate, or promote other sectors. This and the stickiness of leading sector-specific institutions limit the state's ability to restructure.

Societal Actors' Capacity for Collective Action

Low/low sectors comprise myriad tiny, geographically dispersed, mutually competitive firms managed by isolated small businesspeople. They draw unskilled workers from mixed communities and employ them in tiny, dispersed sweatshops under the

High/high sectors comprise a few big firms run by sophisticated, well-connected professionals practiced at collusion. They give steady employment to large numbers of workers who labor in large work gangs and live in homogeneous supervision of owners adamantly opposed to labor organization. Collective action by firms or workers is unlikely, and neither of them packs political clout.

communities. Alhough distributional issues divide them, labor and management have grounds to cooperate. Collective action is easy, making leading sector firms and workers potent political actors.

Autonomy

Leaders enjoy great autonomy when facing low/low sectors. Firms can be monitored and regulated by general-purpose agencies without need for expertise from below. The dispersion of economic activity and the state's difficulties in raising revenues kill incentives to penetrate the state. Asset/factor flexibility and the state's institutional capacity permit leaders to define a national interest autonomous from sectoral interests.

Leaders lack autonomy before high/high sectors. The complexity of operations and of monitoring and regulating them demands close ties among state agencies, management, and labor, making it hard to control the channels of interest representation. The absence of alternatives outside the leading sector and the concentration of wealth in the state give everyone incentives to penetrate the state. Asset/factor inflexibility and weak institutions bar leaders from defining a national interest autonomous from sectoral interests.

Relative Capacity

States with low/low leading export sectors have good prospects relative to restructuring and the opposition. Production and asset/factor flexibility moderate the crises they face and make restructuring tractable. Leading sector opposition is weak, and leaders possess both the autonomy to formulate a restructuring program and the institutional capacity to implement it.

States with high/high leading export sectors cannot restructure because, relative to the task at hand and the opposition, they lack what it takes. Production and asset/factor inflexibility make the crises they face crushing and the restructuring project daunting. Opposition by leading sector actors is intense and well organized, and leaders have neither the autonomy to formulate a restructuring program nor the absolute capacity to implement one.

KOREAN CONTRASTS

Given Korea's dazzling growth since the 1960s, it is easy to forget the pessimism about its prospects that prevailed at the time. After forty years of Japanese occupation and a decade of rule by Syngman Rhee, during which "more energy was spent plundering the existing surplus than producing more," Korea's prospects did not look good (Amsden 1989: 38–39). But in the aftermath of the 1961 Park Chung Hee coup, Korea took off. Investment, exports, and growth surged as Korea built an export-led growth drive on a labor-intensive light manufacturing base comprised largely of tiny firms. In the 1970s, government policy embodied in the Heavy and Chemical Industries Development Plan (HCID) again restructured the economy, transforming Korea into a major exporter of heavy manufactures by the mid-1980s. Today, tiny Korea is the thirteenth-largest industrial exporter in the world, selling more than three times as many manufactures abroad as Brazil does.[4] How was this miracle made?

Alternative Explanations

Explanations abound, most of them useful but none satisfactory. First are those that identify enabling conditions such as land reform, American aid, or foreign investment. Land reform, for example, was a necessary condition for development but cannot explain the explosive growth that began more than a decade after it was completed. American aid also helped but did not *cause* Korean growth; it peaked in 1957 and fell so rapidly that "70% of investment growth from 1960–62 onwards was financed by Korea's efforts . . . fueled largely by the growth of both exports and national savings, which were substantial enough to support large increases in output while simultaneously replacing foreign savings as the dominant factor in development" (Kim and Roemer 1980: 51, 58). Finally, foreign direct investment has played only a minor role in Korean development, financing just 1.2 percent of gross domestic capital formation from 1962 to 1979, peaking at 2.2 percent from 1972 to 1976, and falling to 0.6 percent by 1979 (Hamilton 1986: 45; Amsden 1989: 100–110).

What else might explain growth? The most common explanations focus on Park's strong state and the policies it pursued (Cole and Lyman 1971: 93; Amsden 1989: 8; Wade 1990: 337). Park revitalized the bureaucracy and built strong, insulated institutions for economic management backed by the full authority of the presidency (see Shafer 1994: 102 and Fields in this book). He also initiated a system of "government-directed development" in which "the hand of government reaches down rather far into the activities of individual firms with its manipulation of incentives and disincentives" (Mason et al. 1980: 254; for details, see Fields's Chapter 5 in this book). Such policies gave all Koreans a stake in state actions,

---

[4] For details, see Chapter 5.

however, and therefore required "a state strong enough to battle whoever stood to suffer from a loss of government support" (Amsden 1989: 18). After all, the policy shift hurt those already in business: Interest-rate reforms raised the cost of money for disfavored sectors, import-substituting firms were squeezed by rising costs and import competition, and everyone had to compete according to economic criteria. Not surprisingly, businesspeople became obsessed with policy. Likewise, the push into light manufacturing required an ability to control labor and labor costs, which gave the burgeoning working class an equally strong interest in policy.

What is striking, then, is how little influence business or labor wielded. Despite the importance of business success for the regime, government had the whip hand. Indeed, "private enterprise has been merely a delegate of state power and the principal agent of the state directed development" (Mason et al. 1980: 262–63; Choi 1983: 328–29). Those in control of big business were asked for information, but according to an early Economic Planning Board (EPB) official, their influence was negligible (Chung interview). Workers also had no say; for despite their numbers, labor organization, protest, and power were negligible until the late 1970s.

But such explanations are incomplete. It is not enough to cite coercive capacity; as Rhee's failure shows, an authoritarian state does not guarantee development. Nor is it enough to add leadership interest, for even many export-oriented authoritarians fail. The same can be said for citing the policies pursued: They have been tried in many places only to be abandoned. At issue are questions of timing and state-society relations over time. These have been raised under the rubric of development sequencing. Some such arguments emphasize the supposedly auspicious timing of Korea's insertion into the world economy. But they ignore that fact that Korea's adoption of an export-led growth strategy coincided almost perfectly with the imposition of the first of many increasingly restrictive multilateral protectionist regimes in textiles, Korea's export of preference.

A second, more compelling development sequencing argument focuses on domestic conditions. Fortuitous circumstances permitted Park to forge a development-oriented business-government relationship dominated by the state. The "big pockets," as Koreans call big businessmen, thus stayed at center stage, but "in a kneeling position," while the state could demand that even the biggest firms meet exacting performance standards of its own making (Amsden 1989: 72–74; for details, see Shafer 1994: 105 and Chapter 5 in this volume). The small size of the business community in 1961 and the fact that its growth followed Park's reforms further limited business power because most firms were new, small and weak. Finally,

Park's reforms also preceded the development of strong business organizations (interviews with Chung, Whang, Cha, and Lim). Equally important, labor was limited by a repressive labor regime that predated the export drive (Choi 1983). Park could thus exclude labor from his political calculations because in the absence of any existing labor organization he had no incentive to include it. Industrial labor became important only as a result of the economic growth sparked by his reforms.

But development sequencing arguments are misleading. They imply that, given this leg up, the state is forever favored and therefore offer no way to understand *shifts* in state-society relations or the effects of state action on them. To fix these limitations, let us turn to sectoral analysis.

THE INTERNATIONAL DIMENSION

Light manufacturing is a low/low sector marked by high production and asset/factor flexibility. There are few barriers to entry: Capital requirements are slight; economies of scale are unimportant, and production is divisible; skill requirements are low; technology is standardized and available; access to distribution channels is easy; and infrastructure requirements are unspecialized. Easy entry means that new firms arise quickly when demand surges, barring windfall profits. It also discourages MNC investment, leaving an even field for all producers. Being open to all, however, the market is extremely competitive, and competitiveness is exaggerated by high buyer concentration and low switching costs. Profit margins are tiny, and firms are demand driven.

Under such conditions, neither firms nor countries can control the market; what matters is a capacity to conform to it. There are no monopoly rents available and no incentives for collusion, which is barred anyway by the number of firms and intense competition. What matters is a capacity to seize marginal advantages when ephemeral opportunities appear and survive inevitable market downturns. Firms must be price competitive, able "to comply with clients' detailed specifications, to implement and maintain a stringent system of quality control, and to ensure that all shipments meet their tight delivery dates" (Morawetz 1981: 33). Given market volatility, seasonal demand for many products, and constant changes in style and technical specifications, firms cannot seek efficiencies in specialization but must cultivate flexibility.

Firms can pursue external and internal flexibility. To achieve external flexibility, firms must diversify product lines and customer base to cut dependence on specific products, market segments, or buyers (Ansoff 1986: 56–58). But such efforts are often beyond the power of small firms. Internal flexibilities are thus the key to success. Light manufacturing firms are, of course, flexible by virtue of lower debt, fixed costs, and specificity of assets. Because these advantages are common to all light manufacturing firms, however, competitive flexibility depends on the quality of management and labor. Indeed, "the shopfloor tends to be the strategic focus of firms that compete on the basis of borrowed technology" (Amsden 1989: 5).

But what could the Korean state could do to enhance national firms' ability to meet these challenges, outperform the competition, and generate the benefits of export-led growth? Luckily, the answer was a lot, for the dominance of market-conforming strategies locates all the critical variables within the grasp of firms and the state.

Korea Takes on the Challenges of Light Manufacturing

Korean policymakers developed a wide range of policies and institutions to support firms as they took up export production and intervened to assist targeted industries and individual firms. Although the latter goal attracts most attention, "Korea's successful export performance . . . derives primarily from initiatives taken by firms acting within a decentralized system and in response to generalized incentives" (Westphal 1982: 36). Let us focus on the initiatives that set the policy environment in which all would-be exporting firms operated.

In a market where price, quality, and on-time delivery are critical, firms must receive timely, undistorted market signals. Openness is essential, and the first key element of openness is the exchange rate; for without consistent, competitive exchange rates, firms cannot compete—as Korean firms could not compete under the exchange-rate regime maintained by the Rhee government. The establishment of a unitary floating rate in 1965, however, gave firms accurate signals on prices and removed exchange-rate disincentives to export production, launching the export boom.

Firms also require timely access to equipment and quality inputs at competitive prices. Given the seasonal nature of light manufactures, late delivery of inputs can spell disaster, while poor materials or equipment can lead to buyers' rejection of shipments. Moreover, despite high labor intensity, raw materials account for 35 to 60 percent of production costs; if they are unavailable at competitive prices, firms are lost (United Nations 1966: 44; Morawetz 1981: 92; United Nations 1969: 56). Again, under Rhee import restrictions and high-cost, poor-quality local inputs killed exports. After 1961, however, firms received tariff exemptions on equipment and raw materials for export production, a choice between domestic and imported inputs, and even automatic credit for the purchase of imported inputs upon receipt of an export contract (Jones and Sakong 1980:

94–96; Balassa 1978: 27–28). Such measures put Korean firms on an equal footing with firms elsewhere.

But equality is not enough to succeed; a competitive edge is required. In Korea, state institutional measures provided this edge. Policymakers first had to persuade firms to try exporting. To do so, they shifted incentives to favor production for export and assured exporters high initial profits, much reducing their reluctance to make the leap. But to succeed, would-be exporters also needed help to meet the challenges of light manufacturing. The Park government thus intervened to enhance firms' competitiveness by reducing their production costs. It offered low-cost investment funds and assured the timely provision of working capital; created a fund to convert firms to export production; financed imports needed to meet export orders; granted exporters discounts on electricity and railway freight rates; provided management and technical consulting services; fostered industry-supporting R&D; established industrial parks; and invested in the transportation, communication, and power infrastructures needed for an efficient export manufacturing sector. Still other initiatives, such as the creation of the Korean Trade Promotion Corporation (KOTRA), cut information costs and helped firms penetrate distant markets by lowering downstream barriers to entry.

In short, the key to Korea's international success was the domestic capacity to restructure: to trade up and reallocate resources to new industries. To understand this ability to restructure, however, we must shift our focus to the domestic political economy of light manufacturing.

THE DOMESTIC DIMENSION

The place to start is with the relative ease of restructuring, for light manufacturing's high production and asset/factor flexibility mean that restructuring posed few problems. Production flexibility reflects the core characteristics of light manufacturing. Low fixed costs mean that firms can cut production to meet market downturns without jeopardizing debt service. Similarly, workers are unskilled and easily trained, permitting firms to hire and fire as demand dictates. Finally, light manufacturing facilities are unaffected by shutdowns, and there are few costs associated with temporary closings if demand slumps. In addition, because most light manufacturing is divisible without loss of scale economies, firms can partially shutdown without suffering greatly increased unit costs.

Asset/factor flexibility is also high, and the barriers to exit are low. Although Korea built an extensive transportation, communication, and power infrastructure, it was neither specialized nor concentrated. Similarly, light manufacturing technology, capital equipment, and facilities are unspecialized and can often be redeployed at little cost. This does not, of course, apply to power looms, for example; but here the range of textiles that they can produce (and the heterogeneity of light manufactures generally) increases flexibility. As for labor, skills are limited and widely applicable, giving workers little attachment to specific jobs or industries. So, too, small firm size and the wide geographical distribution of production mean that working-class communities are heterogeneous and farflung, spreading the impact of restructuring. Finally, firms' small size and recent origins mean that most have rudimentary management organizations and managers have only general business skills. Thus, investments in complex organizations and specialized training do not inhibit change.

Flexibility was a boon for Korea. Production flexibility let firms respond to shocks with market-conforming behavior. This kept them competitive, softened the impact on the state, and slowed the speed with which it was felt. Firms with the flexibility to survive in light manufacturing could take evasive action and help themselves without costly state aid. The heterogeneity of light manufacturing firms and products also meant that market downturns seldom touched all segments simultaneously or in the same degree, further easing the blow to export earnings and state revenues (Lyman 1975: 249). And when firms needed help, they required not defense from the market but more of the same competitiveness-enhancing policies central to the export-promotion program. Thus, even aid to firms in trouble could be an investment in future growth and competitiveness.

Asset/factor flexibility had equally important long-term benefits, permitting Korea to restructure in the face of protection. The lack of specialized infrastructures meant that little had to be written off to accommodate change. Cheap incremental improvements such as road widening and better freight facilities bought a lot of growth, limiting major new investments to a few specialized facilities. Similarly, given general-purpose equipment and facilities, and the extent to which progress involves better ways of organizing and doing rather than fancier machines, firms could trade up incrementally and at low cost. The management skills honed to achieve internal flexibility were also those needed to trade up and even to change businesses, while unskilled workers were also mobile and could be trained incrementally at low cost.

Asset/factor flexibility had political benefits. Without big sunk investments, restructuring did not put business's backs to the wall. Indeed, the low cost of modernization, low barriers to exit, and the state's export-promotion package—generous depreciation schedules, cheap investment funds, consulting services, and marketing assistance—gave business-people reason to view the state as a partner in development (Jones and

Sakong 1980: 75). And when they *were* hurt, businesspeople needed more of the same, not adjustment-dulling protection. The pain for labor could be severe because workers bore the burden of adjustment. But the heterogeneity and geographical distribution of light manufacturing and working-class communities meant that even big changes did not dislocate large areas or provoke sharp opposition.

Absolute Capacity

But the relative tractability of the restructuring project that policymakers faced is only part of the answer to our question. We also must examine how light manufacturing shapes the state's capacity and autonomy to undertake it.

When the export drive began, the Korean state already had an autonomous, powerful, competent, deeply penetrating bureaucracy. But the state's initial institutional endowment alone does not explain its exceptional absolute capacity—the pattern of institutions developed to support export-led growth, their capabilities, or the flexibility they later showed when called on to support restructuring. The sectoral characteristics of light manufacturing, however, help explain all three.

Resource Extraction

The Park government inherited little extractive capacity from its predecessors. The economy of the 1950s was tiny, as was the tax yield from it. All this changed under Park. By the early 1970s, tax receipts had risen fifteen-fold since 1962, and the tax yield had doubled as the soaring gross national product (GNP) and better tax collection pushed revenues through the roof. Indeed, despite a rapidly growing budget and the virtual end of foreign aid, current revenues surpassed current expenditures by 1964–65 (J. Kim 1975: 266–67; Kim and Roemer 1980: 54; Mason et al. 1980: 107). In part, rising revenues reflected the continued importance of customs duties on hugely increased imports. But officials feared the market-distorting impact of indirect taxes and tariffs' threat to the competitiveness of high-import content exports and so to export-led growth. They therefore cut tariffs and raised direct taxes' share of revenues to a level that was 50 percent higher than expected for a country of Korea's income (T. Suh 1981: 17; Mason et al. 1980: 316; Chelliah 1971: 278, 283).

Raising direct taxes depended on the state's ability to collect corporate and personal income taxes, administratively and politically the most costly of all taxes. The key was the deeply penetrating, highly flexible Office of National Tax Administration (ONTA) created in 1966. ONTA opened offices across the country, expanded the cadre of tax collectors and auditors, modernized assessment and collection, and built a computerized data base of corporate and individual records. ONTA's semiautonomous status protected its operatives from interference while it set "tax collection targets or quotas by geographic area and tax items" and rewarded or punished tax collectors "for exceeding or falling short of the targets" (Whang 1985: 14). New laws also gave ONTA big sticks to wield against tax evaders.

Why go this route? Given a light manufacturing base, the people to be taxed were mostly poor and the firms to be taxed were numerous, small, marginally profitable, and widely scattered. Individual returns were thus tiny, which meant that raising revenue from direct taxes required a country-wide presence. Moreover, because individuals were poor and firms were pressed by competition, everyone had incentives to evade taxes, which meant that the state also required an extensive audit and enforcement capacity. Finally, the heterogeneity of light manufacturing required that ONTA personnel be generalists and that ONTA be able to assess and collect taxes from all kinds of industries and businesses.

ONTA also enhanced the state's capacity to use fiscal policy to (re)direct development. Limited efforts to do so had begun in 1961, but without ONTA they were at best clumsy. The 1965 Law on the Regulation of Tax Deductions and Exemptions then gave the state broad powers to favor select industries; and ONTA's creation in 1966 made its implementation possible, setting the stage for measures such as the 1967 provision of investment tax credits for targeted industries, the 1969 tax credit for foreign-market development costs, the 1973 tax credits for losses on operations in foreign markets, and the many tax incentives offered as part of HCID (Jones and Sakong 1980: 94; J. Kim 1975: 267).

Finally, ONTA's flexibility protected the state from catastrophic revenue losses and ensured revenues even during restructuring. Its ability to tax a wide range of firms softened the impact of downturns in individual market segments and allowed the state to offer relief to depressed industries and find replacement revenues elsewhere. Indeed, the existence of ONTA permitted Korea to raise revenues even while restructuring. Thus, revenues from light manufacturing continued unabated in the 1970s, permitting huge tax credits to firms investing in heavy industries—and sustaining the state when it found itself overextended in the early 1980s.

Monitoring, Regulating, and Redirecting the Economy

The Korean state also has the institutional capacity to monitor, regulate, and redirect the economy. In part, this reflects past circumstances and institution-building efforts in the early 1960s, but the general-purpose nature of these institutions reflects the characteristics of light manufacturing as well. Korea's brief bout of import substitution industrialization (ISI) left the state unencumbered by institutions devoted to servicing big firms, and the Park government showed "a sophisticated bias ... toward the promotion of light consumer-goods industries amenable to small investments and simple technical processes" (J. Kim 1975: 257). The large number and small size of the firms that sprang up, the range of industries they represented, and the array of markets they serviced made direct government control impossible. Policy aimed instead to establish "a permissive framework for the realization of comparative advantage" (Haggard 1990: 67).

The Korean state thus required highly flexible institutions exemplified by KOTRA and the Korean Traders Association (KTA) (Lim interview). KOTRA promoted *all* Korean exports, the diversity of which forced it to develop a general export-supporting organizational mission and capabilities. Assisting KOTRA were the KTA, which is not organized along industry lines but along functional ones, and, below it, associations representing different export industries. These provided the state and members with timely, detailed information about production, sales, exports, and foreign markets. They also extended the state's regulatory arm deep into industry at little cost (see Chapter 5 this book). KOTRA, KTA, and the associations gave the Korean state the ability to monitor domestic and foreign developments relevant to all current and potential exports, regulate firms' export activities, and redirect them if needed by helping identify new opportunities and easing the costs of entering new markets.

Business's and Labor's Incapacity for Collective Action

To grasp the Korean state's success in restructuring, we must also consider the interests of business and labor and their capacity for collective action. Here, too, sector matters; for whereas the characteristics of light manufacturing made the Korean state strong and flexible, they hobbled business and labor.

In the early 1960s business's weakness was partly circumstantial. ISI had not gone far enough to give Korea a large, inefficient industrial sector able to demand protection by virtue of its size and weakness. The fall of the Rhee regime also temporarily discredited the "big pockets." Although organizations such as the Korea Chamber of Commerce (KCCI) and KTA existed, they were small, divided, and disinclined to lobby. Finally, the business community was still tiny; its explosive growth followed the outward reorientation of government policy. But these initial disadvantages do not explain business's continuing weakness. Korea's light manufacturing base does.

Korean growth built on the production of a huge number of widely scattered small firms. In 1963 firms with fewer than two hundred workers accounted for 98.7 percent of Korea's 18,310 registered firms, while in 1966 firms with ten workers or less employed 43 percent of the work force (Jones 1980: 53; Oshima 1971: 165). But although these tiny firms were family businesses, sweatshops equipped with primitive technologies, their share of Korean exports grew from 18.6 percent in 1963 to 31.4 percent of a far larger total in 1968. Such firms are widely dispersed; just 17 percent are in Seoul—a percentage that increases rapidly with even small increases in firm size (Han interview; Ranis 1973: 404; Oshima 1971: 167–68).

These characteristics barred collective action. Low barriers to entry and government policy enticed thousands of entrepreneurs into the ring. They all suffered the plight of small firms in a tough international market, but their numbers and the heterogeneity of their products and markets limited contact among them and encouraged free riding. While their numbers grew by 40 percent in 1962–74, life at the bottom of the entrepreneurial pyramid was nasty, brutish, and short (Jones and Sakong 1980: 170–71). The result was cutthroat competition for survival, not collusion, and complaints by businesspeople that Korean firms were too competitive with one another to cooperate in lobbying. Further, KCCI, KTA and the Korean Federation of Small Businesses (KFSB) could not help because the heterogeneity of light manufacturing and their members' interests left them internally crosspressured (interviews with Lim, Cha, Han, W. Minn, and C. Minn). Whatever their entrepreneurial talents, small businesspeople also lacked the time, skills, resources, and contacts to lobby.

As I have already noted, the Park government also had early advantages over labor (for details, see Shafer 1994: 105–6, and Choi 1983). Thus, despite a burgeoning industrial work force, miserable working conditions, and low wages, collective bargaining failed in the 1960s, strikes fizzled, and employers violated labor laws with impunity. Although real wages rose after 1968 as a result of a tightening labor market, productivity increases outstripped wage growth, indicating a falling share of profits for labor (Ogle 1981: 504–5; Deyo 1984: 270; Choi 1983: 480). But labor's real problem was that growth, especially job growth, occurred in light manufacturing where sectoral characteristics undercut collective action, insulating business and the state from labor pressure. Indeed, labor protest was limited to skilled, heavy-industry workers, while 70 to 75 percent of employment growth in the 1960s occurred in the light manufacturing export sector marked by unskilled, labor-intensive, small-unit production (Ogle 1981: 503).

Light manufacturing workers face high barriers to collective action. The smallness and dispersion of firms, exaggerated by labor laws requiring firm-based unions, discourage worker solidarity. Firms hire and fire unskilled employees at will, leading workers to see each other as competitors, not companions. The dispersion of workplaces even within urban settings and the rapid influx of new workers in the 1960s resulted in highly heterogeneous communities unconducive to organization. Finally, intense competition, the centrality of labor costs, and the need for flexibility made owners fight unions tooth and nail.

Intersectoral variation in unionization, protest, and wages shows the importance of sectoral characteristics. Thus, in 1974, 50 percent of miners and 37 percent of workers in heavy industries such as chemicals, petroleum, rubber, and cement were unionized but just 18 percent of textile and apparel workers were. Furthermore, heavy industrial workers have long shown a capacity to mount effective strikes. By contrast, protests in light manufacturing have been small, scattered and unorganized and marked by despairing acts of symbolic violence such as self-immolation that by their nature suggest the lack of effective means of protest. Finally, wages are lowest in light manufacturing, with textile and apparel workers making half as much as shipyard workers do. In fact, Korea "has one of the largest manufacturing wage dispersions between light and heavy industry" in the world (Deyo 1984: 282–83; 1989: 176; Amsden 1989: 10).

But the Korean state's capacity to restructure was not merely a matter of its absolute capacity nor of the incapacity of business and labor. What counted was the relationship between them. To understand that relationship, we must examine officials' autonomy to formulate policy and relative capacity to implement it.

Autonomy

Unique circumstances help explain the Korean state's high degree of autonomy, but sectoral characteristics are also critical. Business's and labor's lack of effective organizations and lobbying skills hindered interest articulation and eased the task of controlling the channels of interest representation. The state's role in fostering industry and the simple technologies employed minimized state dependence on business for expertise, narrowing business's access to policy-making (Jones and Sakong 1980: 67). The general-purpose nature of the institutions serving light manufacturing and the sector's heterogeneity also limited access by minimizing capture and denying industries advocates within the state, while the small size and large number of industry groups meant that none could demand attention.

Sectoral characteristics also explain the limited pressures to penetrate the state's autonomy. International competition led to intense interest in state support—but of the sort already provided. The dynamism of the export economy and opportunities in the private sector also minimized incentives to mine the state, while the state's travails with revenue extraction and the openness of the foreign exchange and trade regimes minimized the profitability of doing so. In short, being inaccessible and under little pressure, officials could make policy without reference to special pleading by societal actors; witness their capacity to use state "power to discipline not just workers, but the owners and managers of capital as well" and to invest rather than spend state resources (Amsden 1989: 64).

This autonomy allowed Korean leaders in the 1960s and 1970s to define the state interest in terms compatible with restructuring. They were motivated by political necessity and the economic—and political—logic of export promotion. But sectoral characteristics explain their ability to act because asset/factor flexibility cut the costs of trading up and the sector's heterogeneity ensured that even in transition the economy continued to thrive. ONTA's flexibility ensured that revenues also grew, and other agencies' flexibility meant that restructuring gored no bureaucratic interests and that the state could manage it. In short, restructuring threatened neither state revenues nor institutions, freeing officials to define a state interest approximating the national interest.

Exercising Relative Capacity

Still, by the late 1960s Koreans had reason to worry despite rapid growth. Of special concern were the economic and political vulnerabilities born of success and overspecialization. Real wages were rising, reducing competitiveness vis-à-vis second-tier NICs, while export success was provoking protection. Inflation was on the rise, but devaluing to control it aggravated balance-of-payments and debt-service problems. Finally, the Nixon administration's 1971 call for troop cuts led Korean officials to weigh the wisdom of building an arms industry.

Park responded to the resulting tensions with a preemptive exercise of state power culminating in the authoritarian Yushin Constitution of 1972. But only continued growth, not coercion, could solve Park's problems. Indeed, in the short term all he could hope for was that a new growth spurt would legitimize his actions as it had the 1961 coup. Going for growth, however, also meant confronting Korea's changing international position. And for Park and his advisers this meant shifting the sectoral base of the economy from light to heavy manufacturing. Luckily, the developments of the 1960s had given them "a state that was iron-fisted at home and, therefore, capable of restructuring the domestic economy and supporting sustained growth" (Woo 1991: 116). Their blueprint for

Korea's restructured future was laid out in the Heavy and Chemical Industry Development Plan (HCID) announced in 1973.

HCID aimed to reposition Korea in the international division of labor. The plan did not follow Korea's comparative advantage but used state interventions to lead the market. HCID policies thus encouraged monopolistic production to achieve scale economies, reduced tariffs on capital equipment, protected infant industries, offered incentives for R&D and worker training, and created the National Investment Fund to provide cheap loans to meet the new industries' huge investment needs.

HCID radically redistributed incentives for business. Indeed, "the main goal of Korea's finance was to hemorrhage as much capital as possible into the heavy industrialization program" by setting "financial prices at an artificial low to subsidize import-substituting heavy, chemical and export industries" (Woo 1991: 159). Between 1977 and 1979 "80% of total investment in manufacturing went to heavy industry," an allocation managed by gutting investment in light manufacturing (Haggard and Moon 1986: 11–12). As a government report explained, "labor intensive manufacturing . . . has been left to fend for itself" because policy favored big firms over the small ones on whose success the first phase of Korean growth had depended (Korea Exchange Bank 1980).

But there is irony in the Korean state's success. Its absolute capacity, its autonomy from small firms, and their inability to defend their interests made restructuring possible. But the state's success also had economic costs. More important, it changed the interests and improved the collective-action capabilities of business and labor, giving both the ability to hit back and reducing state autonomy and relative capacity.

Reaping the Dragon's Teeth

HCID had major economic consequences, both good and bad. Where the higher short-term profits of light manufacturing would have discouraged investment in heavy industry, thus reinforcing Korea's existing position in the international division of labor, HCID offered businesspeople incentives to invest in building future competitive advantage in heavy industry. These incentives—combined with stringent performance criteria—sharply increased heavy industries' share of manufacturing output and exports. Steel, for example, absorbed 40 percent of all loans to heavy industry in 1975–82; but steel production capacity increased fourteenfold, and Korea is today one of the most efficient and profitable steel producers in the world. Likewise, shipbuilding, a major consumer of steel, received massive state support "and then proceeded to capture more than 20% of all new orders in the world market." Korea's machine tool, automobile, defense, chemical, and electronics industries have fared equally well (Woo 1991: 133–38).

Even economically, however, HCID created problems. Although the World Bank now argues that "it is difficult to demonstrate that an alternative policy would have worked better," Korea suffered in the short term (World Bank 1987: 45). In part, the causes were exogenous, but HCID itself promoted overinvestment in capital-intensive industries, distorted domestic prices, widened the productivity gap between protected and unprotected industries, and aggravated threats to Korea's comparative advantage in labor-intensive industries. Real wages rose twice as fast as labor productivity; and inflation, foreign debt, and the current account deficit shot up, while GNP and export-growth rates plunged (S. Suh n.d.: 11, 16–17; S. Kim 1982: 64; Haggard and Moon 1990: 216).

By late 1978, many people were demanding changes. Trading partners wanted Korea to cut aid to exporters and open its markets, and insiders called for liberalization to reignite growth and reduce the threat of protection. In April 1979 EPB advanced a plan to cut inflation and undo the monopolistic structure of HCID-sponsored heavy industries by liberalizing trade and increasing the market's role in pricing and resource allocation. Implementation was interrupted by the second oil shock in July and Park's assassination in October; but Park's team of planners remained in the Chun Doo Hwan government, and the effort continued.

The Chun government's stabilization policies succeeded remarkably. A devaluation in 1980 raised competitiveness, growth in government spending was cut, a public-sector wage freeze was imposed; and wage increases were held below labor productivity gains. Inflation fell and the balance-of-payments deficit improved as growth rates rebounded and exports rose (Haggard and Moon 1986: 20–22, 36). The state also began a second outward turn and an effort to correct HCID-induced distortions, liberalizing import controls, rationalizing industries, shifting lending priorities to again favor light manufacturing, and abolishing preferential tax rates for heavy industry (Kim interview).

How were these successes achieved? The damage done and the difficulty of undoing it were limited by HCID's short life and the fact that the state had exacted high performance as well (Kim interview). In part, too, success reflected the continued autonomy and capacity of a state with powerful policy instruments at its command. But it also reflected the continued importance of advantages born of the sectoral characteristics of Korea's economic base. The state could force adjustment costs on the largest firms because, despite HCID, it had allies in the still vital light manufacturing sector. Indeed, reembracing light manufacturing offered important political benefits to a beleaguered Chun, who was desperate to distance himself from his predecessor; it not only reduced the power of big business but also contributed to employment and helped the middle class, both of which are closely tied to light manufacturing.

HCID supplemented, not supplanted, the established core of the economy. Despite heavy industry's growing share of GNP and exports, light manufacturing firms stayed at center stage because their productivity and output growth exceeded that of the big firms in the 1970s (C. Kim 1985: 59). Thus, although motor vehicle exports, one of the most visible successes of industrial deepening, rose from $300 to $1,000 million in 1979–85, the textile industry "still employed 30% of manufacturing workers, churning out 39% of total exports and 22% of value added." Shoes and apparel accounted for another 13 percent of exports, and exporters selling less than $100,000 worth of goods per year shipped another 12.2 percent of total exports (Woo 1991: 131; Lim interview). More generally, despite being starved of investment and otherwise disfavored, light manufacturing remained substantially more profitable than heavy industry throughout the 1970s and 1980s (Amsden 1989: 89). In sum, the vitality of light manufacturing permitted the state to reverse course when the costs of HCID were perceived.

Nevertheless, it is also clear that restructuring had reduced the relative capacity of the state by raising business's and labor's capacity for collective action. The change is clearest in the HCID-spurred rise of the *chaebol*, or conglomerates, which by 1981 had made Korea "one of the world's most concentrated economies" (Amsden 1989: 121; Woo 1991: 14–15, 150). Rising *chaebol* strength altered state-business relations. In the 1960s the state faced thousands of tiny firms and a few vulnerable big ones; now it faces huge firms organized in a unified, potent lobbying organization called the Federation of Korean Industry (FKI) (interviews with Lim, Cha, Kim, Chung, and Cho; Fields, Chapter 5 in this book). The chaebol's dependence on protection, monopoly markets, cheap loans, preferential tax treatment, and export subsidies give them an intense interest in state policy. Conversely, their precarious financial positions and importance in the economy limit state leverage and force the state "into the role of lender of last resort" because the bankruptcy of a chaebol "would threaten not only the financial but the economic stability of the country" (Woo 1991: 149). Further, the chaebol now have access to the state. Public-private joint ventures, and the growth of specialized state agencies and ties between big business and bureaucrats have opened channels of communication and given the chaebol advocates inside the state (Kim interview).

The chaebol have joined the policy process and can resist policies that hurt their interests. Indeed, they forced actual concessions in the stabilization and restructuring program. For example, a key aim was to staunch the flow of preferential loans to heavy industry. But when the chaebol felt the pinch, FKI howled, and the state offered bailout loans (Woo 1991: 170). Even when the state did cut credit, "the relative share of preferential financing out of total bank credit . . . increased [and] the primary beneficiaries of the new policy loans were, once again, big business. . . . [A] further credit squeeze was enforced on all other sectors, including particularly small and medium-sized firms" (Haggard and Moon 1986: 32–33). In short, the chaebol forced an outcome diametrically opposed to the state's interest in rebalancing the relationship between big and little firms and among sectors.

Ironically, liberalization—by which the Chun government hoped to discipline big business—has also backfired because of the chaebol's state policy-induced power (Kim interview). Some trade liberalization did occur but only in return for the state's acquiescence to the chaebol's demands that it cut its control of the financial system. The state thus reduced regulation of nonbank financial intermediaries (NBFIs), many of which are controlled by chaebol, and began to privatize banking. As a result of deregulation, NBFI deposits soared; but despite formal limits on equity ownership, chaebol gained control of individual banks. Armed with vast new financial resources, the chaebol went on a buying spree, sharply increasing economic concentration and their political power. "Korea, Inc." had given way along with the relative capacity of the state as "the government's forcefulness and credibility declined and private business groups augmented their power" (Amsden 1989: 134–36).

The fall of state strength relative to labor is no less striking. In the early 1980s, unions still could not defend workers effectively. But the growth of high/high heavy industry had already fundamentally altered the conditions affecting labor's capacity for collective action, because the huge size of workplaces facilitates organizing. Workers in the new industries are also highly skilled, often at jobs for which they have had to receive extensive on-the-job training, and so possess real leverage. Further, their stable employment prospects and good advancement opportunities give them incentives to invest in labor organization. Finally, stable employment, the geographical concentration of heavy industry, and the size of firms have led to the creation of stable working-class communities, many of which are company towns.

Managers' attitudes toward labor have also changed. Big investments in training, the need for labor discipline and uninterrupted production, and the fear of sabotage gave managers a vital interest in worker retention and loyalty; and labor's small share of production costs gave them room to negotiate. Thus, grudgingly but steadily, Korea's heavy industrial firms have allowed the growth of unions to "stabilize a highly mobile work force by providing new sets of organizational and interpersonal commitments and by providing institutional alternatives to quitting in response to job-related problems or grievances" (Deyo 1989: 146). The number of union shops and union members soared in the 1970s. Today union density is highest in HCID industries, and there is even a Korean Employers Association (representing the chaebol) to foster industrial peace through "cooperation with the FKTU" (Deyo 1989: 77; see also Choi 1983: 55; 165–66; 387–91).

State-labor relations have changed, too. From the exclusionary labor regime of the 1960s, policy moved in a corporatist direction—for heavy industrial workers. Since the mid-1970s, for example, FKTU leaders have even been included in the Economic Plan Coordination Committee, which prepares the five-year plans, and in the Export Promotion Conference, chaired by the president. These changes reflect recognition of heavy industry workers' potential power and aim to offset it. They also grant labor access to the policy process.

Waves of successful strikes against Korea's biggest firms during the 1980s demonstrate heavy industrial workers' clout. While light manufacturing workers' protests fizzled even during the stormy period between Park's death in August 1979 and the Chun coup in May 1980, strikes wracked heavy industry. These won workers higher wages, better working conditions, and more state spending on housing, roads, and amenities. (Deyo 1989: 78–79; S. Kim 1982: 64). Intense repression then cut strike activity until 1984, when it exploded again as heavy industrial workers demanded not only material gains but also changes in the labor regime and the political system itself. They formed independent regional labor associations to help them organize and forged ties to student, church, and other opposition groups, giving these organizations the manpower and economic clout they had long lacked (Haggard and Moon 1990: 233–34).

The best proof of the state's reduced relative capacity, however, is the tidal wave of strikes that swept Korea in 1987 and helped force a return to democracy. They did not mobilize the light manufacturing workers on whose backs the Korean miracle was built. They mobilized the skilled workers of the biggest, most modern firms in the new heavy industries built under the aegis of the state's own restructuring program. Workers took on the state and big business—and when business balked, the state supported labor. Workers won better wages and benefits and the right to organize independent unions. They demanded, and got, humiliating public apologies from the CEOs of Korea's biggest companies. And with their student and middle-class allies, they made the demand for democracy irresistible.

Even as neat a natural experiment as the Korean case provides cannot be conclusive. I would therefore, like to offer two, admittedly stylized, comparisons to other cases, both explored in more detail elsewhere in this book. Specifically, I would like to assay the extent of intrasectoral variation and so test my core contentions: that sectors have an optimal, or at least typical, economic organization and pose distinctive economic challenges to all producers and states, and that states with similar sectoral bases face similar political constraints when they address these challenges, do so from similar institutional positions, and arrive at similar policy outcomes. To this end, I would first like to examine the case of the Taiwanese state, which, despite starting from a remarkably similar light manufacturing base, restructured in ways and with consequences very different than Korea's (for more details, see Fields in this book). Second, I would like to examine the apparently anomalous case of the Coffee Federation of Colombia (FNC), which, despite the low/low character of the coffee sector, has proved a powerful player in Colombian politics (see Chapter 8).

KOREA VERSUS TAIWAN: SECTORS AND STRATEGIC CHOICES

Few nonexperts distinguish much between Korea and Taiwan. And they do have much in common, but there is a key difference: Korea and Taiwan are divided by firm size and degree of economic concentration. By 1981 "Korea had 10 firms in *Fortune*'s 500 biggest industrial firms outside the United States, while Taiwan had only 2. Only 176 firms in Taiwan had more than 1,000 employees in 1976 [and] over 80% . . . had fewer than 20," not much less than in 1966. The industrial structure has deepened, but firm size has not risen apace. In contrast to Korea, where the number of firms rose by 10 percent in 1966–76 and firm size doubled, in Taiwan the number of firms rose 250 percnet, but firm size rose only 29 percent. Politically more important, Taiwan's business groups are smaller than the chaebol. In 1983, for example, Taiwan's largest business group had annual sales that were one-fifth of Hyundai's and employed less than one-quarter as many people, while "only 40% of the 500 largest manufacturing firms belong to business groups, and most Taiwan enterprises remain single-unit operations" (Wade 1990: 66–70).

There is an easy explanation for this divergence consistent with sectoral analysis: Korea and Taiwan diverged because their leaders chose different policies to effect restructuring (see Chapter 5). Policymakers in both countries could make and implement these choices because, given both countries' light manufacturing political economies, the project was tractable, societal actors were weak, and both states were capable and autonomous. Once made, however, their choices fundamentally altered Korea's and Taiwan's political economies, resulting not merely in divergent forms of industrial organization but, for example, in different prospects for democratization. Korean policymakers chose to restructure by building national champions through the use of policies that encouraged economic concentration. These policies catapulted Korean steel, automobiles, ships, and chips to international competitiveness but reduced the relative capacity of the state; created the chaebol, empowered big labor; and unleashed an overwhelming, society-driven push for democracy. Taiwan chose a different path, driven, as Yun-han Chu explains, by the KMT's fear of business's "potential threat to [its] political dominance at the national level" (1989: 656; see Chapter 5).

Recognizing the threat posed by concentration, the Taiwanese chose policies that fostered restructuring but minimized reductions in relative capacity. Policy "encouraged the widest possible accumulation of industrial capital and untrammeled use of that capital, provided it remains small [and] freed the government to concentrate on preventing big business from organizing in ways that threatened the regime" (Wade 1990: 268). As a result, notes Fields in Chapter 5, business has had organizational challenges "to resolve collective-action problems because of the large numbers of smaller business groups and the diverse interests of these conglomerates." Even where restructuring seems to require large-scale operations, the state seeks to minimize the threat to relative capacity. For example, the Program for Promoting Center-Satellite Factory Systems links final assembly factories and parts suppliers and material suppliers and downstream buyers in order to cut transaction costs, maintain the benefits of specialization, and capture many of the benefits of scale while retaining a base of small, dispersed firms. It thus averts the growth of economically and politically powerful large firms and reinforces barriers to collective action by business and labor.

The impact of such policies contrasts with the situation in Korea. Unlike chaebol workers, Taiwanese workers remain widely dispersed in tiny factories and cannot organize, and a tightly controlled labor regime still keeps unions powerless. Unlike the chaebol and FKI, business, too, cannot organize to lobby government; "even an association like the Taiwan Shipbuilders Association . . . has never been asked to give its views on what appropriate policies for the industry should be" (Wade 1990: 282). Indeed, notes Fields, "unlike official Korean tolerance for symbiotic government-business relations, such intimate interaction in Taiwan has typically been suspect by the KMT regime as collusion."[5] The impact of policy

---

[5] In his contribution to this book, Fields contends that there is, in fact, more government-business interaction than Wade suggests; even so, he notes Thomas Gold's observation (1986) that, unlike the Japanese Keidanren (and the FKI), the biggest Taiwanese business association, the National Council of Industry and Commerce, "has functioned largely as a channel for the government to relay its policies to big business." Indeed, Fields observes

choices shows best, however, in the different evolution of Taiwanese politics in the 1980s. True, Taiwan now has a new middle class interested in politics, and groups have formed to press their interests. But the state remains in control because nothing about this process remotely resembles the democratic explosion that has remade Korea.

This mini-comparison of Korea and Taiwan suggests two conclusions. First, it confirms sectoral analysis. As expected, Korea and Taiwan had the autonomy and capacity to restructure. Further, the consequences of the policy choices they made are best understood as reflecting the resulting organization of industry, thus confirming the recursive relationship between state action, the changing structure of the economy, and its implications for future state action. In other words, Korea and Taiwan demonstrate the opportunity for and importance of strategic choice when sectoral conditions permit. Thus, as their divergent restructuring programs show, their common sectoral starting point conferred the capacity and autonomy to implement restructuring. But while this common starting point informed policymakers' choice of targets, it did not determine the policies pursued, although Taiwanese policymakers did take sectoral variables into account as they sought to restructure without suffering the predicted consequences of moving in the high/high direction.

Second, this comparison indicates a need for more research. Taiwan's ability to deepen its industrial structure without ending up like Korea suggests that there are limits to the contention that sectors have an optimal organization. Indeed, the Taiwan case suggests that efficient factor substitution, organizational innovation, and state support can stretch the bounds of optimality. That is, if optimal organization is more a matter of nurture than nature, then the Taiwan case suggests a more central role for politics and policy choice in the making of sectors and sectoral political economies than existing sectoral approaches (including mine), permit. This is a potentially important observation, given the subject matter of this book, and points to the need for considerably more work.

My observation, which resonates with the conclusions of Doner and Ramsay in Chapter 9, raises two challenges. First, it challenges us to refine and extend sectoral analysis by asking where and under what conditions

---

that even given "both the increasingly technical nature of policy and growing strength and skill of the private sector" in the semiconductor industry in the 1980s, there was "no question that the state has continued to play the leading role in structuring cooperation," while the growth of business associations has not provided "significant bases for organizing autonomous collective action because of both the organizational strength of the state (in terms of autonomy and capacity) and the structural characteristics of the private sector. The large numbers of relatively small-sized exporters face low barriers and exit costs and lack resources and skills for organizing group-based action"—just as sectoral analysis predicts.

factor substitution, organizational innovation, and state support are efficient. Specifically, we must explore where and under what conditions policy can nurture different sectoral forms that are stable and internationally competitive, for it is only in these cases that policy choice independently alters the rules of the game laid out in sectoral analysis. After all, while Taiwan succeeded in this regard, policy-induced disaster is far more common. Consider, for example, the effects of ISI as pursued in Latin America and Africa and of central planning in the Soviet Union and Eastern Europe. In these cases policy, not technical necessity, produced huge capital-intensive firms—none of them internationally competitive and all of them compromising states' relative capacity. In other words, these countries' difficulties offer perverse proof of sectoral analysis, a sort of sectors' revenge.

Turning to the case of coffee in Colombia, we confront an apparent anomaly: The low/low sector-production characteristics of coffee ought to inhibit organization and collective action by producers, yet the FNC has for decades been a powerful political actor. (For an analysis of coffee as a peasant cash crop, see Shafer 1994: chap. 6.) On the one hand, the absence of economies of scale and very low capital requirements make coffee an ideal peasant cash crop; in Colombia 90 percent of coffee farms are smaller than 10 hectares, produce more than 50 percent of Colombia's coffee crop, and actually show higher productivity than larger farms do (Shafer 1994: 190–92). In theory, these widely dispersed, mutually competitive, relatively uneducated, and unskilled peasant producers should have serious difficulties combining for effective action, especially given the extraordinary volatility of coffee markets (Shafer 1994: 194–95). On the other hand, as Thorp and Durand report, the FNC is organized from the local to the national level and has long been able to provide public goods to coffee producers, ranging from warehousing, financing, and services of all kinds, and to wield sufficient political influence to win the power to assess and collect taxes and participate in the mangement of Colombia's ports and financial institutions. The question, then, is simple: Does the inconvenient fact of the FNC falsify theoretically elegant sectoral analysis?

The answer, of course, is no; and to understand why requires sectoral analysis. Two points in particular stand out. First, as expected and despite the rapidly growing importance of coffee in the Colombian economy in the first two decades of the twentieth century, peasant producers could not and did not organize for straightforward, Olsonian, collective-action reasons. Instead, they were organized by politicians who, as Robert Bates observes, "at key moments themselves bore the costs of collective action, provisioning the coffee sector with economic institutions and delegating public powers to coffee interests," which could, as a result, offer the selective incentives and wield the sanctions necessary to curb the opportunistic behavior of individual producers that would otherwise have wrecked the FNC (Bates forthcoming: chap. 3). They did so for reasons of their own born of the structure of Colombian political institutions. Thus, as Bates argues, while the FNC has on occasion exercised decisive power within Colombian politics, this power derives not from the coffee sector itself but is, in effect, conferred upon it from above. By way of proof, Bates observes that the FNC's influence in Colombian politics rises and falls according to the degree of democratic competition—that is, according to how much politicians need coffee-sector voters, not how much the coffee sector needs political assistance (Bates forthcoming: chaps. 3 and 7).[6]

Second, as Thorp and Durand argue in Chapter 8, the FNC may have started as an association of small coffee producers, but today it is a multisectoral peak association interested not in the microconcerns of peasant producers but in the health of the economy as a whole. The reasons for this development, which parallel similar developments elsewhere, are intrinsic to coffee.[7] Precisely because there are virtually no barriers to entry, coffee production per se is highly competitive, offering low profit margins and limited reinvestment opportunities. Successful producers, therefore, have strong incentives either to invest downstream in coffee processing or exporting or to invest outside the industry altogether in banking, manufacturing, commercial ventures, or urban real estate. Few in number, centrally located, and well connected, these successful individuals have faced few barriers to collective action. It is thus not surprising that, as Thorp and Durand observe, "from the early days, the Federation was, in effect, a multisectoral association . . . principally controlled by people whose interests lay in diverse fields, always including the commercialization of coffee, rarely its production except in small scale." In short, while the sectoral characteristics of coffee barred the organization of peasant producers as such, they did give rise to a diversification out of coffee, which in turn gave rise to a politically potent organization *called* the FNC but in fact empowered by its non-coffee character and ties to other sectors.

This reanalysis of the apparently anomalous but in fact confirming Colombian coffee case, like the limits to sectoral analysis in the Taiwan case, brings us back to the big question that gave rise to this book: How do we theorize—the key word—government-business relations in the developing world? Indeed, here we confront the whole problem of explanation. After all, explanation requires both a logic and comparison. This

[6] In Chapter 9 Doner and Ramsay tell a similar story about Thai politicians' incentives for organizing the light manufacturing sector given the structure of political institutions and competition.

[7] For an analysis of the Costa Rican case, see Shafer 1994: 193, 200–201.

is why Rogowski, Frieden, and I are at such pains to eschew both black box, anthropomorphic master variables such as "the state" and tightly focused traditional case studies and instead seek to develop general arguments that link the international and domestic arenas with a single logic and offer a parsimonious typology that encourages structured comparisons among cases. But given this purpose, what are we to make of contradictory or apparently contradictory data?

There are both silly and serious answers to this question. It is not useful, for example, to hide behind the trite observation that all theorizing involves identifying trends that never capture reality in all its muddled glory. To do so denies all prospect of falsification. It is, however, useful to reflect upon the relationship between theory and the meaning and implications of these apparent contradictions. After all, the apparently successful organization of small coffee growers in Colombia raises eyebrows and means something—that is, it is not a mere factoid, only within a theoretical context. The editors of this book note it in their introduction only because it seems to contradict the expectations of sectoral analysis, forcing me to push my argument further and look beneath the surface. Thus, this apparent contradiction really comes to mean something only because it leads me to ask and answer additional questions: Why do Colombian coffee growers not seem to fit expectations? How do they compare with coffee growers elsewhere? Is the supposed sectoral logic wrong? How? What better explanation is there?

Although I have laid these specific questions to rest, many more await me and the other authors in this book, for this is just the start of a bigger project. The contrapuntal presentation of chapters serves its purpose, which is to clarity the contradictions that give rise to the big questions. But this book and the contradictions, both empirical and theoretical, that it highlights constitute not the end of the story but the beginning of the real work. Put into the context of sectoral analysis specifically, these apparent contradictions should make us pose a whole series of researchable questions: Can they be explained as resulting from unique, fortuitous, local conditions? Is there other, similar evidence from other countries? Does closer examination reveal a sectoral logic at work below the surface—that is, are these exceptions that prove the rule? Does the evidence require a modification of sectoral analysis that otherwise works? Do these contraditions in fact falsify sectoral analysis? If they do, what next? And this, of course, is the real punch line; the real challenge, for as we push this enterprise forward, it is essential that we keep focused on our fundamental purpose: to fashion a superior alternative to current theorizations of government-business relations in the developing world that better accounts for both the details provided by all the new work being done and the variation across all the cases.

INTERVIEWS

Bae, Ie-Dong, Deputy Director, International Department, Federation of Korean Industries

Cha, Sang-Pil, Executive Vice President, Korean Chamber of Commerce and Industry

Cho, Kyu-Ha, Senior Managing Director, Federation of Korean Industries (previously with Bank of Korea)

Choi, Jang-Jip, Assistant Professor, Department of Political Science, Korea University

Chung, Jai-Suk, Dean, Graduate School of Management Information Systems, Hankuk University of Foreign Studies (previously with Bank of Korea and the Ministry of Reconstruction; first director of the Economic Planning Board; Minister of Commerce and Industry)

Han, Jae-Yuel, Executive Vice President, Korean Federation of Small Business

Kim, Kihwan, President and Chairman, Ilhae Foundation (previously Vice Minister of Trade and Industry)

Lee, Kuy-uch, Senior Fellow, Korea Development Institute

Lim, Dong-Sung, Managing Director, Korean Traders Association (previously with Bank of Korea)

Minn, Choong-Kee, Director, International Affairs Department, Korean Chamber of Commerce and Industry

Minn, Wan-Kee, Director, Marketing Department, Korean Chamber of Commerce and Industry

Sung, H. J., General Manager, Trade Cooperation Department, Korean Traders Association

Whang, In-Joung, Senior Fellow, Korea Development Institute

CHAPTER FIVE

Strong States and Business Organization in Korea and Taiwan

KARL FIELDS

In the final analysis, an economic partnership must be based on a political alliance.

—Chu Yun-han

Bureaucrats and capitalists in South Korea and Taiwan have created the two most successful instances of peripheral economic development in the postwar era. Democratically elected governments now preside over increasingly sophisticated and relatively equitable economies in these two countries, which less than fifty years ago were war-devastated basket cases. In 1949, Taiwan had a per capita income of $224 and an inflation rate of more than 3,000 percent. In 1953, South Korea's inflation rates rivaled those of Taiwan, and its per capita income was only $145. Taiwan's per capita gross national product (GNP) surpassed the $10,000 mark in 1993 with negligible inflation and virtually full employment. Korea, at nearly $7,000, was keeping pace.[1]

How does one account for these stunning economic performances? Scholars and pundits alike point to shared attributes, from neo-Confucian ethics to neoclassical economics, as the common cause of their success. But among the more promising explanations focusing on shared characteristics are those falling under the rubric of new comparative polit-

[1] *Free China Journal*: various issues. Here and throughout the book, dollar amounts indicate U.S. dollars unless otherwise indicated.

ical economy or new institutionalism (Evans and Stephens 1988). In fact, much of the most recent and most useful analysis of East Asian political economy in general, and Korean and Taiwanese development in particular, has been done under this banner of institutionalism.[2]

Chalmers Johnson argues that Korea's and Taiwan's stellar economic performance has been a direct result of their having refined and perfected Japan's institutional enigma, which combines bureaucratic autonomy and state administrative guidance with closely linked large-scale private enterprise groups (1987). Amsden similarly attributes Taiwan's and Korea's economic success (and the relatively less successful performance of other late developers) to the dynamics between two key institutions: "the reciprocity between big business and the state . . . and the internal and external behavior of the diversified business group" (1989: 150–51). Evans also lauds the embedded autonomy of these two developmental states that combines well-developed internal networks of bureaucratic coherence with external networks connecting the state and large private enterprise (1992).

But more careful focus on the specific institutions of these two political economies reveals substantial and causally significant variance. Moreover, this divergence comes precisely at the institutional nexus between public bureaucracy and private capital that institutionalists point to as an explanation for their comparable success. But rather than wholly undermining the institutional embeddedness argument these institutionalists put forth, this juxtaposition allows us to refine it by beginning to specify these differences and disaggregate the resultant, and variant, economic and political outcomes.

In Korea, a highly centralized authoritarian state created and nurtured large private conglomerates known as chaebol, and maintained with these chaebol a long-term collaborative relationship of *public-private reciprocity*. In Taiwan, on the other hand, an equally hard authoritarian state limited the growth of private conglomerates and formally structured with them a more distant and less institutionalized relationship of *mutual adjustment*. In his study of Taiwan, Wade concludes that Taiwan meets Johnson's developmental-state criterion of bureaucratic autonomy but not the requirement of public-private cooperation (Wade 1990: 295). Evans, too, acknowledges this disparity, noting that Korea pushes "at the limit to which embeddedness can be concentrated in a few ties without degenerating into particularistic predation," while Taiwan demonstrates the opposite concern "in which the relative absence of links to private capital might seem to threaten the ability of the autonomous state to secure full infor-

[2] For a survey of the application of this new institutionalism in studies of Korea and Taiwan, see Fields 1995.

mation and count on the private sector for effective implementation" (1992: 163–65).

This chapter demonstrates that cooperation between public bureaucrats and private capitalists has been crucial to the formulation and implementation of effective industrial policy and the pace of economic development in both Korea and Taiwan. But unlike "lumpier" studies that note institutional similarities in East Asia, this chapter argues that such isomorphic convergence, even among fairly similar political economies in the same region, is neither rapid nor inevitable. Rather, historical legacies, situational imperatives, and regime dynamics peculiar to each of these political economies have given rise to different forms of cooperation. Political leaders and policymakers in similarly strong states in Korea and Taiwan have adopted distinctive industrial strategies, fostered particular patterns of industrial organization, and structured specific institutional arrangements that have enhanced public-private cooperation with positive but variant developmental outcomes.

Military and civilian political leaders and technocrats in Korea fostered a relationship of quasi-internal collaboration with a handful of rapidly expanding industrial chaebol.[3] Oriented toward the well-defined and nonideological goal of rapid, Fordist economic growth, the state gained the compliance of the chosen chaebol with its developmental goals by offering them massive financial subsidies and other incentives.[4] The nascent industrial giants thrived in this favorable environment, developing first as junior clients to the state and ultimately as full-fledged symbiotic partners.

In Taiwan, ideological and political motivations prompted the transplanted minority Nationalist (KMT) regime to adopt a dual strategy of industrialization. This included promoting an internal Fordist, public-enterprise sector at the commanding heights of the economy while fostering a more distant but supportive relationship of coordination with smaller private conglomerates and a host of small- and medium-sized enterprises pursuing an industrial strategy of flexible specialization.[5]

[3] Chung Lee argues that the Korean state and chaebol form a "quasi-internal organization" with an internal capital market that has reduced communications costs, uncertainty, and opportunism, allowing the government to efficiently implement industrial policies (1992). Schneider defines collaboration as a relationship in which "bureaucrats and capitalists share a great deal of information, exchange state subsidies for improved business performance (reciprocity), and ultimately trust each other" (see Chapter 7 in this book).

[4] Paul Hirst and Jonathan Zeitlin distinguish between ideal-typical models of Fordist mass production and flexible specialization, defining the former as "the manufacture of standardized products in high volumes using special-purpose machinery and predominately unskilled labour" and the latter as "the manufacture of a wide and changing array of customized products using flexible, general-purpose machinery and skilled, adaptable workers" (1991: 2).

[5] Under conditions of Fordist mass-production industrialization, collaboration is both a

Contrary to Wade's conclusion that Taiwan does not meet the developmental-state requirement of public-private cooperation, the state's ties with Taiwan's less concentrated private-business sector have been substantial and important but decidedly more particularistic, diffuse, and distant than those in Korea.

Streeck argues that different production patterns can be functionally equivalent responses to common economic challenges and that both state- and privately created institutions can facilitate economic efficiency and equity.[6] Although Doner and Ramsay argue in Chapter 9 that private-interest governance in the form of private banks in Thailand have been key to resolving collective-action problems, strong developmental states have made the difference in the Korean and Taiwanese cases. But the divergence in these two regimes' strategies and the consequent variation in links to differently organized private sectors have led to significantly different types of industrial organization with variant opportunities for future growth and consequences for political power.

This chapter analyzes these differences. The following section examines the strength of the respective economic bureaucracies and their motivations for pursuing their particular developmental strategies. The next section contrasts the resultant patterns of enterprise organization in each political economy, and the final section compares the specific nature and extent of cooperation between bureaucrats and capitalists in each case. Although largely beyond the scope of this chapter, the political consequences of these variant (and dynamic) economic structures and social cleavages will be raised in the conclusion.

STATE STRUCTURES

State formation—first colonial, then republican—preceded significant industrialization in both South Korea and Taiwan. Evans notes that the "combination of historically accumulated bureaucratic capacity and conjuncturally generated autonomy" allowed these states to "dominate (at least initially) the formation of the ties that bound capital and state

---

feasible, and the optimal, mode of public-private cooperation because it depends on relatively small numbers of large firms working closely with government officials on micro issues of production and marketing. Flexible niche production strategies, on the other hand, are best served by cooperation through looser coordination, wherein officials work closely with business in determining support levels in terms of infrastructure and inputs (see Chapter 2 in this book).

[6] As cited in Kuo 1994: 6. In a comparative study, Doner concurs, arguing that it is necessary to understand how and why public and private institutions are supplied because similar problems can have different institutional responses (1992: 430–31). This is precisely the case with Korea and Taiwan.

together" (1989: 575). This strength does not, however, presume bureaucratic harmony and omniscience, nor does it deny the growing evidence of both failed state policies and crucial input and occasionally even leadership by private business in many of these policy successes.[7] Much like a tango, both cooperation and development require two parties. But while either can falter, typically only one can lead.

There is no guarantee that strong states will produce optimal or efficient policies, and they should be—institutionally speaking—even more effective predators (Haggard and Moon 1990: 214–15). Haggard notes that the "main problem with the institutionalist approach is it addresses the capacity of the state but not its motivations," and he argues that we must ask why the state chooses to do what it does (1994: 7). This "strategic choice" is a variable at least partially independent from the structure of power. Wade argues that the "difference between Taiwan and Mexico, for example, is less in the structure of power as in the choices made by the political leadership" (1990: 296).

Regimes in Korea and Taiwan have been interventionist by nature and developmental in motivation but have made very different strategic choices about how to organize industry and cooperate with the private sector in achieving developmental goals. Although the Nationalist regime in Taiwan was even more autonomous and nearly as capable as its Korean counterpart, its ideology and historical experience gave the state different priorities. This in turn led political leaders in Taiwan to delegate both industrial policy-making and production differently and constrained them from taking steps similar to their Korean counterparts' in fostering and tying the regime's own fate to large-scale private industry.

Korea

Amsden argues that in all late industrializing countries, the state deliberately subsidizes domestic industry to distort relative prices in order to stimulate economic activity. The Korean state, she contends, has differed from other late developers not in providing subsidies but in being able to impose performance standards on the private firms that receive these subsidies. This Korean capacity and its absence elsewhere "does not reflect differential abilities among policymakers. It reflects differences in state power" (Amsden 1989: 145).

---

[7] Moon and Prasad 1993; Fields 1989. Wade usefully distinguishes four categories of government intervention in the market: *small followership*, helping firms to do what they would have already done; *big followership*, assisting firms significantly to extend the margin of their investments; *small leadership*, providing assistance with too little resources or too little influence to make a difference; and *big leadership*, providing initiatives large enough to make a real difference to investment and production patterns (1990: 28).

Discussion of state power in Korea often obscures the fact that, although the Korean state was more interventionist than its counterpart in Taiwan, this was partially a result of its political vulnerability and its ultimate dependence on business (for both regime legitimacy and financial support). Although colonial precedent and wartime militarization enhanced the institutions and instruments of state power, the Rhee regime (1948–60) was largely unable to capitalize on these potentialities for state power separate from particular societal interests and "incapable of the autonomy to direct growth" (Cumings 1987: 67). Authoritarian in its draconian policies of social control, the regime was beholden initially to a traditional agrarian elite and increasingly to nascent capitalists who skillfully "played on the urgent need for political funds on the part of politicians and the prevalent corruption of high-ranking bureaucrats" to ensure the continuation of state policies guaranteeing windfall monopoly rents (K. Kim 1976: 468).

General Park Chong Hee, after seizing power in 1961, capitalized on public disgust with these corrupt ties between the Rhee government and private capital and assembled both a popular mandate and the institutional means to assure an autonomous state capable of guiding economic development. Answerable only to the military, Park was not initially dependent on support from either the landed or the capitalist classes, as his predecessor had been. Park concentrated virtually all state economic powers in the Economic Planning Board and the Council of Economic Ministers and reserved for these institutions exclusive budgeting authority and very broad authority to coordinate fiscal, monetary, trade, and industrial power. He nationalized the commercial banks and placed them under the direct control of the Ministry of Finance (MOF). In sharp contrast to Taiwan, Park also gave the ministry direct control over Korea's central bank, the Bank of Korea (BOK). Under the immediate supervision of the president, the MOF effectively determined the reserve ratios, loan and investment volumes, and, most important, the interest rates of all formal banking institutions (Fields 1995).

Park staffed this economic bureaucracy with talented personnel bound in a Weberian sense by a shared confidence in their own skills and their national mission. Korea, like its Sinicized neighbors, has a long bureaucratic tradition based on relatively meritocratic civil service appointments. This legacy, Evans notes, provides "legitimacy for state initiatives and non-material incentives for the 'best and brightest' to consider bureaucratic careers." Although neither as elitist nor as prestigious as its Japanese counterpart, the economic bureaucracy selects its personnel from among the most talented members of the most prestigious universities. Only 2 percent of a growing pool of those sitting for the annual higher civil service exam are accepted (Evans 1992: 159).

With firm control of financial capital and economic policy-making, Park and his bureaucratic general staff confiscated ill-gotten private assets of big business and gained control over virtually all resources vital to business. From this position of dominance and institutional capacity, the government devised and implemented its strategy of export-oriented industrialization. Trained under the Japanese, Park consciously patterned this strategy after Meiji Japan's, emphasizing large-scale, privately owned mass production. He argued that "mammoth enterprise," coordinated and supervised by the state, was "indispensable" to Korean development (Park 1962: 228–29). The chosen chaebol learned quickly that to "go along with the state was to get along" (Mason et al. 1981: 265) and thrived with state support in successive strategic industrial sectors. Over the course of Park's rule, the regime's legitimacy became inextricably tied to the fate of the economy, and the fate of the economy increasingly depended on the burgeoning chaebol. While maintaining the upper hand over business, subsequent regimes have all reneged on early promises of taming the chaebol and have pursued pro-growth strategies relying on the chaebol as the engines of that growth.

This growing mutual dependence was a direct result of the state's choice of developmental strategies and the political consequences of this choice. Korea's dearth of private entrepreneurs to draw upon and a state-owned sector much smaller than that which the Nationalist party-state inherited from the Japanese upon its arrival in Taiwan led the Park regime to seek the cooperation of a handful of big private capitalists in its Fordist developmental plans. Politically, the military government lacked a party apparatus to provide a basis of political support. As the legitimacy of successive regimes declined and popular pressure to shift to democratic rule swelled, the government faced increasing demands for political funds that could only be supplied by the rapidly expanding chaebol.[8] And while each of Park's successors has come to power pledging to limit the expanding tentacles of big business, all have retreated from these promises when faced with the economy's overwhelming dependence on the chaebol for output and employment. The relationship has clearly shifted from state dominance to symbiosis and increasing conflict as Park's protégés ponder if they will remain partners in a hegemonic pact or become gravediggers for the developmental state (E. Kim 1988; Evans 1989).

[8] Not surprisingly, the period of highest growth for the chaebol was during the Yushin period of high authoritarianism as the political support coalition narrowed (Haggard 1994: 12).

Taiwan

Taiwan's Nationalist party-state has been remarkably autonomous from Taiwanese society. Leninist in organization, backed by loyal military and security organs, and cleansed of many of its former corrupt officials and collusive activities when transplanted to Taiwan in 1949, the regime began its rule there from a position of remarkable strength and relative honesty. Unlike Korea, Taiwan had no strong local class to compete with Nationalist rule. Colonial and Nationalist land reforms and the decimation of the local intelligentsia left Taiwanese society "leaderless, atomized, quiescent and apolitical" (Gold 1986: 52). Additionally, there was a de facto division of labor between the newly arrived mainlanders and the local Taiwanese: Mainlanders occupied all responsible political and government positions and left the bulk of the economic sector to the local Taiwanese. Linguistic and cultural differences compounded this subethnic division and increased the Nationalist state's insulation from Taiwanese society.

The Nationalist regime established a series of economic pilot agencies for administering its economic policies. These agencies developed a "little understood but apparently vigorous policy network" (Wade 1990: 295) that Chu characterizes as "fairly elaborate and resourceful" (1989: 656). These administrative organs, however, were much more decentralized and did not have either the autonomy from political leaders or the longevity of their Korean counterparts. The reason was neither societal penetration of the state nor a lack of skilled personnel but political conflicts within the governing structure over regime priorities.

Impressed by the streamlined efficiency of Park Chong Hee's Economic Planning Bureau, the Nationalist regime sent a research team to Korea in 1977 and at its suggestion merged several agencies into the Council for Economic Planning and Development (CEPD). This extraministerial organ has proven to be an effective body for advising the economic policy-making process, although, like its predecessors, its autonomy and influence has varied depending on the relationship between the CEPD's leadership and the political elite. Unlike Korea's central bank, which is dominated by the Economic Planning Board (EPB) and the Ministry of Finance, Taiwan's Central Bank of China (CBC) exerts a strong and conservative influence on the economic bureaucracy. Still stinging from their bout with hyperinflation on the Chinese mainland, Nationalist political leaders invested great power in the central bank's conservative officials and gave the bank autonomy from and authority over planning technocrats in the CEPD and the Ministry of Economic Affairs (MOEA). The more decentralized hands-on implementation of industrial policy and the gathering of information from the private industrial sector is carried out in large part by the MOEA's Industrial Development Bureau (IDB), although Chu contends that the IDB has enjoyed "little clout in the overall economic bureaucracy, and has limited influence over fiscal and credit policy" (1989: 656).

The primary goal of the Nationalist Chinese (KMT) regime since its defeat on the mainland and relocation to Taiwan in 1949 has been to strengthen Taiwan militarily and politically by fostering economic development under conditions of price stability and relative social equity. Inspired by Sun Yat-sen's quasi-socialist ideology of "people's livelihood," the Nationalist regime has consciously and assiduously limited the concentration of private capital. This ideological motive was reinforced by the ethnicity-based division of labor between the minority mainlander government officials and Taiwanese capitalists. While growth eased Taiwanese opposition to national political exclusion by providing economic outlets, it raised concerns among Nationalist leaders that increasing economic power could be translated into political clout.

Learning from its defeat on the mainland, and as an exogenous minority regime, the Nationalist state sought legitimacy not from a landed aristocracy nor from a coterie of privileged capitalists but from the multitude of small producers and smallholders that its growth with equity policies fostered (Cheng 1990). Unlike Korea, the Nationalist state adopted a strategy of coordination with the private sector, granting incentives to manufacture and export across the board not limited to a handful of premier firms. Financial regulations, tax and labor laws, and other state policies provided strong incentives to limit firm size and encouraged flexible specialization (Deyo, Doner, and Fields 1993; Biggs and Levy 1991).

At the same time, the Nationalist state used as its developmental vanguard a large stable of state- and party-owned enterprises over which it had greater control. Moreover, this state- and party-owned enterprise sector gave the Nationalist party-state a much higher degree of independence from private capital than its Korean counterpart had. These firms have provided the regime with both political donations and training grounds and pasturage for ascending and descending economic bureaucrats and politicians (Chu 1994a: 13).

The regime's political independence from a relatively less concentrated private sector has effectively curbed the political influence of capital in the past. But as in Korea, distributional demands of democracy and the concentration of private capital have been on the rise. Ironically, the declining significance of the subethnic distinction and the consequent indiginization of the Nationalist party have made a conservative coalition along the lines of Japan's "corporatism without labor" more likely in Taiwan than in Korea (Chu 1994a).

ENTERPRISE ORGANIZATION

The Korean state's greater political dependence on the private sector encouraged "closer institutional linkages between the state and business, more explicit political exchanges (in the form of various 'political funds'), more direct government support for industry, particularly through the financial sector, and a more concentrated [private] industrial structure" (Haggard 1994: 13). The Korean state subsidized the development and expansion of these huge horizontally and vertically integrated business conglomerates. In Taiwan, on the other hand, while private business groups still contribute significantly to the local economy, they are much smaller and very different from their Korean counterparts in terms of capital, scale, control of their own trade, and government connections.

In Taiwan and Korea, although group firms often share economic or financial ties, they typically have no overarching accounting or management systems that coordinate the activities of the member firms. Rather, the diversified groups are usually connected through the ownership or control of all the firms in the group by an individual or small group of individuals linked by family ties or other personal relationships (Hamilton et al. 1988: 5). Patterns of business group organization are quite isomorphic within Korea and Taiwan; however, the scale and relative significance of the groups vary dramatically between the two countries.

Korea's largest five groups alone had total sales of $44 billion and employed nearly half a million workers in 1983. Taiwan's largest five groups, on the other hand, had roughly one-tenth the sales of Korea's top five and employed less than one-third the number of employees in that same year. The relative significance of the groups is even more stark when measured in terms of centrality to their respective economies. Sales of Taiwan's top five business groups accounted for only 10 percent of Taiwan's total GNP for 1983, while the figure for Korea's top five groups was over 50 percent. Sales of the top ninety-six groups accounted for nearly one-third of Taiwan's GNP, paltry when compared to Korea's top fifty, which accounted for sales equal to nearly 94 percent of Korea's 1983 GNP (Hamilton et al. 1987).

Taiwan's top five groups have grown substantially over the past decade, with combined annual revenues of more than $22.2 billion in 1992, more than four times the 1983 figure (*Juoyue,* September 1993). Taiwan's national economy, however, has grown apace; revenues still represent just over 10 percent of Taiwan's total GNP. Korea's top five lost ground slightly but still had sales worth $116.6 billion in 1991, accounting for just under 50 percent of Korea's 1991 GNP.[9] By comparison, the top five business enterprises in both France and Germany had sales equal to 12 percent of GNP, more than Taiwan but less than one-fourth the concentration of Korea. The same figure for the United States was 7 percent, roughly one-seventh of the Korean totals. Korea's Samsung Group alone had sales worth 15 percent of Korea's 1991 GNP; the American equivalent (in terms of sales weight) would need to combine sales of the top twenty American firms (including GM, Exxon, Ford, IBM, GE, and fifteen others).[10]

It is misleading, however, to characterize Taiwan's economy as atomized. Although firms employing fewer than three hundred workers accounted in 1990 for more than 70 percent of the work force and more than 60 percent of the nation's exports (*Economic News*, December 24, 1990), Taiwan's private business groups are nonetheless significant players in the marketplace. A recent survey found that the one thousand biggest private firms (most of them members of business groups) accounted for 25 percent of aggregate capital in 1992. The top ten firms accounted for nearly 40 percent of earnings in their sectors (*Free China Journal*, June 8, 1993).

More important, if state- and party-owned enterprise networks are included, the level of Taiwan's economic concentration is substantial. Clustered in the upstream, capital-intensive, and oligopolized sectors, these firms have served as both sources of government revenue and vertical suppliers to the private conglomerates and plethora of smaller firms.[11] Internally linked to the Nationalist party-state, these huge public enterprises gave the state control of strategic industries and industrial inputs and have in many ways functioned as equivalent developmental

---

[9] Sales figures for top five Korean groups are taken from the *Economist*, June 8, 1991.

[10] *Fortune*, July 1992. GNP figures from KOTRA 1992. A partial list of the activities of the fifty-five affiliated firms of Korea's Samsung conglomerate includes textiles, electronic assembly and equipment, semiconductors, fiber optics, ceramics, precision equipment, detergents, petrochemicals, military equipment, shipbuilding, wholesale trade, land development, construction, insurance, stock brokerage, a newspaper, broadcasting, a hospital, and a university (Fields 1995: 35).

[11] These large-scale public enterprises serve as upstream suppliers of raw materials and in many cases technology and finance as well. Taiwan's upstream petrochemical, plastics, steel, and textile industries are all dominated by large suppliers. Wade notes that "major concentrations of private productive capital are mostly in sectors which depend heavily upon upstream public enterprises" (1990: 179). Concerning loans, Taiwan's banks direct the lion's share of their funds to large public and private firms, who then lend money for equipment and working capital to smaller downstream customers, subcontractors, and suppliers at higher rates through trade credit and loans on the informal curb market (Biggs 1991: 194).

institutions to the Korean chaebol (although with different sociopolitical consequences). From the 1950s to the 1970s, the share of value added by firms employing more than five hundred workers was greater in Taiwan than Korea and 80 to 90 percent of all other non-Communist countries (Chu 1994a: 119; Amsden 1991: 1,122; Wade 1990: 272). Despite recent privatization efforts, sixty state-owned enterprises (SOE) accounted for 15 percent of aggregate capital in 1992, and the Nationalist party controlled enterprises with an estimated value in 1993 of $4.5 billion dollars.[12] A 1992 survey ranked the Nationalist party enterprise system as Taiwan's sixth largest "private" conglomerate (*Juoyue,* September 1992).

Wade concludes that the public-enterprise sector in Taiwan is "an exception to the familiar thesis that government-owned corporations tend to deplete rather than add to government revenues," adding that profit rates have "generally been positive." The result, he contends, is a "dualistic" and "densely interconnected" industrial structure in which "the export success of the smaller, direct exporting firms cannot be understood independently of the productive performance of the big firms" (1990: 70). Amsden concurs, arguing that without these large-scale and domestic sources of upstream inputs, Taiwan's flexible production system of subcontracting based on small-lot purchases would not be feasible (Amsden 1991).

With firm control over their respective financial systems and bureaucratic policy-making apparatuses, strong states in both Korea and Taiwan determined the developmental strategies of their respective regimes and limited the capacity of business as capital to constrain industrial policy choices. In Korea, Park and his successors directly controlled economic policy-making, delegating this authority to a highly centralized and extremely powerful economic bureaucracy. Park's strategic choice to promote Japanese-style concentrated private capital made the Korean state less wary about institutionalizing a relationship of collaboration with the beneficiaries of these policies as long as the government retained the upper hand. The nature and success of this collaborative relationship has, however, made the state more susceptible to chaebol arm twisting as these mature clients have become symbiotic partners and potential gravediggers (Evans 1989). Financial liberalization and political democratization in Korea over the past decade have further weakened the government's

[12] The figures for the state-owned enterprises are from *Free China Journal,* June 8, 1993, and for the party-owned enterprises from *Time,* August 23, 1993. Some estimates are even higher. A 1990 study produced by scholars sympathetic to the opposition Democratic Progressive party valued state-owned assets at eight times that of the top five hundred firms in 1988 and estimated the combined revenues of state- and party-owned enterprises that year at nearly $80 billion, fully 30 percent of GNP (*Economic News,* May 21, 1990).

hold on the chaebol and sharpened the political debate between pro- and anti-chaebol forces.

Painfully aware of the predatory and collusive capacity of private capital and armed with an ideological justification for restricting it, the Nationalist regime bolstered its political and bureaucratic autonomy by retaining control not only of the banks but of large industrial capital as well. The regime further insulated key economic decision making in an independent central bank answerable only to top political leaders and formally distant from private business interests. Internal collaboration between party-state bureaucrats and public enterprise was supplemented with coordination between these two institutions and a less concentrated and less organized private sector. We now turn to these link.

INSTITUTIONAL LINKS

This book hypothesizes that cooperation between government and business under conditions of deep state intervention ameliorates collective-action problems by facilitating information sharing, reciprocity (subsidies for performance), and ultimately trust between bureaucrats and capitalists.[13] This in turn enhances the quality of industrial policy and improves the prospects for national economic development. This chapter confirms that hypothesis but argues that there has been significant variation between the two cases in the nature and consequences of this cooperation.

Strong states in both countries have fostered specific formal and informal institutional ties with private business that have enhanced public-private cooperation. These states directed the flow of information, set the terms of reciprocity, and determined the distance between them and private business. Speaking specifically of the role of business associations in Korea and Taiwan, Anek Laothamatas observed that they "appear to have served much more as channels through which government policies were relayed to the business community than as vigorous representatives of business demands." He concludes that, even at its most intimate, this relationship has been determined by "a state run 'for' capitalists rather than a state run 'by' capitalists" (1994: 207). The previous two sections have introduced both sides of this relationship; in this final section we examine the relationship itself and the evolving nature of their institutional links as private business groups in both Korea and Taiwan have increased their financial independence and political influence.

[13] See Schneider, Chapter 7 in this book.

Korea

Policy-making in "Korea, Inc." has been characterized by "close consultation between the highest ranking state officials and top business leaders through both interpersonal links and formalized channels and by consultation between responsible state agencies and state sponsored industrial associations" (Chu 1989: 654). The organizational structure of Korean business enhanced the exchange of information and reciprocities through these state-structured informal and formal links. The multisectoral diversification of the chaebol made them less resistant to the state's proposed shifts in industrial structure and sectoral priorities.[14] The concentration of the chaebol also enhanced collaboration because of shared interests between the state and a relatively small number of elite business groups. This hegemonic pact began to break down, however, as these behemoths became less financially dependent on the state and their interests began to diverge from those of a democratizing government. Under these circumstances, the chaebol's sheer economic clout and limited numbers have enhanced their capacity to use these same formal and informal institutions of collaboration to protect their interests vis-à-vis the state and privately resolve collective-action problems. We turn first to formal organizational links and then informal networks.

Several chapters in this book emphasize the role of formal business associations in mediating relations between government and business. Korea has more than two hundred business associations, most of which are functionally differentiated associations organized along trade and industry lines and under the guidance of the relevant economic ministry.[15] All are licensed by the state and granted a representational monopoly in government decision-making bodies (Park 1987).

The Park government required all firms in Korea to join industrial associations established at the initiative or by the encouragement of the state for the purpose of gathering information and mobilizing support for government policy. Mark Clifford notes that "very small companies could conceal from the government and the association what they were doing, and very big companies could browbeat the associations, but for the most part this structure gave the government extremely effective control over the economy" (1994: 63). The associations proved to be effective conduits for passing information from business to the economic bureaucracy

[14] This was particularly the case because the chaebol had learned through experience that government policies tended to favor them even when the business groups did not exert their influence (M. Park 1987: 908).

[15] There is also a singular peak association with compulsory membership, the Korean Chamber of Commerce and Industry.

and the president himself and for transmitting orders, regulations, and guidelines to specific sectors and firms. The associations' administrative staff, often peopled with a number of retired military officers (particularly those associations connected with the construction and transportation ministries), in essence provided the bureaucracy with "subordinate bureaucracies made up of association staff paid for by the member companies" (Clifford 1994: 63).

In his study of interest-group representation in Korea, Moon Kyu Park argues that these state corporatist associations are "extremely susceptible to government manipulation" and largely react to the government's policy drafts rather than initiate policy. In interviews, business leaders told Park that their associations would point out problems in drafts, offer suggestions, but not insist on any fundamental changes. Park found no business leaders willing to acknowledge that their association had opposed government policy (1987: 906–7). Mun-boo Cho claims that business association input is only selectively incorporated in bureaucratic decision making and that "their collaboration is essential for policies to be implemented, but their consent is not necessary for policies to be adopted" (1992: 172).

The exception to this rule of business association as mere government delegate is the handful of associations, councils, and other institutionalized forums that have brought together the scions of the largest chaebol and top bureaucrats and political leaders. Several of these organizations emerged independently of the government during the 1950s in an effort to deal privately with collective-action problems at a time when the government was hesitant to give overt support to business associations. These pioneering associations include the Korean Chamber of Commerce and Industry, the Korean Traders Association, and the Korean Federation of Textile Industries, all of which still stand out for their levels of organization and financing and the reputations of influence they enjoy (Park 1987: 904–6).

By far the most influential of these elite organizations is the Federation of Korean Industry (FKI), organized as "a self-defense interest and lobbying organization" for the chaebol to protect their own interests" (Clifford 1994: 40). Like the associations noted in the preceding paragraph, the FKI's founding preceded the Park regime. Seventy-eight top industrialists first organized the FKI as the Korean Economic Council (KEC) in 1961 in anticipation of the Illicit Wealth Decree formulated by the short-lived Chang Myon regime and carried out by his successor Park Chong Hee.[16] Support for this decree stemmed from widespread frustra-

---

[16] I am indebted to David Satterwhite for pointing out the origin of the Illicit Wealth Decree (personal conversation).

tion with the political corruption and economic stagnation that resulted from collusive activities between private economic interests and the Rhee government during the 1950s.[17] The well-connected recipients of these windfall profits became fitting (and wealthy) targets for those seeking to replace Rhee. Park exploited this shift in the political position of business and responded by implementing a policy to clean up the "illegal and unfair profiting" of these chaebol entrepreneurs less than two weeks after taking power. He immediately arrested prominent chaebol leaders and other company heads (thirty in all) and ordered them to return all profits gained through unfair and illicit activities since the signing of the Korean War truce in 1953.[18]

Within the week, nine of Korea's most prominent businessmen "voluntarily" offered to donate their entire fortunes to the government. Because of this submission, and also because the government quickly realized its own dependence on these entrepreneurs as the only viable agents for developing the country, the Park junta backed down and cut a pragmatic deal. Having initially threatened the wealthy capitalists with execution, jail, fines, and confiscation of property, Park reduced the total fines by 90 percent and within months cut that amount in half again. Further, instead of requiring the businessmen to pay these reduced fines, he asked some to build strategic factories (with government financing) and then donate them to the state. Clifford notes that "in the end, most of the factories were not built, no shares were turned over to the government and businessmen settled their obligations by paying only about US$16 million in fines." Nonetheless, he concludes that this government "bullying [and] . . . Confucian coercion . . . set the pattern for a close, if stormy, marriage between business and government" in which Park was "determined to discourage wasteful economic activities by forcing businessmen to invest in the productive economy of the country" (Clifford 1994: 39).

The Korean Economic Council, FKI's predecessor, was instrumental in softening this decree and negotiated the ultimate bargain with Park. Although Park's decree technically dismantled the council, Park himself recommended that the thirteen top chaebol leaders reorganize as the Economic Reconstruction and Promotion Association. The name changed again to the Korean Businessmen's Association and then ulti-

---

[17] The following discussion draws on Jung 1988, E. Kim 1988, K. Kim 1976, Clifford 1994, and Haggard 1994.

[18] Those activities designated as constituting illicit and unfair wealth included tax evasion, illegal contribution to political funds, illicit purchase of national vested properties, extraordinarily preferential monopoly of contracts for construction and supply activities, unusually large and monopolistic allocation of foreign capital, misallocated foreign funds, and other capital illegally taken out of the country (K. Kim 1976: 471). Kim notes that it was primarily those entrepreneurs who had accumulated monopoly profits dealing in the lucrative "three powders"—flour, sugar, and cement—who were affected (Kim 1988: 107).

mately to the Federation of Korean Industry. Although its lobbying strategies have varied as its favor with the state has waxed and waned over three decades, the major goal of the FKI has remained relatively consistent: preventing government confiscation of chaebol wealth.[19] Often billed as a weaker equivalent of Japan's *Keidanren*, the FKI is, according to Clifford, the primary formal "transmission belt for corporate-government communication"; and he argues that, although the state was willing to listen to advice from the private sector, the state was clearly the dominant partner: "Park in the 1960s was good at listening to suggestions, but orders ran in only one direction, from Park's presidential Blue House to the bureaucracy and business" (Clifford 1994: 40).

Despite this "information up, orders down" reputation, the FKI has been an effective lobbying group for chaebol interests. Straining under huge debts and the burdensome servicing of these debts in the early 1970s, the chaebol, via FKI, persuaded the Park regime to shift this burden of interest repayment from the chaebol to small savers by freezing the curb market, reducing corporate taxes, and slashing interest rates (Eckert 1990–91; Woo 1991: 111). During the 1980s, the FKI expanded its organizational capacity to provide policy proposals to the state by creating a number of policy formation and policy research groups.[20] Focusing on issues of taxation, trade, and foreign economic relations, the FKI has made an average of thirty to forty formal policy recommendations a year to the economic bureaucracy since the 1980s. Julia Fox claims that the government implements approximately 30 percent of these proposals within one year and another 40 percent within three years (1992: 10). Shafer argues that by the 1990s the FKI was no longer just a delegate of state power but had become a potent lobbying institution that has joined the policy process as full participant. He contends that the government now accepts 90 percent of the FKI's policy recommendations (Shafer 1994).

The FKI is not the only formal organization representing big business in the policy-making process. In 1965, Park initiated a monthly trade promotion meeting as a forum between government and business. Committed to promoting exports, Park religiously chaired these high-profile meetings, which included trade-related ministers, business association leaders, heads of major financial institutions, and representatives of major export firms (H. Kim 1992: 102). The Korean Traders Association, rep-

---

[19] Fox 1992: 9. See also Moon 1994, Woo 1991, and Kirk 1994.

[20] These have included the Korean Economic Institute, Korean International Economic Institute, International Management Institute, Businessmen's Club, Korean Information Industry Association, and the Korean Technology Development Company. The FKI also helped to form the Korean Development Finance Corporation, a private financial institution, in 1967 (Fox 1992: 10).

resenting the chaebol-affiliated general trading companies, made 176 recommendations to the government in 1974. The government adopted, at
least in part, 76 percent of these proposals.[21]

The export industry was not the only strategic sector to which the state
gave special audience and influence. In his study of Korean auto producers, Chu argues that they were also directly involved in the formulation and implementation of sectoral policies through their sectoral
association, the Korean Automobile Industry Association (KAIA). He
claims that the state-sponsored KAIA, like the FKI and KTA, served as
more than just an intermediary between the state and auto manufacturers. The association played an important role in creating consensus
between the two sides on policy goals and implementation mechanisms,
frequently submitted industrial policy proposals either on demand or on
its own initiative, helped the economic bureaucracy conduct industrial
surveys, devised industry standards, and enforced government regulations. In addition, senior executives of the private producing firms met
regularly with midlevel officials of the Ministry of Trade and Industry
(MTI) and experts from the Korean Institute of Economics and Technology (an MTI-affiliated industrial policy think tank) (Chu 1994b).

These types of business-bureaucrat-technical expert meetings have
been institutionalized in many strategic sectors in the form of Japanese-
style deliberation councils and decision groups. Kim notes that these
channels facilitate the exchange of information and are used by business
to resolve problems and delays in firms' dealings with the economic ministries, who in turn use these institutionalized channels to gather information, administer export and other incentives, and adjust policies and
other administrative arrangements. Kim concludes that, through this flow
of information from the enterprises to the government and the flow of
guidance in the opposite direction, the state significantly reduced the
costs of policy implementation and opportunities for free riding (H. Kim
1992: 102).

In addition to these formal organizations, policymakers and the business elite have relied on extensive informal channels of communication
and cooperation. Chu notes that the formal institutional links in auto production were enhanced by "informal, crosscutting interpersonal connections between the business elite and high ranking state officials." In fact,
most of the chaebol owners involved in auto production "enjoyed direct
access to the presidential office" (1994b: 141). Park argues that, because
business associations are typically weak and dependent, many chaebol

---

[21] Jones and Sakong 1980: 70–71. These proposals concerned government plans to create
and nurture general-trading companies out of the existing trading arms of the chaebol
(Fields 1995).

owners rely instead on "personal relationships, power brokering, outright corruption, and political contributions." These personal efforts through informal contacts, he notes, are most effective in seeking firm or group-specific distributive benefits, such as arranging for a specific exemption to a tax hike (rather than trying to join a collective effort to lower the rate across the board) (M. Park 1987: 907).

These personal connections between public officials and private capitalists can include blood and marriage ties, a shared birthplace, or a common school (Cho 1992). Of the latter two, regional bonds are seen as stronger than alumni ties, with the "TK mafia" their most significant manifestation.[22] As in Japan, however, having attended the same high school or college can also be an important ascriptive link; and bureaucrats and businessmen who boast of, for example, the "K-S mark" have at least the basis for cultivating a collaborative bond.[23]

The Korean bureaucracy also practices its version of descending from bureaucratic heaven into chaebol corporate boardrooms. This "special recruitment" (*tuk chae*) of high-ranking military officers and civil servants, like its Japanese (*amakudari*) and French (*pantouflage*) counterparts, provides an important source for chaebol managers and ongoing channels of communication (Kim and Kim 1989; Chang 1988). A 1984 study of the top twenty chaebol found that 31 percent of executive officers were family members, 29 percent were professional managers promoted from within, and the remaining 40 percent were recruited from the outside. A large portion of this latter category were former high-ranking officials or retired generals, hired not for their managerial skills but because of their personal and political influence (Yoo and Lee 1987). According to one estimate, some 20 percent of the Daewoo group's senior management was recruited from the military (Shin 1991). Park also notes that the government often arranges to give leadership posts in business associations to retired government officials as rewards for past services. The associations usually accept these recommendations readily because they provide informal access to the inner circle of policy-making (1987: 906).

Even more widespread, although less well documented, is the common corporate practice of giving "gifts" (*chonji*), or bribes, to political leaders and economic policymakers. Since the Rhee regime, entrepreneurs have used these bribes and kickbacks to assure political favors. In 1987 hearings before the national assembly, the FKI president and patriarch of

---

[22] This refers to a particularly cohesive and influential regional affiliation comprised of military, political, and corporate elite hailing from the city of Taegu and the surrounding northern Kyongsang Province in southeastern Korea (*Far Eastern Economic Review*, May 13, 1993).
[23] The "K-S mark" consists of degrees from Kyunggi High School and Seoul National University, Korea's best schools (C. Chang 1988).

Korea's largest chaebol acknowledged that he alone had donated close to $2.5 million to the past three presidents of Korea and also donated to the ruling party "always in the amount asked" (Woo 1991: 199). A recent biographer of this capitalist claims that his confession was "on the low end of the scale" (Kirk 1994: 315).

These formal and informal connections add up to what Chung Lee terms a "quasi-internal organization" that allowed for a more direct exchange of information than is possible through market channels (1992: 189). Dense and symbiotic in nature, these collaborative ties and mediating organizations functioned as the bureaucracy's liaison to the private sector, "transmission belts" for implementing state policies (Chu 1989: 654), and increasingly even as mechanisms of interest representation for the chaebol elite (Woo 1991: 200).

Taiwan

Haggard argues that Taiwan's industrial structure must be considered both "cause and consequence" of the arms-length relationship between public bureaucrats and private capitalists in Taiwan (1994: 11). This chapter has argued that political leaders' anti–big capitalist bias and ethnic suspicion of the Taiwanese majority led the state to structure a more distant and less dense relationship of coordination between Taiwan's public and private sector. The state, however, effectively supplemented these more diffuse—but still substantial—ties with a much more intimate relationship between bureaucrats and the managers of public enterprise. This dual structure has given Taiwan an extremely flexible but relatively independent private sector and a public sector in which hierarchy (in the form of internal collaboration) has substituted for trust and information and reciprocity are more easily managed and more readily controlled. The private sphere, on the other hand, has had challenges organizing to resolve collective-action problems because of the larger numbers of smaller business groups and firms and the diverse interests of these conglomerates.[24]

Industrial policy-making in Taiwan has normally taken place "within a narrow coalition" including technocrats and ministers of the central economic bureaucracy and senior managers of public enterprises and state research organizations (Wade 1990: 275).[25] As in Korea, political and military leaders have veto power (Pang 1992); however, in Taiwan even the biggest private firms are on the fringe of this power structure and deci-

---

[24] Shafer argues that low barriers to entry and the heterogeneity of products and markets characteristic of small-lot export sectors hamper collective action and reward free riding (Shafer 1994).

[25] The following two paragraphs draw heavily on Wade 1990: 275–95.

sion-making process (Chu 1989).[26] Institutional ties between central economic officials and public enterprise officials, on the other hand, "tend to be close" (Wade 1990: 275). Evans comments on the "vigorous policy network" that links the central economic bureaus with the public enterprises and public banks (1992). It is these state- and party-owned enterprises that have "taken all the major initiatives in building up the capital intensive sector" and served as the point men in many of the state's policy initiatives (either by design or default) (Chu 1989: 656). Chu concludes also that in Taiwan "intimate institutional links seldom emerge between responsible state agencies and major industrial sectors, with the exception of a few sector-specific policy networks in which state enterprises or parastatals occupy a strategic node" (1994b: 143). Business as capital becomes quite compliant with state proposals when it is state-owned capital.

Many senior bureaucratic officials previously worked for a period of time in either state- or party-owned enterprises. These appointments are viewed as important steps in the career ladder for those aspiring to ministerial positions in economic or industrial affairs. Most economic affairs ministers have had management positions in state-owned enterprises. Similar to the Korean or Japanese descent from heaven, many of these officials and political executives reenter the public-enterprise sector upon retirement. Five of the top twelve state-owned enterprises in 1980 had board chairmen from either military, political, or high government official circles (Wade 1990).

Unlike official Korean tolerance for symbiotic government-business relations, such intimate interaction in Taiwan has typically been suspected by the KMT regime as collusion. Economic planners typically maintained an aloof posture toward private business and allowed minimal direct private-sector input in policy-making because the solicitation of such input went against the "prevailing ethos within the state economic bureaucracy that leniency toward private economic actors often constitutes favoratism, and this is an act of impropriety."[27] Particularly as the Nationalist regime has begun to bring more Taiwanese into government and party

---

[26] Wade argues that the American Chamber of Commerce in Taiwan probably has had more of a consultative role than its Chinese counterpart has had (1990: 282).

[27] Chu 1994b: 143. Although many of these suspicions are certainly not without merit, developmental initiatives and opportunities have been regularly thwarted by overly suspicious political elite. Taiwan's two most important developmentally oriented policymakers, K. Y. Yin and K. T. Li were both censured at separate times by Taiwan's Control Yuan and Legislative Yuan for suspected corruption in their efforts to foster new enterprises (Liu 1987; Pang 1992; Evans 1992). Both were subsequently cleared of all charges. For valuable, although dated, discussions of the extensive corrupt activities between local government officials and entrepreneurs and other private interests in Taiwan, see Cole 1967 and Lerman 1977.

positions over the past two decades, the regime has feared this would lead to "the swamping of the state by concealed patron-client and kinship solidarities" previously held in check by the subethnic cleavage (Wade 1990: 287). A former minister of finance noted efforts by President Jiang Jingguo to institute "ten commandments" regarding government officials' relations with private businesspeople. Among these was the requirement that any government official attending a social engagement that also included private businesspeople was to report it to the government's Bureau of Personnel.[28] Wade notes that Jiang put great emphasis on the "cleanness" of reputation and "induced fear in the central bureaucracy not just of taking bribes, but also of being seen in bars, dance halls, and expensive restaurants" (1990: 287).

Chu contends that a true coalitional relationship between the Nationalist state and private Taiwanese capital has been prevented by "the latter's potential threat to the former's political domination at the national level." This lack of an "extensive web of channels" to the private sector, he argues, has constrained the ability of economic bureaucrats to implement programmatic plans (1989: 656). There is no tradition of amakudari from the public to the private sector, and the civil sector is closed to the inflow of middle- or senior-rank transfers from the private sector. Wade concludes that there is no private industrial input or institutional means for conveying such information on either fiscal investment incentives or tariff rates (1990: 276).

Evans also notes the striking "extent to which the Taiwanese private sector has been absent from policy networks," calling historical links between the state and private capital "sufficiently distant" to threaten the ability of the state to secure information and implement its policies. He nonetheless concludes that the "lack of embeddedness should not be exaggerated"; while informal links are less dense than in Korea, "they are clearly essential to Taiwan's industrial policy" (1992: 161). In the following paragraphs I examine the extent of this embeddedness. For in spite of both formal and substantive constraints, policymakers have frequently guided and communicated with the private business sector on both a formal and informal basis. Taken individually and juxtaposed to the Korean case, these ties appear diffuse and distant. Collectively, they form an effective supplement to the more dense links between policymakers and the public-enterprise sector.

As in Korea, Taiwan's private industry is "intensely organized" through a network of state-corporatist business associations (Wade 1990: 271). Any sector with more than five firms is required to form a government-approved association; and each association is a "singular, compulsory,

---

[28] Interview.

non-competitive, state-sponsored organization enjoying exclusive membership and endowed with specified regulatory authority" (Chu 1994a: 119). All national, provincial, and municipal trade associations belong to one of two national business associations—the National Federation of Industry (NFI) or the National Federation of Commerce (NFC). Wade notes that the "government, and behind it the party, appoints the secretary of all the important associations" and that these secretaries tend to be ex-military, security, or government officers "whose loyalty is unquestioned" (1990: 272). Chairmen of the NFI and NFC, since their founding, have all been Nationalist Party members and have all held positions on the party's Central Standing Committee (Hsiao 1993).

This network of business associations has served as the "handmaidens" and "arms and legs" for both the economic bureaucracy and the Nationalist Party. Economic policymakers (particularly in the MOEA's Industrial Development Bureau) use the constituent industrial associations to gather data on production capabilities, conduct industrial surveys, disseminate business information, negotiate overcapacity production reductions, solicit policy inputs, and implement government policy initiatives such as export quotas. The ruling party, in turn, has used the associations to penetrate, organize, and demobilize various segments of society. The Nationalist Party, through its Department of Social Affairs, supervises the elections for leadership positions, and the paramount political leader handpicks the leaders of the peak associations (Hsiao 1993: 158; Chu 1994a; Wade 1990).

Wade admits that the associations do lobby the government for import protection but concludes that Taiwan's associations have much less power than their Korean counterparts do in determining the level and type of imports. He contends that they "do not provide significant inputs into policy-making," have "too little independence to constrain the actions of government," and have little power to regulate the behavior of their members. Like their Korean counterparts, the associations are structured to require business to "respond to suggestions and instructions from above, not, whenever there is a conflict, to act as spokesmen for the interest of their members" (1990: 271–82).

As in Korea, however, the exceptions to this rule have been in those associations representing the premier business groups and those representing powerful and strategic sectors of the economy. The most influential of all associations has been the National Council of Industry and Commerce (NCIC), which, like Korea's FKI, includes virtually all of the elite business groups (both Taiwanese and mainlander).[29] Leading private

[29] This is also translated as the Chinese National Association of Industry and Commerce or the National Association for the Promotion of Industry and Commerce.

capitalists established NCIC in 1952, with the ruling party's blessing, as a corporatist mechanism for integrating and co-opting native Taiwanese business elite (Hsiao 1993). It was chartered with the express purpose of enhancing communication among business leaders and promoting economic growth "by rallying the support of business and industry for government policies" (Li 1988: 95). Because of its membership, economic policymakers have maintained close links with the association, and the state has awarded it a number of exclusive representational prerogatives in decision-making bodies. Chu notes that a weekly breakfast meeting held under the NCIC's auspices became and remains "the most important institutionalized channel of communication between business leaders and government officials" (1994a: 119). Both Hsiao and Gold argue, however, that unlike Japan's Keidanren, even the NCIC has functioned largely as a mechanism for mobilizing and controlling the big business sector and as a channel for the government to relay its policies to big business (Hsiao 1993: 158; Gold 1986: 71).

In an effort to co-opt the new generation of rising business elites, the Nationalist Party recently sponsored a business leaders' training program and handpicked participants from among Taiwan's younger successful entrepreneurs. From this program, a fourth cross-sectoral business association—the Association of Industrial and Commercial Development (AICD)—was organized. The association provides this cohort of younger businessmen (and often proprietors of smaller businesses) with a channel to political influence and gives the party a means to influence the younger business class in an increasingly competitive political environment (Hsiao 1993: 167).

Several associations representing important industrial sectors have also had relatively more influence. The Taiwan Textile Federation, the umbrella association for eighteen textile associations, has a staff of two hundred personnel and has been a significant source of policy ideas for the textile sector. The Manmade Fiber Association, largely because its membership is small and contains Taiwan's most powerful private industrialists, can also gain the attention of the bureaucracy (Kuo 1994: 9; Wade 1990: 283). Because of the strategic importance of the electronics industry, the Taiwan Electrical Appliance and Manufacturing Association (TEAMA) has also become a high-profile association. The state often convenes large-scale consultation meetings with producers under the auspices of TEAMA, and high-level bureaucrats and even cabinet ministers attend TEAMA annual meetings (Kuo 1990).

In addition to business associations, other forms of public-private co-operation in sectors that are intensive in capital and R&D have taken on new importance because of the smaller scale of Taiwan's private firms. The state has set up numerous technical research centers and advisory task forces designed to assist firms in acquiring technology and technical skills for upgrading their production. This includes the government-owned and operated Industrial Technology Research Institute (ITRI) and its laboratory arm, the Electronics Research and Service Organization (ERSO). The latter is now at the center of Taiwan's $8 billion electronics industry, creating spinoffs of its own, including public-private, joint-venture fabrication firms such as Taiwan Semiconductor Manufacturing Corporation (TSMC) and United Microelectronics Corporation (UMC) (Mody 1990; *Far Eastern Economic Review*, March 25, 1993).

So that it will not rival smaller, private firms, TSMC is forbidden to design products of its own. Instead, it relies on more than forty special-ized private firms (many started by defecting ERSO engineers) that con-tract their manufacturing to the larger fabrication firms, especially TSMC and UMC (*Far Eastern Economic Review*, March 25, 1993). Many of these firms, both public and private, have set up shop in the government-established Hsin Chu Science-Based Industrial Park (HSIP). Here foreign and domestic high-technology firms operate in close proximity to ITRI, and the government lures new ventures with its promise to invest up to 49 percent in joint ventures (Wade 1990). These relatively dense ties in the semiconductor sector are now being reproduced in other emerging high-technology industries such as machine tools and biotechnology.

These efforts have been supplemented by the creation of deliberation and advisory councils in several high-technology sectors since the 1980s. Such councils have earlier precedent: As early as the 1950s, some top eco-nomic policymakers took it upon themselves to formalize contacts with local capitalists in order to carry out economic policies. K. Y. Yin invited a number of local capitalists to advise the powerful Industrial Develop-ment Commission in 1950s, but they "had no right to say anything about the decisionmaking aside from offering the information that the eco-nomic policymakers needed and obeying the policy that the economic policymakers decided" (Pang 1992: 114). In the 1960s, Yin's Foreign Exchange and Trade Control Committee sought private-sector input through monthly meetings with textile producers to discuss the develop-ment of the industry (Kuo 1990).[30] Wade notes that IDB officials spend much of their time out in the industrial trenches monitoring policies, col-lecting information, and learning from the private sector (1990).

[30] Li Guoding, Sun Yunxuan, and Zhao Yaodong, all important economic policymakers, made similar attempts to reach out to the private sector with varying outcomes. See Noble 1987 and Arnold 1989 for two less successful attempts. Chu argues that the nature of gov-ernment-business relations in Taiwan has meant that successful industrial promotion in Taiwan has required "personal commitment of a minister-level policy entrepreneur, typically the head of MOEA, to assert leadership over the private producers, mobilize support and resources within the state economic bureaucracy, win the trust of finance officials, and defuse interagency conflict" (1994b: 144).

But reflecting both the increasingly technical nature of policy and the growing strength and skill of the private sector, the advisory panels formed over the past decade represent a qualitative shift in the nature of government-business relations. In the early 1980s, the MOEA established both the Industrial Policy Advisory Board and science and technology advisory panels. These brought together industrial association representatives, civilian scientists, experts from state- and privately sponsored think tanks, and state policymakers to review and appraise new policy proposals. Chu argues that these forums, for the first time, incorporated private-sector views in a serious fashion into the formation of economic policy. Nonetheless, the state did not loosen its control over agenda setting, and the influence of the private sector depended on the willingness of particular ministers to receive external input (1994a). Constance Meaney also concludes that there is no question that the state has continued to play the leading role in structuring cooperation in the semiconductor industry (1994: 189).

These formal institutional organizations and channels have not yet become significant institutional bases for organizing autonomous collective action because of both the organizational strength of the regime (in terms of autonomy and capacity) and the "structural characteristics of the private sector" (Chu 1994a: 120). The large numbers of relatively small-sized exporters face low entrance barriers and exit costs and lack the resources and skills for organizing group-based action (Shieh 1992). Similar to the Korean case, the diversified nature of Taiwan's conglomerate groups has prevented collective action even in the sectors and associations in which the groups dominate. Chu argues that such collective action would benefit rivals in the industry as much as or more than a particular group's own firms outside of that sector. Informal personalized ties with high-ranking bureaucrats or party leaders, on the other hand, tend to accrue benefits directly and exclusively to group-member firms. Finally, the groups' political weakness (at least historically) has also made them hesitant to pursue any autonomous collective action that may damage these carefully cultivated informal ties (Chu 1994a: 119–20).

Therefore, despite the bureaucratic norm of distance to preserve autonomy, as in Korea, some of the most important ties linking government and business in Taiwan are informal. Because of the potential payoff, private business devotes substantial time and effort to building up personal contacts with the government. The larger groups and firms in particular try to secure personal, clientelistic ties with high-ranking government or party officials and use these private channels to seek particularistic solutions to their problems. Chu notes that, while these ties are typically neither close nor powerful enough to secure exclusive privilege, they can often nullify specific policies that may infringe on their vital interests (1994b: 143).

As in Korea, individual firms and entrepreneurs use common ties of kinship, school, military, or county of origin (Wade 1990: 286). Several of Taiwan's largest private groups are owned and operated by families of mainland, not Taiwanese, descent and have received government favors because of the privileged access this subethnic affinity provided. Similarly, most Taiwanese conglomerates have hired token mainlanders as "public relations managers" whose primary if not sole responsibility has been to facilitate communication channels with the party and state (Cole 1967; Gold 1981). Kuo notes that the government and KMT have also encouraged businesses to hire retired government officials, party cadres, and military men in exchange for access to preferential loans (1992: 92).

Ichiro Numazaki argues that the same kind of affect-laden *guanxi* (connections) networks that are so important within Taiwan's (and all Chinese) economic and social relations link businesspeople and bureaucrats as well. He cites a particular group of business, bureaucratic, and political elite who, by virtue of sharing the same lunar calendar birth year (*tongnian*), met and dined together once a month for nearly two decades. Spanning the mainlander-Taiwanese gulf, this twelve-member group included several financial bureaucrats and some of Taiwan's wealthiest and best-known businessmen (Numazaki 1991). Kuo, too, speaks of the formation of business clubs accessible only to business and political leaders (1994: 11).

Early on, the Nationalist party seated several of Taiwan's largest native industrialists on its ruling Central Committee, providing them with direct access to the president and significant input into and even influence on the policy-making process. Because the Nationalist party handpicks the top leaders of the premier business associations, business leaders have also jockeyed for these positions because of "the opportunity they provided to develop intimate personal ties with high-ranking economic and party officials" (Chu 1994a: 119). Increasingly, business leaders are also assuming positions in city councils and provincial and national assemblies as both Nationalist and opposition party representatives. The patriarch of one loyalist Taiwanese family has been the chairman of NCIC since 1958 and a member of the Nationalist party's Central Standing Committee since 1981 (Pang 1992). Taken collectively, these links of cooperation are impressive: dense ties to public-sector firms; formal links to the private sector through corporatist associations, parastatal high-technology centers, and advisory panels; and informal clientelistic ties through a variety of ascriptive and more mechanical particularistic connections. These diverse and decentralized connections have provided the regime with the means of gathering information and feedback and implementing policy and monitoring compliance. As in Korea, these links will also give private business increasing leverage and influence, at least in some sectors. But while the state must take into account the reaction of the private sector, it still maintains the initiative behind most economic reforms because of the organizational weakness of the private sector. Chu concludes that the "business elite still craves particularistic ties and proprietary returns from political investment, and shuns the task of building the permanent organizational base and impersonal links necessary for broad-based collective action" (1994a: 130).

In both Korea and Taiwan, the state has been—and in many key areas remains—the dominant force in determining the structure and influence of business as firm, network, and association and has therefore managed the distance, density, and nature of cooperative ties. Institutionalized cooperation between (and among) public bureaucrats and private capitalists has been crucial to the formulation and implementation of effective industrial policy and the pace of economic development. Specific state strategies have in turn depended on the ideologies and capacities of the political elite and their bureaucratic apparatuses. It should not surprise us that state-led developmental collaboration has worn different stripes in these two nations, given the particular historical, sociocultural, and political environments in which each political economy is embedded. Nor should it surprise us that these ties have also evolved (and continue to do so) as prevailing power and ideologies—both economic and political—shift over time in each country.

In Korea, symbiotic collaboration between powerful bureaucrats and giant chaebol achieved the mutually beneficial objective of rapid, Fordist economic growth. But the social and political consequences of this developmental strategy and the increasing strength and financial autonomy of the big business sector have significantly altered the nature of state-big business relations and the mutuality of benefits. At the same time, democratization—with its distributional demands—and the current regime's anticorruption campaign have increasingly called into question the legitimacy and survival of this elitist developmental coalition. But even as the increasingly democratic government of Korea comes under growing pressure to rein in the chaebol, the economy remains dependent on their continued success, and politicians crave the conglomerates' deep pockets. The logical conclusion of this process has already occurred: Korea's wealthiest chaebol tycoon formed and funded his own independent political party in Perot-like fashion in 1992, campaigning on an antigovernment platform.

In Taiwan, bureaucrats have relied more on collaboration with public enterprises, which, as Wade notes, has made "long-term strategic bargaining with important private economic groups difficult (though not impossible)" (1990: 296). In the absence of a Korean-style intimate bargaining framework with the private sector, the Nationalist government has emphasized economic stability and predictability and fostered a relatively less concentrated and more flexible private sector. Monetary authorities prevail over industrial bureaucrats who use coordinative policies over collaborative ties, emphasizing trade controls and tax incentives at the macroeconomic level.

More recently, three different processes have been eroding the autonomy and capacity of the Nationalist state and may prove to upset the delicate balance of Taiwan's embedded autonomy. First, an increasing majority of key Nationalist politicians and technocratic policymakers are of Taiwanese descent, including now the Nationalist party chairman and president and much of his cabinet. The ethnic, linguistic, and regional affinities between the new public-sector elite and the predominantly Taiwanese private-sector elite have already led to a lessening of the division and a widening of private business group leaders' access to political influence. Second, economic and financial liberalization has privatized the banks into the hands of the conglomerates, weakened the state-owned and party-owned banks as revenue sources, and made private capital flight a powerful bargaining lever in the hands of private capitalists. Taiwan's wealthiest tycoon got his pick of industrial sites, huge tax breaks, and an expanded entrée into the previously exclusive state monopoly of upstream petrochemical production in exchange for dropping his plans to build the complex on the Chinese mainland.

The third related process is that of democratization, wherein the interests of the Taiwanese majority, and particularly the interests of the capitalist class, will have greater voice. This concurrent Taiwanization of the Nationalist Party, liberalization of the economy, and democratization of the political system promises a resolution to subethnic tensions; but it will also strengthen large capital and compromise the autonomy of the state. As in Korea, although from more humble beginnings, the diversified business groups in the hands of native Taiwanese are increasingly becoming the most important economic and political actors in this new pluralist environment.

Business groups in neither Korea nor Taiwan, however, are yet able or even desirous of going it alone. As state autonomy and developmental resolve weaken in the face of economic, democratic, and demographic changes, and the economic and political influence of private capital grows, both developmental collaboration and particularistic rent seeking will increase. In fact, reciprocal ties between state and capital (Evans's "immersion") can easily facilitate collusion in the absence of the developmental motivation, relative autonomy, *and* capacity at the bureaucratic level that are essential for avoiding the crippling clientelism and collusive activities under conditions of deep state intervention. Although the discipline of recent political and economic liberalization in these countries may temper rent seeking, it also threatens the informal ties of elite collaboration that have been essential to their developmental states. Under these circumstances, distributional goals—of either a particular or universal nature—will increasingly compete with developmental objectives in the political and economic marketplace.

CHAPTER SIX

Business Elites, the State, and Economic Change in Chile

EDUARDO SILVA

Analyses of the Chilean case have overlooked an important aspect of its neoliberal economic restructuring process, one that has broad comparative implications for Latin America and elsewhere. Most analysts conclude that a strong dictatorial state and a cohesive group of technocrats sufficed to push through successful reforms (Frieden 1991; Campero 1984; Foxley 1983). Evidence, however, shows a closer interaction between policymakers and business groups than is generally asserted. The data suggest that shifts in the structure of that interaction and changes in the composition of the business groups and policymakers involved must be included as necessary factors in the explanation of Chile's economic transformation. A comparison across three policy periods, two during the dictatorship and one in the contemporary democratic period, shows that the initial form of interaction between business and the state contributed to policies that had a relatively negative impact on investment and production during a process of neoliberal reform. Subsequent forms correlated with more beneficial effects. The form of the relationship was important because it influenced the confidence and credibility of businesspeople that their general interests were being taken into account.

An earlier version of this chapter was published under the title "From Dictatorship to Democracy: The Business-State Nexus in Chile's Economic Transition, 1975–1994" in *Comparative Politics* 28 (April 1996), and the material appears here with the permission of *Comparative Politics*. Research was funded by the Social Science Research Council, the Fulbright-Hays Program, and the University of Missouri–St. Louis. For constructive criticism I thank Ben Ross Schneider, Robert Kaufman, Sylvia Maxfield, Rosemary Thorp, James McGuire, and the reviewers for Cornell University Press.

As a model for other Latin American countries, Chile offers some hypotheses about how different forms of interaction between policymakers and business groups affect investment and production in processes of economic liberalization. To begin with, the case suggests that an excessive degree of state autonomy is not necessarily conducive to good policy. Among other factors, the isolation of technocratic policymakers generated policies that, while not completely inhibiting investment, concentrated it in speculative financial activities that contributed to sharper economic decline than might have otherwise occurred in 1982. By the same token, closer connections between policymakers and more institutional forms of business representation helped to shape economic recovery measures that stimulated greater levels of investment as a percentage of gross domestic product (GDP) than in the previous period and directed more of it to production than to speculation.

BUSINESS, THE STATE, AND NEOLIBERAL ECONOMIC RESTRUCTURING

Until recently, studies have largely ignored the impact of the business-state relationship for the outcome of neoliberal restructuring, especially in terms of investment and production. Instead, both critics and supporters of such policies have tended to focus on two things: the proper functions of the state for healthy economic development, and the design of correct policy instruments as well as the fine tuning of their sequence and timing. These traditional views, however, obscure the fact that, in both market and mixed economies, good policy design by itself does not necessarily lead to optimum results. Much depends on how business-people react to the signals that government officials send: whether they invest and what they invest in (Onis 1991). In some measure this hinges on the quality of the relationship between businesspeople and state officials. When it is mired in bitter antagonism, no policy design, no matter how correct, will elicit the desired response from capitalists. Similarly, if the relationship is too cozy, it may degenerate into collusion and an inefficient allocation of scarce resources through corruption (Schneider 1993b). The interaction between businesspeople and state officials is crucial for investment and production because, among other factors, it influences the private sector's confidence to commit resources. Business elite's participation in policy formulation and implementation stages of the policy process enhances the credibility of government policy and business's belief that the policies will actually work.

According to Rosemary Thorp's observations of Colombia, the long-standing involvement of top capitalists in the policy process generates trust that solutions to thorny policy issues will be reasonable (Thorp 1991). Trust is deeper and more pervasive than confidence and credibility. Chile's recent experience with closer connections between business elites and policymakers comes on the heels of deep-seated historical traumas that produced a great dial of mistrust between the business community and democratic policy processes. As a result, the higher levels of contact between the private and public sectors induced more confidence and credibility in government policy but not trust. As far as Chilean capitalists are concerned, vigilance is necessary to protect their interests. As long as they participate fully in policy formulation and implementation, they believe that they will be able to do so successfully and to their benefit.

Varying degrees of confidence, credibility, and trust, as well as their effects on economic activity, are influenced by (among other factors) the structure of the relationship between capitalists and the state, which is central to the construction of what Peter Evans calls embedded autonomy (Evans 1992). State institutions and officials require certain characteristics to avoid undue influence by particularistic influences in the policy process, beginning with the setting of development goals. Yet if they are isolated from businesspeople, they are likely to err in policy design, meaning that the desired investment may not be forthcoming. Dense networks of communication with the private sector provide important information on what policies capitalists are likely to find workable.

This concept applies to both *dirigiste* and liberal states. In the case of neoliberal restructuring in Latin America, the idea of embedded autonomy suggests a need for a sharper focus on how different forms of business-state interaction encourage or inhibit increased investment in production. This requires an examination of the characteristics of business organization—at both the associational and the firm levels—as well as state institutions. Research must also investigate the interaction that occurs between them in the policy process and whether it is personalistic or institutionally based.

In terms of institutional arrangements the Chilean case suggests that a tight, hierarchical state structure and participation by encompassing business peak associations are functional for investment-inducing interaction between large-scale capital and policymakers. A well-ordered hierarchy among ministries contributes to coherence in the policy process because it controls the delegation of authority from a lead-line ministry to others. The lead-line ministry acts as a gatekeeper, and in Chile the lead lines are the Ministry of Finance and the central bank. This structure sharply reduces the porosity of state institutions to particularistic interests. It allows policymakers to dominate agenda setting and tightly circumscribe participation in policy formulation by social groups. In addition, encompassing peak associations backed by the nation's leading business concerns provide an arena for aggregating the interests of large-scale capital. They furnish a forum for the formation of business policy coalitions that participate in the formulation and implementation stages of the policy process. This is particularly the case during the period in which a nation is designing a comprehensive policy of economic restructuring to over-come a deep economic crisis. Business participation in policy formulation is also helpful when policymakers seek to alter established policy agendas—for example, when Patricio Aylwin's administration decided to raise taxes on business and revise the labor code. On both occasions it consulted with business organizations in policy formulation in order to assure smoother and more effective policy implementation by the private sector.

The interaction between business and state officials under these con-ditions contributes to investment in production through a dual process that builds confidence that policy will address the needs of both the economy in general and firms in the various economic sectors in partic-ular (Thorp 1991). With access to the policy process, Chilean business-people since 1984 have felt confident that solutions to national economic problems would not be at the expense of their interests. Policymakers have benefited from the private sector's participation in policy formula-tion. They get a much better idea of how business elites will react to a policy. This occurred in Chile during the last seven years of the military government and it has helped smooth a potentially conflictual relation-ship during the new democratic period, where political opposition to the dictatorship—which the business sector once vilified—has governed so far.

The last section of this chapter looks at Chile in comparison to Venezuela and a stylized version of the East Asian model. A brief exami-nation of Venezuela highlights the differences between Chile's style of embeddedness and its lack in other cases of neoliberal restructuring. The contrast with East Asian NICs (newly industrializing countries) offers some interesting suggestions about the characteristics of bureaucracy necessary for a fruitful relationship between business and the state in the construction of liberal societies and economies. A final reflection centers on the limitations of Chilean-style embeddedness and refers to extending participation on a more equal footing to other class-based social groups.

BUSINESS-STATE NETWORKS IN CHILE, 1975–1994

The following sections compare three periods of Chilean political and economic history in relation to the forms of interaction between business and the state and how they contributed to patterns of investment and production. This internal comparison permits analysis to focus on these factors while controlling for general background variables. For example, the contrast between the radical neoliberal policy period (1975–82) and the pragmatic neoliberal phase (1983–89) bring into sharp relief the significance of shifts in business-state relations for investment and production. Both policy periods took place within the same political regime: the military government of General Augusto Pinochet. The final policy period (1990–94) highlights the importance of key elements of continuity in business-state relations in the transition from dictatorship to democracy. Those continuities clearly moderated what might have become a conflictual relationship between long-repressed political elites and a business community that, for historical reasons, was highly suspicious of its intentions.

Business-State Networks during Radical Neoliberalism, 1975–1982

After the overthrow of the socialist Salvador Allende in 1973, Chile's military government implemented a neoclassical economic restructuring program in which policymakers replaced state intervention with market incentives. These policymakers believed that markets allocated resources far more efficiently than bureaucrats did and that markets disciplined economic agents to become more productive. They also assumed that neutral, across-the-board policy instruments worked better than industrial policy and discretionary state powers (Ramos 1986; Edwards and Cox-Edwards 1987). This neoliberal economic restructuring took place over three distinct policy periods in authoritarian Chile: gradual, radical, and pragmatic (Hurtado 1988). Due to space constraints I examine only the latter two and the democratic period that followed.

Between 1975 and 1982, Chile experimented with radical neoliberal policies in the construction of a liberal economy and society. Those policies included draconian economic stabilization programs (shock therapy) and the rapid, thorough liberalization of capital markets, prices, and trade with little regard for their effects on industrial and agricultural sectors, which had difficulty adjusting. The introduction of a fixed exchange rate in 1979 became the centerpiece of a system of automatic economic adjustment, after which the top policymakers believed that their main role would be to act as gatekeepers against interest groups that wanted to change the rules of the game (Foxley 1983; Edwards and Cox-Edwards 1987). Market logic also informed social policy in the new labor code as well as the privatization of health insurance and pensions (Arellano 1981; Campero and Valenzuela 1984; Ruiz-Tagle 1985; Raczynski 1983).

After an expected sharp economic decline in 1975, economic activity and investment resumed. Yet investment as a percentage of GDP failed to reach pre-1970 levels. Nor did the reforms do much to stimulate investment in productive enterprises despite the fact that between 1977 and 1981 Chile experienced an unprecedented influx of foreign savings. Between 1977 and 1981 Chile's external debt rose from $5.8 billion to $15.7 billion; the share going to private debtors increased from 22 to 64 percent (Ffrench-Davis 1989). Yet during the best year, 1981, investment only rose to 19.5 percent of GDP, not quite the 20 percent average of the 1960s.[1] Meanwhile, industry's share of GDP declined from 24.6 percent in 1970 to 21 percent in 1981. An index of industrial production (1980 = 100) showed that at 94.4 in 1979 it had barely surpassed the 1970 level of 90.5. During the same years, the share of agriculture dropped from 8.2 percent to 7.5 percent, while those of the commercial and service sector, especially financial services, expanded (Teitelboim 1987). By the same token, imports rose sharply, especially in finished and intermediate industrial goods (Ffrench-Davis 1989). Most telling, nonmineral export performance was not stellar, further reflecting a relative lack of investment. Between 1975 and 1979, a period of high dollar inflation, the export of sea and agricultural products expanded by $30 to 50 million a year in current values. With the fixed exchange rate, that expansion slowed to $25 and then $10 million between 1980 and 1982 (Ffrench-Davis 1981).[2]

After 1979, in a period of high international liquidity, the fixed exchange rate (which made the dollar very cheap) along with rules that stimulated dollar indebtedness, encouraged financial speculation, commercial exchange, and real estate over productive investment. Although for a brief period Chile's economy boomed, in 1982 its unregulated and immature markets broke down. A deep economic depression engulfed the nation as GDP shrank by 14 percent in 1982, the financial system collapsed in 1983, the largest conglomerates were broken up as their holding companies went under, and unemployment climbed to 25 percent of the work force and eventually to more than 30 percent (Whitehead 1987). Investment as a share of GDP plunged to 12.9 percent in 1983 even as the public share of total investment climbed from 26 percent in 1981 to 37 percent in 1983. The industrial production index plummeted from 100 in 1980 and 1981 to 85 in 1982 (Teitelboim 1987).[3]

---

[1] The composition between public and private shares of total investment changed significantly. The public share averaged 52 percent between 1960 and 1970 and 36 percent between 1975 and 1982. Nevertheless, increased private investment could not make up for the fall in the public share.

[2] Also see Banco Central de Chile, *Boletín mensual,* selected issues.

[3] Also see Cieplan data base on investment indicators, obtained in 1992, courtesy of Cieplan.

A substantial literature covers the economic reasons for this debacle, focusing heavily on mistakes in the use of specific policy instruments (Brock 1992; Edwards and Cox-Edwards 1987). But the structure of the interaction between government policymakers and top capitalists also affected the outcome. Evidence suggests that in processes of neoliberal economic restructuring damaging policies may result when a highly autonomous state overinsulates ideologically rigid technocrats with organic links to a narrow range of business interests operating outside the confines of business peak associations. These characteristics can lead to harmful policies too skewed for healthy economic growth and that, in Chile at least, ended in economic disaster. It is constructive to examine the contrast in investment and growth patterns during the following policy period, which took place within the same military government but with a different system of collaboration between policymakers and business represented by peak associations within an encompassing organization; productive investment as a percentage of GDP increased steadily.

What were the characteristics of the system of interaction between the public and private sectors between 1975 and 1982 and how did they contribute to economic problems? To begin with, a highly autonomous state—Pinochet's system of one-man rule—insulated key policymakers from virtually all pressure groups (Valenzuela 1991). By giving his ministers unconditional backing in the context of a highly repressive authoritarian regime, he shielded them from reaction to their unpopular economic policies. The military government also concentrated economic decision making in government financial institutions, principally the Ministry of Finance and the central bank, thus further reducing points of access for business interest groups. In addition, it diminished the capacity of other ministries to contest the decisions of key policymakers and made it virtually impossible for ministers to use their locus of authority as a springboard to create clientelistic followings.

The characteristics of the economic policymakers themselves were also significant. They were not elite career bureaucrats in a meritocratic system, as they tend to be in more successful dirigiste or developmental states. Instead, they were a cohesive team of highly ideological technocrats from civil society schooled in neoclassical economics—often called "Chicago boys" because many had studied at the University of Chicago in the 1960s (P. Silva 1991; Gabriel Valdés 1989). Given their training, they possessed a distinctive and rigid vision of policy goals and instruments. In the context of a highly autonomous state, this inflexible, ideological approach led to economic restructuring policies that showed no mercy for threatened economic sectors and emphasized financial intermediation and real estate over investment in production (Foxley 1983; Hurtado 1988).

Many of the key Chicago boys, however, had links to a narrow range of internationalist conglomerates that tended to concentrate their holdings in financial intermediation, companies that were internationally competitive, and trade (E. Silva 1996).[4] Key economic ministries and institutions, such as Finance (top of the hierarchy), Economy, the central bank, and the budget office, were headed by men who had close ties to the Cruzat-Larraín, BHC, and Edwards conglomerates. These links gave the top directors of these international conglomerates—especially Cruzat-Larraín—privileged access to policymakers.[5] That access allowed them to discuss policy reforms with the policymakers; and according to one government official of the period, "the directors of privileged conglomerates participated with increasing frequency in key policy meetings, and that clique eventually froze out all opposition to their views."[6]

At first, meetings included technocrats linked to the Christian Democratic Party in contact with select representatives of more traditional business groups and their associations. In the end, however, only the more radical Chicago boys and the directors of a narrow range of conglomerates formulated key policies related to the privatization and deregulation of the financial system, privatization in general, and the rate of decline in levels of protection for industry. The radical Chicago boys included these directors in policy formulation because they were friends who shared similar training and views. Because they were real businessmen with real managerial experience, they also supplied the Chicago boys with valuable information about how new sectors of the economy—which they controlled or could quickly gain domination over—would react to the proposed policies. Policy discussions were free-flowing in terms of the exchange of ideas about policy design and its effects between the technocrats and the conglomerate directors.[7] Other government officials and

[4] For another study that distinguishes the importance of private-public sector networks for policy-making, see Schneider 1993a.

[5] They had been either executives, advisors, or members of the professional staff of those conglomerates before taking office, and most returned to those positions after they left government service (Dahse 1979; E. Silva 1996). Significantly, these were the same conglomerates that had organized business resistance against Allende in the Monday Club and collaborated with the military in the conspiracy to overthrow Salvador Allende (O'Brien 1983).

[6] Author interview with the Christian Democrat Juan Villarzú, budget director from 1974 to 1975, Santiago de Chile, December 1988. This view was corroborated by Andrés Sanfuentes, an early Christian Democratic civilian economic advisor to the military government (author interview, Santiago de Chile, April 1989).

[7] Author interview with Juan Villarzú, former budget director, Santiago de Chile, December 12, 1988.

businesspeople were simply not informed about these meetings. When summoned to "official" policy discussions, they only learned out about decisions already taken to which there was no appeal.[8]

In short, the directors of those internationally oriented conglomerates participated extensively in policy formulation. This gave them insider information regarding key economic policy decisions with initial results that seemed very positive. With access to international credit in a country starved for capital, this knowledge allowed them to set up financial intermediation firms before other, more traditional economic groups. Thus, they were able to buy public assets that were being privatized before them. In other words, the privileged access of conglomerate executives in the policy formulation stage helped them to play a vital role in policy implementation as well. Their aggressive strategy of corporate expansion at the expense of more traditional business groups promoted high GDP growth, spectacular expansion of the financial sector, and some growth of economic sectors in which Chile had comparative advantages. Because the policies seemed to be working, policymakers believed that rapid growth and drastic market economic restructuring based on an almost exclusively technocratic approach could go hand in hand. The "right breed" of new entrepreneurs was responding aggressively to the new policies. As soon as the rest followed their example, all would be well.

Ultimately, however, the activities of the new conglomerates were damaging. They based their expansion on highly leveraged buyouts and clearly emphasized profiting from financial intermediation and real estate over investment in production. The conglomerates were organized around financial institutions that captured domestic and international savings, as did their flagship industrial companies. The importance of this is reflected in the myriad investment companies that they set up to channel their funds. A substantial amount of those funds were used to acquire more firms, as evidenced by the rapid buildup of these economic groups. The two largest by far—Cruzat-Larraín and BHC—grew from eleven and eighteen companies in 1974 to eighty-five and sixty-two respectively by 1977. By 1978 they were in control of more than 37 percent of the assets of the 250 largest Chilean firms. By contrast, the next two largest (Matte and Luksic) controlled just 12 percent. Significantly, most of the expansion was based on the acquisition of exiting firms rather than

---

[8] Author interview with Juan Ignacio Varas, private-sector representative to the Tariff Review Board at the beginning of the military government, Santiago de Chile, November 2, 1988. Orlando Saénz, president of the Sociedad de Fomento Fabril (SFF) during the Allende years and the first years of the military government, said that radical Chicago boys would receive organized business but never listened to their position. Organized business was reduced to sending letters to ministers, which were ignored (author interview, Santiago de Chile, September 14, 1988).

investment in new companies. Moreover, by the end of 1977 Cruzat-Larraín and BHC alone controlled 40 percent of private-sector banking assets and almost 30 percent of credit from *financieras* (nonbank lending institutions) (Dahse 1979). A substantial amount of the savings they captured went to loans for their companies (de la Cuadra and Valdés 1992). In addition to self-lending, these conglomerates, and smaller ones like them that mushroomed overnight, made substantial profits in the spread between low international interest rates at which they borrowed from abroad and the high internal rates at which unrelated firms and consumers borrowed.

These tactics worked as long as there were no major shrinkages in international liquidity and international interest rates remained reasonably low (de la Cuadra and Valdés 1992). When those conditions changed after 1980, economic disaster struck. Studies have shown that overindebtedness was the major reason for the wave of bankruptcies that swept Chile in the early 1980s. Firms went into debt to expand (mainly to acquire other companies) to obtain working capital to stay in business if they were in internationally uncompetitive sectors and to pay back existing debts (Mizala 1985).

The increase in international interest rates and the fall of loanable funds to Latin America hit the new aggressive financial conglomerates hard. Because they had built their expansion on debt, they had to capture an even higher proportion of available credit to keep from going under in the early 1980s. As a result, they began to drive up interest rates even more in an effort to crowd out competing borrowers and made it impossible for policymakers to control those rates. Meanwhile, in the rest of the economy, firms began to go under as interest rates climbed beyond what they could afford. Smaller, more precarious financial groups went belly up as their customers in real estate, commerce, industry, and agriculture went bankrupt. The financial institutions of the larger conglomerates were no longer solvent either, but they kept borrowing from themselves to stay afloat as they crowded others out of the credit markets that they controlled. The government finally put them into receivership in early 1983 (de la Cuadra and Valdés 1992). In one fell swoop the military regime unwittingly found itself in control of a large portion of Chile's largest and most heavily debt-ridden companies as the nation's financial sector collapsed.

In addition to these well-documented international and domestic factors, the form of interaction between ideological technocrats and a small group of capitalists produced a policy rigidity that contributed to the economic debacle of 1982–83. By 1979, the web of connections between top economic policymakers and the largest financial conglomerates had expanded, largely through a revolving-door system. Policymakers resisted devaluation as pressure on the peso mounted far beyond what was prudent, in part because of its effect on financial-speculative–driven investment in a dollarized economy where the top conglomerates stood at the apex. When economic storm clouds gathered in 1981, new ministers of finance and economy continued to be associated with those conglomerates. Presumably they knew their structure and could devise the best economic adjustment strategy—one that least affected those conglomerates because everybody knew that, if they went, so would the financial system they dominated.

In sum, as others have argued, bad policy design and errors in the timing and sequencing of the reforms, coupled with the impact of external shocks, clearly affected the collapse of the Chilean economy in 1982. My argument here is that during policy formulation the highly insulated relationship of radical free-market technocrats and a narrow group of businessmen who shared their views helped to shape policies that emphasized investment in short-term financial gain over investment in production, which, as so many other studies have shown, contributed to the severity of the economic crisis that followed. The policymakers believed that markets governed by neutral policy instruments were the solution to renewed investment. The privileged conglomerate heads believed that they could gain the upper hand in the intracapitalist struggles over assets that would follow a strategy of shock therapy. The policy focus on the financial sector suited their purposes splendidly. Conversely, a broader range of principled business participation in policy formulation in an agenda of economic liberalization might have introduced policy instruments capable of stimulating more investment in production and less in financial speculation during the process of economic adjustment. Policymakers would have had the benefit of a much broader range of information regarding the medium-term consequences of their policies for investment and growth; and 1982 may have had a softer landing, as it did in Colombia.

In addition to contributing to policy design, the system of interaction between business and the state during this policy period affected investment patterns because of differentials in the level of confidence about the business climate among business groups. It infused some groups with confidence in the future and left others confused and disoriented. Businesspeople connected to the conglomerates with access to the policymaking process had insider knowledge and thus confidence—although not certainty—that they could gain a competitive edge over more established rival business groups. In short, they probably did not design initial liberalization policies for their own benefit. But knowing what the design was, and as a new breed of entrepreneur, they believed that they could spearhead the capitalist modernization of Chile. Hence, they invested in areas that would allow them to grow rapidly.[9] With hindsight, much of their reckless expansion can be attributed to a fierce competitive drive to force the old guard into relative economic insignificance. Thus, the new entrepreneurs could block opposition to rapid market transformations by destroying the economic base of the potential opposition.

The autonomy conferred upon the Chicago boys and their narrow circle of business allies was probably rooted in two factors: Pinochet's maneuvering to consolidate one-man rule and the desire to break organized labor. In the policy period immediately after the coup (gradual adjustment in 1973–74), business organizations and members of the Christian Democratic Party participated more in the policy-making process. They ensured that neoliberal restructuring took a gradual rather than a rapid and drastic course. Moreover, organized business and the Christian Democrats saw the military junta, of which Pinochet was the head, as an interim government, one that would remain long enough to purge Marxists, reestablish order, and then return to a democratic form of government. Pinochet, however, regarded the petty wrangling and policy obstructionism of organized business as one of the conditions that had led to Salvador Allende's election, and he viewed their support for a quick return to a protected democracy with suspicion. As Pinochet consolidated his dominance within the junta, with the aim of remaining in power indefinitely in order to discipline society and extirpate Marxism, he needed an independent power base in society. Consequently, he increasingly elevated and insulated the ambitious Chicago boys because they were not connected to organized business but were intimately linked to the potential economic power of new, modern entrepreneurs, thus possessing the potential for capitalizing on rapid and drastic neoliberal economic reform. In short, they could provide the initial investment to implement radical economic change (E. Silva 1996). Moreover, thorough economic transformation would not only change the structure of business; deindustrialization would also help to break organized labor more effectively.

By early 1975, organized business was effectively shut out of the policy formulation stage of the policy-making process and was relegated to polite, after-the-fact meetings with ministers and undersecretaries in fruitless attempts to influence policy implementation. Often, all organized business could do was to send protest memos, which were similarly ignored. Policy changes were applied in a very draconian manner, and there was no compensation for the losers. Under the circumstances, they sought to adjust as best as possible. Nevertheless, because many of the

---

[9] These entrepreneurs constantly lionized themselves in the press (which they controlled) as the harbingers of modernity (see *Qué Pasa* [weekly] and *El Mercurio* [daily], passim).

leaders of the industrial sector were linked to multisectoral conglomerates, albeit with a concentration in production for domestic markets, the industrial association did not protest too openly. But the landowners' association, dominated by traditional landowners, did openly oppose agricultural policy up to 1978, largely through a media campaign and mobilization in southern Chile (Campero 1984). The military government repressed the mobilization, and the Chicago boys' response became legend: "Let them eat their cows." The encompassing peak association of the private sector, the Confederación de la Producción, stayed out of these policy disputes; and the commerce, construction, and mining chambers were not opposed to the new policies. Industrialists and landowners were too split on the issue of tariff protection to present a common front (E. Silva 1996).

As a result of this situation, the directors of the more traditional established conglomerates and the leaders of the business associations of the industrial and agricultural sectors reacted to policy decisions with caution and uncertainty, often finding themselves at a competitive disadvantage to the new conglomerates, who bought up their assets whenever possible. Under these conditions, as they so often warned, they were not likely to invest. After 1979, however, policymakers' commitment to opening the economy, the fixed exchange rate, and the sudden surge of available credit convinced the rest of the private sector that the time had come to stop resisting and join in.[10] Ample international liquidity provided credit for more traditional producers to adjust or change economic activity from production to importing, commercial distribution, or speculation in financial markets. In short, by 1979, the rapid expansion of the radical conglomerate heads in the policy loop provided a model of success and behavioral code for the new, modern entrepreneurs. Many who followed that path came to grief in 1982.

In conclusion, this policy period suggests that investment and confidence, usually associated with successful economic performance, can lead to disaster if they are only shared by a small group of capitalists and if policies are faulty (which presumably they would not be if policymakers listened to a broader spectrum of business interests). Rapid economic liberalization with an emphasis on neutral policy instruments leaves virtually all aspects of policy implementation to the private sector. If

[10] Author interviews with Jorge Fontaine, former head of the Confederación de la Producción (CPC); Efraín Friedman, former director of the Sociedad de Fomento Fabril (SFF); Alfonso Mujica, former director of the Cámara Nacional de Comercio (CNC); Orlando Sáenz, former president of the SFF; and Manuel Valdés, former vice president of the Sociedad Nacional de Agricultura (SNA). Interviews conducted in Santiago de Chile on August 6, 1989; November 16, 1988; January 19, 1989; April 19, 1988; and March 29, 1989, respectively.

policymakers inclined toward radical neoliberal economic restructuring only consult with a narrow, homogeneous group of capitalists interested in rapid expansion and short-term financial gain, policy and its timing and sequencing may be disproportionately skewed in their favor with little or no attention to contributions of other sectors of the economy. In other words, inflexible outsider ideologues with a small circle of capitalists contributed to policy rigidity in Chile between 1975 and 1982. The emphasis was on quick stabilization and recovery based on investment in highly volatile short-term financial instruments. By the same token, investment stayed low until 1979 in part because capitalists excluded from the policy loop were uncertain. The incomplete feedback loop—the fact that officials only talked to a narrow group of businessmen—contributed to policy rigidity and financial collapse in 1982–83.

Business-State Networks during Pragmatic Neoliberalism, 1983–1988

In the final analysis, Chile's economy did not prosper in the context of a highly autonomous state, a small cohesive group of inexperienced ideological technocrats drawn from civil society, and a narrow network of contacts between them and the executives of conglomerates in which they had been employed or linked to. In 1984, the economy began to recover under a much more flexible approach to the construction of a liberal economy, one that Chileans dubbed *pragmatic neoliberalism*. Policymakers in the financial institutions still preferred neutral policy instruments. But they acknowledged that the state also had a duty to intervene in markets, particularly to stabilize prices and boost domestic production, albeit with the most market-friendly instruments available. Thus, the government saw to it that real exchange rates remained high, interest rates were reasonable, agricultural and mining activities were protected by price floors, and manufacturers received protection from unfair external competition as well as incentives to export (Fontaine 1988; Hurtado 1988; Whitehead 1987).[11] Yet price supports and other sectoral policies were set at levels that provided a minimum of protection to keep businesses from succumbing to predatory international competition. Thus, Chile's basically liberal economy set relatively high performance standards for industry because competition remained fierce despite some protection.

Regime type and state structure remained virtually the same during this policy period. Pinochet retained his system of one-man rule, and the hierarchy of ministries and their quotas of authority essentially persisted. As

---

[11] For agricultural and industrial supports, see *El Campesino* and *Revista Industria,* the industry journals of landowners and manufacturers, respectively.

a result, this second policy period highlights the point that a different system of interaction between capitalists and policymakers can have a positive impact on investment and economic growth in a developing liberal economy.

On the state side, the system of interaction now featured a mixture of experienced, well-trained, career bureaucrats in financial agencies that still stood at the apex of the hierarchy of economic bureaus. Between 1984 and 1985 some businessmen occupied the top positions in the financial and economic ministries. The available evidence suggests that Pinochet did this to recover the loyalty of business elites, and is to keep an industrial faction from joining the moderate opposition. But after Chile's economy and political upheaval stabilized in 1985, the top economic policymakers of those principal agencies were almost exclusively drawn from the ranks of experienced, technocratic, flexible, civil service officers. As in the previous policy period, they set general policy guidelines, which continued to emphasize economic liberalism. Beneath them, however, prominent businessmen headed the sectoral ministries (Economy for industry and commerce, Agriculture, Mining, and Public Works) (Campero 1991). Their economic interests included a mixture of financial and international and domestic market-oriented ones.[12] For example, ministers of economy and finance might simultaneously be on the board of directors of companies not linked through conglomerate structure in private pension funds (finance), supermarket chains, food processing, commerce, or construction; ministers of agriculture operated farms that produced traditional grains for domestic markets (hard-hit during the radical neoliberal policy period) and fruits for exports as well as being involved in the import-export business. Thus, it was unlikely that they would consider policy proposals that zealously pursued any one activity to the exclusion of another. Moreover, those ministers tended to be less closely linked to specific conglomerates than had been the case in the previous policy period. For the most part they did not appear in the directories of conglomerate structures. Instead, most were prominent businessmen who managed their own large firms, either in construction, commerce, manufacturing, or agriculture. When tied to conglomerates, they chose well-established ones that had not gone into financial speculation, had managed to survive the adjustment period of 1973–83, and possessed connections to pre-coup conservative political currents. Moreover, they might be directors of firms in more than one conglomerate rather than exclusively identified with a single one.

The ministers maintained fluid channels of communication with cohe-

---

[12] Based on prosopographical data gathered by the author in Santiago de Chile between July 1988 and June 1989.

sive and highly representative business peak associations at two levels. First, the umbrella organization of large-scale business associations, the Confederation for Production and Commerce (CPC), routinely discussed exchange-rate, interest-rate, and general monetary policy with the minister of finance and the central bankers. According to Jorge Fontaine, president of the CPC in the mid-1980s, "we had excellent access to ministers, even the president himself. The ministers were much more receptive to our point of view once the Chicago boys were no longer in charge."[13] Second, sector-specific peak associations participated in the formulation and implementation stages of the policy process in close contact with the ministries in charge of their sector. In the words of the director of studies of the Construction Chamber, "As a condition of accepting the Ministry of Finance, Modesto Collados demanded a free hand in the implementation of the triennial plan that he had drawn up when he was president of the chamber."[14] At both the general and sector-specific levels, then, the public and private sectors for the most part negotiated on the basis of technical criteria rather than personal favors, clientelism, or political threats.

This system of business-state interaction did not emerge as end in itself. Rather, it arose in a situation of greater government weakness: the crisis of the military regime in 1983–84, when mass mobilization and economic depression threatened the stability of Pinochet's rule. The economic debacle of 1982–83 revived opposition unions, professional associations, and political parties. Beginning in May 1983, a series of monthly mass demonstrations rocked the capital city and the rest of country. Centrist political parties quickly took control of the movement and attempted to oust Pinochet and redemocratize Chile through negotiation with disgruntled business sectors (basically industry) and some factions of the armed forces, principally the air force and the national police. The idea was to build a broad multiclass coalition against continued inflexible rule by Pinochet and the Chicago boys.

The strategy came close to working with the business sectors. For them, the deep economic crisis and the military government's refusal to enact reflationary policies constituted as grim a threat to their survival as any economic mismanagement by the moderate opposition. As a result, both the CPC and the industrialists' association issued veiled threats of joining the political opposition unless economic policy changed. Drawing on the rhetoric developed during the campaign to destabilize Allende's administration, they pointed out that the private sector only rose against governments when they posed a threat to the survival of private enterprise.

[13] Author interview with Jorge Fontaine, April 19, 1989, Santiago de Chile.
[14] Author interview with Pablo Araya, Santiago de Chile, May 3, 1989.

They quickly added that the current economic crisis posed such a threat (E. Silva 1996).

It is striking that only after this announcement did Pinochet replace Chicago boy–oriented economic ministers with businessmen who were clearly identified with Chile's more traditional economic circles and conservative political parties. This suggests that Pinochet appointed them to defuse opposition by recapturing the support of the key social base for his rule (E. Silva 1993). As part of that process, the military regime entered into a system of negotiation with the CPC and the sectoral organizations that had devised a policy proposal for economic recovery.

Throughout this whole process, then, the CPC, an encompassing peak association of sectoral business organization, was crucial in the development of a policy alternative to radical neoliberalism. During the 1982–83 economic crisis, the leaders of the CPC began a series of meetings to formulate an alternative policy package to counter the radical Chicago boys. These leaders consisted of the presidents of the six sectoral business organizations, who effectively represented the interests of Chile's large-scale businessmen. In charge of their directorships were men who were top managers—or their agents—of Chile's largest corporations, many of them linked to important conglomerates. Surmounting sectoral differences, they hammered out a consensus over general economic policy for the nation, policies that would stimulate investment and economic recovery. These included a commitment to an open-market economy, high real exchange rates, and low interest rates to stimulate exports and domestic production. They also advocated countercyclical deficit spending to restart the economy as well as some specific sectoral policies that fit within the framework of the general policy lines (Confederación de la Producción y Comercio 1983; Campero 1984).[15]

Under the leadership of Modesto Collados, president of the Construction Chamber and later minister of finance, each sectoral business organization put together detailed plans for policies that would stimulate investment in their sectors over a three-year period. This was the so-called triennial plan. For example, the builder's chamber recommended public spending for construction, and the industrial association outlined a mechanism to stimulate exports of manufactured goods and marginally raise levels of protection from imports. The landowners designed a system of price floors and ceilings to boost production of cereals, cattle, and dairy products. The mine owners detailed a mechanism for price floors for copper production.[16]

[15] Also see related documents presented by member associations.

[16] The sectoral planning groups of the triennial plan drew heavily from the programs that the individual peak associations had elaborated for the *Recuperación Económica* program of the CPC.

In sum, the economic crisis of 1982–83 threatened all business sectors. The military government's steadfast adherence to procyclical economic policies provided the catalyst for collective action among businesspeople. If the government would not adopt reflationary policy, then the private sector had no recourse but to craft a coherent alternative set of policies and convey the seriousness of their intent to Pinochet by presenting a united front via the CPC. The process was not easy. It took six months, and the industrialists' insistence on reviving the issue of differential tariffs almost brought the effort to grief. But all of the other business and landowners' associations presented a solid coalition against the industrialists on this point, and they were forced to drop the issue. This underscores the point made by Schneider and Maxfield in Chapter 1, that encompassing organizations are more likely to press for policies that favor the economy as a whole rather than particular sectors. Pinochet, however, ignored them until significant elements of the private sector threatened to align with the moderate political opposition thus jeopardizing his hold on power.

Once the military government sacked the Chicago boys, the new ministers worked in close connection with the CPC and the sectoral peak associations. They based their interaction on the CPC's economic recovery plan that moderated the radical neoliberal approach but did not overturn it. All of the proposals were relatively moderate departures from orthodoxy that the business community felt would stimulate investment and production. During this period, the CPC's main role was to keep the policy consensus among the sectoral organizations from disintegrating, to make sure that sectoral interests did not clash with the general outline of market economic transformation. This was important because major lobbying initiatives had to be conducted in the name of the CPC, not of individual sectoral organizations. Otherwise, technocratic policymakers dismissed them on the basis that narrow, selfish, sectoral interests were attempting to undermine the general good. Major lobbying initiatives basically consisted of high-level meetings between the president of the CPC accompanied by the presidents of the sectoral peak associations who formed its board and top economic ministers and financial agency officials of the government. In this arena agreements were reached concerning the size of the fiscal deficit, devaluation and interest rates, protection for industry and agriculture, and the instruments to achieve it.

According to this schema, intersectoral representation of economic interests among both government officials and business organizations avoided the formation of Olsonian distributional coalitions. This result depended on several factors. As I have previously described, the economic ministers possessed interests in many areas of the economy, and these did not by and large link up in a single conglomerate with a marked concentration in a given activity. By the same token, the CPC was an encompassing business organization whose executive board consisted of the presidents and vice presidents of the six major sectoral peak associations. Its policy stances and recommendations represented the results of negotiation that often involved sharp discussions over how best to avoid skewed distribution in favor of any particular sector—or firms that dominate it. Therefore, it was important that the main policy outline should be the product of bargaining between the CPC and top economic ministers.

After the CPC negotiated major points with policymakers, the sectoral associations worked closely with their respective ministries to hammer out specific policies. This was the case with drawback rules for industry, housing projects for construction, price floors for agriculture and mining. All of this presupposed a high technical capacity on the part of the sectoral associations. They had to justify their petitions with detailed economic modeling of their proposals and its expected impact on investment and production.[17] In short, after an agreement had been worked out between ministers and business leaders, the respective technical staffs hammered out the technical details.

This new system of interaction between policymakers and business elites contributed to the adoption of policy instruments that facilitated economic recovery from the 1982–83 debacle. Without the benefit of international liquidity and laboring to repay external obligations, overall investment rose steadily from 17 percent of GDP in 1986 to 20 percent in 1988 (*La Epoca*, August 18, 1993). After a reflationary surge of public investment to 49 percent of the total in 1986, it declined to 34 percent in 1989, the last year of the military government, and 32 percent in 1990, the first year of the democratic government that followed.[18] Industrial production indexes rose to higher levels at a higher rate than during 1975–82. By 1986 the general index had already exceeded the level of 1981, the best year for the previous period (Teitelboim 1987). By 1989 it was thirty-six points higher than in 1981 (Banco Central de Chile 1992b). During a period of low international inflation, exports surged significantly. Agricultural and sea-product exports expanded by $100

---

[17] Author interviews, all conducted in Santiago de Chile, with Gustavo Ramdohr, president of the Nontraditional Exporters Association (ASEXMA), August 25, 1988; Manuel Valdés, president of SNA, March 21, 1989; Efraín Friedman, member of SFF, November 16, 1988; Lee Ward, director of the National Commission for External Commerce, Ministry of Economy, December 13, 1988; minutes of the meetings of the Subcommission for Drawback Legislation, National Commission for External Commerce; Jaime Palma of the National Commerce Commission, Ministry of Economy; Carlos Recabarren of the Cámara Nacional de Comercio, January 24, 1989.

[18] Cieplan data base.

million to $150 million each year. Industrial exports rose by two-thirds from their peak in 1980 (Banco Central de Chile 1992a). Those exports were strongly tied to agribusiness and timber.

These figures underscore the fact that much of post-1983 investment was in productive enterprises in agriculture (packing companies) and industry, both internationally and domestic-market oriented (timber, fishing, manufacturing, communications). The financial sector recovered its health but no longer overshadowed other activities. A substantial proportion of foreign investment went into joint ventures with the holding companies of Chile's largest and best-established surviving conglomerates, particularly in timber, agriculture, and fishing (Rozas and Marín 1989). All of these factors strengthened Chile's robust economic expansion at an average GDP growth rate of about 8 percent until 1988 (*La Epoca*, August 18, 1993).

The private sector's participation in policy formulation contributed to the emergence of investment-enhancing policies. Businesspeople responded by actually investing in production, which in a market economy amounts to policy implementation. Interview data suggest that two additional conditions bolstered their resolve to commit their resources: their inclusion in those processes also increased the credibility of proposed policies, and close interaction with government officials buoyed their confidence in the nation's economic future. According to the president of the CPC during that period, "Hammering out a consensus within the CPC was a difficult process. But once completed, we knew that these policies would stimulate production, not the financial speculation of the past. Once the authorities began to listen to us, our hope in the future rekindled. Although we don't get everything we want, we can trust the rules of the game that emerge. As long as they remain stable, they encourage us to invest."[19] A member of the merchants' association confided, "Once the president of our association became minister of economy, we knew that things would work out. He understands our problems, and that gives us confidence in the future."[20] Pointing to a large conference table, another added, "Government officials sit down with us here to go over the design of policy instruments for the commercial sector. We can flag anything that is really bad for us. This gives us confidence that our sector will not be neglected."[21] Similar expressions emerged from interviews with leaders and members of the industrial and

[19] Author interview, Jorge Fontaine, former president of the CPC, April 6, 1989, Santiago de Chile.
[20] Author interview with Humberto Prieto, member of the Executive board of the CNC, January 19, 1989, Santiago de Chile.
[21] Author interview with Carlos Recabarren, director of studies of the CNC, January 14, 1989, Santiago de Chile.

landowners' associations: "The Chicago boys were too isolated, too ideologically rigid. We industrialists kept telling them that their policies were not conducive to investment. They ignored us. Now things have changed. We don't dictate policy, but dialogue allows policymakers to avoid the worst mistakes. This gives our people the confidence they require to commit their resources."[22] "Things are much better now in agriculture. We can talk to these people, work things out. As long as things continue as they are, the sector will expand."[23]

In sum, this policy period was characterized by interaction between more adaptable policymakers and a much broader spectrum of business interests. The result: a much more flexible approach to policy-making that gave rise to pragmatic neoliberalism, a policy orientation in which the market provides essential signals for the allocation of resources but where specific regulations and small-scale protections and subsidies induce modernization and rationalization of more traditional economic sectors rather than simply letting them sink. In short, economic policy seeks balance among different sectors and the healthy internal development of each. On the state side of this system, policymakers set the agenda and opened policy formulation to the private sector. After the dust settled in the wake of the political repercussions of the 1982–83 economic debacle, top economic ministers tended to be career bureaucrats with an interest in overall conditions for capital accumulation. Line ministers tended to be capitalists from the same economic sector that the ministry oversaw but with wider economic interests. Moreover, these ministers were not closely identified with any single, specific conglomerate. This gave them an interest in more flexible policy that balanced the needs of different economic sectors. On the side of capitalists, business organizations essentially represented their interests and negotiated with policymakers.

Two conditions promoted flexibility and balance in this arrangement. First, the major policy positions emerged after negotiation between the sectoral peak associations. This mitigated the possibility that policy recommendations could completely run roughshod over the interests of any given sector, as they had in the radical period. Second, sectoral peak associations then developed specific policy documents as a basis for negotiation with the respective authorities. This far-more-complete feedback loop between policymakers and a broad spectrum of capitalists gave business elites credibility in government economic policy and confidence in the country's economic future because policies now addressed their perceived needs.

[22] Author interview with Pedro Lizana, member of the board of directors, SFF, October 25, 1988, Santiago de Chile.
[23] Author interview with Raúl García, member of the board of directors, SNA, January 23, 1989, Santiago de Chile.

Business-State Networks in Democratic Chile, *1990–1994*

The center-left democratic opposition bloc that took over the Chilean government in March 1990, the Concertación de Partidos por la Democracia, had long pledged its commitment to the development of a liberal economy and society during the transition to democracy. It explicitly promised not to tamper with the general economic model—pragmatic liberalism—developed during the last years of the dictatorship (E. Silva 1996). Because it had been the opposition during the dictatorship, however, the Concertación faced the problem of convincing investors that it was sincere. The problem was how to maintain investor confidence and avoid an antagonistic relationship with business. As we will see, the party resolved the problem through a strategy that used business as association to contain business as capital.

The administration of Patricio Aylwin established a system of close interaction—consultation—with the business peak associations whenever the new administration wished to introduce changes in the pragmatic neoliberal model founded under Pinochet. This approach fundamentally applied to tax- and labor-code legislation that Aylwin's administration wanted to pass in order to make economic growth compatible with social equity. But it also included discussions of more sector-specific problems as they arose. For example, one director of the Industrial Development Society (SFF) confided, "On matters large and small, we have excellent access to the ministries. All I have to do is pick up the phone, and we arrange a meeting right away."[24] This system was an integral part of the Concertación's consensus politics.[25] It was a means to make good on Finance Minister Alejandro Foxley's assertion: "We have given businessmen every assurance that we will respect their fundamental interests. We will not countenance a return to populist policies. Chile needs to retain the conditions that foster private sector investment because that's the only path to healthy development."[26]

Although the system of interaction was not institutionalized, top policymakers regularly consulted and negotiated with the leadership of business peak associations on major economic-policy issues from the policy formulation stage on down. As we have previously seen, the main agenda had already been set with the participation of business elites under

---

[24] Author interview with Pedro Lizana, then on the executive committee of the SFF (later its president in 1993), June 10, 1992, Santiago de Chile.

[25] This pattern also represented a continuity in the consensus style of interaction with business that the Alianza Democrática (AD), and later the Concertación de Partidos por la Democracia, developed during the transition to democracy. As early as 1984, AD had explicitly included business sectors in the discussion of economic, social, and political policies in democracy. See Centro de Estudios del Desarrollo 1985.

[26] Author interview with Alejandro Foxley, August 29, 1988, Santiago de Chile.

Pinochet. The new authorities had taken it upon themselves to set an agenda for changes at the margin. Taxation and labor-code policies were among some of the major initiatives on the table and thus were subjects for consultation with business leaders. According to Manuel Feliú, then president of the CPC, "tax and labor code changes were negotiated settlements with the government."[27] A brief discussion of the style of interaction on these policy issues follows.

The Aylwin administration proposed legislation for a tax on corporate earnings and increases in the value-added tax (VAT) in order to fund greater spending on social programs. It was widely believed that the private sector would resist the measure and find it to be a disincentive to investment. These expectations fit closely with theorizing that proposals for tax increases reduce investment (Przeworski and Wallerstein 1988). To overcome these difficulties, top policymakers of the Ministry of Finance consulted closely with the CPC, as well as with the major conservative party in the congress, Renovación Nacional (RN), in the policy-formulation stage. Finding ways to assure the business community and RN that proposed taxes were not going to work against anyone's survival—that they would not be confiscatory—was key to the government's effort. The exchange of information revealed that a tax on profits of between 10 and 15 percent should not dampen investment, given the high profitability of most Chilean firms. To overcome suspicions over government use of the revenue, policymakers built in sunset clauses and tied the new revenue to specific programs. While some businesspeople remained unhappy about the measures—notably industrialists—the taxes were not so onerous as to induce business as capital to use its veto power.[28] As I will show, investment and production did not abate. Moreover, neither interviews nor the available evidence suggests that investment would have gone up significantly further in the absence of a tax increase.

A similar, albeit more drawn-out, process took place in the reform of the labor code. The government wanted to equalize labor-management relations.[29] That involved key issues such as job security, collective negotiation, and unionization rights. From the outset, the Labor Ministry involved the CPC in the policy process. Policymakers passed draft legislation to the CPC and then held a series of meetings with top business leaders to discuss their observations. As a result, the government began to moderate what the business community felt were excessively pro-labor

[27] Author interview with Manuel Feliú, June 1992, Santiago de Chile.
[28] Author interview with Manuel Marfán, architect of the Ministry of Finance's tax reform strategy, July 7, 1992, Santiago de Chile.
[29] Author interview with Joseph Ramos, special consultant to the Labor Ministry, July 3, 1992, Santiago de Chile.

elements of the bill.[30] The government compromised most on collective negotiation and unionization rights (Herschberg, forthcoming). It was a bit more successful with respect to job-security measures such as severance pay and increased protection from dismissal. Part of the success was related to the fact that the policymakers possessed detailed impact studies that they shared with business organizations. These studies showed that such measures would not substantially raise costs for firms. When conservative think tanks came up with the same projections, the business community relaxed.[31]

The clear subordination of labor to business interests in state-society relations became apparent in the negotiations over the labor code, which played a significant role in providing the state-business nexus with relative autonomy from labor and contributed to the effectiveness of accords between policymakers and capitalists. Labor was indirectly represented in the Concertación through various political parties, principally Christian Democrats and Reformed Socialists. At first, the Labor Ministry fought hard to obtain as much of the union's platform as possible in tripartite negotiations among state, business, and labor. Business nervousness about this turn of events led the president to balk, and he ordered the minister of labor to offer more substantial concessions to business. Eventually, the government backed out of the negotiations, abandoning a very weak organized-labor sector (the result of the dictatorship) to bilateral talks with a very strong organized-business sector. Once the political parties of the Concertacíon abandoned labor, their fate was sealed; for they had no other avenues of protest. Strikes were not a viable alternative in the view of labor leaders.

So far we have examined the willingness to compromise that resulted from closer interaction between policymakers and business elites. What were some of the characteristics of the top policymakers and the business peak associations that helped to reduce tensions between business and the Concertacíon? Some of the traits of the policymakers changed from the days of pragmatic neoliberalism under the military government. The top ranks were no longer composed of a combination of career bureaucrats and businesspeople. Instead, most were highly trained economists from think tanks linked to the major political parties that formed the

[30] Author interview with Antonio Guzmán, president of the CPC, June 16, 1992, Santiago de Chile. Other interviewees agreed: Manuel Feliú, president of Banco Concepción, past president of the CPC; Pedro Lizana, executive committee member of the SFF; Raúl García, secretary general of the Sociedad Nacional de Agricultura; Alfonso Mujica, vice-president of the Cámara Nacional de Comercio. All interviews conducted in Santiago de Chile between June and July 1992.

[31] Author interview with Joseph Ramos, Labor Ministry consultant, July 3, 1993, Santiago de Chile.

opposition bloc (P. Silva 1991). This suggests that having businesspeople in the cabinet was not absolutely essential for investor confidence in Chile. But according to both government officials and business leaders, a commitment to building a liberal economy and society, along with technical capability, was crucial. Flexibility in policy stance after feedback on policy proposals was also important.[32]

Similarly, the existence of an encompassing peak business association— the CPC—facilitated interaction with top policymakers on policy measures that affected the whole business community. The CPC acted as a filter that allowed only the most central and crucial points of divergence to emerge for discussion. This facilitated negotiation and dispute resolution. The CPC also promoted consensus within the business community with respect to proposed policy. In the end, individual sectoral organizations may not have been happy with some of the results, but none was so disgruntled that it began to disinvest or sought to affect policy independently. Of course, on sector-specific issues, policymakers dealt directly with the appropriate business organization.

How did authorities and capitalists participate in the policy-making process? In this period, top policymakers set the agenda for incremental changes. After their technical commissions drew up draft legislation, it was circulated to the appropriate peak association. For each initiative the business organizations formed a technical commission to study the proposal and make observations. Policymakers and business leaders then negotiated on the basis of those reports. The exchange of information on the basis of technical evaluations facilitated accommodation. According to a member of the executive committee of the Sociedad de Fomento Fabril (SFF), "we meet often to technically evaluate policy proposals. We then make counter proposals and accompany our directors when they negotiate with government officials. Ever since we began discussing policy on a more technical basis, we have had better relations with government, and better results."[33]

This arrangement has contributed to impressive economic results. Investment, reported at 25 percent of GDP in 1992, continued to flow into the country; and the economy has enjoyed sustained high production rates and export figures. This has contributed to high aggregate-growth figures of about 7 percent per year since 1986 (*La Epoca*, August 18, 1993). As was the case for 1984–89, the interview data with business leaders suggest that the system of interaction between business and poli-

[32] Author interviews with Manuel Marfán of the Ministry of Finance, Joseph Ramos of the Ministry of Labor, Antonio Guzmán of the CPC, Pedro Lizana of the SFF, Alfonso Mujica of the CNC, and Raúl García of the SNA, all conducted in Santiago de Chile between June and July 1992.
[33] Author interview with Pedro Lizana, June 10, 1992, Santiago de Chile.

cymakers instilled enough confidence in the private sector to invest. Easy access to the executive branch, a flexible attitude there, and a commitment on the part of the Concertacíon to do what was necessary for growth with low inflation bolstered trust among capitalists that the Concertacíon indeed intended to keep its promise to adhere to the main tenets of pragmatic neoliberalism. In virtually every interview, business leaders acknowledged that this system allowed them to alter proposed legislation in ways that favored their interests.[34]

The finding is especially significant because the relationship between business and the Concertacíon was not naturally harmonious but fraught with the potential for investment-dampening conditions. For capitalists, the policymakers belonged to a political bloc tied to a statist past who had to prove their capacity to maintain a good business climate. Business leaders were on their guard, ready to challenge deviance and defend the gains made during the dictatorship. In public debates it sometimes seemed that the relationship is highly conflictual.[35]

Nevertheless, interviewees were careful to point out that, underneath the occasionally belligerent public stance, private negotiation with authorities was fruitful. It generated confidence to invest more than they might have without close ties. According to one source, "at first [in 1990] we worried about the Concertacion's capacity to manage the economy. We feared that their policies might reduce investment opportunities in Chile and that the nation would suffer an economic setback. Fortunately, the administration's economic team has been very prudent. They meet with us frequently to discuss policy, at either our initiative or theirs. The policymakers are serious, highly trained, and capable individuals, with the ability to learn from the interaction between us and to translate that learning into the design of effective policy instruments. This lends credibility to their policies and gives us the confidence we need to continue to risk our resources in the service of Chile."[36] In short, close ties between capitalists and policymakers convinced business as association to accept the fact that the Concertación would compromise, perhaps not on all issues but often enough to keep business as capital from rebelling and engag-

[34] Author interviews with José Antonio Guzmán president of the CPC; Manuel Feliú, president of Banco Concepción, past president of the CPC; Pedro Lizana, member of the executive committee of the SFF; Raúl García, secretary general of the Sociedad Nacional de Agricultura; and Alfonso Mujica, vice president of the Cámara Nacional de Comercio. All interviews conducted in Santiago de Chile between June and July 1992.

[35] This was also the case when the Concertación contemplated some constitutional amendments that would weaken authoritarian protections for conservatives. These were holdovers from the authoritarian constitution of 1980 fashioned under Pinochet, which is still the law of the land.

[36] Author interview with Pedro Lizana, member of the executive committee of the SFF, 1992. Antonio Guzmán corroborated such views in a separate interview. Both interviews conducted in June and July 1992 in Santiago de Chile.

ing in investment strikes and to keep capitalists investing at rates similar to the last years of the dictatorship.

Policymakers agreed that the interaction with business was crucial to calming the fears of investors. Through reiteration of the negotiation process—consensus politics—they hoped to prove to capitalists that they were technically capable of running an economy and compromising with the private sector in the interests of maintaining a good business climate. They wanted to prove that democracy, and the Concertación in particular, did not pose a threat. No one's fundamental interests would be gored.

Before moving on to the conclusion, let me summarize the conditions of benign collaboration in Chile, both during the dictatorship and under democratic rule. It seems clear that the pattern is not uniform; no one, single formula appears with respect to the characteristics of top policymakers, although other factors are more constant. In the period after the economic debacle of 1982–83, career civil servants occupied most of the top posts in the policy-making hierarchy of state institutions (the Ministry of Finance and the Central Bank) while businessmen with multisectoral economic interests who were not completely identified with a specific conglomerate occupied line ministries. During the democratic period, technocratic party appointees, many from recognized (if opposition) think tanks, occupied the highest positions in the state economic policy-making hierarchy, while businessmen with ties to the administration's political parties often headed line ministries. In both periods, the formulation of economic-reform policies and their implementation (in the form of investment and production) benefited from a working relationship with organized business as opposed to multisectoral conglomerates alone.

It seems, then, that whether career bureaucrats or party technocrats occupy the top economic agencies of the state is not crucial for neoliberal reform. What is important is that they be highly trained, not dogmatically ideological, and flexible. The difference in the two periods may rest on political factors and institutional development in processes of democratic breakdown, authoritarian rule, and redemocratization. The first cohort of new career bureaucrats after the overthrow of Allende and subsequent purges just had time to emerge by 1984. That served Pinochet's purposes. But they were all closely linked to the dictatorship and the political parties that supported it. The Concertación had its own political agenda and could not rely on bureaucrats politically beholden to the civilian groups that backed authoritarianism. They had to put their own people in charge. They necessarily had to be from outside the bureaucracy, from the shadow government born in semiclandestine opposition to Pinochet. Perhaps in another ten years a new generation of less politically compromised career bureaucrats might appear. But this seems unlikely given the low level of salaries and general lack of prestige of public service. Professionals often begin a career in the government and then move to the private sector once they gain experience. Later successes, party affiliation, and reputation usually determine whether one occupies high office.

The pattern of interaction between top policymakers and business elites also remained constant across the last two policy periods. The heads of the Ministry of Finance and the central bank, as well as the Ministry of Economy, generally collaborated in the formulation of general economic policy with the heads of the encompassing organization of business (the CPC). Within the confines of that general policy (macroeconomic measures and overall levels of mild protection and subsidies), line ministries hammered out sector-specific implications with sectoral peak associations. At all levels, discussions were usually based on technical criteria elaborated by the departments of study of both private- and public-sector institutions.

COMPARATIVE CONCLUSION

This section briefly addresses three issues. First, on the basis of limited available evidence, it examines whether processes of neoliberal transformation in Venezuela contributed to the kind of embeddedness that the Chilean state has achieved with business elites and the likely consequences of that embeddedness. Second, it suggests that the requirements for optimum state-business relations differs somewhat in cases of neoliberal economic restructuring as opposed to developmentalist ones, such as some of the East Asian states. Third, it argues that Chilean-style embeddedness has limitations. It is an exclusionary arrangement in which, for the moment, neither policymakers nor business elites appear to have strong incentives to include other social groups meaningfully.

Venezuela under Carlos Andrés Pérez began a process of neoliberal restructuring in the late 1980s. How it structured state-business relations, however, was not conducive to forging the kind of embeddedness that Chile exhibited after 1984. Rather, it resembled the Chilean situation between 1975 and 1982. That is, policymakers with close links to specific conglomerates churned out liberalizing decrees without significant participation from other business interests. Thus, although investment rates rose somewhat during the Pérez administration (1989–94) compared to previous recessionary periods, that rise was on the basis of volatile international financial capital or shot-in-the-arm investment blips in newly privatized companies. Domestic capitalists basically remained wary. In short, a steady stream of stable investment in production by the national bourgeoisie was not forthcoming, meaning that, hard-won macroeconomic stability rests on very uncertain ground. Moreover, as we will see, the fragmentation of business organizations and the willingness of powerful capitalists to defend their own sectoral interests directly before ministers of state make Venezuela's future development of the Chilean pragmatic coalition difficult. This might be a serious obstacle to building Chilean-style state-business relations and reaping its benefits for investment and production.

The Pérez administration undertook its program of neoliberal restructuring against a backdrop of state-business relations that was virtually the opposite of Chile's. In Chile, during the economic crisis of 1982–83, highly cohesive state institutions bargained with a fairly cohesive private sector. Venezuela met its economic crisis, which began roughly in the same period, with a system of state-business relations in which fragmentation and particularism within both the government and the private sector seems to have been its main characteristic (Gil Yepes 1981). This made Venezuela's economic policy-making institutions more porous than Chile's and facilitated corruption and private deal making on the part of capitalists and government decision makers alike, both before and during the economic crisis. It also encouraged competing particularistic coalitions of state institutions and capitalists (Martz and Meyers 1977; Blank 1973).

The system worked after a fashion once democracy was consolidated in the mid-1960s and before the economic crisis hit in 1982 because public investment (from oil revenues) drove Venezuelan private investment. The government targeted industries for growth and offered subsidized credits and other incentives for their development. Private investment followed. As oil wealth increased, so did investment as a percent of GDP, although the private share was always higher than the public share. The translation of that investment into higher production figures (industry performance) and GDP rates, however, was sluggish for several reasons. First, those government resources were not conditioned on expectation of better performance by capitalists. Second, successive administrations—and semiautonomous parapublic institutions—constantly redefined the priority sectors. As a result, Venezuelan capitalists continually diversified their holdings in new industries where they had little experience and favored short-term gains over long-range planning (Escobar 1984; Naím, 1984, 1988; Francés 1988). Third, in the context of the myriad regulations and controls associated with the ISI development model, the fragmented system of collaboration between government policymakers and capitalists encouraged corruption. The director of a leading pulp and paper company said, "We lobby government officials by offering stock options, a job when they get out of office, and other incentives."[37] The president of an insurance group added, "The most important businessmen regularly strike private deals with politicians over prices, contracts, and exceptions to policies they don't agree with for their firms."[38]

Business peak associations played a secondary role in this situation. They were weak and divided among themselves (Salgado 1987; Gil Yepes 1981). Their weakness primarily stemmed from fact that they did not really speak for large-scale business (Sweeney 1989).[39] The leadership of the peak associations was not composed of businesspeople with executive capacity. They mainly worked out the details of policy implementation, especially in regulations and prices (Gil Yepes 1981).

Given the relative lack of importance of business peak associations following the oil boom of the early 1970s, the main channels of access and communication between the state and capitalists were on a personal level between large-scale businesspeople and ministers of state. Business peak associations might agree on a general position on a given problem with government officials. After that, the most important businesspeople of a particular industry would privately seek out their friends in the respective ministry (Naím 1988).[40] They would either negotiate an exception for their firms or block or modify proposed regulations or prices for the entire industry in accord with their individual needs. The insurance group president said, "The peak associations work out a position. Then the owners of the largest corporations in the sector sabotage it by making private arrangements with friendly politicians. We won't get anything done until this situation is reversed."[41]

On the government side, business association leaders and top capitalists dealt with top policymakers who could be either party politicians or important businesspeople. They directed the Ministry of Finance, the Central Bank, the Ministry of Development, the Planning Ministry, the Venezuelan Investment Fund, and the Ministry of Mines and Energy (oil). All of these agencies made important investment decisions in a relatively decentralized manner. As a result, their goals were sometimes in conflict as well. In a sense, they had their own clienteles in the private sector that they dealt with directly. The decentralized economic decision making and the discretionary pots of money for industrial policy that different semi-

---

[37] Confidential author interview, July 1993, Caracas.

[38] Author interview with Iván Landsberg, Venezuela, July 1993, Caracas.

[39] Antonio Francés of the Instituto de Estudios Superiores de Adminis tración (IESA) and Roberto Bottomme, editor of *Veneconomía*, confirmed this view in author interviews in June and July 1993 in Caracas.

[40] Author interview with Pedro Palma, vice president of Booz-Allen & Hamilton, an international business consulting firm, July 1993, Caracas.

[41] Author interview with Iván Landsberg, noted financial-sector businessman, July 1993, Caracas.

autonomous institutions wielded encouraged fragmentation in the private sector. They were also disincentives for top capitalists to work within business associations.

As Thorp and Durand show in Chapter 8, this system ceased to be even moderately functional for investment and production once oil revenues were no longer sufficient to drive the Venezuelan economy. With the debt crisis of the early 1980s, the end of the fixed exchange rate for the bolívar, plummeting oil prices, and increasing economic instability, Venezuelan capitalists stopped investing. Capital flight, much of it through corrupt and illegal movements, reached scandalous levels (Maxfield 1989; Frieden 1989, 1991).[42] Private-sector investment levels dropped below public-sector investment for the first time in democratic Venezuela (Escobar 1984; Baptista 1993). Public-sector investment also declined as fiscal spending concentrated on fueling populist social spending programs or bailouts for financially strapped companies with good political contacts (Naím 1993).

In response to the economic crisis, the second administration of Carlos Andrés Pérez (1988–93) initiated an economic stabilization plan and liberalizing economic reforms. The system of interaction between business and the state that emerged closely resembled that of the radical period in Chile. Pérez appointed to top policy-making positions a narrow group of businesspeople and technocrats interested in radical liberal economic restructuring (Naím 1993).[43] Mostly by decree, they pushed through price and trade liberalization along with privatization and a high real exchange rate.[44] Again, as in Chile, the capitalists involved were associated with large conglomerates that concentrated their holdings in internationally competitive industries; and some had long supported tariff reform. Many of these businessmen/technocrat policymakers were "on loan" to the government, as Venezuelans phrased it. Moreover, quite a few had been associated with a working group established in the early 1980s—the Grupo Roraima—dedicated to finding a liberal solution to the crisis of the populist state.

If the relationship between a narrow band of capitalists, technocrats, and the president proved fragile in authoritarian Chile, it was even more so in democratic Venezuela. Unlike Chile, those adversely affected by economic adjustment and restructuring had means with which to defend

[42] About one-fifth of total capital flight between 1976 and 1985 ($6 billion) occurred between 1983 and 1985. The amounts lost to capital flight between 1976 and 1982 were also very high ($25 billion).

[43] Author interview with Janet Kelly de Escobar, academic director of IESA, May 1993, Caracas.

[44] It may be worth examining these relationships in other cases, such as Peru, Bolivia, Ecuador, and Mexico. This may be a stage in the process of adjustment. For a description of adjustment policies in Venezuela, see Naím 1993 and Toro Hardy 1992.

themselves: the congress. They stalled supporting legislation intended to deepen privatization and market liberalization (Tarre Briceño 1993). With the impeachment of Pérez in May 1993, the fate of the reforms became uncertain. This does not mean that economic restructuring cannot be accomplished in democracies. The Argentine case shows that Pérez's main problem was that he did not control his own majority party in the congress. Conversely, the vice-president of a leading business consultant suggested that Pérez's "biggest failing was not to have built a broader business coalition first. He should have communicated better to the different sectors the costs and benefits of economic change. If he had, they would never have turned on him this way."[45]

Meanwhile, the bulk of the investments for Venezuela's high growth levels in the early 1990s came from abroad. The absence of a cohesive capitalist policy coalition capable of negotiating a new form of articulation to the state made the Venezuelan private sector very cautious. They were not certain of the rules of the game, and most did not have the funds to gamble in the long term.[46] The relative porousness of the Venezuelan state coupled with the fragmentation of weak peak associations were not incentives to forging a capitalist coalition like the pragmatic one in Chile. Instead, top capitalists still sought private deals with top policymakers or key congressional leaders, depending on the circumstance.

In conclusion, the equivalent of Chile's pragmatic coalition and its relationship to the state did not appear in Venezuela. Instead, the state mirrored Chile's situation during the radical restructuring phase—a core economic team in close contact with a core of top capitalists from a select number of multisectoral conglomerates that could take advantage of rapid change. As in Chile during that period, the major areas of economic activity were in financial intermediation, privatization deals, real estate, and commerce. Domestic investment was not particularly stimulated, certainly not in production. In Chile, this turned out to be a fragile situation and did not end well. Venezuela's situation has already changed, as the new government of Rafael Caldera attempts to moderate some of the Pérez reforms.

The Chilean Case in Light of the East Asian Experience

Much of the initial impetus for the study of the interaction between state officials and businesspeople arose from analyses of the East Asian

[45] Author interview with Pedro Palma, vice president of Booz-Allen & Hamilton, an international consulting firm, July 1993, Caracas.

[46] Author interviews with Cristina Rodríguez, president of Metroeconomía, a high-powered business-consultancy firm, July 1993; Pedro Palma, vice president of Booz-Allen & Hamilton. For overall investment figures, see *Metroeconomía* 1993; Naím 1993.

developmental states, especially South Korea and Taiwan. Analysts such as Karl Fields have found states that played an important role in shaping the economy, carried out aggressive industrial policies, and in some cases favored public enterprise (see also Amsden 1989; Deyo 1987; Wade 1990). Their studies focus on the characteristics of bureaucracy that promote effective policy-making and discourage collusion.[47] They point to the need for the formation of elite, meritocratic, professional career civil servants on the assumption that training and esprit de corps facilitate good policy-making. To promote efficiency, as they also note, bureaucrats attach performance criteria to industrial subsidies (Evans 1992; Schneider 1993a).

In terms of the relationship of top policymakers to business elites, those same studies have found that bureaucrats should be highly autonomous from pressure groups in order to formulate industrial policy but not isolated from contact with the nation's largest conglomerates or intersectoral encompassing business associations. Contact with multisectoral conglomerates provides a window into policy design that cuts across economic sectors. It also furnishes potential allies in policy implementation—firms with investment capacity that can shift resources more easily than can companies dependent on the health of a single economic sector (Onis 1991).

The prescription for Latin America, however, has been to dismantle the developmental state—to forge liberal states with minimal involvement in the economy. At most, fiscal and monetary policy should be used to send general signals to private economic agents, who then take such action as they see fit. Industrial policy is to be avoided. But even the World Bank in recent years has begun to realize that a minimalist, night-watchman state needs to be an effective state. As a result, it began a campaign to promote an effective bureaucracy. The principle prescription is a meritocratic, technocratic career civil service (World Bank 1991). But neither the World Bank nor similar institutions and consultants have paid much attention to the interaction between the state and capitalists in the liberal economies of developing nations. It is generally assumed that the state and the private sector have their own spheres of activity, and the less interaction between the two the better.

The evidence presented here calls such assumptions into question. Chile is widely perceived as a model for neoliberal economic restructuring; yet the form of interaction between capitalists and policymakers clearly mattered for policy design, investment, and production. The case suggests that liberal developing economies also require a state characterized by embedded autonomy. Of course, some of the specific features of

---

[47] France is another case that has received some attention in this respect (Zysman 1983).

embedded autonomy in liberal states will differ from those of developmental states.

The Chilean case has at least two differences from the East Asian cases. First, Chile has taken a liberal path to economic development, while a number of East Asian countries have opted for industrial policies that require more direct state intervention in the economy. This means that some of the requirements for efficient bureaucracy in East Asia may not be strictly necessary in cases that follow a liberal developmental path. To begin with, the successes in East Asia are partially attributed to the formation of an insulated, meritocratic career civil service or bureaucracy. In Chile, however, most of the top policymakers were political appointees, members of the parties of the governing coalition. Nevertheless, a functional equivalent may exist between these two divergent patterns. In both, top policymakers possess an intense professionalism and high levels of technocratic expertise. The Chileans had those qualities because their top economic policymakers had advanced academic degrees from elite, foreign universities. That training and leadership functions in academically styled think tanks linked to political parties were the wellsprings of their stance. The main reason for this difference may lie in the following condition. Career bureaucrats may not be essential in countries where liberal states have less discretion over the allocation of resources. A caste-like insulation from the temptations of particularistic or captive relationships, or outright corruption, seems less necessary under conditions in which policymakers have fewer favors to dole out. Solid technical competence to manage general macroeconomic conditions, however, appears to be crucial.

The Chilean case also reveals something that is not discussed in the literature on East Asia, which focuses so much on the state, but that was crucial to the success of interaction between business and the state in Chile: Learning in the business community was also important. Business organizations developed technical expertise in their research departments in order to speak a common technical language with professional, technocratic policymakers. Otherwise, government officials tended to ignore them because business leaders were seen as defending parochial interests in ignorance of wider economic consequences.

Second, the Chilean case suggests that negotiation with encompassing peak associations functions better for processes of neoliberal reform than do dealings with multisectoral conglomerates. This is different from cases such as South Korea, where bureaucrats engaged in the design and implementation of industrial policy dealt directly with such conglomerates. In cases of liberal reform, where the state is not directing the flow of investment, it appears that reliance on a few conglomerates sparks intense inter-business competition that can dampen investment because those business sectors on the "outs" tend to withhold investment as they struggle for survival. This may be at the root of the investment problem in production in countries undergoing liberal economic reform processes, such as Argentina and Mexico, and may be part of the problem in Venezuela. Those cases relied on short-term external financial flows and foreign direct investment in privatization schemes to help stabilize their economies. But they have had little success in convincing their own private sectors to invest in production. The available data reveal that policymakers in both Argentina and Mexico have interacted mainly with the leadership of a few carefully selected conglomerates.

The Limits of Chilean-Style Embeddedness

This chapter has focused on the characteristics of successful and not so successful collaboration in Chile. Some of the key features of the discussion and the framing of its terms, however, raise additional difficult questions. For some time now, the issue of economic efficiency has tended to dominate mainstream academic discussions of economic development on the periphery. Thus, the current debate about the consequences of collaboration is defined in terms of rates of investment and economic growth. Not too surprisingly, the evidence reveals that successful collaboration requires single-minded dedication to providing a good business climate, of favoring growth to the exclusion of other values. This focus crowds out other questions. What, for example, are acceptable trade-offs between equity and growth in developing countries (Thorp 1991)? How can capitalists be induced to continue investing once governments begin to address the social question in terms that challenge neoliberalism (E. Silva 1996)?

The Chilean case highlights some of the difficulties involved. The Concertación certainly paid more attention to social equity than to the military government did. It has also induced capitalists to contribute more for social programs than they would if left to their own devices. This was evidenced by very mild tax and labor-law reforms in the early 1990s. Laudable as these efforts were, they never challenged the core of the dictatorship's neoliberal social reforms (E. Silva 1996). Increased social expenditures were channeled through the same welfare framework designed in the early 1980s. As in the dictatorship, services remained targeted for the extreme poor. There was no pretense of universality (Vergara 1994). Similarly, changes in the labor code were carried out in essentially bilateral accords between business and labor. In this arrangement labor did not gain much, certainly nothing substantive. On a number of occasions, business groups took very strong stands and made the government back down on proposed reforms.

In short, the neoliberal version of social welfare and labor law remains essentially intact in Chile. The mild reforms that have been undertaken look good, but that is only because they are contrasted with those of the dictatorship, a nadir. The real test is the comparison to the pre-Allende period. Compared to the two decades before Allende, the statistics do not appear quite as impressive. Chile has essentially only caught up with itself. The available estimates on income distribution also lag behind those of East Asia. In part, that is because Chile, and other Latin American countries, lack effective land reforms, which skews the curve. In part, it is because East Asian states concentrate in labor-intensive export manufactures as opposed to primary-product exports. Whether Chile and other Latin American countries can follow that route remains unclear; so does whether they should. For in the absence of well-developed welfare provision, the move to capital-intensive production in East Asia appears to be skewing income distribution in an unfavorable direction.

Despite these shortcomings, compared with the period of the dictatorship and to many other Latin American countries, the increases in spending and effectiveness of targeted programs for the extreme poor make Chile a model for neoliberal welfare reform. Within the confines of the model, increased social spending without negative effects on investment seems possible. Countries in which the welfare systems set up in the 1950s are under stress or that never really established any system in the first place look to Chile for ways to structure changes (Angell and Graham 1995).

The crux of the issue, however, lies in the Concertación's inability to move beyond a liberal conception of the welfare state (Esping-Andersen 1990). This is what the targeted programs for the extreme poor are: They set up a dualistic system of provision of services—stigmatized, substandard ones for the very poor, and everybody else must rely on their ability to pay for private insurance. Moveover, it is a system that leaves individuals unprotected from the labor markets in which they have little power. In other words, people will need to work at whatever price the "free" market offers and under virtually any condition if they want to survive. This fits business's conception of efficiency and its desire for the most flexible labor arrangements possible. Needless to say, there are welfare and labor-market systems that move away from such positions and offer the individual a modicum of increased protection from the market in which business has far greater power than they do. In that sense, perhaps Costa Rica and Uruguay would be better laboratories for investigation, maybe even Venezuela after Pérez.

In conclusion, all modern states, especially democratic ones, have a welfare function. The question is under what principles will they be structured. In this sense there are principles consonant with (neo)liberalism—

least protection of the individual from the market—and other forms, including the Social Democratic one, that offer different arrangements. Chile's mild reforms fit the liberal model.

There are serious obstacles for moving beyond this in Chile, which I and others have written about. One is the structure of Chile's political institutions as inherited from the dictatorship (Loveman 1991). The congress, particularly the Senate, gives conservative forces virtual veto power over all legislation. Thus, from the outset, bills have to be couched in ways that will be acceptable to the faction. Moving away from liberal principles is not acceptable. Another obstacle is related to the form of interaction between business and policymakers, also inherited from the dictatorship. The pragmatic capitalist coalition was forged during the military government and gave good results for economic investment and growth. The Concertación pledged basically to uphold those arrangements. Business holds them to their promise in an aggressive manner. If the Concertación were to deviate, investment strikes might follow. In this, an open capital account further fortifies the influence of business, augmenting its veto power over reforms. Moreover, Chilean capitalists have become accustomed to a relationship with the state in which other social actors are kept either absent or in extremely subordinate positions that will not threaten the privileges and prerogatives of business, a situation that business claims is necessary if Chileans want their investment. For the time being, this is the equilibrium outcome in Chile.

Part III

COLLECTIVE BUSINESS ACTION AND WEAK STATES

CHAPTER SEVEN

Big Business and the Politics of Economic Reform: Confidence and Concertation in Brazil and Mexico

BEN ROSS SCHNEIDER

For several decades before the debt crisis of 1982, Mexico and Brazil pursued roughly similar development strategies, based on closed economies and extensive state promotion of industry. By the late 1990s their development strategies were again converging, this time around open and freer markets; yet the paths from one strategy to the other were quite different in the two countries. Mexico was one of the leaders in neoliberal economic reform in Latin America, Brazil one of the laggards. In the decade after 1982, Mexican governments controlled inflation, liberalized trade, deregulated, and privatized most state firms. Through the mid-1990s Brazilian governments had yet to stabilize despite more than a decade of almost annual shock programs. Since 1990, governments liberalized trade and privatized by fits and starts, but neoliberal reform was still uneven and incomplete by mid-decade. In 1995 the comparative performance of the two economies changed dramatically as the peso crisis of December 1994 rocked the Mexican economy while the Real program in Brazil reduced inflation without recession. Yet the Zedillo government did not roll back reform in response to the peso crisis, and the Cardoso government continued on the path of gradual and piecemeal liberal reform.

Why was neoliberal reform in Mexico more radical, in the sense of

I am grateful to the Center for International Studies at Princeton University and the Kellogg Institute at the University of Notre Dame for research support. Edward Gibson, Scott Mainwaring, Sylvia Maxfield, Jaime Ros, and Kathleen Thelen made helpful suggestions on earlier versions of this chapter.

being earlier and more comprehensive?[1] And why was the implementation of these reforms more rapid? My overall argument for Brazil and Mexico is that variations in the timing, scope, and implementation of economic reform depended heavily on relations between business and government. Within this overall framework, there are two specific arguments. First, a deeper investment crisis in Mexico prompted officials to undertake more radical reform. Second, once reforms were enacted, concertation or organized cooperation between business and government sped the implementation of reforms (although not necessarily the resumption of sustained development). These arguments illustrate the utility of the distinctions in the fivefold typology in Chapter 2. In my first argument, business as capital drove reform. Business as firm, sector, association, and network played at most minor roles in pressuring state officials to enact neoliberal reforms. In my second argument, business as association facilitated implementation and thereby lowered the costs of reform. In the process of reform, credibility, flexibility, and what one observer called the "coordination of expectations" are crucial; and as we discussed in Chapter 1, ongoing negotiations between business associations and state officials can enhance them all.

Other analyses of the political economy of neoliberal reform, for Brazil and Mexico as well as other developing countries, often either neglect or misconstrue the multifaceted and dynamic interaction between big business and top state officials.[2] Many explanations focus largely on state characteristics such as bureaucratic coherence and capacity, state autonomy, leadership, party strength, and policy design to explain variations in reform (see, for example, Williamson and Haggard 1994; Nelson 1990). These variables can be used to construct a first, rough explanation for the contrast between Brazil and Mexico: An autonomous Mexican state, staffed by a cohesive group of skilled technocrats, facing minimal opposition from parties and legislators, enacted a coherent reform package. In contrast, policymakers in Brazil's new democracy and enfeebled state lacked autonomy and cohesion. These state characteristics are central in any immediate explanation, given that reform policies originate in the

---

[1] Neoliberal reform comprises interrelated programs of macroeconomic stabilization and market-oriented structural adjustment (especially deregulation, privatization, and trade liberalization). Williamson (1990) dubbed the neoliberal package the "Washington consensus" and listed nine major areas of reform: fiscal discipline, public spending, taxes, financial liberalization, exchange rates, trade liberalization, foreign investment, privatization, and deregulation. Roughly, radical reforms are those that encompass major market-oriented changes in at least five of the nine policy areas that are largely implemented within five years.

[2] For extensive reviews of the literature on economic reform, see Haggard and Webb 1994, Haggard and Kaufman 1992, Haggard and Kaufman 1995, Smith et al. 1994, and Bates and Krueger 1993b.

state; yet they are incomplete. State or institutional autonomy explains some variation, but it is at most a permissive variable. Officials in an autonomous state or insulated agencies have more independence, but institutional analysis alone cannot explain how or when they will use it.[3] At the moment when reforms are adopted, the conventional political factors are key; but a full understanding of the crisis preceding reform and the essential cooperation of big business during implementation requires close attention to business-state relations.

While statist perspectives are often incomplete, analyses that do bring in business often misspecify their influence by concentrating on business as a lobby or interest group (usually based on sectoral interests) and argue that neoliberal reforms, or their absence, were largely the result of business pressure. So, for example, big firms push reform more than small firms do (Rivera Ríos 1992), firms with liquid assets favor reform more than those with dedicated assets do (Frieden 1991), and firms engaged in intra-industry trade want liberalization more than firms not so engaged do (Wise 1993b; see also Valdés Ugalde 1994). Theories of rent seeking and distributional coalitions also deduce decisive business influence on policy but in the opposite direction, to block reform (see Olson 1982; Nelson 1994: 179–80). In these theories firms collecting existing rents should be better organized and have more intense preferences than those who might benefit from reform. But neopluralist arguments that place business at the center of reform politics have some severe faults. Theoretically, some are implicitly, or even explicitly, tautological; those groups that benefited from reform (or its absence) must have been the ones who pushed it through government (or blocked it).[4] Empirically, the evidence does not support neopluralist arguments. In a book with case studies of eight developing countries, "one of the most surprising findings . . . is the degree to which the intervention of interest groups fails to account for the initiation, or lack of initiation, of policy reform" (Bates and Krueger 1993a: 455).

In sum, this chapter seeks to move beyond one-sided statist or neopluralist perspectives to provide a fuller examination of the diverse roles

[3] More disaggregated statist approaches argue that the source of reform lies less in overall state characteristics and more in small autonomous groups of technocrats, what Waterbury (1992) dubbed "change teams" (see also Stallings and Kaufman 1989). True, most reforms can be traced back to small groups of powerful, independent technocrats, but again a full explanation needs to show how they got their power. In appointive bureaucracies, the question remains as to why the neoliberals were appointed in the first place (see Schneider 1991b, 1996). The coincidence of investment crises with the rise to power of reformist change teams suggests that a full explanation requires looking beyond bureaucratic politics.

[4] Frieden argues, for example, that "where we see policy favoring interest groups that logic and theory tell us are most likely to bring pressure to bear on policymakers, it is appropriate to infer, at least provisionally, that there is a line of cause and effect that relates lobbying pressure and policy" (1991: 11).

played by business and state elites and the dynamic of their interaction over the course of economic reform (see also Evans 1992; Nelson 1994). First, I examine investment crises in Mexico and Brazil, especially shifts in aggregate investment, capital flight, and business confidence. The investment crisis was more severe in Mexico, and policymakers used radical neoliberal reform in their efforts to restore business confidence and investment. Then I study business-government relations in implementing reform. In Mexico concertation sped the implementation of stabilization and trade liberalization. In Brazil there was only one significant case of concertation, but it had many of the same benefits manifest in the Mexican cases. A comparison of these cases suggests that successful concertation depends on political stability, strong business associations, and shared perceptions of vulnerability. Finally, I briefly consider some broader conceptual implications for the analysis of preference formation and power resources of business and state elites.

INVESTMENT CRISIS AND RADICAL REFORM

Wholesale revisions in development strategy rarely occur in the absence of profound or protracted economic crisis. But what is often lost in the depersonalized language of macroeconomics is the role of big capitalists as agents in deepening or mitigating crisis. Investment crises usually entail more or less simultaneous contraction in capital flows from abroad, public savings, and private investment. Regardless of the source of the most severe contraction, the net result is to increase state dependence on nonstate sources of funds—domestic business in the case of the debt crisis in Latin America. Nevertheless, the magnitude of the crisis and the resulting dependence varied across countries.

An investment crisis is defined by a medium-term drop in aggregate productive investment accompanied by dramatic increases in competing claims on investable funds such as government borrowing and capital flight. A crisis in business confidence is another essential component of an investment crisis.[5] An investment crisis greatly increases the dependence of state actors on private investors and prompts them to do something drastic. Explaining why something was neoliberalism rather than

---

[5] Because it depends on information, perception, and composite indicators, a threshold for an investment crisis is not easily quantified. At a minimum it would require a decrease of 20 percent or more in aggregate investment over a period of three or more years (compared to the average rate over the previous five years) accompanied by competing claims over three or more years greater than previous private investment. The causal force of an investment crisis seemed to fade over the course of the 1980s; it was often not as severe in late-reforming countries in the 1990s.

Table 7.1. Investment in Brazil and Mexico, 1970–1991 (gross fixed investment as a percentage of GDP, in current prices)

	Brazil			Mexico		
	Total	Private	Public	Total	Private	Public
1970	18.8			19.8	13.2	6.6
1975	24.4			21.4	12.4	9.0
1980	22.9	15.1	7.8	24.8	13.9	10.9
1981	22.8	14.1	8.8	26.4	14.3	12.1
1982	21.4	13.9	7.4	23.0	12.8	10.2
1983	17.9	11.9	6.0	17.6	11.0	6.6
1984	16.4	10.8	5.7	17.9	11.3	6.6
1985	17.0	10.9	6.1	19.1	12.5	6.6
1986	19.2	12.9	6.3	19.4	12.9	6.5
1987	22.2	15.0	7.2	18.4	12.9	5.5
1988	22.7			19.1	14.7	4.4
1989	24.8			18.2	14.4	3.8
1990	21.5			18.6	13.7	4.9
1991	18.9					

SOURCES: Brazil: 1970–75, IBGE 1987: 568; 1980–87, Dinsmoor 1990: 62; 1988–91, IBGE 1992: 1034. Mexico: 1970–89, Pfeffermann and Madarassy 1992; 1990, Banco de México 1993: f.

some other development strategy is beyond the scope of this chapter. My working hypothesis is that the choice of development strategy is related to its effectiveness in calming investor anxieties (see Schneider 1996).

At first glance the data on investment show roughly similar crises in Brazil and Mexico in the 1980s (see Table 7.1).[6] Private investment initially dropped more in Brazil than it did Mexico but then recovered in the late 1980s. Public investment dropped by almost a third in Brazil from 1981 to 1983 and by almost half in Mexico. In the late 1980s public investment recovered somewhat in Brazil but declined even further in Mexico. More important, the competing claims on investment resources and the crisis in business confidence were far more severe in Mexico. Reform initiatives often coincide with changes in government, but in Mexico the

[6] Data on aggregate investment vary greatly depending on the source and method of estimation. In particular, investment rates begin to diverge markedly in the 1980s, depending on whether they are calculated in current or constant prices. The rate of investment in Brazil in constant prices shows steady deterioration over the 1980s. For example, at constant prices, it declines from 22.8 percent of GDP in 1980, to 16.2 in 1984, recovers to 18.7 in 1986, and then declines steadily to 14.4 percent in 1992 (see IESP 1993: 44). Comparing these figures with those in Table 7.1 shows that the rate of inflation for investment goods is greater than that for the economy overall. I use the data on investment at current prices because they reflect investor willingness to spend, which is more relevant for my argument than what investors really get (fewer investment goods at a higher cost). I am grateful to Jaime Ros for help with these data.

government enacted radical reform in 1985 in the middle of a *sexenio* the President's six year term) after several years of gradual and uneven liberal reform. This shift in midstream highlights the explanatory power of the investment crisis rather than other political changes. In Brazil, reform efforts through the end of the 1980s tried to address the multiple debt, fiscal, current account, and inflation crises. The overall investment crisis was less severe, however, especially in perceptual terms; and policymakers did not attempt wholesale revision of the development strategy.

In Mexico competing claims on investable resources began increasing even before the debt crisis and grew rapidly thereafter. From 1982 to 1987 average annual external debt service was 9 percent of gross domestic product (GDP) for Mexico, 4 percent for Brazil (IDB 1992). The international debt crisis quickly evolved into a domestic fiscal crisis (see Bresser Pereira 1989, 1992). Mexico's public deficit averaged 13 percent of GDP compared to Brazil's 5 percent (1982–87, IDB 1992). By the mid-1980s, debt service rose to half of government revenues in both countries (Banco de México 1990; Galleta 1988). In Mexico oil revenues contributed more than a third of government revenues in the early 1980s. When oil prices fell by half in 1986, the fiscal repercussions were dire (Kaufman et al. 1994: 366, 368). Massive government borrowing to cover the deficits diverted resources from productive investment. By the mid-1980s in Mexico "the banking system . . . became dedicated almost entirely to financing the government" (Cline 1991: 25). Finally, capital flight was much greater from Mexico than from Brazil. Mexican capital had more opportunities to flee because of the two thousand mile border with the United States and close integration into international financial markets (see Maxfield 1990), and more reasons because of political uncertainties over property rights and abrupt policy changes. Cumulative capital flight (1976–88) accounted for 28 percent of Mexico's GDP in 1986 compared to only 8 percent of Brazil's.[7] For 1983–84 the Mexican private sector invested abroad all of "its *net* real savings" (Ros 1987: 106). Capital continued to hemorrhage at a net rate of about $5 billion a year throughout the rest of the decade, and net repatriation started only after 1990 (Oks and van Wijnbergen 1993: 206, 219).

Given the competing claims on resources, it is remarkable that investment, especially private investment, stayed as high as it did. Several factors

[7] For Mexico the average of three separate estimates for cumulative capital flight from 1976 to 1988 was $47 billion or 56 percent of increase in foreign debt. In Brazil the cumulative capital flight was $27 billion or about a quarter of increase in foreign debt (Anthony and Hallett 1992: 543). Other estimates put Mexican capital flight at $30 to 40 billion for 1977–87 (Cline 1991: 18); $64 billion for 1973–84 (Ros 1987: 107); $25 billion for 1976–82, and $35 billion for 1983–87 (Dornbusch 1990: 323). For Brazil, others have estimated capital flight at $6 billion for 1976–82 and $25 billion for 1983–87 (Dornbusch 1990: 323).

maintained aggregate investment. Firms have to invest a great deal just to maintain the status quo. In Mexico total depreciation ranged from one-half to three-quarters of gross investment from 1983 to 1989 (Banco de México 1993: f). Surveys in the manufacturing sector revealed that one-third to one-half of investment went for replacement in the 1980s (Banco de México 1994). The replacement rate was higher in the early 1980s than at the end of the decade. In addition, government incentives or conjunctural quirks buoyed private investment artificially. For example, in Mexico, the government offered generous tax incentives (accelerated depreciation) for investment in the early 1980s, but many firms took advantage of the incentives to renovate their auto fleets. In 1984 two-thirds of an estimated 9 percent increase in investment went for vehicle purchases (Ros 1987: 100–101). In sum, even when total investment does not fall by much, the kinds of investments that create jobs and enhance productivity can all but vanish.

An investment crisis is also a matter of perception and confidence (see Bresser Pereira 1993: 51). Here, the contrast between Brazil and Mexico is even greater. Nearly all studies of economic policy in the 1980s in Mexico emphasize the goal of restoring business confidence.[8] Mexican officials worried openly about the investment climate and capital flight.[9] In the wake of the nationalization of the banks in 1982, the incoming de la Madrid government instituted a monthly survey of key capitalists to assess their views on fuzzy issues such as the investment climate and expectations for coming years.[10] Jesús Silva Herzog (finance minister, 1982–86) claimed that economic policymakers felt they needed to improve relations with the private sector in any way they could. This goal figured prominently in the early privatization program (interview, July 3, 1989; see also Lustig 1992: 104; Schneider 1989). More than three-quarters of businesspeople appreciated the gesture, even though it had no direct impact on their businesses (Alduncin Abitia 1989). In a lecture in 1992 Manuel Camacho (then regent of Mexico City and a contender to succeed Salinas) extolled the virtues of economic reforms in Mexico. When asked

[8] In the index to an otherwise conventional economic book, Nora Lustig (1992) has seventeen references to "business confidence."

[9] Broad crossnational studies usually conclude that economic crisis is a necessary but not sufficient condition for radical reform because some governments preside over prolonged economic decline (Bates and Krueger 1993a: 452–54; Williamson and Haggard 1994: 563–65). But adding in a specifying condition that government elites feel their legitimacy and survival depends heavily on economic performance makes economic crisis a sufficient condition for a policy response, although not necessarily a successful one. Nondemocratic governments that stake part of their legitimacy on economic performance have strong incentives to respond to economic crisis.

[10] Since 1983 the Banco de México has had a special research department responsible for conducting these surveys twice a year. Interview with Ricardo Reyes Araiza, Banco de México, September 27, 1994.

why the reforms did little for the poor, Camacho thought for a moment and responded simply, "Capital is mobile" (Princeton University, March 2, 1992). A more concrete measure of business confidence and political uncertainty is the risk premium in interest rates. One study estimated that as late as 1990 the country risk still added 7.5 percent risk premium and the currency risk another 36 percent (Reisen 1993: 152).

In Brazil one rarely heard similar concerns about business confidence from either industrialists or government officials. In fact, what was surprising was continued investment and relatively low capital flight despite very high inflation and periodic unorthodox shock programs. Historically, Brazilian investors had experienced fewer politically based crises of confidence; and for a variety of historical and contemporary reasons, big business in Brazil was not overly preoccupied with property rights and government commitment to capitalism (see Leff 1968). Moreover, the political dynamics in Brazil in the mid-1980s were quite different from those in Mexico in ways that influenced economic diagnoses. During the transition to civilian rule in 1985, much of the debate on economic policy revolved around the errors of the military regime and the expectation, shared by many in the business community, that the civilian government would be able to fix these errors without radically altering the development strategy (see Sola 1991). Some positive signs in growth and trade in 1984 and 1985 "led most economists to conclude that the crisis was over and the country was ready to grow again" (Bresser Pereira 1993: 47–48). The initial success of the Cruzado plan in 1986 seemed to confirm the assessment that radical changes in development strategy were unnecessary. It was not until the late 1980s that a clearer crisis of confidence began to emerge, and even then it was less severe than in Mexico.

Those who think that domestic economic crisis drives reform disagree on which aspect of the crisis is key. Although cumbersome, the composite indicator of investment crisis has advantages over other variables such as balance of payments, fiscal deficit, or inflation for identifying when a triggering crisis exists.[11] Governments have no choice but to respond to a deficit in the balance of payments but usually stop short of wholesale reform. In other instances business and state elites tolerate very high levels of inflation or fiscal deficit without resorting to neoliberal reform. Investment crisis is a useful tool in crossnational comparison because it filters out peculiar characteristics in particular economies, such as depen-

[11] Bates and Krueger found three different crisis triggers in their eight cases: balance of payments, inflation, and the "withering away of the state" (1993a: 442). Bresser Pereira argues that the fiscal crisis of the state drives reform. A fiscal crisis exists when the state can no longer finance its deficit in a noninflationary way (1993: 7). Such a crisis implies a broader investment crisis; if not, state elites could reform the state without necessarily adopting a new development strategy. See also Haggard and Maxfield 1996.

dence on raw materials (as in Mexico) or a high tolerance for inflation (as in Brazil) to focus on the common motor of the economy.

Others analyses of neoliberal reform emphasize the role of international influences and the conditionality imposed by multilateral lending agencies (see Stallings 1992; Kahler 1992; Vacs 1994). Policymakers in Mexico in the 1980s were particularly susceptible and receptive to pressures from international financial institutions in Washington and New York (Heredia 1996). But this influence should not be understood narrowly in the context of a bilateral relation between international creditors and debtor governments because it is strongly mediated by relations between government officials and *domestic* capitalists. First, of course, the dependence of government officials on international creditors (and financial bailouts by international financial institutions) is partly the result of prior decisions by domestic investors, especially decisions to take their resources abroad.

Second, when international resources are marginal to overall adjustment, as in Mexico and Brazil, then the critical impact of international pressures, especially from private and multilateral banks, comes indirectly through its effect on the "animal spirits" of domestic investors. When domestic business elites view the unwillingness of government elites to make international settlements with creditors as a critical signal of government disregard for property rights and business confidence, then state elites have incentives to pay greater heed to the international financial community. José Córdoba, Salinas's main economic adviser, wrote that a major benefit of Mexico's debt agreements was to generate "greater confidence among national and international investors" (1991: 37). Robert Kaufman, Carlos Bazdresch, and Blanca Heredia argue that "the group most concerned about a moratorium was the *Mexican* financial establishment [which] ... feared that confrontation with creditors would be linked to populist policies directed against them and allied sectors of big business" (1994: 405n; emphasis mine).

In fact the Brady plan gave Mexico only modest relief in terms of international debt service but provoked a dramatic decline in Mexican interest rates and a rapid increase in private investment and repatriation of flight capital. One econometric study found that "the impact of debt relief on uncertainty is a more important channel through which debt relief influences the macro economy" (Oks and van Wijnbergen 1993: 208). Specifically, the Brady deal prompted an immediate 16 percent reduction in the interest rate attributable to the currency risk premium (Cetes versus Pagafes) and a further 4 percent reduction due to the general country risk (Pagafes versus U.S. Treasury bills) (Oks and van Wijnbergen 1993: 209).

In sum, the investment crisis of the 1980s was more severe in Mexico than in Brazil. In the Mexican crisis, domestic business elites were the key interlocutors for reformist officials and the core economic agents whose confidence needed restoring. Other analyses that emphasize the structural power of capital in prompting policy change (see Chapter 2) often leave off at the moment when reforms are enacted. But business-government relations are also key to the success of implementing reform. The next sections analyze how organized cooperation between business (as association) and state elites facilitated implementation and accelerated consolidation.

CONCERTATION AND THE IMPLEMENTATION OF REFORM

For my present purposes, concertation is defined as a process of regular meetings between representatives of business associations, the government, and sometimes labor unions to negotiate the details of policy implementation.[12] This is more or less the usage of *concertación* in Mexico. In Brazil the more common term is *social pact*. Concertation can contribute decisively to several problematic aspects of implementation in many of the ways described in Chapter 1.

For example, two contradictory components of successful implementation stand out in the literature. First, reforms must be credible to succeed, and noncredible reform can be worse than no reform at all (Rodrik 1989). Concertation is one of the few ways to generate credibility in the short run because government officials can commit themselves in person and in writing to particular economic targets. Second, others argue that flexibility is essential to implementation (Bates and Krueger 1993a: 460). This was one of the main lessons of the Chilean failure of the 1970s, where the government put great stock in its inflexibility (Stallings and Brock 1993). The conundrum is that flexibility and responsiveness undermine credibility (see Rodrik and Zeckhauser 1988). In principle, concertation can help reconcile these conflicting imperatives by allowing government officials to negotiate adjustments in one area without diminishing the overall credibility of the reform program. Altering a reform program without the extensive communication permitted through concertation gives business little idea of whether the adjustment signals just an adjustment or the begining of the end of reform. If, in contrast, the government makes transparent just how far it is willing to bend, then business can assign probabilities to further adjustments.

---

[12] My definition does not necessarily include labor as an equal participant, as concertation does in Europe. It also differs from Chilean concertation, which refers to party and electoral alliances.

Politically, reformers need to win friends over the course of implementing reforms. As Tocqueville noted, tyrannies have an advantage at the beginning of a war, but democracies gain the upper hand over time. Likewise, authoritarian regimes may have some advantage in initiating reforms but not in consolidating them (Haggard and Kaufman 1992). Coalition building by reformist political leaders, especially in the business community, is essential to sustain reforms over the medium term (see Haggard and Kaufman 1995). Concertation is a useful means for shaping business preferences and building consensus in favor of reform (which in turn also enhances the credibility of reform).

In institutional terms, concertation requires a well-organized private sector. By the mid-1980s the private sector was much better organized in Mexico than in Brazil, especially along two crucial dimensions: coordination among sectoral and regional organizations through a peak association, and exclusive articulation among the biggest of the big. In Brazil relations between business and the state were, to borrow a term from finance, disintermediated. Business organiations from different sectors had no peak association. On occassion business elites in Brazil convened ad hoc meetings or pooled efforts for particular purposes, as in the lobbying of the Constituent Assembly in the late 1980s, but never created a lasting peak association (see Dreifuss 1989; Weyland 1992; Schneider, forthcoming). In Mexico sectoral organizations created a formal peak association, the Consejo Coordinador Empresarial (CCE), in 1975. The CCE remained a loose federation into the 1980s and had a small staff and budget. Nonetheless, the president of the CCE regularly spoke for the whole private sector, and in the 1980s the CCE became the key interlocutor with government.

In addition to the CCE, big business in Mexico also had more exclusive and informal organizations to aggregate their interests. The Consejo Mexicano de Hombres de Negocios (CMHN) organized the owners of about thirty of the largest groups in Mexico, who by some estimates controlled 20–30 percent of GDP. In addition, the "holy fathers" or Group of Ten organized the biggest industrialists in Monterrey. These associations have no staff or offices, but their members regularly break bread and exchange views with ministers and presidents. The owners of the biggest Brazilian groups have even less articulation of this kind. Some members thought that IEDI (Institute for the Study of Industrial Development, discussed later) had pretensions of becoming a Brazilian Keidanren, but if so, the hope never materialized (interview with Paulo Villares, January 28, 1993).

The following subsections examine stabilization and trade policies in greater detail to show how concertation enhanced the implementation of neoliberal reform in Mexico, where organized business elites provided public support and private cooperation for the reforms. In Brazil stabilization came late, and the implementation of structural reforms such as trade liberalization was slow and uneven. Government officials rarely attempted to enlist business collaboration in implementation, with the significant exception of some sectoral accords, and hence reaped few of the advantages observed in Mexican concertation.

Stabilization through Concertation

In December 1987, after several weeks of consultation with business leaders, the Mexican government created the Pacto de Solidaridad Económico to negotiate an incomes policy (wage and price adjustments). This pact was meant to be temporary, but meetings continued throughout the Salinas government before collapsing along with the peso in 1995. The Pacto (the exact name changed several times) received much of the credit for accelerating the demise of inflation.[13] Eliana Cardoso concludes that "as a result of the *Pacto*, monthly inflation rates dropped from an average of about 15 percent in January 1988 to only one percent for the second half of the year" (1991: 175). Annual rates of inflation dropped from a record high of 159 percent in 1987 to 52 percent in 1988 and 20 percent in 1989 (Kaufman et al. 1994: 368). Much of the praise for the Pacto used terms similar to those discussed in Chapter 1, such as exchange of information, flexibility, credibility, and reciprocity.

Formally the Pacto looked like European-style tripartite bargaining among representatives of business, labor, and government. In fact, labor had little real influence, and business had little choice but to participate. Participation was officially voluntary, but 99 percent of firms eventually signed on, in part because, if a firm opted out, its unions would not be bound by the terms of the pact (interview with Santiago Macías, director general of SECOFI (Ministry of Commerce and Industrial Promotion), November 1993). The government also threatened business with audits, inspections, labor unrest, and withdrawal of government contracts (*Proceso*, April 4, 1988, 30; Centeno 1994: 196). Business was initially skeptical; but after 1988 large majorities of businesspeople surveyed favored maintaining the Pacto, even after inflation dropped below 10 percent a year in 1993.

---

[13] Kaufman et al. 1994 provide the full story on the first year of the Pacto and include an appendix on why it worked so well. For other favorable reviews, see Chine 1991, Lustig 1992: 55, and Córdoba 1991. Córdoba lauds concertation but notes that incomes policies only facilitate orthodox measures and that, in the Mexican case, fiscal overadjustment, strong external accounts, and prior alignment of relative prices were necessary preconditions for the Pacto (1991: 35). For an early recommendation for an incomes policy, see Ros 1987.

The Pacto contributed to the success of the stabilization plan in multiple ways. Concertation, especially through the Price and Monitoring Commission, provided information to policymakers so they could anticipate problems (Lustig 1992: 54). Government officials watched carefully for shortages, which were rare, certainly compared to the Brazilian experience with the Cruzado plan. By providing information on the contribution of each party to the accords, concertation reduced incentives for free riding (see Córdoba 1991: 35). Concertation enlisted firms and business associations in the tasks of monitoring and enforcement (see Streeck and Schmitter 1985). The government signed numerous concertation accords with particular firms, groups of firms, or associations and created a tripartite Price and Monitoring Commission that met weekly to assess compliance. Of the associations, those representing retail trade, cement, chemicals, and autos were pivotal. In retail trade, members of the National Association of Self-Service and Department Stores (ANTAD) controlled 35–60 percent of the retail market and they bought only at prices authorized by the government (Kaufman et al. 1994: 388–89).[14]

Concertation greatly enhanced the credibility of the stabilization program; it "coordinated expectations" (Cline 1991: 14). The memories of the turbulence at the end of the terms of Presidents Echeverría and López Portillo led capitalists to expect the worst in the last year of a sexenio. The last quarter of 1987, after Salinas had been "fingered" as the government's candidate, looked like the beginnings of a nasty repeat performance: The stock market crashed, capital flight picked up, and inflation accelerated. In this context, the Pacto became a crucial conduit for communication, especially on government intentions. In particular, the government used the Pacto to demonstrate commitment to fiscal discipline (despite election-year pressures) and overall policy continuity. The commitment to fiscal austerity was one of the core components of reciprocity for business: "both publicly and in interviews, representatives of the leading business organizations identified quantified commitments to reduce expenditures as a key condition for their participation in the pact" (Kaufman et al. 1994: 382).

Concertation also permitted more flexibility, especially in adjusting individual prices without irreparable damage to credibility (Cline 1991; Kaufman et al. 1994; Córdoba 1991: 35). Price freezes always get some prices wrong, and concertation provided a means for adjustment without apparently damaging the overall credibility of the Pacto. The government in fact did not make open-ended promises on exchange rates and public

---

[14] In an earlier draft, Kaufman, Bazdresch, and Heredia wrote that "the large majority of the businessmen interviewed . . . said they had kept their prices relatively stable as a result of their participation in the Pacto" (1992: 15).

prices, precisely to maintain credibility after the inevitable adjustments. In principle, the terms of the Pacto were subject to revision at each meeting: "this was a precaution to preserve government *credibility* in the event conditions were not sustainable" (Lustig 1992: 54, emphasis mine). Finally, the incomes policy in the Pacto reduced the social costs associated with the more orthodox elements of the stabilization program and thereby made the program more politically sustainable (Córdoba 1991: 34). Some businesspeople found the concertation relationship so cozy that they criticized the leaders of major participating associations of being "Ministers of the Private Sector" (*Proceso,* April 11, 1988, 10). While levied as a criticism, this transformation is precisely what concertation is designed to do—to broaden the horizons of business leaders and enlist them in the task of providing collective public goods.

The crisis of 1995 demonstrated that the Pacto was not the panacea some thought it to be. The full story of the crisis is beyond this chapter; suffice it to note that by 1994 stabilization and trade reform were complete and eclipsed by multiple political crises, including the Zapatista uprising, Colosio's assassination, and the weakness of the presidential candidate of the PRI Institutional Revolutionary Party. The Pacto ceased in 1994 to be a sufficient channel for sustaining government credibility and supplying adequate information on government actions (international reserves and short-term borrowing, especially). That the Pacto was difficult to revive in 1995 was due in large part to the instability of the peso; in an increasingly open economy, none of the parties could commit to fiscal, price, and wage targets without a predictable exchange rate. These limitations thus help specify more clearly the preconditions necessary to gain the benefits generated by concertation in the late 1980s.[15]

In Brazil, discussions about social pacts appeared frequently in the press in the 1980s and 1990s. Top officials in the Sarney, Collor, and Itamar Franco governments invited representatives of business and labor to Brasília for informal discussions. These meetings, however, never resulted in systematic concertation because the government often was not willing to negotiate anything (see Schneider 1991a) but, more structurally, because business and labor had no authoritative peak associations (see Roxborough 1992; Kingstone 1994: chap. 7). Concertation alone could not have saved earlier stabilization programs from their political and economic miscalculations (see Bresser Pereira 1993), and the Real plan was

---

[15] As of early 1996, reviews of pacts in the Zedillo government were mixed. A survey of 453 businesspeople at the end of 1995 found considerable skepticism, as had been the case in the first months of the first Pacto, about the benefits of the renamed Alliance for Economic Recovery (*La Journada,* January 19, 1996). Leaders of the CCE and Coparmex, in contrast, lauded the new pacts (see, respectively, *La Jornada,* April 5, 1996, January 18, 1996).

successful despite the lack of an incomes policy. Nevertheless, all or some of the benefits attributed to concertation in the process of stabilization in Mexico would have been a boon to policymakers in Brazil. Beginning in the late 1980s, officials did experiment with sectoral agreements (*câmaras setoriais*). The câmaras had little influence on aggregate price levels, but, as discussed in the next section, they facilitated adjustment in some sectors to the trade liberalization.

Negotiation in Trade Liberalization

In Mexico consultations between business and government about trade policy began before the Pacto and grew more intense as the liberalization proceeded, especially after the government entered into negotiations over the North American Free Trade Agreement (NAFTA).[16] In 1986, after the opening began, representatives of business and government met to discuss the planned four-year schedule for tariff reductions. In 1987 the government accelerated the tariff reductions unilaterally but made trade liberalization an integral part of the stabilization program and an item on the agenda for Pacto meetings. When the Mexican government announced plans in March 1990 to pursue NAFTA, the CCE (with government approval) quickly created Coordinadora Empresarial de Comercio Exterior (COECE). COECE and the government in turn created advisory committees comprised of five or so officials and eight to ten representatives from business to accompany negotiations in about twenty sectors. In the two years following the March 1990 announcement, various groups of representatives of business and government negotiators had 1,333 meetings, roughly a dozen a week (Puga 1994: 9). Business representatives were not allowed at the bargaining table with United States and Canada but were figuratively "in the room next door" (*cuarto de junta*; interview with Raúl Ortega, COECE, November 16, 1993; Puga 1994).

Concertation through these multiple forums, especially through COECE and the NAFTA negotiations, contributed to consolidating trade reform by building support in the private sector, increasing the flow of information between business and government, and allowing business the opportunity to propose complementary and compensatory policies. The acquiescence of business to trade liberalization was surprising, considering that business blocked Mexico's entrance into the GATT (General Agreement on Tariffs and Trade) in 1979 (Story 1982; Kaufman et al.

---

[16] The government was willing to discuss the opening but not negotiate its overall implementation. Salinas's main economic adviser, José Córdoba, thought negotiations before implementation were risky and likely to end up canceling the reform (1991: 41).

1994). Other factors contributed to muting opposition, but the fact that business felt consulted and included in negotiating the opening was also significant.[17] Government leaders felt such consensus building was important enough in the 1990s to invest a great deal in campaigning in favor of liberalization by sending officials out to talk with business groups (interview with a SECOFI negotiator, November 1993). Business support for NAFTA was nearly unanimous by 1993.

Concertation increased the flow of information from business to government and vice versa. Generally, the advisory committees allowed for much communication (everybody was link by E-mail) and mostly harmonious negotiation between business and government.[18] When NAFTA negotiations began, young government negotiators knew less about North American business and trade than did Mexican exporters. Beyond this familiarity, the government needed more systematic data, which COECE and member associations set about to collect. Initially, the government relied on the CCE's research unit to conduct a first national survey to find out what business wanted from a trade agreement (Puga 1994: 7). Over time, sectoral associations began collecting more complete data on their respective sectors to use in the negotiations (Puga 1994: 15).[19]

From the business side, concertation gave investors a better sense of where the government was headed and hence provided greater certainty for planning and investment (interview, Fernando Canales Clariond, vice president of IMSA, November 19, 1993). Before 1988 business had been skeptical about the opening because previous attempts had been aborted. After 1988 "the private sector was at last convinced that the trade opening would not be abandoned or delayed" (Kaufman et al. 1994: 396). Concertation enhanced the credibility of trade policy.

Over time, business leaders increasingly used the Pacto meetings to make requests for complementary and compensatory policies to help with

---

[17] Interview, Fernando Canales Clariond, vice president of IMSA, November 19, 1993. Other factors include the coercive powers of the state, the control of business associations by big business sympathetic to reform, the link of stabilization with liberalization, and the preexisting support for trade liberalization (Kaufman et al. 1994). As early as the late 1960s significant pluralities of large Mexican industrialists ($N = 143$) opposed government policy on the pricing of raw materials (54 percent), customs duties (50 percent), and import policy generally (40 percent). In a larger sample of industrialists ($N = 332$), only 12 percent listed increased protection as a top priority for government policy (Derossi 1971: 61, 63).

[18] For a favorable review of COECE and concerted trade liberalization from the business side, see Coparmex's magazine *Entorno,* June 1991, 12, and the interviewees cited in Puga 1994: 10.

[19] Through these negotiations, the state enhanced business capacity for interest intermediation. Within various advisory groups, representatives of upstream and downstream firms realized that they had to work out differences before taking joint proposal to government, otherwise business would lose influence (interview with Raúl Ortega, COECE, November 1993). See Puga 1994 for further analysis of the profound impact of the NAFTA negotiations on Mexican business associations.

the trade opening (interview with Fernando Villareal Palomo, director general, CAINTRA (Chamber of Manufacturing Industry), Nuevo León, November 18, 1993). For example, in 1993 business leaders complained that the energy prices charged by state enterprises were higher than those in the United States and other trading-partner nations, which put Mexican business at a competitive disadvantage. The government agreed to reduce energy prices in return for corresponding price reductions in pesos (interview with Santiago Macias, director general, SECOFI, November 1993). By 1994, CONCAMIN (Confederation of Industrial Chambers) and the CCE were even making general demands for more active industrial policies (Puga 1994: 14). COECE was due to close after the negotiations ended in 1993, but it survived in part to accompany negotiations over other possible trade agreements. Moreover, the model of consultation in COECE was so popular that government and business leaders favored extending it to other areas. For example, in 1994 the government revived the Comisión Mixta para la Promoción de las Exportaciones (COMPEX), which brought together representatives of government and business to discuss regulating and promoting exports (Puga 1994: 16).

In Brazil government officials consulted ocassionally with business about trade policy but never institutionalized concertation on an industry- or economy-wide basis. Trade liberalization started slowly in the Sarney government and accelerated rapidly after 1990 in the Collor government. In 1990 FIESP (Federation of Industry of the State of São Paulo) published its manifesto for the incoming Collor government, *Livre para crescer* (Free to grow), which endorsed a program of radical market-oriented reforms, including trade liberalization. On its own intitiative the CNI (National Confederation of Industry) began surveying members on their views of trade policy; but the surveys were not commissioned by the government as in Mexico, nor is there evidence that the government called on other associations to help collect data.

For some industrialists, liberalization was simply a negative policy in Collor's general offensive against big business rather than part of a project to make Brazilian industry competitive. This kind of dissatisfaction prompted a small group of Brazil's largest industrialists to create the Instituto de Estudos de Desenvolvimento Industrial (IEDI) in 1989 (treated in Schneider, forthcoming). By 1993 IEDI had thirty-three members and an operating budget of about $350,000 (interview, Mauro Arruda, executive director of IEDI, December 15, 1993). Although restricted to industry, IEDI resembled the Mexican Council of Businessmen (CMHN) in that it was voluntary, open by invitation only, and restricted to the owners of the largest industrial groups. The purpose of IEDI was to participate in devising new industrial policies, especially to complement the trade opening, but successive governments were not interested in their proposals. Overall, Brazil's trade liberalization was more controversial than Mexico's and its implementation less smooth. Opinion surveys of business continued to show majority support for liberalization, yet the objections raised by IEDI and some FIESP leaders revealed powerful pockets of resistance.[20]

Government officials were more open to multiple forums for concertation in particular sectors. In 1991 and especially 1992 the Collor government turned to sectoral accords to smooth adjustment to unfreezing prices and international competition. At the end of the Sarney government and the beginning of the Collor government, officials had discussed various sectoral arrangements, sometimes including labor. These arrangements did not, however, materialize until they received decisive support from top government officials, specifically Antônio Kandir in the Ministry of the Economy and Dorothea Werneck (then minister of labor), and from labor leaders in CUT, the leftist labor confederation associated with the Workers Party (PT). The support from labor intensified when a delegation of union leaders in the auto sector returned from a sobering trip to Detroit, where they learned that the future of the Brazilian industry was clouded by the trade opening. Hence, labor was willing to invest in a sectoral entity that would negotiate the adjustment of the industry to international competition. Discussions advanced rapidly in the automobile sector; and in March 1992 representatives of government, business, and labor signed the first sectoral accord, a *câmara setorial* (subsequently renewed several times), which committed the government to reduce taxes; business to reduce profits and prices, maintain employment, and increase investment in restructuring the industry; and labor to wage moderation and no strikes.

The reasons for investing in collective action in the câmaras varied across the key actors. For business and labor, the key motivation was the threat of international competition.[21] Another accord was signed early on in the toy sector, where business leaders also acknowledged strong pressure from international competition (interview with Synésio Batista da Costa, executive director of ABRINQ (Brazilian Toy Association), May 23,

---

[20] See CNI 1990, 1991, 1992 and Barros and Oliveira 1992 for surveys of business. Interviews with Nicola Jeha and Sergio Bergamini, directors at FIESP, January 1993; Paulo Villares, member of IEDI, January 28, 1993. See *Isto E/Senhor,* December 1, 1993, pp. 5–7.

[21] When asked why negotiations proceeded faster in the auto sector than in other sectors, José Roberto Ferro, a consultant who helped set up the auto accord, said that the threat of the trade opening gave both unions and managers strong incentives to come to an agreement (interview, December 16, 1993). See Kingstone 1994: chap. 7, Diniz 1995, and Arbix 1995 for a full discussion of the câmaras.

1995). Government officials had multiple motives, ranging from industrial policy (enhancing competitiveness), to macropolicy (restraining price increases), to coalition building.[22] It was in part this multiplity of state objectives that made the câmaras vulnerable to subsequent changes in government personnel and priorities.

Concertation in the auto industry appeared to have a dramatic impact. In 1993 and 1994 the auto sector set all-time records for production. In 1993 the sector grew by 30 percent (which fueled overall growth because the sector accounts for 12 percent of GDP), and prices fell by 30 percent; growth in 1994 was another 14 percent.[23] Critics charged that production would have increased without a câmara setorial and that therefore the accord amounted to little more than a massive government subsidy to wealthy consumers. Econometric studies show that at least some of the increase in production can be attributed to the accords (Fazenda 1994; Toledo Neto 1994). Moreover, interviewees in the sector emphasize the stabilizing impact the accords had on prices, wages, employment, and hence overall labor relations. This effect was significant in a sector that had been rocked throughout the 1980s by often vicious strikes and stoppages. At Autolatina (a joint venture between Ford and Volkswagen), worker-hours lost in 1989 rose to 11 million, dropped to 2.2 million in 1991, but then averaged only 89,000 for the three years of the accord (1992–94) (Arbix 1995: 240). Union representatives were struck by how participation in the câmara in the accord shifted their negotiations at the firm level, where they began to discuss subcontracting, modernization, and Mercosul (the trade agreement between Brazil, Argenting, Paraguay, and Uruguay) (Arbix 1995: 238–39).

In 1995 the auto câmara broke down along two fault lines. First, the companies could not agree on tax rates for various-sized cars, especially the smallest (called the "popular car"). Second, the government subsequently acted unilaterally to stem the flood of imported cars by raising tariffs and then imposing quotas. Ironically, the câmara that was established to ease adjustment to international competition was displaced by a government that rescinded the trade opening to reduce the trade deficit. Just as the Pacto in Mexico fell victim to more pressing electoral concerns, the auto câmara in Brazil was sacrificed to more immediate pressures on the macrostabilization program.

---

[22] Kandir pushed the câmaras in part as a concession to the PT in the hopes of gaining their support for amendments that the Collor government wanted to make to the constitution (interview, May 1995).

[23] *Veja*, March 9, 1994, p. 94, and Arbix 1995: 253. In addition to the sectoral accords, the government provided further tax incentives for small cars, and the trade opening encouraged further price moderation.

Benefits and Sources of Concertation

A comparison the reform experiences in Brazil and Mexico and of concertation in the Pacto, NAFTA negotiations, and the câmaras setoriais suggest several general conclusions. First, concertation is neither indispensable nor a panacea. In both countries governments implemented some reforms without concertation while concertation did not keep others from being derailed. Second, in other instances concertation did provide significant benefits, especially in reforms that required coordinated actions by numerous economic agents. Third, concertation was a fairly flexible arrangement that could be constructed quickly and deployed to address a variety of problems in the implementation of economic reform. Finally, concertation collapsed quickly as well, especially when the state withdrew from it.

Further comparative analysis is necessary to specify the benefits of concertation and the conditions that make it possible and successful. In other countries economic reform occurred without the organized collaboration of business in the process of implementation. Governments in Bolivia, Argentina, Peru, and elsewhere reduced inflation without significant concertation (see Smith et al. 1994). Were there costs to foregoing concertation? A first probable cost is greater rigidity in implementing reform. In the absence of other means of establishing credibility, governments often adopt stringent measures to tie the government's own hands. The Cavallo plan in Argentina, for example, welded the peso to the dollar and put constitutional limits on the emission of money. This rigidity worked in the first years of the plan and in achieving the primary goal of reducing inflation but imposed heavy costs on tradable sectors as the peso appreciated and later circumscribed the government's margin of maneuver in 1995 when portfolio investment drained out of Latin America.[24]

Another potential cost of foregoing concertation is delay. In stabilization policies speed is of the essence in order to shorten associated recessions. Using demand management alone to fight inflation generally causes "extraordinary depression" (Dornbusch 1990: 317).[25] One of the most remarked-on features of Mexican stabilization under the Pacto was precisely the speed at which inflation decelerated. In the case of structural adjustment, the key is to convince investors to shift investment in

---

[24] As we discussed in Chapter 1, the stock of credibility enjoyed by governments depends partly on characteristics of the government and the state (reputations of top leaders and officials, for example). The Mexican case suggests that the deficit in credibility depends on the nature and depth of a preceding crisis in investor confidence. Given these multiple dimensions of variation, the range of circumstances under which concertation achieves maximum results in terms of credibility may be limited.

[25] Incomes policies, negotiated or not, greatly speed stabilization, especially at very high levels of inflation (see Bresser Pereira 1993: 58; Ros 1987).

line with activities favored by the new development strategy. If investors have doubts about whether the reforms will last (as they did after the Belaunde government in Peru and the Pérez government in Venezuela), the rational response is to wait and see and to withhold investment (see Rodrik 1989). Such delays can either undermine reforms or significantly postpone the benefits expected from the new development strategy.

Comparisons with other countries also highlight the conditions favoring successful concertation, namely formal relations between state officials and organized business, political stability, and a shared sense of economic or political vulnerability. As Silva shows in Chapter 6, the comparison of failed reform in Chile in the 1970s versus success in the 1980s highlights the importance, holding regime type and state strength constant, of consultation with organized business. The key difference between the two periods of reform is less the absence of contact in the first than the almost incestuous relationship between top officials and a handful of the largest business groups before 1983 versus the more formal contacts between government and business associations after 1983.

The formal organization of business seems especially important in the absence of Weberian bureaucracies. Neither the Salinas nor the Collor governments will be remembered as models of public propriety, yet significant and apparently uncorrupt concertation emerged in each.[26] What kept the corruption that permeated other relations between business and government from seeping into concertation? Concertation was at least partly shielded by the fact that decision making was relatively transparent and monitoring by member associations was cheap and easy. In the case of the price accords achieved in the Pacto and the auto câmara, participating associations had strong incentives to watch that firms in other sectors did not deviate from the accords. The participation of labor did not ensure an equal distribution of the costs or benefits of adjustment, but it did add another group of motivated monitors and hence an additional restraint on the rent-seeking tendencies of other participants.

The collapse of the Pacto and the auto câmara in 1995 revealed the political fragility of concertation. Concertation seems to require sustained political investment and relative political stability (see the chapter by Thorp and Durand). Frequent changes in personnel in Brazil, another consequence of the lack of Weberian practices in the upper reaches of

---

[26] To date, there have been no major charges of corruption in the Pacto, NAFTA negotiations, or câmaras setoriais. The general picture, however, is quite different. In an index of corruption compiled by Transparency International in 1995, Brazil and Mexico were ranked respectively as the fifth and tenth most corrupt countries out of forty-one surveyed (*New York Times,* August 20, 1995, E3). I am grateful to Peter Katzenstein for bringing this survey to my attention.

the bureaucracy, were sometimes devastating for sectoral negotiations. To the extent that concertation is motivated by conjunctural political or economic threats, continued political investment is less likely once the threat has passed or been eclipsed by another. In Mexico in 1988, capital flight was a predominant preoccupation of state officials; by 1994 it was still a concern but less intense than winning a relatively clean election. In other countries considered in this book, long-term vulnerabilities (geopolitical in postwar Korea or economic for Colombian coffee), combined with longer periods of political stability, generated more continuous investment in collective action.

Other governments lack both the capacity and well-organized interlocutors necessary to reap the benefits of concertation (see Stallings and Kaufman 1989; Rueschemeyer et al. 1992: 293). As we considered briefly in Chapter 1, however, creative state actors may be able to use concertation for temporary pacts or to establish piecemeal and partial concertation (as in the sectoral pacts in Brazil) and over the longer term to strengthen business associations. The key here may be the common perception of threats to political leaders, workers, and capitalists. The threats to business leaders and workers were clearest in the instances of trade liberalization. The political threats were greatest to Mexican leaders in 1987 and to both government and opposition (PT) leaders in the case of Brazilian autos. The delicate political task is to harness these anxieties to collaboration in arrangements that do not overtax the institutional capacities of participating states and associations.

FURTHER IMPLICATIONS

Borrowing Hirschman's terms, I argue that Mexican and Brazilian business elites interacted with state elites primarily through exit and voice (see Hirschman 1978). By exercising the exit option—withholding investment—business as capital makes state actors feel they have to do something. The greater the recourse to exit from productive investment, the more often that state officials take faster and more dramatic measures to woo back capital. Once reforms are adopted, the greater the capacity on the part of business for organized voice, the greater the likelihood of consolidating stabilization and new development strategies. On both counts, exit and voice, big business in Mexico had greater impact; it induced more rapid reform through exit and helped to implement and consolidate it through voice. In this view state elites are quite dependent on private investment (business as capital); but because they have the policy initiative, they influence the way business organizes and defines its preferences (business as association) and hence the tone and volume of its voice.

This perspective on economic reform in Brazil and Mexico has several implications for conceptions of the preference formation and power resources of both state and business elites. First, it is essential not to lose sight of the dependence of officials on private investment. Even when state actors are exercising policy initiative, they are not doing so in isolation. Some authors trace the adoption of neoliberal reform to the deep-seated beliefs of political leaders. Others see the delegation of authority to technocrats and the building of insulated institutions as a resolution of the "politicians' dilemma" of how to keep from spending themselves out of power (Bates and Krueger 1993a: 464–65). These motives may be present, but the selection of neoliberalism and the delegation of authority to insulated groups of foreign trained economists cannot be divorced from attempts to maintain credibility and restore business confidence (see Schneider 1996). Reformers try to induce investment; and to do so means choosing discourses, personnel, and institutions that restore business confidence, improve the investment climate, and make policies credible. Autonomy and insulation may be essential to implementing economic reform, but creating and sustaining insulation is often designed in the first place to calm investors. To borrow the language of classic debates on the capitalist state, reformers create instrumental autonomy in order to respond to structural imperatives.

This structural power of business as capital is not necessarily matched by organized, proactive input into policy formulation. A past member of the elite Mexican Council of Businessmen put it this way: "the only group with any real influence in Mexico is the private sector. But our influence can be measured by the degree to which we can limit the activities of the state. We can't achieve what we want in a positive direction. What I mean to say is that we can limit its action in terms of the resources we control, and in this we are very strong, but we can't achieve new and constructive policies on the part of the government" (Camp 1989: 113). In other words, business exercises structural veto power but cedes policy initiative to the state. As I noted at the outset, in Mexico, Brazil, and elsewhere, business lobbies or interest groups neither imposed nor blocked economic reform. One main reason that business associations are absent from the making or braking of reform policies is the ambiguity of business preferences. It is reasonable to make assumptions about what capitalists want—profits—but not about how they intend to get them—their strategies. To the extent that business preferences are not predetermined, business politics become more dependent on context and contingent on state actions.[27]

---

[27] Payne (1994) develops a similar pragmatic approach to business preferences in Brazil regarding democracy and authoritarianism.

The ambiguity of business preferences with regard to neoliberal reform arises from both patterns of business organization and the context of reform. In most developing countries business is dominated by huge diversified groups whose strategies are flexible, contingent, and complex (see Chapter 2). Given the diversity of their holdings, any particular reform will benefit some parts of the group and hurt others, and it is therefore difficult ex ante to categorize such groups as pro- or antireform. In terms of context, gauging the impact of reform, even on less diversified businesses, is not always straightforward. For example, when reforms come simultaneously, businesses may not know for some time whether they stand to gain or lose overall (see Rodrik 1994; Bates and Krueger 1993a: 456). In highly uncertain and politicized contexts, capitalists may even be willing to trade their rents for stronger property rights (Frieden 1991). As Bates and Krueger conclude, "under conditions of uncertainty, people's beliefs of where their economic interest lie can be created and organized by political activists" (1993a: 456).[28]

While a focus on exit highlights the weakness of the state, the ambiguity of business preferences restores to state actors the potential for exercising greater power. If business preferences are amorphous and contingent, then state officials can use their substantial powers of agenda setting and persuasion to convince capitalists that something like neoliberal reform is in their long-term interest. Moreover, as discussed generally in Chapters 1 and 2, state officials can have a decisive impact on business organizations and through them on interest intermediation because they control some of the key benefits and regulations on which associations depend. State actors in Brazil and Mexico influenced business associations by strengthening the CCE, encouraging the creation of COECE, and forcing the association of the big auto firms to negotiate with other business associations.

Concertation, or listening to business voice, does not mean simply a zero-sum loss of state autonomy or power to business. In concerted implementation the state does cede some prerogatives through negotiated compromise. State actors trade some autonomy for greater capacity, in the sense that concertation speeds the implementation of policies. But to come full circle, to the extent that concertation and voice impede exit, concertation can enhance the structural autonomy of the state (from business as capital). Moreover, even before representatives of government and business sit down at the table to initiate concertation, state actions will have been decisive in shaping business articulation (hence the orga-

---

[28] They also credit ideologies with a great deal of influence under conditions of uncertainty. Nevertheless, activists and ideologies rarely have much influence without institutional backing by organizations in the state and private sector. See also Mansbridge 1992.

nizational capacity of business to participate in concertation) and business preferences (hence business inclination to engage in concertation). From this perspective, state strength is less a function of the ability of state actors to overpower societal resistance and more the consequence of redeploying state powers to bring societal preferences and their articulation in line with state preferences. From one angle this is a kinder, gentler, more compromising state; from another it is potentially a more sinister state that more thoroughly dominates civil society.

CHAPTER EIGHT

A Historical View of Business-State Relations: Colombia, Peru, and Venezuela Compared

ROSEMARY THORP AND FRANCISCO DURAND

In the first chapter, Schneider and Maxfield focus our attention on two questions: *how* business-state relations may enhance performance, and *why* there are exceptions to the general rule, which appears to be that close congenial relations lead to rent seeking and shade into corruption, misallocation, and inefficiency. This chapter takes three Latin American instances of business-state relations over the long term as a way of exploring these questions. The three cases are similar in size but distinct in their resource base: Colombia was until recently a mono-export economy based on coffee, Venezuela is an oil economy, while Peru has had an unusual export diversity with a substantial base in mining.

The economic history of our cases leads us to define the dependent variable not as growth per se but as management of change. Over the long run, for economies still dependent for their motor of growth on primary exports, the growth rate is very much a function of international market conditions; and Venezuela and Peru outdid Colombia because oil and mining exports over the long haul have been more buoyant than coffee. The fascination of the comparison, however, turns out to be centered not in the periods of buoyant exports but in the periods when change has to be negotiated if reasonable progress is to be secured and sectoral shifts are needed. Over the long run, Colombia grows less spectacularly but more consistently, and we seek to explore why.

The detailed historical story pushes us in one direction for an explanation: The heart of the difference appears to lie in that capacity to negotiate structural change, which in turn appears to be rooted in the nature of business-state relationships as it emerges out of the different export economy histories. One history, Colombia's, produces an encompassing business association with special characteristics that influence both of the questions Schneider and Maxfield pose: how such a business-state relationship influences economic management and performance, and why it persists as a positive relationship over time, providing a framework rather than an obstacle for negotiating change. Interestingly, the Colombian state is *not* an insulated bureaucracy—far from it—nor is the state a strong one. In general, Colombian politics follow a clientelistic mode, wide open to rent seeking, corruption, and special interests. We seek insights into why Colombia nevertheless appears to be the exception to the rule, comparing its export economy history with two others similar in size and without strong states but different in their natural resource base.

Our study seems to fall under the second category of the classification in Chapter 2: a sectoral approach. But appearances are misleading. Our argument does not share the technological determinism identified by Haggard, Maxfield, and Schneider as characteristic of sectoral studies; rather, the historical approach leads to a focus on the institutional consequences of different sectoral characteristics. The approach links more naturally to their fourth and fifth categories: business associations and networks that evolve (or do not) as crucial intermediating agencies with the state. We use the Evans concept of embeddedness and find that most, but not all, of the components identified by Schneider and Maxfield are important: reciprocity, trust, monitoring, and information exchange.

The sectoral focus is also misleading inasmuch as for Venezuela. In fact, the point is precisely that business interests lie *outside* the leading sector, oil, which is in government and multinational hands. This makes business associations and networks fundamentally weaker and dependent on government. An encompassing association emerges because multisectoral alliances are crucial given the strength of the government position. A lack of capital specificity develops because of the need to preserve options as the solidity of the oil-based model weakens. At this point the business-as-capital framework—the first category—becomes relevant.

The emphasis on the sectoral stories coincides with Shafer's in Chapter 4, as does the centrality of the issue of the management of change. But the role of the sectors is distinct. Where Shafer is seeking to explain the *constraints* on the ability of the state to restructure, we find that history yields insights about different sectors' need for government of different kinds, with consequences for institutional development and therefore in due course for policy styles, coherence, and efficacy.

Because we have found that the export economy histories influence in a complex way both of the issues raised by Schneider and Maxfield, we have given the chapter the following form. First, we provide a summary of each export economy history, its connection to the emerging business-state relationship, and the relevance of that connection to the management of change. We then turn to a comparative analysis of why Colombia is the exception to the rule. Our underlying framework owes much to Douglass North and other writers following him (see North 1990). The appropriate institutions to facilitate structural change (in their wide Northian sense) do not come from nowhere or automatically. Different export economy structures provide different needs for and impetus to the development of institutions. Path dependency is important, particularly because the institutions responding to the needs of a period of export expansion may or may not be helpful when the issue becomes one of structural change. The response to the needs and impetus of the different periods has much to do with dealing with transactions costs and externalities at the microlevel. We find, however, that the need for collective action may be as much at the macro- or mesolevel (such as pressures for appropriate exchange rates) as it is at the microlevel. Transactions have costs—for example, seeking information or convoking other actors to secure a united bargaining front. They also involve prices that may be to a greater or lesser extent negotiated—for example, by behind-the-scenes pressure for an exchange-rate change—where it is mesolevel collective action that is required. Thus, the costs of managing the terms of transactions may be as important as direct transactions costs per se and associated externalities.

We find that institutional evolution responds to two sets of variables—power and control on the one hand, trust and reciprocity on the other—and that these may interrelate in an interesting way. For example, a highly oligarchic and paternalistic society may use vertical relations of trust and reciprocity as instruments of control, and this may explain certain characteristics of institutions as they develop.

Finally, we focus on export economy histories but acknowledge that many other factors intervene as well that go beyond the scope of this chapter. We signal some, such as the role of crisis and the threat of social upheaval, but recognize that our coverage is not adequate. The chapter should be regarded as no more than a building block in a complex edifice.

COLOMBIAN COFFEE: CONSERVATISM AND COOPERATION

Colombia is an extreme example where the nature of the export economy explains the generation of rather successful institutional development. Predominantly in the hands of small-scale farmers from the 1910s on, the expansion of coffee presented a strong challenge that met with an exceptional response. Colombian coffee is of very high quality;

and its successful marketing, when produced on a small scale, requires careful warehousing and quality control despite distances and large numbers of producers. The transactions costs implicit in the associated monitoring activities and the economies of scale possible in warehousing formed an impetus over time to institutional development of an exceptional kind.

The international situation was also important: from the turn of the century Brazil began to intervene in the coffee market with attempts to buy up stocks and hold up the price. Brazil's search for collaboration in its attempts to restrict supply was a further incentive to producer interests in Colombia to develop ways of responding coherently. From the earliest days, the large coffee firms were already answering some of these needs—in particular, the Casa López.[1] But early in the 1920s these needs produced a more formal and eventually more wide-ranging response. Significantly, it was the government of Antioquia, the state at the heart of the recent expansion of small coffee producers, that convened a coffee congress backed by municipal governments and agricultural societies (Bates, forthcoming). The Congress called for the formation of the Coffee Federation of Colombia—the FNC.

Under the aegis of the FNC, there followed a rapid expansion of warehousing, financing, and services of all kinds. Here, the ability to command political influence was crucial: Coffee was widespread, and even in non-coffee departments, the role of coffee in the business of the ports and financial institutions was crucial.

Government backing of the federation was important. From the start the federation had the right to collect taxes, which resolved a typical collective-action dilemma by providing resources. Hence, from the very beginning it reaped the rewards of political influence and in due course became even more influential in the public sector, from the national to the local level. Coffee committees existed at all these levels, right down to the municipal; and farmers found their committees vital in intermediating their relations with the state, not simply in regard to direct production needs but gradually extending to a wide range of services. Among both large and small producers, a solid tradition grew up of maintaining a positive and beneficial relation with the state that extended far beyond coffee. The benefits of belonging, and the all-encompassing nature of the federation's activity, meant that from an early date the exit costs were, and were perceived to be, high.

Initially, the federation did little direct marketing where it had to carve its way. The private exporters formed their own association in 1933 in

[1] President López claims that his family's firm was from an early date playing many of the roles that the federation went on to play more comprehensively (interview, April 30, 1996, London).

response to the need to defend themselves against the FNC. Even here, however, the FNC gradually assumed an important role, its market share rising to 30 percent of coffee exports by the 1960s and a peak of 95 percent by 1980.[2] The relation with non-FNC exporters was always one of both conflict and symbiosis. The private exporters were useful to the federation because the United States would never accept trade with a single producer and the federation would at times have found it difficult to buy the entire harvest. The FNC was useful to the private exporter because it intervened effectively in economic policy in the interests of the whole sector, developed technology and new markets, and bargained effectively in the International Coffee Organization (once it was formed). At the same time, naturally, the private sector resisted the controls and taxes imposed by the FNC, and the FNC tended to view the private exporters as free riders or speculators.[3]

Thus, the federation began as an association representing producers. Nevertheless, it is crucial to understand that the FNC was principally controlled by people whose interests lay in diverse fields, always including the commercialization of coffee but rarely its production except in small scale. From the early days, the federation was in effect a multisectoral association. What contributed to this was the fact that coffee production in itself requires little subsequent investment once the plantation is established. There was thus a need for deployment of surplus funds in other ways. From early on, important coffee people were also looking for outlets in commerce, real estate, industry, shipping, and finance. It was only logical that the federation should put its funds into an institution with responsibility for developing activities far beyond the direct productive interest of the coffee sector.[4] This move interacted with the fact that macro variables such as the real exchange rate were crucial for the health of the coffee sector: federation leaders had a strong motivation to seek influence in policy formulation, and the political importance of the first leaders of the association gave it to them.[5] This importance was consolidated as the association's activities reached into every aspect of economic life and was maintained by the credibility of the federation. The FNC has

[2] FNC, *Boletín estadístico*, various years. The situation has changed since then under pressure from the multilaterals and the prevailing neoliberal consensus, which sees it as inappropriate that the FNC should dominate the market and play the two roles of policy management and direct seller in the market.

[3] Interviews conducted by Martha Delgado in Bogotá in April 1996 with Gabriel Rosas, Roberto Junguito, José Leivobich, Manuel Banquero, and Sergio Clavijo. We are indebted to Martha Delgado for her assistance.

[4] On the history of the Fondo Nacional del Café, see Junguito 1978, Junguito and Pizano 1993, Beyer 1947, Palacios 1979, and Arango 1982. Each of these sources has an extensive bibliography.

[5] The general manager has been a member of CONPES, the key policy-making body, from its inception. But the real influence has been informal and personal, and predates CONPES.

been justly famous for having had only three general managers in the course of its nearly seventy years of life—all of them people of enormous stature and quality. The professionalism of the federation rapidly became a visible source of its credibility, creating a self-reinforcing process.

Three other outstanding characteristics of this political economy are relevant to our analysis. First, we need to consider the significance of the absence of foreigners in production. The major export sector was thus locally controlled. Needs that might have been answered if foreign investment had been present (such as the building of railways and roads and the acquiring of management know-how and skills) required a domestic response. So the incentive to lobby the state, find funds for public works, and insist they be continued even in the face of the Depression was undiluted by easier options.

Second, the regional diffusion of coffee, plus its production characteristics and its local control, led to a remarkably wide stimulus to industrialization; the consolidation of a number of regional centers of industry; and, with that consolidation, regional elites. Colombia is today one of the least centralized of Latin American states. Ocampo and Reveiz (1979) attribute the sophistication of political management in contemporary Colombia in part to the resulting need to develop political transaction mechanisms between regional elites.

Third, notwithstanding this regional strength of elites, the whole system coheres into a tightly knit and stable oligarchic political system in which its members all speak to and know each other. The closeness of the elite, even across the party divide, also allows experts to join rival-party administrations with remarkable freedom, which assists quality and continuity. This results in tight networks and security of access: "The private sector feels it has—and has had—excellent access to the public sector. The professional associations—particularly ANDI [Asociasión Nacional de Industriales]—are enormously influential. There is equal and amazing access under *any* presidency—even to the president himself."[6]

ANDI is invited by the government to hold forums on issues such as tax reforms; its role in molding opinion is consciously used and respected. Of course, the degree of influence of different sectors varies with different regimes; the manufacturing sector was not center stage during the Turbay or Lopez regimes, for example. Yet it is striking that all sectors insist that access remains good: "There is a widespread confidence that the web of friendships and contacts is such that interests will be sensibly looked after. Thus with regard to an import control policy, for example, there is trust that the system will be 'reasonably' operated. This does not mean that some abstract and neutral system will arbitrate, but that rea-

---

[6] Interview with Fabio Echeverri, president of ANDI, July 1987, Bogotá.

sonable common sense and practicality will prevail" (Thorp 1991: 197–89).[7] Entering government is prestigious and further develops networks; thus, individuals move frequently between the state and the private sector.[8]

We cannot stress too heavily, therefore, that coffee interests interact with a political system and a social structure that preceded coffee. First, what coffee has done is to stimulate the building of a strong organization at the heart of the institutionality of the sector, providing a focus of trust and reciprocity at the elite level that has cemented the oligarchic system. Second, the fact that the dominant interests in that organization have *not* been producer interests but spread across commerce, finance, and industry has aided the way in which coffee development has meshed with the growth of the economy. Third, the nature of the organization has built a system of co-optation down the line to very small producers, allowing a system of vertical trust and reciprocity to be used for power and control. Fourth, over time, the productive needs of the key interests have centered the organization on securing good private and public management. Colombian bureaucracy is little different from the Latin American norm when it comes to mismanagement and corruption, but this is widely acknowledged not to be true of the highest levels of management.

If we now turn to observe our dependent variable—the management of change—we find in comparative terms some exceptional results. The 1930s presented the first major challenge: Colombia practiced pragmatic Keynesian policies earlier and more coherently than anywhere else in Latin America.[9] By the 1940s those Latin American countries far enough advanced to be involved in import-substituting industrialization were implementing policies that discriminated heavily against agriculture and the primary sector in general, at great cost for the future. Colombia was unique in the way in which it avoided such pitfalls, finding ways to build in the interests of both industry and agriculture in response to the encompassing nature of the interests behind the FNC (Thorp 1991: 18). The exceptionality of Colombian performance is too consistent to be ignored.

Such examples have a fairly direct relationship to productive interests. But there are also instances where sound policies may require immediate distance from productive interests yet the autonomy so evidenced needs to leave intact the credibility and wider relations of trust that sustain the

---

[7] The interviews on which this section is based were carried out in 1987 by Thorp.

[8] Rodrigo Llorente tells how a Frenchman, looking at his curriculum vitae, exclaimed in horror at his number of moves. When Llorente recounted the story to President Alberto Lleras, Lleras explained his bottle theory: In most countries, one can think of a particular career as a bottle, with many insiders fighting to make it to the top of the bottle and few succeeding. Colombia has discovered that one advances much better by jumping from bottle to bottle (interview, Rodrigo Llorente, 1987, Bogotá).

[9] This is demonstrated in Thorp and Londoño 1984.

confidence of business groups. Colombia seems to have been able to walk this tightrope. One outstanding example is the policy of foreign borrowing in the mid-1970s. At a moment when every other Latin American country with any international credit standing was rushing to borrow abroad, the core policy team in Colombia decided this reaction would be foolish and would endanger Colombian development of internal sources of finance. The team implemented a policy that was extremely unpopular with the business elite and indeed with many elements in the wider public sector. But with hindsight it has been clearly recognized as a prudent policy and has played its part in building the credibility of Colombian macro policy-making in general. Another example is the management of devaluation in 1985: To achieve the amazing result of a 30 percent devaluation in one year with no acceleration of inflation, complete secrecy had to be observed and the gains negotiated away from the hands of coffee producers to avoid demand effects. The story (told in detail in Thorp 1991) is remarkable for both its subtlety and the relative autonomy it reveals. Again, it served to reinforce the image of coherence and efficacious policy, so much so that the use of secrecy apparently did not damage trust.

In building this evident degree of trust, confidence, and credibility, there was both a necessary degree of relative autonomy and a degree of trust and confidence. Combining professional top-level policy management with a high level of trust and credibility has produced the possibility of policies that are relatively autonomous from immediate interests that yet do not damage relations of trust and confidence or security of access.

The issue thrown up by this discussion, and one demanding research, is the nature of rent seeking in this undoubtedly clientelistic but still relatively functional system. Doner and Ramsay provide interesting comparative material on Thailand in Chapter 9. They argue that the competition in corruption—competitive clientelism—keeps distortions and inefficiencies within bounds because favors can be obtained from more than one government agency. This is not the Colombian model. Rather, we suggest that the force of a common culture and interest in growth, plus the professionalism of the FNC, provide relative insulation from clientelistic pressures in key areas of economic management.[10]

The fluid and effective relations at the elite level that we have described are quite distinct from the social capital concept elaborated by Putnam (1993a) to explain the difference between northern and southern Italy.

---

[10] An interesting area for speculation is the effect of having sizable opportunities for illegal profit at hand in the form of the drug industry. It was suggested at the second workshop for this volume that this might lessen pressure for directly unproductive activities in the legal section of the economy.

Putnam argues that effective government can be causally linked to relations of cooperation and trust that permeate far more deeply into a society than the case we are discussing here. He is describing horizontal association at a civic level: Colombia has been characterized by essentially vertical clientelistic relationships in general but with this orizontal elite-level characteristic of cooperation and reciprocity. The vertical element uses trust and reciprocity to maintain control. This opens up deep issues of what the business-state relationship in and of itself can and cannot explain, a point we return to in the conclusion. For now, we underline that there are important reservations about what sounds like an ideal system. First, in the past decade many of Colombia's characteristics have been changing toward a less stable and probably less efficient situation. Discussion of this situation needs more space than we have available but is a fundamental qualification. Second, many actors both inside and outside the public sector are extremely critical of policy-making and the state apparatus. The system is run in the interests of a fairly narrow elite, and those interests extend only to a select range of issues. Social policy in Colombia is not progressive.

Peru: Conflict and Incoherence

In sharp contrast to Colombia, Peru's export history has been dominated by a diversity of products and has been fast growing in expansion periods of the world economy. The richness of Peru's mineral wealth brought foreign investment at an early date: The close relationship between coffee and the state in Colombia was replicated by the relationship between the private sector and foreigners in Peru. The state was important to maintain order and a liberal regime attractive to foreign capital, but basically the opportunities for the local business elite to cooperate with foreign capital and make money meant that they could afford to neglect the building up of coalitions to press for diversification of the economy or even for infrastructure for exporting. Foreign capital built the railroads, provided the know-how and the contacts for marketing and technological improvement, and allowed Peruvian businesspeople a place in the sector. The symbiotic relationship thus established in, for example, the copper sector contrasts with the case of Chile, where groups excluded by foreign capital formed the basis for pressure for policies to provide opportunities elsewhere in the economy. Thus, where the Colombian state was gaining experience in intervention and management as early as the 1930s, a laissez-faire government in Peru followed classical policies and waited for the recovery of the international market. When an administration did attempt intervention, as with the Bustamante regime of the 1940s, the lack of a coherent base behind the policies and the lack of experience meant that the episode was disastrous and pushed policy-making choices firmly back to laissez-faire.

As a consequence of this pattern of development, the nurturing of business associations and traditions of collective lobbying and other forms of collective action were never of principal importance to the key elite actors; and the role of such associations therefore remained weak and peripheral. The strong presence of foreign firms and close links of individuals with such firms filled the need that in Colombia required collective action. The important Cuerpo de Ingenieros de Minas (Peruvian Engineers' Association) of the first decade of the century declined as foreign interests took the lead in the mining sector, and it was never rivaled in its strength and coherence by any subsequent organization. Various factors contributed to this fact. The key elite interests required relatively limited roles of the state, had excellent access for such manipulation as they required without formal organizations, and tended to have interests in several sectors as a natural risk-minimizing strategy. Diversity was in evidence in the 1920s and 1930s, when any significant figure in the mining sector would also have interests in, for example, sugar and commerce/industry. The resulting groups were characteristically built around a single core family, an informal network as identified by Schneider and Maxfield.[11] This emerges clearly in the first study of such interlocking interests, carried out in the 1960s (Malpica 1968). The solidity of the elites' network with international capital reinforced internal class structures and further weakened the chance of business associations' emerging to prominence. As one participant said, "The oligarchy look down at us and many at the SNI [Sociedad Nacional de Industrias] were afraid to challenge their power in the 1960s."[12]

The efficiency of the way in which the elite achieved informal access and control reduced the importance of building formal organizations to secure it. The modus operandi of the elite can be observed in a particularly illuminating document from the 1940s and 1950s: the Klein correspondence. This is a correspondence file from the Gildemeister sugar estate now held in the Centro de Documentación Agraria, Lima. The file is labeled "Klein" because many of the letters concern the 1949 visit of the foreign consultancy group known as the Klein-Saks mission. The letters involve the correspondence of Augusto Gildemeister with Pedro

[11] Examples are Wiese (mining, hotels, and import commerce), Bentín (real estate, cotton platations, and breweries), Brescia (grain farming, urban land, and mining), and Romero (cotton export and plantations). See Vásquez 1995.

[12] Interview by Durand with an industrialist and member of the SNI, May 1986, Lima.

Beltrán, a businessman with his principal interest in cotton and, in the 1940s, Peruvian ambassador in Washington, and with Douglas Heddon Allen, a New York business consultant with interests in the Amazon. In the letters we observe, for instance, how foreign pressure is mobilized over the exchange rate. Beltrán is asked by Gildemeister to mobilize Cerro de Pasco Copper Corporation in New York: "Perhaps we might get them as allies so as not to be the only ones who are complaining about putting the brakes on deliveries of dollars" (A.G. to P.B., August 10, 1948). Care is taken that such pressures should appear to be independent. The U.S. Chamber of Commerce is persuaded to cable approval of the freeing of the exchange rate (November 11, 1949). The Klein mission is carefully supervised, directly and indirectly (D.H.A. to A.G., November 21, 1948; A.G. to P.B., November 3, 1950), and used to apply pressure for the lifting of import controls.[13]

The importance of the diversity of export products is that, rather than build an overt campaign on a point of sectoral interest, it was often more rational to switch and develop other activities. The core of such activities was always the family. (The development of such family groups has been documented by Vásquez 1995).[14] These groups provided classic networks of trust and reciprocity.

Only crisis served to break the pattern of lack of interest in any kind of institutionalizing of an encompassing association. Twice, in 1930 and again in 1945–48, fear of mass mobilization and a sudden unaccustomed need to build relations with the incoming government led to collective-action initiatives. In 1930 Pedro Beltrán and the Sociedad Nacional Agraria (SNA) formed the Unión Social, together with the Sociedad Nacional de Industrias and the Cámara de Comercio. Once the danger passed, interest lapsed. Similarly in 1945 a committee of eight trade associations led by the SNA was formed to stop unionism, the then-left-wing Aprista party's influence on the Bustamante government, and the threat of interventionist policies. Again, with the conservative military coup of 1948, the danger passed and the effort faded.

As Thorp and Bertram (1978) explain, this model broke down in the 1960s, when the period of easy supply-side expansion came to an end and the next stage of expansion demanded more in terms of entrepreneurship and management than the system could provide. The politics of the model also broke down with growing discontent with the oligarchic system and the division of spoils. In the chaos of the next twenty years, when the weak institutions and weak state inherited from the previous model tried and failed in numerous different manifestations to put the economy and

---

[13] These are only a few of many examples; the correspondence is reviewed in Thorp 1974.
[14] Vásquez documents how groups interacted with the state over time.

society back on an even keel, various disasters turned what had previously been a low-level relationship between business elites and government into a strong and antagonistic relationship.[15]

The decisive factor was the takeover of export interests by the new military elite, which came to power in 1968. A new system began to evolve whereby control of export resources was used by state elites to impose from above a pattern of noninstitutionalized conditional relationships with different segments of the business class, which was itself too disarticulated to find a coherent strategy in reply. The increasingly bad relationship and the lack of channels of communication, accentuated by the lack of strong professional organizations able to provide expert advice and convoke a broad membership, played a part in the weak economic management and poorly constructed policies of this twenty-year period.[16] On the side of business, the sector has typically had little vision and has sought particular and often personal benefits. The level of party involvement has always been low. A prominent entrepreneur said: "We have concerned ourselves with having the right connections and looking for our friends in government so that we can obtain price increases, foreign currency and credit facilities" (Gabriel Lanatta, *El Comercio*, April 17, 1987). Government, on its side, has sought to make the most of the divisions in the movement to weaken further the associations' role. Velasco began this with what became known as his sausage policy: taking the business sector by slices. He would isolate trade associations who opposed reforms and give preferential treatment to those willing to support the government. Co-optation of individual businesspeople occurred with invitations to membership in advisory committees or the president's inner circle. The basic characteristics of the "slicing" policy continued through Morales Bermúdez and Belaúnde into García's government. García sought alliances with certain elements sometimes precisely to exclude others (Durand 1994: 122).[17] As business associations were weakened and the environment became more unpredictable, the family groups remained and became more defensive and adaptive in their strategies (Vásquez 1995).

At the same time the perception of the business sector, with reason, was that the government did not understand or in any way seek to use the sector for the skills and advice it could give. The government did not seek to inform, nor did it trust the sector. Basically, investment was simply

---

[15] See Wise 1993a for a vivid description of this deterioration, in which the role of Velasco was crucial. See also Durand 1982.

[16] The following paragraphs draw on Durand 1994.

[17] Manuel Ulloa, minister of finance and a businessman himself, said at the annual meeting of entrepreneurs (CADE) in 1980: "El Perú es un país archipiélago, se negocia con cada quien por separado [Peru is like an archipelago; you negotiate separately with each bit]."

expected to occur without the prior establishment of credibility. Thus, policies were not transacted with the business sector or attuned to their needs. From interviews conducted in the García period, we sensed an unbridgeable gap, a lack of communication: "No one in the government understands the world of business."[18]

As time passed, the weakness of the institutions within the business sector and the lack of consultation became a vicious circle. A key actor in the recent reform of Superintendencia Nacional de Administración Tributaria (SUNAT), the tax administration, stated: "We didn't dare open the gates to negotiation. We knew we'd be overwhelmed." Without mature bodies of negotiators with clear proposals and agendas, and with no tradition of consultation, it appeared impossible to proceed.[19]

Perhaps the climax of the deterioration, as well as a vivid demonstration of its costs, came in 1987. Initially, Garcia had considerable goodwill to draw on because the experience with the previous government had been so bad that businesspeople longed to believe in the new alternative. There was also an effort to consult. But it proved impossible to change the institutional fabric: As one businessman commented, "there's a tremendous gap between the concept and its execution. People hear this marvelous stuff about 'concertación' and the Fondo de Inversiones, but when they go to COFIDE, to the price control committee, to the BCR for imports, they get a negative response."[20] The end of that particular period is well known: García lost all patience and decided to nationalize the banks, and relations broke down completely.

Again, however, crisis stimulated a response—this time, it appears, a more permanent change. As early as 1984, deepening crisis led to the formation of Confederación Intersectorial de las Empresas Peruanas (CONFIEP), an umbrella business organization. With "the battle of the banks," CONFIEP became consolidated and more articulate and was thus able to establish a stable relationship with Fujimori from the beginning of his government in 1990. Once the political and economic instability of the late 1980s and early 1990s was overcome, institutional consolidation became possible. Most legislation approved by Fujimori from the start was closely coordinated between government elites and CONFIEP's policy experts.[21]

The extreme lack of confidence resulting from this disastrous public-

---

[18] Interview, Gabriel Seminario, May 1987, Lima.

[19] This is based on the personal experience of Francisco Durand, director of SUNAT during the reform.

[20] Interview by Thorp with a leading industrialist, Juan Francisco Raffo, May 1987, Lima. COFIDE (Corporación de Finanzas para el Desarrollo) is the Development Funding corporation; the BCR is Peru's central bank.

[21] Interview by Durand with CONFIEP's manager, Arturo Tello, May 18, 1995, Lima.

private relationship is only, of course, part of the explanation of Peru's problems, but it is certainly significant. A policy such as import controls can be accepted in Colombia; in Peru it is dreaded, and with reason. In Colombia, virtuous circles operated; in Peru, the reverse. The more the mismanagement, the more the discrediting of policy and the less the willingness to take on a public-sector job. The rebuilding of the situation has to begin with fundamental political renovation and reconstruction of institutions. A viable state-business relationship can only come later as credibility is restored.

Venezuela: From Incest to Divorce

Like Colombia, Venezuela is an instance of a mono-economy; but unlike Colombia, it is characterized by abundance and fast growth of the source of foreign exchange over several decades, driven by direct foreign investment that for many years was seen as completely essential. As in any oil-led boom, the expansion of oil in the 1920s seriously weakened the profitability of agriculture and industry. Rural landlords moved their surplus to commerce, real estate, finance, and in negligible quantities to industry. An important consequence was that traders lost their profitable export business and had to rely on imports, using the state as the source of foreign exchange.

In fact, an industrial sector grew, despite the 1939 Treaty of Commercial Reciprocity with the United States, which committed Venezuela to forgoing tariffs on 50 percent of imports in return for quota access for oil to the U.S. market. World War II induced evasion of the treaty, and industry grew, protected by quotas. The impact of oil abundance was reflected in the assumption that there was room for everybody. The institutionalization of private-sector relations with government moved forward in an important step in 1944 with the formation of an umbrella organization, Fedecámaras, drawing together and reinforcing the chambers for industry, agriculture, and commerce. Industry-agriculture agreements were now set up, providing protection down the chain. Clear examples are textiles and canned vegetables. Cotton textile producers could only import cotton once the domestic supply was used up, but domestic supply was subsidized with cheap credit and favorable input prices. Garment producers likewise faced a quota on textile imports, but support to the textile producers made sure they found the situation manageable. Importers found the imposition of quotas manageable because imports in total were not falling. It was easy to shift into supplying local industry and sometimes to move further into direct production, often alongside commercial activity.

Organizations were created to implement all this. The Junta para el Fomento de la Producción Nacional had been created in 1944, the Corporación Venezolana de Fomento (CVF), in 1946. Fedecámaras not only had its own representatives on the board but also controlled the making of public-sector appointments. The political economy of this early period is thus rather clear. The state had the resources to provide something for everyone, and the private sector had ample access to the flow of benefits. Although the notion of "sowing the oil" was expressed as early as 1946, the driving force was one of seeking privileged access to the benefits of oil rather than any more coherent vision of Venezuela's long-run needs.

During the oil boom of the 1970s the corruption of abundance really came into play, with effects on the coherence of policy-making and the public-private relationship. The result of the oil boom was an explosion of fiscal revenue, pronounced overvaluation, and profound political economy effects. The availability of funds led to an explosion of state organizations. At the same time there was a growth in individual and personalistic relations with the state. The power of the executive grew with the concentration of revenue, and parties and congress were weakened. Meanwhile Fedecámaras was less central: it lacked mechanisms for reconciling conflicts between the various sectors it represented. When the important emerging industrial firms sent their managers to the Fedecámas meetings, they tended to rely on direct access to powerful decision makers, while new medium-sized interests entering Fedecámaras fought with established interests (Moncada 1995).

With this increased confusion and growth in personalism and patronage came a weakening of the model of accumulation. Dutch Disease Venezuelan-style took the form of protection through tariffs and quotas but with a flood of subsidized credit, which simply led to the accumulation of highly mobile funds elsewhere in the economy, leaving the economy vulnerable to subsequent capital flight. Meanwhile public enterprises borrowed abroad, and total debt and foreign exchange reserves rose. Oil was nationalized in 1976.

The increasingly disjointed political economy went along with the collapse of what Ricardo Hausmann describes as "the rules of the game" over a long period of Venezuelan economic history. He explains how for many years the simple fixing of the exchange rate and the interest rate and a public-sector rule of spending what you have served Venezuela remarkably well as straightforward ways of resolving values for macrovariables that the society lacked the institutions to resolve in a more complex and subtle fashion (Hausmann 1990: 341).[22] After 1973, exchange-rate stability in nominal terms led to increasing overvaluation; and "spending

[22] The exchange-rate stability dates from the previous century, with the exception of 1960.

what it got" was overwhelming as oil revenue soared and endless possibilities of funds from abroad seemed to open up. From 1978 on, the interest-rate side also became more complex as international rates adjusted upward. Responding to both overvaluation and a growing interest-rate differential, and feeling the impact of technological change and institutional developments that were drawing Latin America irrevocably into operating in world capital and finance markets in a new way and into an international sphere of operations, the everpresent phenomenon of capital flight took on new dimensions. Rather than mirroring in Frieden's analysis—more specificity equaling more threat (see Chapter 2)—it was the reverse: The increased *lack* of specificity allowed the threat of exit.

The 1980s were disastrous years of mismanaged controls and capital flight. There was an abrupt change from a stable and viable political economy of fixed rules to one that Hausmann—hopeful but ironic—calls an "excellent" political economy. He is referring to its outstanding characteristic of something for everyone (Hausmann 1990). Nevertheless, because it was underpinned with no mechanisms for softening or rationalizing interventionist policies and had a deteriorated set of institutions after the personalism and clientelism of the 1970s, it was *no* political economy, given the swings in key variables. The only easy survival route or defense mechanism was a dollar portfolio. To survive such an unstable environment and manage a productive enterprise needs planning ability and a long-run view of the economy. This was not Venezuela in the 1980s.

Basically, the story we are telling is one of a classic oil-economy relationship, with the business class highly and profitably dependent on the state for protection and subsidy. Under the influence of extreme bonanza and subsequent mismanagement, this relationship deteriorated into the worst kind of short-term and individualistic rent seeking and profit taking, with extensive use of capital flight and virtually no domestic investment or productivity-increasing measures. The chaos and corruption were such by 1989 that the "Gran Viraje," or turnaround, of the new president, Carlos Andrés Pérez, was understandable. The only solution appeared to be the ending of every possible form of rent seeking by ending controls and as far as possible every type of government intervention. Under the influence of a team of technocrats led by Miguel Rodríguez, the decision was to go for a radical market model.

As is now widely acknowledged by the actors involved, the political economy of this shift was a disaster, akin to going from incest to an abrupt divorce instigated by one partner with no attempt at counseling or intermediation. The failure to understand the needs of the business sector was paralleled by the utter failure to understand the social situation in which the adjustment was occurring. On neither front was there any communication. This was vividly expressed by one member of the team: "The language was new, almost incomprehensible to most producers. It made them feel inadequate, dumb. They felt insulted" (Coles 1993: n.p.). There was also a failure to understand the need to build consensus and the importance of the relationship with the private sector.[23] Another member of the team said: "We thought we had Superman on board and that was enough. Unfortunately we didn't realize that Superman no longer had his party's backing and that this would matter" (Interamerican Development Bank 1993: 19). The assumption in regard to the business sector was expressed in an interview with Pedro Tinoco. He had no doubts about entrepreneurs' capacity to respond to the stimulus of market forces in Venezuela: "When you loose a mad dog, it is remarkable how fast people learn to jump over a wall."[24]

The significance of the clear move to absence of relationship is huge and was demonstrated in the reversal of policies with the next government. As Silva argues elsewhere in this book, the situation paralleled the first phase of Chilean neoliberal policies. On top of the shared false assumptions that Silva documents, we would add the specificity of oil: To combine oil and a market economy is to take on an exceptionally delicate task. The past means that tradables other than oil are extremely underdeveloped. There was little investment in industry in the 1980s and, as we have seen, years of declining productivity. There was thus a backlog of investment required if enterprises were to compete on the world market. At the same time many elements of a modern economy were missing. Technology policy, for example, had not adapted to the conditions of modern technical innovation. And Venezuelan business groups hold substantial assets abroad. In addition, when the exchange rate is determined by oil prices, as is still the case for Venezuela, businesspeople need special reassurance that commitment to the market will not leave them exposed to the vagaries of the oil market, with its constant threat of overvaluation. In many interviews and conversations in 1993, Venezuelan businssmen were quite clear that conditions in no way existed to bring money back: "We have *no* relations with government."

FINAL REFLECTIONS: THE NATURE OF THE INSTITUTIONAL
CHALLENGE AND RESPONSE

Every sectoral story reveals that an institutional challenge is there in principle, whether it be how to diffuse oil revenues through the economy, how to maintain the quality of coffee, or how to market good-quality

---

[23] Silva eloquently documents this failure in Chapter 6.
[24] Interview with Thorp, 1992, Oxford.

cotton successfully. But the stories we have told here suggest that only under quite special conditions does this challenge take a form that leads to effective building of institutions in the crucial area of public sector-private sector relations. More case studies are needed to build a strong analytical picture, but a number of elements can be discerned from the case studies we present.

First, it is notable that even in our most favorable instance of spontaneous generation of institutionality—the FNC—the catalyst was the departmental government of Antioquia. The response relied at least in part on an impulse from the state. Giving the right to collect taxes was a further significant impulse from the national level.

Second, it is important to whom the revenue accrues. The fact that Venezuelan oil revenue is received in the public sector, initially as tax and subsequently via direct ownership, means that the state in economic terms is autonomous. This implies that the private sector has to concentrate its efforts in institution building on constructing and securing access routes to rents. No such issue arises in the case of coffee growers. The fact of foreign ownership precipitated in the Peruvian case the seeking of alliances to get access to profit opportunities and diverted attention from the state as an ally. Velasco's assumption of control over export sectors was crucial in the ensuing redefining of relations with business.

This is reinforced by the third factor, the role of the foreigner. The fact that foreign firms can build infrastructure and provide marketing skills again diverts attention from the Peruvian state. The lack of interest of foreigners in coffee production makes the state a crucial ally in providing infrastructure—for example, in building Colombian rail and road networks in the 1920s. Relations with the state must therefore be invested in and developed with care.

A fourth factor is the weight of a particular sector in the economy. Coffee was determinant for Colombia at the macrolevel: The pressure on the state could therefore be successful in a way that the needs of Peruvian sectors that were typically only 20 percent of exports could never be. The coherence of interests given by the common link of coffee added a solidity to the relationship of trust and reciprocity constituting the embeddedness of the business-state relationship in Colombia that would have been hard to replicate with the diverse base of Peru. Coffee-related interests in Colombia managed to have the best of two worlds because they were both sectoral and encompassing. There is a down side to export diversity. Copper or sugar in Peru could be ignored or even taxed where for decades coffee in Colombia could only be taxed by promising all the revenues to the FNC. The down side is allowed to persist by the simple fact that diversity gives producers other options.

Fifth, it also matters how rapidly the sector grows. Fast growth of oil revenues gave Venezuela Dutch-disease problems from an early date: From the 1930s it was not profitable to invest elsewhere in the economy unless support was provided. The close relationship produced by the concentration of revenue in the state was therefore pushed in a rent-seeking direction by the simple fact that little else but rent seeking was worthwhile. The Colombian need for the state was fostered in the healthier climate of relatively slow growth of coffee plus limited investment needs within the sector. The interest of the elite was good productivity conditions in coffee but also elsewhere in the economy.

Sixth, the exact nature of the institutional challenge is important. Does it invite a response emphasizing productivity and inclusion of all producers in whatever institutional arrangements are developed? This seems to have been the logic of the Colombian situation. Thus, the resulting producers' association must in some sense be inclusive. Further, in the Colombian case the nature and importance of the need for monitoring and control were significant in producing the strength of the institutional response. There was no point in the larger producers' controlling the quality and carefully marketing their own production if the reputation of Colombian coffee could be sabotaged by small producers who were not complying with standards. Therefore, what are the specific infrastructure needs? Are such needs within the financial/entrepreneurial capacity of the government? If not, this will encourage actors to seek alliances outside.

Seventh, the political-social structure is relevant. Colombia's elite political system is fundamental to the ease with which various collective-action problems were overcome. Elite producer groups, or elite groups of merchants and financiers in the Colombian case, were rather centralized in character and tended to facilitate collaboration. In addition, the degree of stability or instability is relevant. Compared to Colombia or Venezuela, Peru's greater instability never fostered the establishment of normal, institutionalized business-government relations.

Our eight and ninth points concern path dependence. Its importance is clear when there are strong cumulative elements at work. For instance, an efficient organization emerging out of the initial challenge may go on to assume more roles, such as influence on general macro policy, as with the coffee federation. Success will breed success. The size of surplus in the sector and its reinvestment needs will be relevant. If there is surplus available for investment elsewhere, this will be important in developing a supersectoral character for the institution, which in the course of time may make it well adapted to facilitating and accommodating necessary structural change. Again, we have Colombia in mind.

Finally, crisis (and other factors we may not have identified here) can break patterns. Attempts at disrupting the pattern in Peru have all occurred in the face of threat—and perhaps at last successfully.

These ten elements have emerged out of our three stories to explain how Colombia has been historically the exception to the general rule. Because of the special characteristics of the coffee economy and culture, which interacted with the elite nature of Colombian society, an encompassing association emerged that was unusually qualified by its multisectoral interests, professionalism, and elite relations to transact change. It was able to penetrate policy-making formally and informally and create a culture of positive and fluid relations and a credibility of policy-making that went far beyond coffee. This enhanced performance by generating a learning-by-doing attitude that was never strongly at variance with productive interests. Thus, both of the questions with which we began—*how* business-state relations may enhance performance and *why* on occasion they do not deteriorate into rent seeking—are answered from the same set of special characteristics.

Two important reflections remain, both of them reservations. First, this chapter has argued that the extraordinarily different degrees of efficacy we observe today in the functioning of the business-state relationship in our three cases can indeed be related back to the very different sectoral stories that produced them. But we insist that other elements impinge as well, especially class structures, which themselves are only partially explained by the export economy structures. It still seems that, even for the FNC, the state was a trigger mechanism. Other intangibles also come in: For instance, Colombia's caution in regard to foreigners has been a significant part of that country's political economy; and while that caution is permitted by its export history to a degree difficult for an oil or mineral economy, we do not see that it has been caused by that history. But we hope we have shown that there is enough value in this line of exploration to justify more inquiry.

Second, none of the different export economy histories we have described have been associated with particularly democratic social structures or with social capital à la Putnam. In this they are all similar, which underlines the point just reiterated—that many other elements intervene here. Colombia's clientelistic political structures assimilated and used the relations of trust engendered by coffee and the FNC to reinforce the traditional structures. Effective government has thus been limited to the kind of efficient management the elite considered to be in its interest. Effective social policy has not been a characteristic of Colombia nor has effectiveness in many other areas, such as investment planning or even industrial policy. The rent seeking typical of clientelistic politics has prevailed. Effective business-government relations achieve much, but only so much. As Colombia has moved away from coffee, the lack of effectiveness in other areas has become more evident and more costly.

Chapter Nine

Competitive Clientelism and Economic Governance: The Case of Thailand

Richard F. Doner and Ansil Ramsay

Scholars have associated public-private sector collaboration with strong economic performance in Taiwan and South Korea. This collaboration involves systematic information exchange and reciprocity between a coherent, capable state and groups of entrepreneurs. As such, collaboration can be understood as a form of economic governance—a mechanism through which firms and officials interact to address market failures in the form of resource scarcity, information complexity, and conflicts of interests (Hollingsworth and Lindberg 1985: 221). Collaboration can thus help to resolve collective action dilemmas—to facilitate economic activities that integrate particular interests with broader and longer-term development objectives. Institutions, such as state agencies, business associations, and public-private sector links, are typically critical to the overcoming of collective action problems.

The World Bank grudgingly acknowledges the benefits of these institutions in the northern tier of high-performing Asian economies—Taiwan, South Korea, and Singapore. But institutions are rare in the bank's account of growth in the resource-rich countries of Southeast Asia—Indonesia, Malaysia, and Thailand. High-performing economies in these countries, the bank argues, are largely the result of competitive markets and liberalization, not interactions between organized public and private sectors. Indeed, the bank suggests that such institutional interventions would create distortions in countries where states are incapable of imposing clear performance criteria on those receiving selective benefits and limiting the costs of such interventions (World Bank 1993a: 6). This position is in line with the neoliberal view that, "in settling matters of resource allocation, imperfect markets are better than imperfect states" (Colclough and Manor 1991: 7). This view seems especially relevant to the nations of Southeast Asia, whose states are so much less expert, cohesive, and insulated than those of the East Asian newly industrialized countries (NICs).

We take issue with this politics- and institution-free view of growth as it applies to the case of Thailand. Before outlining our specific arguments, let us stress that much of the neoliberal view does help to explain Thai economic performance. The state has helped to provide limited but important collective goods—infrastructure and macroeconomic stability. Thailand is known for fiscal caution, low inflation, staunch adherence to realistic and stable exchange rates, and successful economic reform during the 1980s (Muscat 1994; Warr 1993; Doner and Laothamatas 1994). Compared to many other developing countries, Thai governments have generally adopted a hands-off approach to the private sector. In many ways, this is fortunate because the Thai political economy has not exhibited the economy-wide systematic exchanges of information, reciprocity, transparency, and trust that facilitated growth in the NICs. The unity, independence, and expertise of Thailand's macroeconomic agencies have contrasted with fragmented political leadership and weak sectoral agencies. The business community, dominated by ethnic Chinese (Sino-Thai), who make up 10 percent of the population, has been politically weak for most of the country's history. Most peak business associations have been private and ineffectual, in part due to lack of support from political leaders and career state officials. Finally, relations between state and private sector have exhibited little systematic exchange. Rather than being dense and institutionalized, public-private sector ties have been diffuse, particularistic, personalized, and thus clientelist.[1]

How, then, do we explain Thailand's high growth rates and impressive structural change (Table 9.1)? More specifically, how do we account for the country's capacity to shift from agriculture to manufacturing, to move out of largely import-substitution production toward export-oriented growth, to diversify markets, and generally to advance from primary commodity exports to export processing assembly to component-supply subcontracting (Gereffi 1995)? This performance is even more puzzling given the well-known tendency of clientelist arrangements to result in either monopoly or dissipation of resources through rent seeking.

In response to this puzzle, we first draw attention to Thailand's particular form of clientelism. We acknowledge the importance of competitive

---

[1] *Density* refers to the number of access points between public and private actors and is a function of the level of government and business concentration and degree of differentiation between the two. *Institutionalization* refers to the degree to which links are systematic and function-based.

Table 9.1. Economic performance, Thailand, 1970–1992 (percent)

Growth rate	1970–1980	1980–1992
GDP	9.2%	4.2%
Agriculture	4.4	4.1
Industry	9.5	10.1
Manufacturing	10.5	10.1
Inflation	n.a.	4.2
Exports	10.3	14.7
Imports	5.0	11.5
Production as percent of GDP	**1970**	**1992**
Agriculture	26.0	12.0
Industry	25.0	39.0
Manufacturing	16.0	28.0
Services, etc.	49.0	49.0
Manufacturing	**1970**	**1991**
Food, beverages, tobacco	43.0	28.0
Textiles and clothing	13.0	24.0
Machinery, transportation equipment	9.0	14.0
Chemicals	6.0	3.0
Other	29.0	32.0
Exports	**1970**	**1992**
Fuels, minerals, metals	15.0	2.0
Other primary commodities	77.0	32.0
Machinery, transportation equipment	0.0	22.0
Other manufactures	8.0	45.0
Textiles and clothing	1.0	17.0

SOURCE: World Bank 1994, Tables 1, 2, 3, 6, 12, 13, 15.

markets, but we also allow for the possibility that markets and access to them are socially and politically constructed.[2] That is, competitive markets themselves require explanation. In the Thai case, competitive markets are in part the result of a particular structure of patron-client relations. Put simply, intra-elite rivalries led to a competitive rather than a monopolistic market for state-supplied goods and services. This pattern had several beneficial consequences. It compelled patrons to keep funds within the country because sending money abroad would have undermined their capacity to maintain support networks. It also opened opportunities for market entry to a variety of private clients. Because rents yielded to private firms through this process have generally been temporary, recipients have had to limit inefficient investments in anticipation of market competition. Indeed, this competition undermined the high rates of tariff protection operating in Thailand until the early 1990s.

But competitive clientelism can result in particularism and a host of related collective action problems. Our second argument is that the Thai

---

[2] On socially constructed markets, see Schmitter 1988.

economy, despite its lack of NIC-like institutions, has benefited from a range of public, mixed, and private institutional mechanisms addressing these problems. Consider first the structure and preferences of the state itself: For historical reasons the macroeconomic officials in Thailand's bifurcated state have been both highly sensitive to the dangers of government deficits and exchange-rate instability and institutionally capable of protecting fiscal decisions from political influence. This has had the important effect of limiting the rents available for deployment by political leaders and bureaucratic officials. In addition, state macroeconomic policies have fostered intersectoral transfers (through taxes on agriculture and limits to competition among large commercial banks), encouraged exports (through special, albeit limited, incentives), and facilitated the growth of local capacity in upstream and midstream sectors of the economy (through support for a giant, quasi-public enterprise group).

In addition to direct, albeit limited, interventions, state officials have influenced economic performance through links with the private sector in those sectors important to national fiscal health. This is in no small part a function of macroeconomic officials' traditional sensitivity to revenue shortages and is thus consistent with Schneider and Maxfield's emphasis in Chapter 1 on vulnerability as a source of pressure for collaboration. When exports and foreign exchange have declined, officials have pursued more systematic relations with business interests and encouraged more collective organization by them. The object of such efforts has been to promote measures (such as clear product standards, reduction in red tape, and national campaigns) that facilitate the country's exports.

Finally, despite its traditional weakness in the political realm, Sino-Thai business itself has been rich in institutions. Private-sector clients in Thailand thus exhibit a collective side. This structure does not obviate the politically atomizing consequences of clientelism found in many developing countries, but it does indicate a capacity for economic governance. Consistent with the arguments of Schneider and Maxfield in Chapter 1, business groups, commercial banks, and trust-based ethnic networks have contributed to economic performance by fulfilling such functions as spreading risks, overcoming labor market imperfections in new industries, and minimizing intersectoral conflict.

Our third argument is that Thailand's combination of competitive clientelism and institutional richness emerged under a particular set of external and domestic conditions. Externally, the menace of colonial powers instilled a fear of indebtedness and a corresponding commitment to fiscal conservatism on the part of state officials. At the same time, opportunities for exports to volatile markets encouraged the growth of a dominant rice sector composed of small farmers linked to foreign markets through ethnic Chinese millers, merchants, and bankers. As a result, a landed aristocracy did not emerge in Thailand. What did emerge was a commercial class whose economic position made it critical to the Thai elite but whose ethnic minority status made it politically subservient.

Very concerned about the dangers of indebtedness but forced to contend with open markets, Thai officials were acutely sensitive to the importance of business as capital, especially trade capital capable of generating critical foreign exchange (see Chapter 2). This pushed the state toward a de facto alliance with Sino-Thai business even as it strengthened the credibility of state macroeconomic agencies on issues of fiscal and monetary stability. Sectorally, the small farmer aspect of Thai agriculture not only deprived political leaders of landed supporters but also removed the threat of an entrenched, capital-demanding oligarchy capable of blocking reforms. The trade-dependent nature of the Chinese, meanwhile, encouraged an outward-looking trade regime. Finally, one also begins to see the importance of business as a range of institutions: as communal networks and associations protecting Sino-Thai interests, and as groups and firms helping both to generate needed foreign exchange and to perform the kind of domestic resource mobilization required by a state facing a leading sector of fragmented producers.

Our emphasis until now has been on the positive consequences of Thailand's competitive clientelism and collective institutional arrangements. Our final argument is that these benefits are limited to productive activities that do not require extensive industrial upgrading. More specifically, the Thai economy has grown by relying on a relatively protected domestic market and on exports of natural resources and light manufactured goods. This shift from primary commodity exports to export processing assembly and even some component-supply subcontracting has required little physical or human resource infrastructure capable of promoting technology absorption or providing intermediate and capital goods. As a result, neither state nor private sector, separately or together, was pressed to develop institutional capacities for extensive collective action. But by the 1980s, the country began to encounter falling commodity prices, agricultural stagnation, and competition from lower-wage neighbors. Thailand now faces the challenge of economic deepening and upgrading into the production of more sophisticated components and even original equipment (Gereffi 1995). But the country is plagued by severe bottlenecks in physical and human infrastructure as well as tensions between upstream and downstream firms. Thailand needs collective goods for which the country's previous growth has left it institutionally unprepared.

The next section explores the preceding issues through a chronological analysis that concludes with an examination of recent collective-action problems. In the final section, we review the main arguments through a comparison with the Philippines.

THAI CLIENTELISM

For most of Thai history, state-business relations took the form of links between Chinese entrepreneurs and individual Thai officials. These relationships were clientelist in the sense that they were particularistic and affective and occurred between individuals with clear status differentials. The higher status position of patrons (in this case, Thai officials) conferred upon them the capacity to control access to the means of production and major markets. Indeed, the core of the clientelist model is a relationship of power (Hutchcroft 1996: 8). It is an exchange relationship in which, on the one hand, "the client 'buys,' as it were, protection against the exigencies of the markets or of nature or of the arbitrariness or weakness of the center, or against the demands of other powerful groups or individuals" (Eisenstadt and Roniger 1980: 71). On the other hand, clients have their own leverage when patrons find themselves in precarious positions, especially in "situations of modernization or development, where the relatively high degree of flow of free resources makes the competition for any specific position intense" (Eisenstadt and Roniger 1980: 70).[3] We argue that Thai patrons experienced high levels of rivalry with each other in part because of an absence of ascriptive, corporate ties but also because they had no source of material benefits besides Chinese clients. As a result, clientelism tended to involve political protection of Chinese clients in exchange for political subordination and, more important, for material rewards from Chinese business.

This structure dominated the Thai political economy through the 1960s. Because it lowered market-entry barriers, clientelism helped to promote the growth of both the economy and the country's middle class. By the early to mid-1970s, economic and social development had undermined clientelism itself. By the late 1970s, the Thai political economy was a hybrid of clientelism, pluralism, and concertation. Economic reform efforts and intra-industry distributional conflicts pushed private-sector

---

[3] Clientelism may or may not involve corrupt practices. Whereas clientelism is, above all, a relationship of power based on status differentials and personal ties of reciprocity, corruption typically refers to the use of public office for private gain. Thus, when a patron occupies a public office and uses that office to extract particular benefits from a client, corruption and patronage overlap. But pure market corruption—that is, a one-time transaction lacking any affective ties or basis in status differential—is not considered clientelistic. For a helpful discussion of these issues, see Hutchcroft 1996: 8.

and state technocrats into extensive consultation during the 1980s. But this consultation focused largely on market expansion rather than industry or sectoral efficiency. And with economic recovery, a flood of foreign investment, and a more open political system, consultation literally evaporated for several years. Efforts at more collective economic governance resumed only in the early 1990s as Thailand began to encounter the challenges of economic upgrading and diversification. We first describe the key aspects of Thailand's political and institutional arrangements and then explore the links between these arrangements and economic growth.

Institutions and Clientelism

The period from the seventeenth to early twentieth centuries laid an initial base for Thailand's distinct combination of patron-client relations and institutional growth. The key development was an ethnic-based division of labor involving large numbers of small-scale Thai cultivators on the one hand and Chinese merchants and tax farmers on the other. This arrangement strengthened clientelism by making the Chinese politically vulnerable but indispensable sources of material benefits for an indigenous elite without links to a landed oligarchy. It strengthened fiscally conservative state institutions by precluding costly demands of a landed oligarchy and providing export revenues without requiring state investments. As we shall see, this division of labor also encouraged the growth of private-sector institutions to address the needs of processing, transport, finance, and revenue collection in an expanding export economy. Beginning in the early twentieth century, relations between Chinese entrepreneurs and Thai political elites became somewhat more organized. Organized clientelism combined with more insulated state macroeconomic institutions to generate significant economic growth after World War II.[4]

Private-Sector Institutions

Sino-Thai business interests themselves became more organized in the early twentieth century. One stimulus was rivalry with Western interests. As their economic role expanded, the Chinese began to confront Western competition in a number of sectors. The Chinese Chamber of Commerce was established in 1908 in response to Western competition and was followed by more specialized associations for insurance, rice merchants, and

[4] Useful summaries of early Thai economic development are found in Ingram 1971 and Brown 1988. On relations between Chinese merchants and Siamese elites, see Cushman 1993 and Hong 1984. The classic and still invaluable work on the Sino-Thai business community is Skinner 1957a.

others (Skinner 1957b: 170–71, 254–55). Associational growth reinforced the emergence of Sino-Thai institutions in banking. Initially acting as compradors—local merchants acting as intermediaries on behalf of foreign firms—for European banks during the late nineteenth century, the Chinese soon created their own banks to finance rice milling, shipping, and related activities. By the early twentieth century, the Chinese used trade associations to create small foreign-exchange banks to avoid the exchange losses suffered by Chinese exporters working with Western banks (Bualek 1986: 35–37). These institutions supported official efforts to reduce Western economic influence.

The threat of growing Thai nationalism constituted a second stimulus for greater organization within the Chinese community. A dramatic increase in Chinese immigrants prompted a fear that Thais would be swamped if high rates of immigration continued, the arrival of married couples resulted in less intermarriage between Chinese men and Thai women, and the growth of Chinese education in Thailand and heightened Chinese nationalism after the Chinese Revolution of 1911 stimulated Thai concerns about the loyalties of Chinese living in Thailand. In addition, nationalist ideas stressing differences between Thais and Chinese and the importance of a Thai nation were brought back to Thailand by students who had studied in the West.

Following the 1932 coup that overthrew the absolute monarchy, Thai governments took a number of steps to limit Chinese influence in the economy and promote indigenous Thai businesses. During the early 1930s, for example, almost all existing Chinese banks were dissolved and replaced by government-backed institutions in what Robert Muscat calls "ethnocentric dirigisme" (1990: 280). The most restrictive regulations were issued between 1938 and 1941 and again in the early 1950s. The result was "strong if intermittent governmental pressure on Chinese businesses" in which "no one knew when his particular trade might be reserved for Thai nationals . . . , when the lease of his shop might be challenged, or when his business might be inspected by revenue officials or raided by the police" (Skinner 1957a: 394).

Uncertainty resulting from these threats to Sino-Thai property rights reinforced both organization within the Chinese community and more extensive clientelism between Sino-Thai businesses and Thai officials (discussed later in the chapter). Internally, the early twentieth century marks the beginning of an institutional shift from vertical guild and speech groups to more horizontal organizations, especially in Bangkok. Political pressures, compounded by Depression-induced problems, led Chinese in almost every trade to organize trade associations. The most widespread type of Chinese organization, these associations constituted arenas through which businesspeople in similar lines of work could exchange information, formulate concerted action in the face of government regulation, operate to avoid excess competition, and restrict entry of new entrepreneurs into the trade.

These associations in turn facilitated the growth of Sino-Thai banks in the 1940s and 1950s (Suehiro 1992: 42–46). Nationalist economic policies initiated in the late 1930s had made it difficult for Chinese to expand rice milling and exporting activities. Commercial banking and related services constituted an attractive alternative due to government regulations promoting local commercial banks as well as the impact of World War II: The war not only resulted in Japanese destruction of Western financial networks but also stimulated anti-Japanese activities by the Sino-Thai community, which sometimes generated commercial and financial opportunities for local Chinese.

Eight new commercial banks and twenty-five insurance companies were established between 1944 and 1951. In 1950, eleven commercial banks were operating, and most financed commodity exports critical to the country's economy and the state's revenue.[5] Ten of these were Chinese dominated. These banks were not one-family operations. They drew instead on a wider circle of leaders and shareholders to create financial groups. Within Thailand, these circles included often overlapping clan organizations, dialect groups, industry associations, and groups organized against Japan's invasion of China.[6] Externally, the circles included overseas Chinese merchants in other major Asian port cities such as Hong Kong, Singapore, and Swatow. The clearest illustration of the importance of external ties involves links between Thailand's leading private financial institution, the Bangkok Bank, and Hong Kong interests. During the 1950s, the Bangkok Bank established the Bangkok Mercantile Company in Hong Kong. The British colony was a top market for Thai rice, and Bangkok Mercantile became Hong Kong's largest private rice importer (Christensen 1993: 188).

Clientelist Relations between Government and Business

The Sino-Thai community and its associations did not dare to engage in open political activities aimed at influencing public policies.[7]

---

[5] Four exports—rice, rubber, tin, and teak—accounted for 86 percent of total exports in 1951. From 1952 through 1957, rice averaged 51 percent of exports, with rubber and tin accounting for another 27 percent (Corden 1967: 133, 168).

[6] Thus, the Bangkok Metropolitan Bank originated in groups of Teochiu Chinese organized in the Teochiu Rice Industry and Trade Compeny, established to support anti-Japanese resistance activities (Suehiro 1992: 46).

[7] There were some exceptions. In 1943, when the Japanese army attempted to recruit Chinese workers for road construction, the Chinese Chamber of Commerce worked with the government to engineer an agreement through which Chinese would be employed, not conscripted (Laothamatas 1992).

Instead, Chinese relations with particular Thai officials became ever more important. "If a merchant knows officials of the Ministry of Economic Affairs well, he gets a number of import permits relatively easily; . . . if he is not personally acquainted with the officials at all, there is no chance whatsoever of his getting a permit" (Skinner 1958: 303).

The Chinese also deepened their links with officials. Abandoning the traditional practices of piecemeal protection and special treatment, leading Chinese businesses sought to secure more permanent protection by establishing explicit business alliances with Thai officials. Beginning in the 1930s and intensifying after World War II, these alliances involved the inclusion of officials on the boards of major Chinese firms and banks and the participation of Sino-Thai managers in state-owned enterprises (Skinner 1957a: 394; Suehiro 1992: 47). Thai political patronage thus facilitated the growth of Sino-Thai economic institutions such as banks and business groups by both providing political protection and creating lucrative links to state-owned enterprises (Hewison 1989: 184). But with the important exceptions of agriculture and banking (discussed later), the state did not encourage the growth of industry-wide associations or their participation in public policy (Laothamatas 1992).

The growth of these clientelistic alliances cannot be understood without reference to the discontinuities and fragmentation characterizing Thai political elites following the overthrow of the absolute monarchy in 1932. The promoters of the coup were a counterelite, a small group of civilian and military officials frustrated with the king's failure to open up senior positions and the broader political system to new faces (Muscat 1994: 29). This group was itself deeply divided along ideological, armed service, and military-civilian lines. These divisions, and the lack of any other source of material support, encouraged alliances between Sino-Thai and even the most left-leaning of the coup promoters. Thus, Pridi Panomyong, author of a Socialist blueprint for Thai economic development, established banks with two purposes: to train Thais in banking and to bolster his own power base. These banks involved extensive Chinese participation, with one led by influential rice and rubber interests (Silcock 1967: 184).

The Thai political elite was also fragmented during the postwar period despite its ostensible unity under one prime minister from 1948 to 1957. After defeating rivals from other military services in 1947, an army-based group itself divided into three cliques, with the prime minister able to remain in power only by playing off the other two cliques against each other. Official policy during this period remained a combination of anti-Chinese rhetoric and support for the state-enterprise sector. Yet the military factions struggling for dominance "began entering into alliances with leading Chinese businessmen willing to pay for the protection that could be provided by powerful patrons," despite the fact that these patrons were espousing anti-Chinese policies (Muscat 1994: 42).

Field Marshall Sarit Thanarat's seizure of power in 1957 initiated a period that should have discouraged clientelism. The political-military elite was less fragmented: Sarit shifted official policy away from state-owned enterprises and anti-Sinicism toward support for private investment (in part because the state enterprise sector constituted an important base of his factional rivals), and government openness to foreign direct investment provided implicit property-rights protection for the Sino-Thai whom foreign investors preferred as local partners (Hewison 1989).

Yet clientelism continued to blossom. On the demand side, the appeals of clientelism for business remained: Sino-Thai entrepreneurs still had little ability to affect public policy. To overcome bureaucratic obstacles and obtain privileges, patrons were necessary. But if Sarit effectively ended interfactional competition, why were members of this elite still available to supply government services?[8] First, by the late 1950s it had become clear that the private sector was a more lucrative source of finance than the numerous state-owned enterprises that had proliferated earlier in the decade (McVey 1992). Second, allowing various members of the elite access to lucrative posts in the cabinet, the military, and the police was a critical instrument through which the victorious Sarit group consolidated its position: "sharing the spoils of political rule became one of the principal mechanisms for continued political stability" (Morell 1974: 846). The result was a situation in which ministries competed to extend their influence in part by linking up with the private sector. Third, competition remained even during the Sarit period. Cooperation among members of the victorious coup group was rapidly replaced by intragroup competition for the rewards of political status. Intra-elite rivalry intensified after Sarit's death in 1963. The spoils of corruption now had to be equally divided among competing factions, "each of which already had a good start while Sarit was alive" (Morell 1974: 846). As H. D. Evers and Thomas H. Silcock note, "the Thai system allows and expects the bureaucratic elite to engage-directly or indirectly-in private business" (1967: 96). By 1969, more than eighty senior military officers were connected to at least one firm. Six top political bureaucrats each had connections with twenty to fifty firms (Laothamatas 1992: 31).

State Institutions

In addition to dense links within the Chinese community and clientelist relationships between Chinese entrepreneurs and Thai officials, Thai-

---

[8] The following discussion draws on Wilson 1962: 258–59.

land's institutional configuration has included a bifurcated state divided between a centralized, insulated, and efficient set of macroeconomic agencies on the one hand and more politicized, fragmented, sectoral agencies on the other. Macroeconomic consolidation occurred during the late 1950s and early 1960s as part of a general shift away from state intervention and state enterprises. Field Marshall Sarit presided over a centralization of the budgetary process under a newly created Bureau of the Budget. Key to this process was a regulation prohibiting government guarantees of private-sector debt (Silcock 1967: 196). All of this meant that the Bank of Thailand, the Ministry of Finance, and the Bureau of the Budget enjoyed significant autonomy from other parts of the bureaucracy as well as from elected officials. The Thai state has thus operated with hard budget constraints. Thai legislators have been unable to initiate money bills and can only cut budgetary outlays, not increase them. They have limited influence over allocations and none over appropriations. Politicians are therefore unable to use macroeconomic policies for social or political objectives (Christensen Dollars, Siamwalla, and Vichyanond 1993; Doner and Laothamatas 1994). This arrangement contributed to a stable macroeconomic environment—low government deficits, positive interest rates, and realistic exchange rates—for Sino-Thai businesses.

Thailand's tradition of fiscal caution and institutional coherence certainly helps to explain the strength of these macroeconomic agencies. The country's disastrous experience with a major state enterprise in the mid-1950s reinforced this institutional prudence: After securing large amounts of state-guaranteed loans, many from foreign sources, the enterprise went bankrupt. The Ministry of Finance honored the debts but effectively mortgaged the development budget for several years. The impact of that experience served to strengthen the belief within the macroeconomic agencies "that an unchecked public sector would be detrimental to Thailand's development" (Muscat 1990: 281).

The macroeconomic agencies had several sources of influence with which to pursue this cautious approach. They were able to use International Monetary Fund (IMF) and World Bank pressure as leverage over other parts of the state, including military officials. Even more important were powerful domestic interests—the commercial banks and political leadership—bolstering the central bank's leverage. The Bank of Thailand engaged in extensive consultation with and supervision of private commercial bankers (see, for example, Maxfield 1994: 12). These relationships were much more systematic than were the clientelist links so widespread in the Thai economy. They reflected both the structural importance of banking as capital and the sectoral focus and resulting policy preferences of the commercial banks. The latters' heavy involvement in agriculture and related export activities translated into a propensity for low capital investments (thus, low government deficits) and realistic exchange rates.[9] These were consistent with the policies espoused by Thailand's central bank and Finance Ministry. Finally, macroeconomic agencies had backing from the political leadership: fiscal caution served Sarit's political objective of weakening his factional rivals, part of whose political base lay in the now-weakened state-owned enterprises.

Sarit did not, however, eradicate patronage. Indeed, the very strength of the "virtuous" part of the state was in part a function of its more penetrated, clientelist component found in sectoral ministries (such as Agriculture, Industry, and Commerce) as well as in the agency established by Sarit to attract foreign capital—the Board of Investments. The ability of military and bureaucratic officials to enrich themselves by granting property rights and market access had two important consequences: It resulted in a fragmentation of decision making with regard to trade and industrial policy, and it provided institutional and political space for the macroeconomic agencies. Sarit's own corruption merits special note here. He obtained funds from the state lottery, illicit ventures in opium trafficking and extortion, and certain commercial banks. Following his death, the value of his estate was equal to roughly 40 percent of 1960 government revenues (Christensen 1991: 34). But because these funds were not drawn from regular ministerial operations, the corruption did not fundamentally conflict with technocratic control over macroeconomic policy. Indeed, Sarit's financial resources allowed him to remain independent from particular clients and helped to protect macroeconomic officials.

Before exploring the benefits of this system, let us note the strengths of similarly bifurcated structures both in Thai history and in the ostensibly "hard" state of South Korea. Historically, one finds the growth of a structure emerging late in the nineteenth century under Rama V, one of Thailand's reformist monarchs. While centralizing funds and introducing strict auditing in the treasury, the king maintained his authority through a system of patronage down through the civil service (Silcock 1967: 172). In South Korea, according to David Kang, a state under Park Chung-hee involved service ministries, staffed by clientelistic appointments and satisfying domestic patronage requirements, and fiscal ministries, functioning to create economic effectiveness and international competitiveness (Kang 1995: 26).

[9] Until the mid-1970s, foreign trade accounted for roughly 30 percent of commercial bank credit (Doner and Unger 1993: 105).

Institutional Sources of Economic Growth, 1950s–1970s

During the 1950s and 1960s, both the Thai economy and the business class grew and diversified.[10] This performance is attributable in part to favorable external conditions. The country benefited from healthy demand for its varied export crops, and Thailand's position on a cold war fault line yielded benefits: The Korean War provided a major boost to Thai economic growth in the early 1950s, and Thailand benefited from extensive U.S. military and economic aid from the 1950s to the mid-1970s as a result of the Vietnam War. More recently, Thailand's close proximity to Japan and the East Asian NICs has resulted in trade opportunities and extensive foreign investment. But external factors provide only a nurturing context within which domestic entrepreneurs may or may not expand. In our view, Thailand's growth through the 1970s was also a function of the institutional factors we have already discussed.

Clientelism

Clientelism promoted Thai growth by discouraging capital flight, encouraging competition, and, as a result, weakening protectionism. In contrast to political leaders of other countries who export funds to Swiss bank accounts, Thai patrons reinvested money gained through patronage in Thailand. Intra-elite rivalry meant that networks of supporters were critical. As David Morell notes, "without money, no network; without network no power; and without the power, no money" (1974: 635).

Just as important, clientelism promoted growth by encouraging "an element of competition, with its attendant pressure for efficiency" in the Thai economy (Leff 1964: 11). With fragmented political patrons eager to obtain extrabureaucratic funds, clientelism facilitated a constant flow of new private-sector claimants on state largesse and thereby weakened tendencies toward the more common result of clientelism—monopoly cronyism. We are not arguing that clientelism is efficient in any general sense. Rather, the particular type of clientelism prevalent in Thailand tended to expand rather than restrict new opportunities. More specifically, the Thai case seems to be one in which "each one of . . . several

[10] Cumulative growth rate between 1951 and 1969 was what Ingram calls a "remarkably high" cumulative growth rate of 6.6 percent per year. GNP grew from 35.2 billion baht in 1951, to 45.6 in 1955, to 56 in 1960, to 79.5 in 1965, to 112.4 in 1969. This growth occurred with only 1.9 percent average annual price rise, one of the lowest inflation rates in the world during this inflationary period (Ingram 1971: 222). Manufacturing's contribution to GDP rose from 10.3 percent in 1951, to 11.8 percent in 1955, to 12.6 percent in 1960, to 14.2 percent in 1965, to 15 percent in 1968. Agriculture became increasingly diversified. The top four exports—rice, rubber, tin, and teak—accounted for 81 percent of exports in 1950 and 50 percent in 1969. Rice accounted for 48 percent of exports in 1950 and by 1969 was down to 20 percent of exports (Ingram 1971: 312). On the growth of Thai entrepreneurs, see Hewison 1989 and Suehiro 1985.

complementary government goods can be supplied by at least two government agencies" (Shleifer and Vishny 1993: 606). This contrasts with a unified monopolist model, as in the Philippines, where Marcos provided all government goods and was able to drive up the bribe level.[11] It also differs from a situation, as in post-Communist Russia, where firms must expend large sums of money purchasing complementary government goods from a series of independent monopolists. In the Thai case, the level of bribes has tended to be reduced because "the market for each government-supplied good is competitive" (Shleifer and Vishny 1993: 607). The following episode is typical:

> Through business ties with officials in the Ministry of Finance, . . . Leader F. T. Ho in February, 1953 obtained all three of the remittance licenses issued as part of a move to bring the remittance business with the China mainland under government control. As it turned out, the Police Department as well as the Finance Ministry was in on the monopolization move, so Leader Chung, the chief businessman in General Phao's clique, later obtained one of the licenses. Not to be left out, another Sino-Thai clique headed by Field Marshal Phin and Leader Yang forced a reorganization whereby Leader Yang obtained another of the three licenses. (Skinner 1958: 304)

Similar patterns led to competitive structures in several important sectors (Muscat 1994: 118). Consider first the all-important rice trade— Thailand's top earner of foreign exchange until 1985 and the country's food staple and principal wage good. Beginning in the 1930s, rival milling and export groups jockeyed for position on the basis of links with various political factions.[12] By the early 1960s, some fifty licensed exporters, led by five large traders, dominated the rice trade. These firms restricted market entry and accumulated rents by operating in a form of export syndicate. Yet they also competed among themselves and, by the late 1960s and early 1970s, were forced to accommodate a new generation of exporters.[13]

[11] For a nuanced view on this issue, see Hutchcroft 1996.

[12] Consider the example of the Thai Rice Company, an ostensibly state-owned firm established in 1938 to take over the rice trade from the Chinese, whose anti-Japanese boycotts were cutting into rice exports and state revenues. Although a state firm, many of Thai Rice's mills were rented from Chinese millers. Its managing director was a former president of the Chinese Chamber of Commerce. The company pushed other Chinese firms out of the rice trade, forcing them to diversify into a number of commercial, financial, and industrial activities. By the mid-1940s Thai Rice itself came under competition from rival milling and export groups associated with various political groups. While the Thai Rice Company gradually failed, its managing director expanded the activities of his own group. As Kevin Hewison notes, "Chinese capital continued to control the rice trade, albeit with new political partners" (1989: 75–76).

[13] One of these newcomers, a provincial rice miller, became Thailand's second largest rice exporter in 1977 and has since become a fledgling multinational firm with investments in Vietnam and China (Christensen 1993: 192).

The sugar industry was more oligopolistic than the rice industry, largely because of contrasting technological features: With the shift to more expensive centrifugal mills (which refine sugar) in the 1950s and 1960s, the number of mills declined drastically from several hundred to three large milling groups. Even these groups, however, were exposed to competition from each other and from imported sugar.

In the auto industry, political entry barriers to local firms have been lower than those of other Southeast Asian countries, especially the Philippines (Doner 1992). In the construction industry, many new firms got their start through rakeoffs and kickbacks in dams, power systems, roads, and irrigation projects during the Sarit period. These activities "laid the framework for later economic growth, while at the same time providing fuel for the political machines of Sarit and his colleagues" (Morell 1974: 685–86). In consumer electronics, protectionism failed as upstart importers were able to create competition through smuggling (Thanamai 1985: 196–208). In textiles and apparel, Thailand's largest export industry since the mid-1980s, twenty enterprises were set up by some sixteen groups of investors (Muscat 1994: 117–18). Critical to the competitive structure was the ability of an upstart Sino-Thai firm, Thai Blanket Industries (TBI), to break into a market dominated by a powerful Japanese joint venture led by a former minister of industry. TBI has gone on to become one of the country's largest integrated textile conglomerates. An important component of the firm's success was its founder's ability to find backers in the Thai Board of Investments (BOI) after having been denied backing from the Ministry of Industry (Doner and Ramsay 1993).

The role of the BOI merits special note because it was established by Sarit to guide as well as attract foreign capital. The board functioned to provide still another channel through which new firms could gain market access. As in the case of the Turkish export promotion process described by Biddle and Milor in Chapter 10, the BOI was "extremely promiscuous in giving away promotion certificates. . . . The end result of this hectic issuing of certificates (an activity in which the BOI took great pride) was higgledy-piggledy growth of Thailand's industrial sector with spotty performance in terms of efficiency" (Siamwalla 1975: 38). The board was "promiscuous" in part from design but largely from bureaucratic weakness. Its lack of funds and internal expertise deprived it of any capacity to monitor promoted firms, much less to impose any clear performance standards on them.

The BOI's weakness was symptomatic of the trade and industrial policy process as a whole (Rock 1995). At least four agencies—the Board of Investment and the ministries of Commerce, Industry, and Finance—controlled trade policy, with the Finance Ministry itself torn between support for export promotion and a commitment to high tariffs as a means of generating government revenue.[14] Five departments in three ministries influenced access to permits and licenses. As a result, industries prohibited from expansion due to excess capacity by the Interior Ministry were able to expand under BOI incentives or high tariffs under control of the Ministry of Finance. Firms that thought they would gain privileged market positions through BOI measures found themselves competing with firms supported by other ministries.[15]

Politically, this pattern of policy-making allowed patrons in a range of agencies to satisfy particular groups of supporters (Christensen et al.: 1992). Economically, it meant that the Thai state was strikingly incapable of imposing capacity controls. Although this weakness resulted in extensive overcapacity in many sectors, it kept entry barriers low and thus helps to explain an important puzzle in the Thai case: the emergence of dynamic export performance not only in agriculture but also in textiles and electronics despite the country's protectionist trade regime.[16] As Thai economists note, there has been "water in the tariffs." That is, domestic prices are often close to cost, insurance, and freight prices as a result of high levels of competition from domestic rivals, smuggling, administrative irregularities, market slumps, temporary lifting of protectionist measures, and the threat of such changes (Muscat 1994: 149; Brimble 1994). This competition reflects the clientelist-based fragmentation and bureaucratic weakness of Thai industrial policy.

This emphasis on the benefits of competitive market structures leaves open two important questions: Who has looked out for the common interest, whether defined at the industry or national level? And how were collective-action problems resolved? In the rest of this section we address the role of state, public-private, and private institutions.

---

[14] Although the Bowring Treaty severely circumscribed Thailand's ability to tax trade in the late nineteenth and early twentieth centuries, the state maintained its solvency through tax revenues on opium and gambling, imposed largely on Chinese immigrants. Between 1926, when Thailand achieved fiscal autonomy, and World War II, import duties rose to become the principal single revenue source. After the war, export taxes came close to equalling import duties but gradually declined in importance during the 1980s. Thus, at no time during 1963–90 did import taxes account for less than 20 percent of state tax revenues (Corden 1967: 165–67; GATT 1991: 48). The importance of trade taxes for state revenues actually grew during the 1980s, from 21 percent in 1980 to 28 percent in 1991, largely as a means of generating revenues during Thailand's debt problems (Waller 1994: 65).

[15] During the early 1980s, for example, the BOI selected one firm out of several contenders to produce compressors for refrigeration units under a guarantee of no competition. Despite the guarantee, the Ministry of Industry gave one of the rejected firms a license to operate (Rock 1995: 10). On failed efforts to control capacity in the textile industry, see Suphachalasai 1992: 17.

[16] Average tariff levels for the region are Singapore, 0; Malaysia, 15.64 percent; Indonesia, 21.68 percent; Philippines, 25.96 percent; and Thailand, 43.83 percent (Stone 1992). For an overview of Thai tariff policy, see Warr 1993: 15–17.

State Institutions

The Thai economy has benefited from several sorts of collective goods provided by the country's macroeconomic agencies. These range from broad macroeconomic stability, to intersectoral shifts, to export incentives, to the promotion of enterprises akin to *zaibatsu*, the giant financial and industrial conglomerates of pre-World War II Japan. Macroeconomic policies have received the most attention: Through low inflation and minimal intervention in foreign exchange and credit markets, the Ministry of Finance and the central bank provided firms with a stable price environment. Through hard budget constraints, these agencies ensured that favors provided to local firms by sectoral agencies did not include subsidies but were limited to measures involving capacity expansion.

But the practice of maintaining low price distortions has not been universal. In one critical area—rice—distortions were systematic. Beginning in the mid-1950s, an export-tax regime composed of Sino-Thai rice traders, commercial banks, and the Ministry of Commerce maintained a "cheap rice" policy for domestic urban consumers through the 1980s. Later, we shall address the interactions of public and private sectors in this institution. Here, we wish simply to note its principal components and consequences. The roots of this arrangement date from the immediate postwar period, when the government attempted to monopolize the rice trade itself. This effort failed as vast rice surpluses and well-established Chinese export networks resulted in parallel markets. In response, the government exited the domestic rice trade but intervened at the border by imposing export duties on a small number of Sino-Thai firms holding export quotas. With rice as the country's principal export commodity until 1985, such levies were an important source of foreign exchange and government finance: Rice export taxes alone accounted for 10 to 15 percent of such revenues throughout the 1960s (Suehiro 1992: 57). Equally important, the Commerce Ministry's power to increase (or decrease) the size of the tax as rice export prices rose (or fell) allowed the government to narrow the size of price fluctuations and effectively maintain low prices for domestic consumers, most of whom were in Bangkok (Muscat 1994: 76). Because the rice traders constituted a government-backed monopsony, they were able to pass the tax on to millers and farmers. The policy thus not only generated significant amounts of government revenue but constituted "the largest single postwar government intervention affecting income distribution in Thailand, regressively falling on the rural sector"(Muscat 1994: 76).

Economically, this tax regime facilitated a shifting of investment funds from the countryside to urban business. Politically, the arrangement generated urban support for the state while reflecting the immediate interests of bureaucratic revenue seekers, rent-seeking exporters, large bankers, and emerging manufacturers. Cheaper rice subsidized urban wage earners and civil servants, thus alleviating pressure on the state to raise wages and subsidizing Thailand's manufacturing elite in Bangkok (Christensen 1993: 184). Although the burden of the system clearly fell on Thailand's rice farmers (who constituted 67 percent of the economically active population in 1970), the impact was alleviated by Thailand's large land frontier: Because the peasantry had access to land, "it was possible to extract resources from agriculture without impoverishing the peasantry and to build an indigenously owned commercial banking system and an import-substitution industrial base in Bangkok behind protective barriers" (Rock 1995: 13).[17]

State macroeconomic institutions also departed from a purely neutral price regime through a limited program of concessionary rediscount rates to large exporters. This instrument did not constitute a large-scale program of selective credit. It never involved large amounts of funds relative to the total banking system and therefore did not distort the allocation of credit. Nor did it involve long-term development financing: Working through the commercial banks, the Bank of Thailand provided the funds as working capital for firms during periods of market volatility or overproduction. The central bank therefore did not offer funds to push firms into new sectors. The funds, however, were clearly targeted. First focused on rice in the 1950s and then broadened to other agricultural products and labor-intensive industrial goods, the system provided different concessional rates for different commodities, with higher rates for raw-material exporters or raw-material–based goods. Allocation of these funds was "based on the Bank of Thailand's own judgment regarding the relative importance of the commodities for the country's development" (Muscat 1994: 143).

The Finance Ministry and the central bank were also actively involved in the promotion and stability of locally owned commercial banks. The state banned new entries and severely limited foreign bank expansion. Working closely with the Thai Bankers' Association, it also bailed out weak commercial banks and imposed ceilings on interest rates. This did not eradicate competition, but it did help to nurture a small number of family-owned commercial banks that in turn supported the growth of large Thai business groups (Rock 1995: 13; Muscat 1994: 114–15). Indeed, a critical result of state interventions has been an economy dominated by large, albeit competitive, firms and groups. By the early 1980s, large firms

---

[17] For a view that questions the argument that Thailand financed industrial development through net transfers out of agriculture, see Muscat 1994: 245–46.

amounted to only 1.6 percent of all industrial enterprises but owned 54 percent of all industrial assets and accounted for 41 percent of industrial employment. Moreover, fifty of the country's largest one hundred manufacturing enterprises belonged to one of sixteen conglomerates. Together, these conglomerates accounted for 90 percent of the total assets of Thai enterprises (Rock 1995: 14).

The state's support for large firms has been indirect, with one significant exception. In the case of the the Siam Cement Group (SCG), the Thai state has directly nurtured a kind of quasi-public enterprise that comes fairly close to a chaebol or zaibatsu. Established as part of the royal family's Crown Property Bureau in 1913, SCG is managed by an official of that bureau under the supervision of a five-person committee headed by the finance minister. Siam Cement began as a producer of construction materials and has evolved into a sort of Thai zaibatsu composed of firms producing iron and steel, metal and electrical products, petrochemicals, construction materials, ceramics, tires and auto accessories, cement and trading, and paper and packaging. SCG has become the wealthiest institution in Thailand, the largest manufacturing conglomerate in the country, and "the largest privately owned, vertically integrated heavy industry and natural resource based business group in Southeast Asia today" (Hamilton and Waters 1995: 102). SCG is equally known for its efficiency, commercial viability, and honesty (it pays its taxes). The group is strategically important—a "source of national pride" and, through its investments in a wide variety of manufacturing, a kind of flagship enterprise for Thai industrialization (Sricharatchanya 1988: 61; Muscat 1994: 259). Backed by the Siam Commercial Bank, Siam Cement has the highest percentage of assets devoted to research and development of any indigenous firm. The firm's reputation for honesty has allowed it to function as a key player in some of the most politically sensitive upstream projects undertaken by the country: In at least two very large petrochemical projects involving extensive foreign capital, Siam Cement has taken a critical 2 percent "balancing stake" to ensure both public and private shareholders that the controlling margin was in responsible hands.

Siam Cement's emphasis on market-based performance reflects at least two factors. First, its links to a highly respected monarchy compel a certain caution: Firms affiliated with the Crown Property Bureau try not to exploit their royal connection "in order to avoid criticism which may subsequently reflect badly on the monarchy" (Sricharatchanya 1988: 62). The SCG group is also constrained by a factor discussed earlier: the dynamism and competitive structure of the broader Thai private sector. Thus, even for a hugely rich group with strong political ties and high status, rents are both temporary and limited.

Public-Private Sector Institutions

The Thai state's sensitivity to the country's fiscal health has translated into an active concern for export revenues and, when necessary, a willingness to collaborate with the private sector in sustaining such revenues. Thailand is thus characterized by a sector-specific pattern of collaboration. The earliest and most significant illustration of this pattern is the already-discussed export tax regime in rice.[18] Here we wish to emphasize the ways in which this arrangement relied on corporatist-like relations between government officials on the one hand and private traders and large banks on the other.

By the mid-1950s, competition in rice and other export commodities became excessive, leading to practices such as breach of contract with foreign importers and the adulteration of products. Fearing damage to the country's reputation and a drop in the inflow of critical foreign exchange, the government established the Board of Trade, a peak association composed of commodity-based associations and led by the Bangkok Chamber of Commerce. The board was empowered to regulate commodity transactions through systematic negotiations with the Commerce Ministry. It encouraged exporters of the same product to form associations within which norms governing trade practices would be worked out. Only group members would receive export quotas. Violators of group norms would lose their export licenses after being reported by the Board of Trade to the Ministry of Commerce. The board also discouraged cutthroat competition by ensuring that each group established a minimal export price in consultation with the Commerce Ministry (Laothamatas 1992: 27).

Rice was, of course, the major focus of such efforts. Within the Board of Trade, some fifty licensed rice traders, led by the five largest firms and supported by the Bangkok Bank, constituted the Rice Exporters Association. Until the early 1970s, this group met weekly at the board to share quotas and agree on and send prices to the Commerce Ministry for approval.[19] This arrangement involved a quid pro quo between exporters and ministry officials: Officials allowed private traders to organize them-

---

[18] Unless otherwise noted, this account is drawn from Laothamatas 1992 and Christensen 1993: chap. 4.

[19] Beginning in the late 1960s and early 1970s, new exporters broke into this cartel as a result of changing external markets and domestic political arrangements. With the closure of Thailand's traditional rice markets by the Green Revolution and competition from subsidized U.S. rice, Thai exporters had to enter new markets with more competitive price and quality. In addition, the shift to electoral politics forced government officials to pay greater attention to farmer welfare and strengthened the capacity of provincial elites, especially millers, to compete with established exporters. Despite these changes, the largest exporters, now comprising nine leading firms, have continued to operate as a syndicate, pooling to set prices and share large deals (Christensen 1993: 220).

selves freely so as to enhance earnings through quota rents. The officials, meanwhile, were able to keep traders in line by their control of (1) exporters' right to participate in highly lucrative government-to-government rice deals and (2) price information that bolstered the market leverage of exporters vis-à-vis provincial millers (Christensen 1993: 186–200).

The behavior of Thai officials in this case showed the state's sensitivity to market volatility and revenue concerns. Despite extensive factional infighting among military leaders during the mid-1950s, the reality of market changes and the threat of revenue losses were viewed as sufficiently serious to stimulate coherent state interaction with and support for private-sector organization. The importance of export revenues was illustrated some ten years later when the government established similar, albeit less extensive, arrangements for the textile and fishmeal industries. In both cases, associations were empowered to allocate export quotas; the textile association was also responsible for organizing imports of certain raw materials (Laothamatas 1992: 29). In both cases, the associations operated essentially as instruments of state policy, leading one observer to call these arrangements "state (authoritarian) corporatism" (Chenvidyakarn 1979).

A final example of systematic links between public and private sector involves the already-noted consultations between the Bank of Thailand and the country's commercial banks. This relationship has been both bilateral and multilateral. The Bank of Thailand has supervisory powers allowing its representatives to sit on the boards of troubled financial institutions. At the same time, the central bank has engaged in ongoing discussions with the Thai Bankers' Association over issues such as interest-rate ceilings, cash reserves, new branch openings, general liberalization, and collective support for troubled financial institutions. Central to these discussions has been the government's concern with financial sector stability. Indeed, beginning in the late 1950s problems of solvency and bank management compelled the central bank to tighten its links with existing members of the financial community and therefore provide implicit support for financial-sector concentration (Doner and Unger 1993).

Robert Muscat argues that the central bank's acceptance of commercial banking concentration constitutes "a major exception to the general policy of free entry and exit that the government applied to most areas of economic activity" (1994: 115). This perspective, we suggest, is only partially accurate if viewed in light of government support for cartel-like arrangements in agriculture, textiles, and fishmeal as well as in institutionalized efforts to promote tourism and general exports in the 1980s. In this context, state links with and support of commercial banks fit a pattern of close public-private sector links in sectors whose health bears on the state's fiscal condition.

Private-Sector Institutions

Public-private sector links have themselves drawn on private-sector governance institutions: business associations such as the Chinese Chamber of Commerce, trading networks, banks, and business groups. These Sino-Thai institutions operated both inside and outside Thailand. Indeed, it was their combination of internal coherence and external links with other overseas Chinese, their knowledge of both modern business techniques and local business conditions that made them such "a powerful resource both for protection and for the mobilization of capital" (McVey 1992: 21). It also made them a major attraction for Japanese investors reestablishing themselves in Thailand after the war.

The specific advantages of such ethnic institutions involve group-based norms of trust and enforcement. These ethnic-specific assets may be considered a public good or social capital that help economize on transaction costs. Ethnic and kinship status/identity indicate degrees of social distance and therefore transmit cheap signals of reputation and trustworthiness of potential contracting parties. Mutual trust between pairs of entrepreneurs can stimulate transitive trust and thus economize on the need to investigate the reputation of indirect partners (Landa 1991; Leff 1979). In these ways, ethnic links allowed Chinese entrepreneurs to cope with both market imperfections typical of developing countries and the specific uncertainties imposed by Thailand's ethnic nationalism and factionalized politics (McVey 1992: 21).

Thailand's commercial banks merit special attention in this regard. During the 1950s and 1960s, Thai commercial banks linked Sino-Thai enterprises by combining credit with kinship and other social ties in response to various collective-action problems.[20] To overcome Thailand's lack of a securities market, commercial bankers often granted credit on the basis of trust, which was based in turn on community reputation and a banker's gut reaction to the borrower.[21] Through these practices, the commercial banks acted as agents "in extending a rather looser form of influence mediated through capital" (McVey 1992: 183).

We can appreciate these functions by beginning with the banks' role in organizing export cartels in sugar, maize, and especially rice (Silcock 1967: 184). We have noted the ways in which the Board of Trade and the Commerce Ministry constituted a syndicate-like structure to govern rice

[20] Unless noted, this discussion draws on Silcock 1967.
[21] The Thai stock exchange was created in the 1960s, restructured in the 1970s, and only became significant during the 1980s.

exports. Here we wish to emphasize that, with support from the ministry, the exporters operated collectively as a self-regulated arrangement to set prices, share quotas, and share risks. This oligopoly was held together by ethnic affiliation and credit and protected by personal connections with leading military officers.[22]

Thailand's largest commercial bank, the Bangkok Bank, played a key role in the provision of these resources. Led by its founder, Chin Sophanpanich, the bank used close ties to the minister of commerce during the 1950s to corner the market on financing Thailand's government-to-government rice deals, one of the most lucrative government business activities of the period. In subsequent years, the bank was flexible in allying itself with diverse and shifting political factions. When a new generation of rice exporters emerged in the late 1960s, a Bangkok Bank official occupied top positions in the Ministry of Commerce to ensure the bank's continued influence over export quotas and financing.

The bank also used ethnic and family connections among the Bangkok Chinese to organize and finance the major rice exporters. (Two of the largest exporters during the 1960s were cousins.) Chin often acquired shares in these firms and reportedly supplied credit "on a personal, case-by-case basis" (Christensen 1993: 189). By pioneering the use of letters of credit, the Bangkok Bank shouldered foreign-exchange risks in the rice trade. And as we noted earlier, the bank developed marketing outlets in Hong Kong and elsewhere in Asia.

Building on rice profits, the Bangkok Bank became the largest source of private credit to exporters and importers in cassava, maize, textiles, and fertilizers as well as the largest source of central bank credits. The bank was thus well positioned to play a number of investment coordination functions beyond rice exporting. It mobilized capital to finance the country's agricultural diversification: In the 1960s this involved a shift from rice and rubber into cassava, kenaf, maize, and sugar and in the 1970s into oilseeds, tree crops, livestock, and aquaculture (Christensen 1992). The banks also promoted large firms and groups involved in this diversification. By the early 1980s, seventeen of the major twenty-eight nonfinancial Thai business groups belonged to agribusiness. These included not only firms involved in traditional products such as rice and sugar but also newer, vertically integrated enterprises dealing in everything from raw materials to shipping (Suehiro 1992: 58–59).[23]

[22] See Christensen 1993: chap. 4, from which the rest of this discussion is drawn.
[23] The outstanding example of this pattern is a major client of the Bangkok Bank, Charoen Phokphand. It began as a seed company in the 1960s and diversified first into an array of agro-industrial concerns (chicken farming, prawns, etc.) and subsequently into industrial (motorcycles, petrochemicals) and commercial activities (retail, real estate) through some two hundred companies in eleven countries (for example, see Friedland 1989). It is now the largest single investor in China.

The Bangkok Bank played a major role in coordinating the shift of resources from agriculture to manufacturing, especially textiles and garments, Thailand's leading export industry in the late 1980s. In a clear case of intersectoral transfers, Chin not only mobilized capital from rice exporters to save Thai Durable Textile, one of Thailand's largest spinning and weaving firms, but also oversaw the sale of the firm to a major textile conglomerate and arranged for family members of three of the largest rice exporters to sit on Thai Durable's board of directors.

Finally, the Bangkok Bank directly helped to resolve collective-action problems within particular industries. In sugar, the bank was involved not only in the early financing of mills and warehouses but also in subsequent successful efforts to reconcile revenue distribution between millers and growers. The bank's role in textiles and apparel stands out in this regard. In the early 1970s, it established its own textile center whose functions included identifying and recruiting Thai engineering graduates for the country's textile industry and resolving overcapacity problems among textile producers. By the mid-1970s the bank was financing 70 to 80 percent of textile manufacturing and supporting efforts by Thai Durable to renegotiate restrictive conditions imposed by Japanese partners.

Although the Bangkok Bank is Thailand's largest, it is neither monopolist nor the only bank heavily engaged in agricultural and industrial promotion.[24] Several banks, for example, have been active in the financing and organization of the sugar industry.[25] Reflecting on these activities, some argue that Thailand's commercial banks as a group have performed "many of the investment coordination functions through financial intermediation that have been attributed to the state in the NICs" (Christensen et al. 1993: 14). While something of an overstatement, this perspective highlights an important statelike role played by these institutions. Building on communal-based reputation and trust as well as support from the state itself, the banks helped to organize and finance a largely private arrangement—the rice export-tax regime—that extracted revenues from a multitude of geographically dispersed and marginally profitable small farmers. This private governance structure effectively substituted for the "flexible, deeply penetrating" *state* tax authorities that Michael Shafer

---

[24] The Bangkok Bank has operated within a fairly competitive oligopoly of five other institutions, most of whom are involved in a similarly wide range of activities. The rate of commercial bank concentration, measured by percentage of assets held by the largest five banks, rose from 56 percent in 1962, to 62 percent in 1972, to 69.1 percent in 1980 and 1990 (World Bank data, cited in Doner and Unger 1993: 106). Citing the same World Bank study, Muscat (1994: 147) notes that rivalry among the large banks limits margins in most areas of business.

[25] For example, the Bank of Ahudhya held 12 percent of shares of the largest sugar export company compared to 7 percent for the Bangkok Bank. Thailand's largest sugar milling group has close ties to several banks (Hewison 1989: 134, 141).

anticipates in countries dominated by a peasant cash crop such as rice (Shafer 1994).

But Thailand's commercial banks, at least up to the 1970s, also resemble German banks in certain respects (Zysman 1983). Structurally, Thailand was a credit-based system of corporate finance in a country whose government, with minor exceptions, has not intervened extensively to affect credit allocation.[26] While Thai banks did not preside over coherent groups (as in Japan's main bank system), they did develop close relationships with particular firms and even industries along lines closer to the German system.[27] This structure, combined with their ethnic links, encouraged extensive bank involvement in agriculture and industrial affairs. More specifically, by completing or improving product and factor markets, the banks facilitated the expansion of agricultural exports and thus capital accumulation overall. The banks also facilitated diversification—intra- and intersectoral resource shifts—and exhibited longtime horizons in industrial growth. And with their multisectoral interests, the commercial banks effectively functioned as encompassing coalitions. As such, they helped to weaken protectionist tendencies and facilitate both economic reform and export promotion. Finally, in addition to satisfying the needs of an urban-based coalition, commercial banks played still another important political role: They reduced the burden of sectoral adjustment on a state ill-equipped for such interventions.

External Constraints and the Decline of Clientelism: 1970s–1980s

The growth facilitated by this combination of clientelism and collective institutions weakened clientelism itself. Thai interest aggregation and articulation generally became more pluralistic and, in some cases, more predatory than in the past. Rather than weakening market competition, however, this transformation further reduced entry barriers to new firms. But when the external environment deteriorated in the latter part of 1970s, Thailand moved toward closer and more corporatist forms of business-government relations. These links reflect a recurring theme of this chapter: Thailand's capacity to mount collective responses to broad eco-

---

[26] This description of Thailand as a credit-based system applies to the first twenty-five years after World War II. Moving into the 1980s, the equity of Thai industrial firms grew more rapidly than their debt, suggesting that the dependence of industrial firms on commercial banks has decreased (World Bank 1990: 106). For a view emphasizing the distinctions between banking conglomerates and industrial groups, see Mackie 1992: 183.

[27] According to Choonhavan (1984: 145), Thai banks have constituted an "embryonic zaibatsu system." Nevertheless, one does not find the banks involved in behavioral manifestations of zaibatsu or chaebol such as deliberation councils. Close bank-firm coordination is also discouraged by the fact that the commercial banks maintain links with a variety of often competing firms. And state officials have not provided any incentives for the banks to exert control over groups of firms.

nomic threats in the midst of a generally fragmented and competitive political economy.

The growth of Thai firms helped to undermine clientelism by promoting the absorption of patrons by business clients. Given the weaknesses of state-owned enterprises and the absence of a landed aristocracy, participation in private firms constituted the safest landing for high officials in case of political adversity (McVey 1992: 23–24). This strategy required that political-military elites take a serious interest in business to oversee their own affairs. The strategy also required effective guarantees for private property; such guarantees, reinforced by the expanding role of foreign investors, weakened the reliance of entrepreneurs on political protectors (Hewison 1989). The strategy worked. The Thai political elite is sprinkled with the offspring of past military leaders who made wise investments (McVey 1992: 23–24).

The counterpart of weaker patrons was greater social and political autonomy on the part of Sino-Thai entrepreneurs. The 1973 overthrow of the military leadership by a student-led rebellion resulted in three years of democratically elected, civilian governments; the growth of parties; and uninterrupted growth of direct business participation in politics.[28] But even before 1973, businesspeople had become increasingly active in politics: They accounted for 20 percent of the House of Representatives in 1952 and 45 percent in 1969. The democratic interlude of 1973–76 witnessed the proportion of businesspeople in Thai cabinets rising to almost 60 percent compared with 11 percent in 1958.[29] During 1973–76, Chinese capitalists also became increasingly active in the creation or funding of parties, although Bangkok-based firms spread their risks by contributing to numerous parties (Christensen 1991). Clientelism did not disappear, but connections had become "a way of increasing leverage over politics, not of sheltering under a patron; and growing pluralism in Thai politics has required that business establish links with a range of bureaucrats and parties rather than one or two powerful protectors. Not only is political connection no longer central to business success, but the most 'political' of the big conglomerates are not the most successful or the most modernized" (Mackie 1992: 175).

The opening up of the political system bolstered market competition by providing opportunities for new firms. The rice, sugar, and auto sectors

[28] The democratic shift was partially reversed by a military crackdown and resurgence in 1976. Military governments ran the country until 1979, when parties reemerged and quasi-democratic regimes emerged during the 1980s.

[29] The percentage of businesspeople in cabinets dropped sharply (to about 5 percent after the military reasserted power in 1977 but then quickly rose to between 30 percent and 60 percent during the 1980s (Christensen 1991: 59). Figures on membership in the House of Representatives are from Laothamatas 1992: 33.

illustrate this pattern. Through greater organization (the Thai Rice Mills Association was founded in the late 1970s) and ties to increasingly powerful rural politicians, provincial rice millers were able to weaken the leverage of the dominant exporters and break into the ranks of the exporters themselves (Christensen 1993: 199). The change in sugar was even more striking. Until 1975, all sugar mills had to export through a single firm dominated by one powerful group. With the weakening of military control, mills were able to establish their own exporting firms (Ramsay 1987). In autos, the political shifts provided backing for local parts firms pressing multinational assemblers to increase local content (Doner 1991).

The combination of economic growth, greater market competition, and more open politics also stimulated private-sector organization. In automobiles, local parts firms organized business associations to lobby for higher local contents requirements and a reduction in makes and models (to achieve larger economies of scale) (Doner 1991). In textiles, associations of spinners, weavers, garment makers, and others became involved in negotiations concerning overcapacity, conflicts between upstream and downstream sectors, and the distribution of export quotas under the Multi-Fibre Agreement. In sugar, well-organized growers' groups emerged to bargain with millers' groups over the price of sugarcane (Ramsay 1987).

These industry-specific negotiations were largely distributional. State officials tended to serve as brokers between upstream and downstream producers rather than arbiters of industrial performance. But a modest growth of more efficiency-oriented associational business-government links did occur at the *peak* level. In the late 1960s, concerns about the limits of import institution prompted leading sectors of business to press for stronger private-sector organization and more extensive consultation with state officials at a national level. Thailand's peak manufacturing group, the Association of Thai Industries, urged both increased protection and more extensive export incentives (Hewison 1987: 56). Sectoral peak associations lobbied for a Federation of Economic Organizations of Thailand (with compulsory membership) and an institutionalized process of state-business consultation (Laothamatas 1992). These initiatives found some support among state officials, especially technocrats in the country's planning body, the National Economic and Social Development Board (NESDB). By the end of the 1960s, the Board of Trade, the Thai Bankers' Association, and the Federation of Thai Industries had links to state officials "almost unheard of even a decade earlier" (Christensen et al. 1992: 11). Representatives of these peak business associations were thus invited to meet with representatives of NESDB to participate in drafting the third national economic and social development plan (1972–76)

(Laothamatas 1992: 29). Increasingly, officials drew on private firms to supply policy-relevant information and resources.

This budding corporatism was interrupted by Thailand's political upheavals and gradual shift to quasi-democracy in the 1970s. Large numbers of strikes and demonstrations weakened state capacity to formulate long-term policy, let alone respond to proposals from business associations (Laothamatas 1992). But by the late 1970s, deteriorating trade balances and relatively high government deficits compelled the country to undertake economic reforms in conjunction with World Bank and IMF loans (Doner and Laothamatas 1994). These constraints, along with a reassertion of quasi-military rule, expanded political space for organized business on the one hand and empowered corporatist-leaning state officials on the other. Business became more organized: The number of associations grew from 48 in 1967 to 233 in 1987 (Christensen et al. 1992: 11). Government technocrats, especially those in the NESDB, gained leverage with the backing of Prime Minister Prem Tinsulanond. Prem's own longevity in office (1980–88) reflected a standoff between the military and political parties. NESDB officials in turn saw support for and cooperation with an increasingly organized private sector as a key means of resolving the country's economic ills.

Under these conditions, business-government collaboration expanded on both industry and multisectoral levels. On an industry level, collaboration was strikingly successful in tourism. Concerned with the need to generate foreign exchange, NESDB officials organized public- and private-sector interests and supervised the creation of an "integrated program of international promotion and domestic investment in . . . [tourist] accommodation and services" (Muscat 1994: 197). Tourist earnings grew from about $1 billion in 1985 to more than $3 billion in 1988, accounting for 15 percent of goods-and-services receipts. This effort ranks, according to Muscat, as the "single most import export policy success" of the government of the period (1994: 197). Multisectoral consultation was also important. Major business groups responded to falling export commodity prices by arguing for a greater emphasis on export promotion through incentives and measures such as customs regularization. Corruption was perceived as counterproductive when exports became more critical. Peak associations pursued these concerns through a series of informal public-private sector consultative groups that culminated in the establishment of the Joint Public and Private Sector Consultative Committee (JPPCC). This body is composed of top state economic officials and representatives of the country's three peak associations (the Thai Chamber of Commerce, the Thai Bankers' Association, and the Association of Thai Industries).

During the 1980s, the JPPCC provided the government with information about a broad range of administrative obstacles to Thai exports and political support for the reduction of red tape and the development of new public-sector supports for exports. These included services to help private-sector penetration of foreign markets, strengthen quality standards, and encourage participation in foreign and domestic trade fairs (Muscat 1994: 196; Laothamatas 1992). The JPPCC was the most systematic and inclusive form of interest aggregation and intermediation seen in Thailand. Labeled "liberal corporatism" and "the workable Thai version of 'Japan Inc.'" (Laothamatas 1992; Muscat 1994: 183), the JPPCC was specifically designed not to allow lobbying by particular interests: "Only matters of general public or business interests would be discussed. The meetings were open to the press and the government side was under pressure, between the press and the prime minister, to respond" (Muscat 1994: 183).

The multisectoral composition of the peak associations and their members, especially the banks, was critical to both of these contributions. This point is illustrated by fact that the business community mounted no serious opposition to a steep (14 percent) devaluation in 1984, despite the move's damage to several large import competing firms and opposition to the devaluation from military leaders. Although some small banks opposed the measure, the Thai Bankers' Association remained passive while its largest member, the Bangkok Bank, simply reduced its foreign-exchange exposure in anticipation of the devaluation. Cross-pressures prevented the peak manufacturers' group, the Association of Thai Industries, from offering any serious opposition to the decision (Doner and Laothamatas 1994: 433). This combination of stabilization measures and public-private sector cooperation to promote exports resulted in clear economic gains. The country put its fiscal house back in order; agricultural exports became more diversified as did the economy overall; industry expanded, and manufactured exports grew (Table 9.1). Rising labor costs and exchange rates elsewhere in the region were important to this shift, but the domestic arrangements we have described allowed Thailand to take advantage of these conditions (Akrasanee et al. 1991).

Business-government consultations of the 1980s were nevertheless limited by weaknesses of the state itself and by the intrusion of fragmenting, pluralist politics. The JPPCC helped to facilitate exports of products already competitive. The committee did not involve the state's provision of subsidies or pressure in exchange for particular types of investment or improved economic performance by business. State agencies had neither the instruments nor the will for such an exchange. The most extensive study of the JPPCC concludes that it "turned out to be a venue for business to forward its complaints or requests to the government, rather than the reverse" (Laothamatas 1992: 70).

The sectoral scope of consultation was also fairly confined. Success in tourism proved to be something of an anomaly, perhaps because the industry was just emerging and its interests less established. The government did launch an automotive engine project in consultation with part of the Siam Cement group during the 1980s. But the effort required extensive protection of multinational investors, and multinational pressures stymied government efforts to expand scale economies and promote efficiency by limiting the number of engine producers (Doner 1991).

More seriously, the government failed in its efforts to restructure inefficient industries through tariff liberalization and rationalization. A top-level Restructuring Committee (RESCOM) was established in the mid-1980s to rationalize a number of specific industries, including autos, electronics, and textiles/apparel. But RESCOM lacked control over tariffs, which were under the supervision of the Finance Ministry. Given that ministry's concern with the country's fiscal health, tariffs would not be lowered during a period of alarming public-sector deficits. Staffed with neoclassical economists, RESCOM also lacked links to and real knowledge about particular industries. Restructuring efforts in textiles and autos generated more private-sector resentment than anything else. Tariff reform was successful only in consumer electronics, where the private sector agreed on the need for liberalization to undercut rampant smuggling (Thanamai 1985; Brimble 1994).

Finally, increasing business participation in the electoral process during the 1980s weakened state and private sector consultation toward the end of the decade. As electoral competition intensified during the 1980s, so did party reliance on financial support from business. The largest Thai enterprises became heavily involved in funding candidates. Yet this did not translate into a collective business voice. It was often not banks that financed parties but individuals or families within banks. In addition, firms and individuals within industry associations often backed rival parties, the better to gain access to particular state services. Indeed, certain sectoral interests have tended to be identified with particular parties due to the latters' access to relevant cabinet positions.[30] This whole

---

[30] The Chart Thai party has exerted strong control over the Ministry of Industry, the agency responsible for regulating the party's major interests (textiles, glass, sugar milling, and so on). The Social Action Party's principal ministerial holdout is the Ministry of Commerce, the agency responsible for handling quotas critical to the party backers from the rice, tapioca, soybean, and animal feed industries. Chart Thai governed the Industry Ministry during almost the entire period from 1975 to 1990. The Social Action Party (SAP) ran the Commerce Ministry in 1975, 1980–81, and 1983–90 and placed members of parliament in the ministry in seven of nine elected coalitions beginning in 1975. One SAP leader complained that he didn't want the job of commerce minister because "of the difficult position it puts you in when the lobbying from exporters starts" (Christensen 1991: 82).

process was encouraged by an expansion in the number of cabinet, sub-cabinet, and advisory positions during the 1980s, a process that in turn served the needs of Thailand's changing electoral system (Christensen 1991: 57). Cabinet posts not only provided extra salaries but also consti-tuted channels through which party leaders could satisfy the rural patron-age requirements of getting elected. Since the 1970s, as elections have became more institutionalized, networks of influential people or "godfa-thers" in rural areas (entrepreneurs involved in smuggling, illegal logging, liquor sales, real estate, and construction) have become critical channels of voter mobilization (Ockey 1992: 134).

The Fragility of Collective Economic Governance

During the post-Prem period Thailand has lurched from a flowering of pluralistic spoils, to autonomous state initiatives, to a partial resurgence of public-private sector consultation. Two important trends have emerged: collective private-sector efforts to contend with a more com-petitive external environment, and a weakened state.

By the late 1980s, regime changes and an economic boom allowed rent seeking to flower. In 1988, Prime Minister Prem was replaced by Chartchai Choonavan, the country's first elected leader since 1976. The Chartchai government presided over intense party rivalry in which numbers of parliament competed for spoils through control of ministries, access to infrastructural projects, and sales of offices.[31] This marked a new step in a process begun earlier in the decade: Formerly, private interests paid bribes to appropriate state goods and services whose volume and scope were limited by the nature of the fiscal process. Now, to support rural patronage networks necessary for elections, they were paying to appropriate the state itself.

The civil service became intensely politicized as senior officials who refused to follow their minister's partisan strategies were replaced by more pliable officials. The new government also curtailed the influence of NESDB officials. The latter had supported the joint public-private sector committees and blocked large infrastructure projects out of concern for their potential for corruption. With these officials weakened, corruption expanded, and Chartchai abandoned national-level consultations. Whereas the JPPCC met almost monthly in the early 1980s, it met five times in 1988, two in 1990, and not at all in 1991–92.

The country's economic boom also weakened incentives for collective economic governance. Strengthened by the macroeconomic reforms of

---

[31] In addition to covering scandals over logging and telephone concessions, the Thai press reported that top police posts were on sale for anywhere from $4,000 to $8,000 apiece at the Interior Ministry (Christensen 1991: 83).

the 1980s and fueled by huge foreign-investment inflows and domestic savings, the Thai economy soared in the late 1980s.[32] In 1987–90, gross do mertic product (GDP) growth rates averaged 11.6 percent annually, and manufacturing grew at more than 16 percent. Manufactured exports, growing at more than 29 percent, led the expansion and exceeded agricultural exports for the first time in 1986.[33] Ironically, this growth undermined industry-level associations and consultation by obviating concerns about market share and access. Auto parts firms, for example, were not only satisfied with their market share but could barely keep up with expanding orders. Local content regulations and model limits became irrelevant. Private-sector organization and public-private links remained strong only where access to foreign markets required collective action, as in quotas for textiles and garments. Even in this case, there were complaints that quota allocation functioned largely to impede new entrants rather than to encourage greater efficiency (Suphachalasai 1992).

By 1991, however, the boom itself had created new strains in the Thai economy. In addition to widening income disparities and worsening environmental conditions (Muscat 1994), Thailand began to experience the effects of its weak infrastructure and technological base. In terms of human infrastructure, new industries exhausted the country's supply of skilled labor and laid bare its traditional neglect of education: Thailand's percentage of secondary school-age children enrolled in school (29 percent) is the lowest in the region, trailing even Indonesia (47 percent) and China (44 percent) (Fairclough 1993: 25). Thailand has three scientists and engineers per one million people in the labor force compared with twenty-seven for South Korea, thirty-four for Singapore, and fifty-four for Taiwan (Brimble and Sripraipan 1994: 42). Firms responded by raiding each other for skilled personnel, while Thailand risked being frozen between low-wage neighbors such as Indonesia and the more developed NICs. Meanwhile, Thai efforts at industrial upgrading have been plagued by severe weakness in science and technology. Private R&D remains "dismally low" (Brimble and Sripaipan 1994: 24). State funding levels are also minimal, and the country suffers from weak links between the scientific community and the private sector. Despite recent institutional changes, those parts of the bureaucracy concerned with science and technology lack leverage. One finds none of the state-supported programs for the private sector seen in the NICs, nor has the state been able to implement a program to encourage technology transfer through more systematic links between local suppliers and foreign multinationals.

---

[32] Net foreign investment went from $263 million in 1986, to $352 million in 1987, to $1.1 billion in 1988, to $1.78 billion in 1989, to $2.5 billion in 1990 (SEAMICO 1993).
[33] By 1991, the value of textile and apparel exports was three times that of rice (Kaosa-ard 1992: 3–12; SEAMICO 1993).

Lack of attention to physical infrastructure has also been a problem. Investment in transport and communications was cut during the 1980s stabilization program. Thus, the acceleration of economic growth later in the decade led to a severe infrastructural bottleneck. Conflicts between elected politicians and macroeconomic technocrats intensified as the need for infrastructural investments grew. Because many activities came under the purview of monopolistic state enterprises, technocrats pushed for privatization. But the bidding process itself became a politicized spoils process under Chartchai (Christensen et al. 1993). The negotiation process was slow and riddled with corruption. These problems were exacerbated in Bangkok, the country's core economic area and largest population concentration, by an utter lack of institutional coherence and accountability (Muscat 1994: 250–51).

Thailand also suffered from major bottlenecks in the supply and allocation of water (Christensen and Boon-long 1993). Water supplies have deteriorated as watersheds have been destroyed and rainfall has dropped. Overuse has resulted from the lack of property rights noted earlier in this chapter: Agriculturalists enjoy free access to water, while urban consumers pay only a nominal fee. Further exacerbating overuse are problems of administrative fragmentation: there are some thirty department-level agencies under seven different ministries responsible for water management, none of which are legally required to inform the others of their activities. Finally, industrial growth has placed new demands on water supplies, particularly in Bangkok, where groundwater pumping threatens to create massive environmental costs and intensifies sectoral conflicts between agriculture and industry. Thus, the range of actors whose interests require coordination has grown while institutional capacities have stagnated. Problems in water allocation have also plagued one of the country's major export industries: textiles and garments. Despite its success, the Thai textile industry is quite dualistic: The upstream and midstream producers of fiber, yarn, and fabric have little to do with the downstream garment firms. Critical to this problem is a lack of dyeing and printing capacity, due in large part to a lack of wastewater treatment.

Finally, the country's taxation system was severely outmoded. Industrial upgrading requires links among firms at different stages in the production chain. This process has been hindered by the cascading system of Thai business taxes. Reflecting the government's reliance on tax revenues, the system imposed levies on the full value of products transacted between domestic firms. As a result, it encouraged enterprises either to import or produce their inputs themselves rather than obtain them from local suppliers. Reform of this system proved very difficult because of the weakness of links between business and the agency responsible for taxes and tariffs—the Finance Ministry.

Increasingly predatory, the Chartchai government was largely impotent in the face of these problems. Rampant corruption prompted broad public support for a military coup against the government in 1991. The new government was led by a respected business leader, Anand Panyarachun, who in turn provided political support for state technocrats.[34] Emboldened by fiscal surpluses, Anand's administration undertook a number of efficiency-related measures, including tariff reforms in autos, capital equipment, computers, and other sectors; the replacement of the business tax by a value-added tax; commitment to membership in GATT and the World Trade Organization (which requires complete tariff liberalization and an end to local content requirements); and leadership in an effort to create an ASEAN (Association of Southeast Asian Nations) free-trade area.

Despite clear achievements, the government had little time to make real progress on issues such as infrastructure, industrial upgrading, environment, and rural poverty. In fact, bureaucratic and political hurdles undermined the government's capacity to spend even those funds already approved for infrastructure projects.[35] Also problematic was the lack of public-private sector consultation regarding trade liberalization. To some extent this was an advantage: Consultation might have blocked the process. Military-backed autonomy was clearly useful, especially for trade liberalization.[36] But the lack of consultation undermined adjustment and coordination measures necessary for Thai industry to emerge stronger from the liberalization process. For example, Thai commitments to tariff reductions under an ASEAN fee-trade area were not accompanied by any effort to compensate losers and strengthen the winners' competitive base. Liberalization thus unleashed a series of disputes between upstream producers such as petrochemicals slated to lose their protection and downstream enterprises anxious to gain access to cheaper petrochemical inputs from neighboring countries.[37] The traditional weakness of links between Finance Ministry technocrats and business leaders discouraged prior consultation on these issues.

[34] Anand actually led two governments. As a result of elections held in March 1992, one of the military leaders of the previous coup government became prime minister. This prompted mass protests that were met in turn by military force. After the death of at least fifty-two people, the military leader resigned to be replaced by another interim government headed by Anand in June 1992. The second Anand government was replaced by a coalition government led by Chuan Leekpai after the September 1992 elections.

[35] The government spent only 70 percent of its 1992 budget, only 40 percent of that going to capital expenditures (S. Johnson 1993: 27).

[36] Note that the Chartchai government, bolstered by a strong budgetary surplus, had initiated the process by reducing duties on capital goods from 20 percent to 5 percent in October 1990.

[37] See, for example, "Industries May Lose Protection," *Bangkok Post*, March 3, 1991, p. 26; "Longer Protection Urged for Petrochem Industry," *Nation*, January 20, 1992, p. B1.

In the long run, however, the move toward greater openness has provoked some beneficial institutional responses, especially on the part of the private sector. Industries are facing not only the inevitability of greater exposure to import competition but also the need to negotiate the speed and terms of this exposure with the key arbiter of upstream-downstream linkages—the ministry of Finance. To deal with this ministry, firms have had to become more professional in their research. In some cases, this involves hiring local research institutions to gather data. In others, it involves closer cooperation with bureaucratic pockets of industry-specific expertise and commitment.[38]

The need for greater efficiency and higher value added has also stimulated broader institutional growth within the private sector itself. Groups of firms in the textile industry have accelerated efforts to promote training and technology institutes.[39] In the auto industry, Japanese assemblers have begun to establish training centers, fund engineering departments of local universities, and intensify the quality-related activities of their supplier associations. Finally, there has been a growth of industrial parks outside of Bangkok, in some cases with industry-initiated support from technology institutes (Brimble and Sripraipan 1994; author interviews).

The key question here involves the supply of state support for these activities. On the positive side, the Ministry of Finance, historically aloof from sector-specific concerns, has become a productive interlocutor with private-sector institutions. The minister of finance under the Chuan government (1992–95) took the unprecedented step of initiating several education projects and actually attending business association meetings to urge members to undertake collective training efforts. On the other hand, the Finance Ministry has avoided any active efforts at reconciling intra-industry differences. More troubling has been a distinct weakening of state agencies. Tendencies toward politicization of the bureaucracy intensified with the June 1995 election of a coalition government headed by a party and a prime minister with especially strong links to rural patronage networks. The new prime minister, Banharn Silpaarcha, began his political career as a wealthy provincial business leader (Ockey 1992:

---

[38] For example, the Association of Thai Industries has used the Thai Development Research Institute to generate data on the impact of liberalization. The Dyers' and Printers' Association has worked closely with the Textile Industry Division of the Ministry of Industry to develop a position on the need for reduction of tariffs on chemicals used in dyeing (author interviews).

[39] After several years, the Thai Garment Manufacturers' Association has finally established a training foundation through cooperation with experts from Thailand's National Institute of Development Administration. The Dyers' and Printers' Association has, with support from the Textile Industry Division, begun to diffuse information on environmentally safe chemicals—this in response to a European Union decision to ban imports of garments dyed with chemicals traditionally used by Thai firms (author interviews).

228–31). After taking office, he alarmed the business community by appointing as finance minister an individual with no experience in a major financial post and as vice-ministers two individuals accused of malfeasance (*Nation*, July 1995, various issues). Even the central bank, heretofore a model of propriety and expertise, has come under financial industry criticism for political interference and favoritism (Fairclough 1996). Retaining personnel is also a problem. With private-sector salaries running many times above those of state officials, the Thai bureaucracy is experiencing a brain drain of sufficient severity to put into doubt its capacity to support, much less promote, private-sector efforts. One emerging response to the personnel problem is the growth of quasi-private organizations: Groups of firms and associations hire experienced state officials to staff institutions financed and directed largely by the private sector.[40] Whether such efforts can succeed in the absence of consistent state support remains to be seen.

CONCLUSION

Thailand has succeeded in maintaining macroeconomic stability, diversifying its agriculture, shifting into industry, and expanding manufactured exports. This success has depended on a set of arrangements that reduced entry barriers for new firms and forced them to compete with each other, even as it provided a certain level of collective goods and extensive macroeconomic stability. These arrangements included (1) a clientelism involving mutual vulnerability and need, (2) community and broader private-sector institutions such as banks and business groups capable of reconciling diverse sectoral interests, and (3) insulated macroeconomic officials whose institutional coherence and ties with export-oriented commercial bankers allowed them to impose hard-budget constraints on the rest of the state. We have also argued that these institutions cannot be understood outside of certain enabling factors, especially a threatening external environment and the absence of a landed oligarchy.

A brief comparison with the Philippines is useful to explore the broader utility of this argument. In the early 1950s, analysts assumed that the Philippines would be the economic success story of East Asia. With its strong U.S.–based educational system, its well-developed entrepreneurial class, and its large number of managers and technicians, the Philippines was slated to leap ahead not just of Thailand but of South Korea as well. By the late 1980s, however, Thailand had clearly outdistanced the Philippines.

[40] This seems to be the pattern adopted by the textile and tool and die industries.

This contrast is explained in part by the weak institutionalization of the Philippine state, especially its macroeconomic components. As we have seen, the Thai state is divided between weak and relatively politicized line ministries and macroeconomic officials substantially insulated from political pressures originating from other ministries as well as social forces working through legislators or political patrons. In the Philippines, we find a more consistent state apparatus, all of whose components have been open to plunder by strong private-sector forces.[41] Selective credit has been not only widespread but also highly vulnerable to political manipulation. During the 1960s, officials in the central and state development banks were unable to resist claims on government funds by powerful commercial banks, which then lent the funds to favored customers, including government officials. President Marcos's "crony capitalism" only exacerbated the weakness of central bank regulators in the face of these abuses. Cronies were, for example, allowed to obtain interest-free deposits of publicly decreed coconut levies. Officials attempting to restrict such practices often found themselves the object of successful lawsuits.

Politicized macroeconomic agencies in the Philippines also undermined the capacity of business groups and commercial banks for provision of collective goods. With the central bank unable to limit the disbursement of public funds and impose positive rates on savings deposits, commercial banks were poor at mobilizing savings but quite good at providing profitable loan portfolios for plunder by directors and stockholders. Although both Thai and Philippine commercial banks supported the fortunes of allied firms in diverse sectors, the control or ownership of such groups was quite narrow in the Philippines case. Just as the state was captured by private interests, commercial banks were captured by particular firms and families within individual industries, thus weakening any capacity toward provision of collective goods as seen in the Thai case.

The textile industry is a good example. A recent study of the Philippine textile industry makes no mention of commercial bank efforts to reconcile upstream-downstream interests, organize the industry's labor market, or negotiate reductions in capacity. Instead, Marcos cronies in the textile industry used political connections to inflate assets of allied commercial banks and, in one major case, fled the country and triggered a major banking crisis after defaulting on some $85 million in debt (Kuo 1990: 234). The Bangkok Bank's contribution to rationalizing the Thai textile industry has no analogue in the Philippines.[42]

Philippine problems are also explained by the country's particular form of clientelism. Clients enjoyed both independent sources of wealth accu-

---

[41] Unless noted, this discussion draws on the work of Hutchcroft 1993, 1996.
[42] See Hutchcroft 1993 and personal communication from Paul Hutchcroft.

mulation and significant political autonomy (through a U.S.–style electoral system and a strong nationalist movement). The result was a very different exchange relationship between entrepreneurial patrons and state-based clients: In contrast to the mutual vulnerability seen in Thailand, Philippine state officials were clearly the weaker party. Before the early 1970s, this resulted in a policy stalemate. Marcos's declaration of martial law only narrowed the range of favored interests. Networks became collusive and exclusive, thus raising bribe costs, reducing the level of private-sector competition, and undermining pressure on private-sector clients to make productive use of their rents.

Two enabling factors help to explain these different institutional patterns. First, the Philippines experienced a less disciplining set of external conditions than did Thailand. The United States provided numerous guarantees of extensive financial support, whether in the form of security support, repeated rescues from balance-of-payment crises, or assured access to the U.S. market for Filipino sugar. Under these conditions, there was every incentive for Filipino political elites to keep on spending regardless of the actual condition of state revenues. Conversely, there were few incentives for the creation of fiscally cautious state institutions.

We are not arguing that revenue constraints lead to fiscal caution in some linear fashion. Rather, revenue shortages can encourage fiscal caution when their threat is of significant duration. The strength of fiscally conservative institutions is also a function of private-sector leverage. Philippine state officials had to contend with an oligarchy that was both landed and politically organized. This oligarchy not only blocked land reform but, as it diversified into protected manufacturing and banking, had sufficient leverage to undermine other institutional and economic reforms as well (Haggard 1994: 86). As we have noted, no such oligarchy existed in Thailand. Separated from land ownership, the interests of Sino-Thai firms were profoundly commercial and export-oriented. Moreover, they needed the backing of Thai political patrons, even as the latter relied on Sino-Thai entrepreneurs both to generate revenues for the state and to provide them with personal finances necessary for a "safe landing in case of political adversity" (McVey 1992: 23).

Institutional and background factors thus help to explain the strength of Thailand's performance relative to the Philippines. Nevertheless, our analysis of recent developments in Thailand suggests some areas of concern with regard to the country's future growth. The first has to do with development tasks. By effectively mobilizing raw materials and cheap labor, the Thai economy has expanded through exports of primary commodities and low value-added manufactured goods (export processing assembly and some component subcontracting). The capacity to shift into original equipment manufacturing requires not just mobilization of existing factors of production but creation and upgrading of new factors and reconciliation of more entrenched groups of firms at upstream, mid-stream, and downstream stages of production. Thailand's institutional arrangements have not shown themselves especially capable of resolving these kinds of problems.

In addition, the country's economic and political developments have themselves weakened the state's capacity to promote and join with an organized private-sector response to the challenge of industrial upgrad-ing. The growth of a dynamic and independent capitalist class has sapped the state of critical personnel. And the country's particular form of democratization has spawned a group of parties whose focus is less on policy issues than on using the state to bolster local electoral networks. These conditions weaken the potential for efficient institutional responses to the country's new set of development challenges.

CHAPTER TEN

Economic Governance in Turkey: Bureaucratic Capacity, Policy Networks, and Business Associations

JESSE BIDDLE AND VEDAT MILOR

A wide range of protectionist policies inspired by an import substitution industrialization (ISI) strategy were prominent instruments of Turkish industrial policy through the 1970s. From the 1980s onward, however, in the context of a gradually liberalizing trade regime, the selective use of incentives and subsidies has played an increasingly important role. These incentives and subsidies, such as exemptions from customs duties, tax breaks, and subsidized credit, have been targeted for a number of industrial policy purposes, including the promotion of regional development, particular industries, and functional activities such as investments and exports.

There is vigorous debate as to whether an industrial policy premised on selective use of incentives and subsidies, as in Turkey, constitutes a coherent means of promoting economic growth and international competitiveness. This debate has recently centered on alternative interpretations of the spectacular economic performance of East Asian developmental states. At question is whether the well-established presence of the selective use of incentives and subsidies are among the causes of superior economic performance or are spuriously or negatively associated. While more orthodox analyses stress the openness and macroeco-

We thank Izak Atiyas, Ben Ross Schneider, Ziya Öniş, and two anonymous reviewers for helpful comments on earlier drafts. The World Bank provided financial support for our research. Research assistance in Turkey was provided by Erkan Erdil and Hakan Batur. Finally, we are grateful for the stimulating comments on our work from various participants in the two workshops on the role of collaboration between business and the state in rapid growth in the periphery.

nomic stability of these economies, there has been an explosion of institutional analyses arguing that East Asian economic performance is, in fact, partially attributable to strategic government industrial policies.[1] Economic modeling can, in fact, demonstrate that under certain imperfect market conditions the use of trade barriers, incentives, and subsidies in a selective industrial policy may lead to optimal solutions. Strategic trade policy, for example, may help increase national market share in concentrated international markets (Krugman 1986).

Irrespective of theoretical models, however, a serious practical difficulty arises with the use of industrial policies. The availability of the rents created by such policies generates incentives for business actors, politicians, and bureaucrats to rent-seek or, as Bhagwati (1982) says, to engage in "directly unproductive activities." Of course, the nature of the policy regime is related to the degree of rent seeking. In particular, an ISI strategy is likely to be subject to higher degrees of rent seeking than one whose aim is to promote externally competitive industries. This is because the policy instruments associated with ISI, such as quotas and tariffs, not only enhance government discretion over resource allocation but also, by reducing competition, encourage the formation of a protectionist business culture bent on asking special favors from the state. Even export-oriented policy regimes, however, are not necessarily free from rent seeking. Even after liberalizing foreign trade, governments often make use of a multitude of other direct inducements, such as preferential credits, discretionary tax breaks, custom duty exemptions, and so on, which engender business demands for favorable treatment. Thus, irrespective of the nature of the policy regime, given that the rents created by industrial policy interventions are the product of decisions made in institutional contexts in which rent-seeking political pressure may be influential, there is an unambiguous potential for industrial policy to be diverted over time toward narrow, private ends. No matter which side one takes in the debate over the merits of selective industrial policies, all sides agree, and comparative empirical evidence demonstrates, that such policies can be easily abused when private economic actors, economic bureaucrats, and politicians are able to channel such policies toward their own ends. The pernicious effects of such rent seeking on economic performance are well established.[2]

---

[1] See Balassa 1981, Lal 1983, and Krueger 1980 for empirical arguments relating East Asian economic performance to expectations of the neoclassical paradigm and theory of comparative advantage. The institutionalist critique is best articulated by Wade 1990. See also Amsden 1989, Deyo 1987, and Onis 1991. Recently, a World Bank study endorsed some of the tenets of the institutional critique, particularly those relating to bureaucratic insularity and state-business networks. See *The East-Asian Miracle: Economic Growth and Public Policy* (1993a) and related bank policy papers, especially those by Campos 1993 and Stiglitz 1993.

[2] On rent seeking with respect to quotas, see Krueger 1974. A generalization of the

This chapter does not concentrate on the contribution of Turkish industrial policy to economic performance during the liberal export-led stage of development in the 1980s. Rather, it addresses the equally important issue of the coherence and effectiveness with which the state delivers such policies in the first place. What are the institutional conditions influencing whether Turkish strategic industrial policies remain focused on publicly oriented goals (such as growth or export competitiveness) as opposed to becoming focused on privately oriented ones? One way to begin answering this question is to view the state-business relationship in the context of an industrial policy as a contract that carries obligations for both parties, particularly for business beneficiaries of incentives and subsidies financed from the public purse.[3] Thus, effective economic policy is closely related to the extent to which these contracts are fulfilled. Focusing first on business as one of the parties, economic analyses suggest that businesses are more likely to fulfill their end of incentive and subsidy contracts when the state establishes an initial screening process for applicants, based on technical criteria monitors the use of incentives and subsidies, and imposes disciplinary consequences (such as penalties) on beneficiaries who fail to meet mutually agreed-upon performance standards.[4] Alice Amsden's (1989) study of industrial policy in South Korea illustrates these points in an empirical context. The Korean state screened, monitored, and, most important, disciplined incentive and subsidy recipients who failed to meet performance standards. These and other East Asian experiences further suggest that business compliance with industrial policy goals may be enhanced by combining the "stick" of disciplinary consequences for poor performers with "carrots" in the form of escalating access to incentives and subsidies for superior performers.

This focus on the monitoring and disciplinary capability of the state and its economic bureaucracy, however, may be putting the cart before

---

argument is offered in Bhagwati 1982. See also Buchanan et al. 1980 and Colander 1984 for various perspectives on rent seeking and associated new neoclassical political economy.

[3] Thus, industrial policies involve what economists refer to as a principal-agent relationship between the state and business. On agency theory, see Alchian and Demsetz 1973, Fama 1980, and Jensen and Meckling 1976. Nontechnical overviews are provided by Moe 1984 and Perrow 1990.

[4] If there is no initial screening process based on technical criteria or, worse still, a selection process based on political criteria, this encourages an adverse selection process whereby less competent and less sincere investors may crowd out more competent and more sincere ones. Moreover, if it is known that the state does not monitor business performance or is unwilling to enforce agreed-upon performance standards of the contract (that is, to discipline program abusers), the moral hazard arises that incentives and subsidies will become giveaways because business recipients may be able to use them with scant reference to their contractual commitments. Finally, to the extent that the state is commonly known to allow investors to renegotiate the original terms of the incentive and subsidy contract, this ex ante reduces incentives for the investor to fulfill contractual obligations (Bolton 1990).

the horse. It presupposes the existence of sufficient competence and will on the part of the state, the other party, to uphold its end of the industrial policy contract. In particular, there is no guarantee that state policy, including the selective provision of incentives and subsidies to business, will remain focused on achieving publicly oriented goals in line with coherently organized industrial policy programs. In fact, industrial policies can be detoured toward the achievement of narrow, rent-oriented goals through the selective misuse of incentives and subsidies. A vigorous political economy literature emphasizes the importance of insulating economic bureaucrats from direct interest-based pressures from business, labor, or other groups in society as well as from pork-barrel political pressures.[5] Such bureaucratic insulation is related to the presence of a small and centralized economic bureaucracy that is endowed with well-defined authorities for certain policy areas and characterized by Weberian traits such as stable career paths and meritocratic recruitment and promotion criteria. Such institutional characteristics allow bureaucrats to develop shared identity and purpose that facilitate unified decision making, deter corruption, and help professionalize the policy process (Rueschemeyer and Evans 1985).

Nevertheless, even though some insulation from political and interest-based pressures helps bureaucrats deliver publicly oriented policies, too much outright bureaucratic isolation from real-world economic issues confronting business actors may hinder industrial policy conceptualization and implementation and slow down needed policy reformulation, given changing economic conditions or policies that were poorly conceived in the first place. Furthermore, the credibility of government industrial policies in the eyes of business, and therefore business's willingness to undertake risks in conjunction with those policies, are undermined when business is out of the policy loop. Thus, the nature of institutionalized state-business relationships, what we call policy networks, may influence the effectiveness of policy formulation, implementation, and adjustment.[6] By policy networks we refer to not only formal consultations between bureaucrats and businesspersons or associations but also the presence and density of informal ad hoc meetings and communications.

While our focus is predominantly on policy effectiveness, let us briefly

---

[5] For recent examples, see Zysman 1983, Shapiro and Taylor 1990, Geddes 1990, Schneider 1993a, and Evans 1995.

[6] The literature on networks is large and varied. See the chapter in this book by Haggard, Maxfield, and Schneider as well as Berry 1989 for a review of political science perspectives on networks; Zeitlin and Ratcliff 1988 for a neo-Marxist analysis of dominant class networks; and Powell and Smith-Doerr 1994 for a review of network approaches in the growing economic sociology literature.

discuss our conceptualization of business as an economic and political actor. We view economic agents as the individual, family, or group that enjoys proprietary control over a firm.[7] In many developing nations, high levels of concentration in the economy means that a small number of such economic agents—"big business"—enjoy proprietary control over large and often many individual firms (see Chapter 2). In Turkey, one observes a pattern of massive conglomerate holdings characterized by multisectoral investment patterns, strong interfirm proprietary ties, and hierarchical managerial control. Such economic agents certainly share a broad class interest in the maintenance of private property relations, as emphasized by neo-Marxists, and certain subgroups may share more specific industrial or sectoral interests (discussed by Shafer in this book). We contend, however, that the simple sharing of economic interests among economic agents may not be sufficiently compelling to overcome the collective-action difficulties identified by Olson (1965) and other rational-choice theorists to be inherent in the rational pursuit of self-interest. For example, businesses active in a given industry—say, autos—may rationally be able to agree that certain long-term advantages would come about with a significant restructuring of the industry but may be unable to cooperate with restructuring efforts because of concerns about the short-term distribution of costs and uneven distribution of future gains. Through collective organization, either formal or informal, such collective-action dilemmas may be overcome.

As Bates (1987) notes, formal collective institutions, such as business associations, can help resolve collective-action dilemmas by changing the individual cost-benefit calculation of economic agents. Industry-level associations may allow for the provision of common goods, such as information about overseas markets, which would be prohibitively expensive for economic agents to pursue individually. Furthermore, encompassing cross-sectoral business associations can help resolve interindustry collective-action problems associated with the uneven distribution of gains and losses associated with long-term economic restructuring policies. As an alternative to formal collective institutions, economic agents may share sufficient beliefs, values, and background assumptions to trust each other enough to make informal collective coordination of economic actions possible. Some have argued that the sharing of such social capital, in what Haggard, Maxfield, and Schneider call natural networks, has been

[7] The determination of proprietary control is complex and difficult because the rise of joint stock corporations, as argued by Berle and Means 1967, raises the possibility that highly dispersed ownership may eventuate in managerial control. Nevertheless, as effectively argued by Zeitlin and Ratcliff 1988, proprietary control is often possible to wield over a firm even in the context of highly dispersed shareholdings, given pyramidal and other shareholding devices that maximize the influence of minority holding interests.

instrumental to East Asian economic success (Dore 1983) as well as to the rapid growth of certain European industrial regions, such as Emilia-Romagna in Italy (Putnam 1993a; Schmitz and Musyck 1994). We believe that the presence or absence of business collective organization, either formal or informal, often reflects historically contingent factors, as in the ready-wear clothing industry in Turkey; therefore, we disagree with approaches that endogenize business's likelihood to organize collectively by reducing it to industry- or sector-specific factors.[8]

The relationship of state-business policy networks to policy effectiveness depends on both the nature of the economic bureaucracy and the nature of the network. Given a bureaucracy that approximates Weberian characteristics, the self-interest of bureaucrats is firmly anchored to institutional goals and thus not easily diverted toward private ends. As Fields discusses in this book, such Weberian bureaucracies are approximated in Korea and Taiwan. In such environments, businesses still have incentive to seek access to subsidies and other bureaucratic favors. Yet such rent seeking, (if the term is still appropriate in such contexts) is channeled toward the meeting of state-defined developmental performance criteria rather than cajoling or bribing bureaucrats to bend the rules governing subsidy access in some private manner. It is reasonable to conclude that a disciplined subsidy allocation process can potentially be growth-promoting, export-enhancing, or otherwise virtuous if it creates a contest among businesses involving the competitive pursuit of developmental goals.[9] In such contexts, state-business policy networks can perform positive functions such as allowing information to pass rapidly among bureaucrats and businesspersons, encouraging business input in policy discussions, and generating greater consensus about policy direction. This combination of a relatively insular Weberian bureaucratic structure with dense, communicative ties to the business community is what Evans (1995) refers to as embedded autonomy.[10] In developmental East Asian states, policy networks appear to be organized both in relatively formal and institutionalized manners, such as Japan's well-known deliberation

---

[8] Such endogenizing of collective-action prospects is characteristic of sectoral approaches. See, for example, Gourevitch 1986; Frieden 1991; and Shafer, forthcoming. See also Chapter 4 in this book as well as the discussion of sectoral approaches in Chapter 2.

[9] Our thanks to an anonymous reviewer for stimulating our thoughts about contests. Of course, deciding whether such contests are inferior, an adequate functional substitute, or even superior to competitive market pressures as a means of stimulating publicly oriented corporate behavior is well beyond the scope of this chapter.

[10] Polanyi (1944, 1957) originally coined the term *embeddedness* to characterize how inextricably bound market interactions are within preexisting institutional and normative frameworks. Granovetter 1985 provides a more contemporary discussion of how market interactions and, by extension, state-business interactions may be embedded in previously existing social networks.

councils and Korea's monthly export promotion meetings, as well as in more informal manners involving regular private contacts among industry, bureaucratic, and political leaders.

In the general absence of a Weberian bureaucracy, however, policy effectiveness may be either hindered or helped depending on the nature of the policy network in question. We disagree with the working assumption of much neoliberal economic analysis, which presumes that state-business ties will inevitably become focused on the delivery of special favors from the state to business. This position is captured well in Olson's (1982) analysis of the growth-inhibiting effects of distributional coalitions and leads to the common neoliberal prescription to minimize the role of the state and remove it from the activity of industrial policy. In contrast, we characterize as growth-oriented those networks in which there is a two-way information flow; established norms of reciprocity, honesty, and trust; and transparency in information sharing and decision making among network members. The two-way information flow may enhance initial policy design as well as allow for more rapid and flexible policy adjustment by helping to ensure that information with respect to "changes in world markets, new trends in technologies, perverse effects of regulations domestically and abroad are all communicated to the bureaucracy by private sector agents" (Campos 1993: 28). Established norms may help reduce transaction costs, generate trust among network members, and facilitate the resolution of collective-action problems confronting network members in the presence of prisoner's dilemma–type situations, where, in the absence of norms, inefficient outcomes are likely to prevail (Arrow 1974; Kandori 1992; Putnam 1993a).

Finally, network transparency is important because it raises the cost, both to members of the state and the business community, of private rent seeking, rendering such actions more easily observed and punished by other network members. The term *transparency* does not necessarily entail widespread public access to knowledge, but it does suggest that actual network members are aware of information and decision-making processes. For example, in a transparent network associated with the disbursal of subsidies in an industrial policy, network members have readily available knowledge concerning a rival firm's access to subsidies; crucially, the procedures or rules governing this access—both for the rival firm and for themselves—are public knowledge. Such transparency, we contend, significantly decreases the attractiveness of rent-seeking efforts by rendering such efforts more easily observable and therefore more risky and costly. Moreover, especially when access to subsidies is linked unambiguously to performance criteria, transparency channels firms' competitiveness away from lobbying government (or business association) officials and toward improving their own performance.

Unlike growth-oriented networks, rent-oriented networks have a two-way information flow and the presence, perhaps, of various norms such as trust (which enables businesspersons, politicians, and bureaucrats to cooperate more easily) but in which the level of transparency is low enough for some network members to develop narrow rent-oriented ties successfully. A rent-oriented policy network may or may not regularly involve corruption, understood as an illegal form of cooperation between public officials and private citizens oriented toward mutual gain. Undoubtedly, the nontransparency of these networks generates incentives for corrupt behavior, particularly if combined, as in Turkey, with considerable bureaucratic discretion over legal and regulatory issues that concern business. In some nations, however (Turkey again is an illustration), public-private cooperation involving narrow legal and regulatory changes that benefit a small number of parties may not only be legal but also regular institutionalized behavior and therefore not corrupt. In either case, a lack of transparency in policy networks is particularly harmful to economic growth because "since the fruits of growth occur in the future, growth creates enormous uncertainty over how its fruits are going to be distributed"; given a lack of transparency, "this creates incentives for various agents to preempt their competitors by bribing pubic officials" (Campos 1993: 28–29). Such a process, illustrated by the auto industry in Turkey, not only harms growth by diverting the energy of businesspersons away from productive activity and toward lobbying but also because it effectively precludes the adoption of longer-term economic strategies—especially industrial restructuring policies involving an unequal short-term distribution of costs—dependent on cooperation among different economic agents.

In the next section we discuss the ineffectiveness of Turkish industrial policy in relation to patterns of state-business relations. We account in theoretical terms for this general ineffectiveness by referring to the lack of insulation in the Turkish bureaucracy empowered to implement industrial policy as well as to a general prevalence of rent-oriented policy networks linking state and business actors. We found an interesting lacuna with respect to the general pattern of rent-oriented state-business networks in the case of the ready-wear clothing industry. Here, we found a growth-oriented policy network characterized by a high degree of transparency in its operation. In particular, the industry associations that mediated between the state and the beneficiaries of the incentive program established rules governing the distribution of incentives that linked member access to benefits with their quantifiable export success and made transparent and trustworthy the process through which members documented their performance. Such transparency in the rules reduced the uncertainties surrounding the future distribution of incentives and subsidies, which was instrumental in freeing members to engage in growth-oriented competition over exports as opposed to competing with each other in lobbying and rent seeking. Such private-sector economic governance allowed for more effective economic policy than would have been possible given Turkish bureaucrats' general lack of insulation from pork-barrel and rent-seeking pressures.[11]

INDUSTRIAL POLICY IN TURKEY

The Turkish Republic, which came into existence in 1923, inherited a strong dirigiste state tradition from the Ottoman Empire. While the existence of a centralized state tradition differentiated Turkey from the bulk of once-colonized countries, the young republic resembled other newly independent nations in the sense that a local entrepreneurial class did not exist. The founders of the new republic believed that the economic and military superiority of Western nations (which had militarily defeated the Ottomans) rested on technological prowess associated with the existence of a dynamic and innovative business class. Consequently, in an attempt to replicate the Western trajectory, they decided to foster a national business class to perform entrepreneurial functions necessary for development. The bureaucratic elite that ruled the country during the single-party period (1923–50) assumed the task of transforming the economic structure through direct participation in capital formation, either through state economic enterprises (SEEs) established in the étatist period of the 1930s or through public-private joint ventures in various industries.

The adoption of an import-substitution *cum* protectionist development strategy coincided with the transition to a multiparty democracy (1946) and the unseating of the Republican People Party's government in 1950 by the right-of-center Democratic Party. Although the Democratic Party's government lasted only ten years, until it was overthrown by a military coup, the various governments that ruled between 1950 and 1980 did not alter the basic parameters of an import-substitution economic policy. While the public sector typically accounted for more than half of fixed capital formation, the state also indirectly intervened in the market via heavy tariffs and quotas, an overvalued exchange rate, price controls, and generous investment subsidies. One legacy of the Ottoman Empire was to leave the new republic with a competent and professional bureaucratic corps forming a well-paid and esteemed status group. But after the tran-

---

[11] Streeck and Schmitter (1985) also found that business associations may sometimes substitute for a weak state in helping to build a growth-oriented economic environment.

sition toward a multiparty democracy and an inwardly oriented development strategy, civil servants began to lose their privileged status. This was especially accelerated in the 1970s when the country was mostly ruled by coalition governments heavily engaged in unrestrained patronage and nepotism. The resulting arbitrary reshuffling of bureaucrats involved all ranks, politicized the bureaucracy, and undermined esprit de corps.

Following a protracted crisis of the import-substitution *cum* protectionist development regime in the late 1970s, a major transformation of the economy was initiated in 1980 in the immediate aftermath of the third—and, we hope, the last—military coup. The new economic strategy, which gained momentum after the return to democracy and the triumph of the neoliberal Motherland Party's government in the polls, was inspired by an outward-oriented development vision and aimed to remove price controls, privatize the bulk of the SEEs, eliminate major distortions except export-promotion measures, and decentralize the economic decision-making process by empowering local governments.

In the meantime, in an attempt to circumvent what it perceived as bureaucratic resistance to its minimalist state vision, the government hired highly paid contract personnel to staff the upper ranks of key economic agencies and created new agencies and autonomous units within the existing agencies to bypass traditional policy institutions such as the State Planning Organization. On the one hand, such administrative reforms gave a freer hand in policy-making to the Motherland Party, whose leaders, typically U.S.-educated "princes," relied on close allies in the bureaucracy in the design and implementation of reforms. On the other hand, because strategic policy powers were centralized and decisions hastily taken by a small number of technocrats allied to the prime minister and involved little consultation with private actors or other public officials, administrative reform measures further added to the overwhelming uncertainty about the rules of the game with regard to established norms and procedures in economic policy-making. Consequently, such actions led to increasing fragmentation and balkanization of the economic policy apparatus and high turnover among top personnel, who often opted for private industry.

Turkish State-Business Relations

Effective policy design and implementation in Turkey has been crippled by not only the absence of coordination among state economic agencies but also the existence of private-sector cleavages. Most notable is the fact that Turkish business in general and industrialists in particular are devoid of a peak all-encompassing umbrella organization able to aggregate various interests, shape policy, and function as a conflict-resolution mechanism among business firms. Its absence is partly due to the fact that private business developed under the explicit guidance of the state. In particular, the political elite, at least until the early 1970s, was reluctant to consent to the formation of independent organizations. Instead, the Union of Chamber and Commodity Exchanges of Turkey, which dates back to 1950, was organized at the behest of the government to undertake stated quasi-legal functions such as foreign-exchange allocation and export processing and the unstated task of supporting the then-reigning Democratic Party government. The politicization of the union reached extreme proportions in the 1960s and 1970s (the heyday of protectionist economic policy) when the reigning right-of-center Justice Party would prepare lists of candidates for election to the board of directors of the union as well as affiliated chambers. This situation and its resulting nepotism also led to the disaffection of large-scale industrialists, who were often bypassed in foreign-exchange allocation decisions in favor of merchants and small-scale businesspeople (Oncu 1980). Consequently, industrialists representing major conglomerates successfully pressured the military government in 1971 to take foreign-exchange allocation out of the hands of the union and place it under the authority of various ministries. In addition, on August 2, 1971, eighty-six industrialists founded the first voluntary business association in Turkey—the Turkish Industrialists' and Businessmens' Association (TUSIAD).

Although TUSIAD's membership and activities increased dramatically over the years, a number of factors cripple this organization's capacity to represent big business effectively, let alone the whole business community. TUSIAD is very much perceived as a "club of the rich" and resented by other members of the community. The Union of Chambers, for instance, does not welcome the association's prominence in economic affairs and resists the adoption of policy initiatives proposed by TUSIAD (such as the formation of a formal concertation mechanism among the state, business, and labor modeled after the French Economic and Social Council). Similarly, anti-TUSIAD feelings have also been widespread among the state elite, who often denounce the association's economic policy proposals on the grounds that TUSIAD is not minding its own business. In addition, frequent friction between member conglomerates and cleavages between large exporters and domestic-market–oriented industrialists concerning which policies TUSIAD should support often interfere with the organization's capacity for collective action. Finally, as Gulfidan (1993) reports, the most powerful members of TUSIAD, who are well represented in the Executive Committee, often find it expedient to bypass their own association in favor of personal contacts with top bureaucrats and politicians in order to find solutions to economic problems that concern them. Consequently, despite pleas by TUSIAD's leadership to establish tightly institutionalized and transparent channels of contact between government and business circles, the particularistic efforts of TUSIAD members breed public cynicism concerning the sincerity of such proposals.

Since the about-turn to a market-oriented economic policy in the 1980s, there has been a proliferation of various business associations at the industry level. These independent associations are generally established at the initiative of leading producers in the relevant industry and provide channels for members to influence the economic policy of local and national governments. In addition, the associations often attempt to function as transmission belts between industry and government and, when necessary, serve as a conflict-resolution mechanism between firms in the given industry. Of course, their developmental role varies. At worst, they can approximate what Olson calls a rent-seeking distributional coalition, which attempts to circumvent the market in order to fix prices and act in a cartel-like fashion to weaken competitors. On the other hand, under certain circumstances, as in the Readywear Manufacturers' Association, these organizations can facilitate economic growth by generating relevant information and facilitating members' adjustment to the requisites of an outward-oriented economy.

From the 1980s on, these industry associations were also active in seeking advantage for their members from various government-backed incentive and subsidy programs. Even after the radical turn in economic policy, the Turkish state continued to provide formal incentive programs for private business as it did before 1980. There was even a procedural continuity: Two formal incentive programs—the investment-incentive and export-incentive regimes—continued to be officially announced each year. Nevertheless, even though export incentives had been in operation since the early 1960s, until the early 1980s they were limited and could be regarded as an attempt to compensate for the distortions of an over-valued exchange rate. After 1980, not only were these incentives widely used, but new instruments were also added to the list of preexisting investment and export incentives. Although the ostensible aim of the incentive program consisted of easing the burdens of adjustment, there was also a quasi-political rationale aimed at rendering painful economic reforms politically palatable by creating direct stakes for them in the ranks of domestic-market–oriented industrialists and broadening the scope of the beneficiaries. In addition, throughout the 1980s the incentives tended to become more widespread rather than more restricted, primarily because modifications to the system were resisted by the beneficiaries and the maximization of the discretionary powers of the state proved expedient for policy-generated rents that could be selectively allocated to reward friends and punish foes.

The Turkish Incentive Regime

It is difficult to summarize concisely the main elements of the Turkish incentive regime for this period because these elements changed regularly. For example, the exemptions from financial tax and stamp duty on investments in priority development regions were introduced in 1984 and were still in operation in 1992, whereas the foreign-exchange allocation scheme was only in operation between 1981 and 1989. Table 10.1 sums up the main elements of the incentive regime during the export-oriented phase of economic development. The fiscal costs of the incentive programs in the 1980s were quite significant, amounting to 4 or 5 percent of the GNP in a given year.[12] The sectoral distribution of both investment and export-encouragement certificates from 1980 to 1992 shows a preference for manufacturing over other sectors in the 1980s. Finally, the incentive system in Turkey aimed to discriminate in favor of investments in priority regions (most of the eastern half of the country) at the expense of developed regions (the area around Istanbul and the eastern end of the sea of Marmara as well as around Ankara and Ionia).

If one assumes that the provision of incentives and subsidies in effective industrial policies involves the reciprocal fulfillment of obligations between the state and business, then the Turkish incentive regime overall can only be described as beset by serious and crippling problems. We drew this conclusion after a comprehensive study on policy effectiveness and business performance in the incentive regime (Biddle and Milor 1995). This is not to say that no pockets of efficiency within the incentive regime structure exist; in fact, incentives and subsidies are delivered efficiently with respect to at least one industry—ready-wear clothing. In general, however, Turkish industrial policy is quite ineffective because the incentive contracts are routinely violated by business recipients without consequence and business renegotiation of contracts is easy and common. Not surprisingly, actual business performance is usually a far cry from business's initial commitments made in exchange for access to incentives or subsidies.

On the surface it seems that business access to incentives and subsidies in Turkey is regulated by the state in a formal and transparent manner and the contractual obligations are clearly spelled out. In 1968, a specific bureau, the Directorate of Incentives and Implementation (TUD), was established within the State Planning Organization (SPO) and charged with administering investment and, later, export-encouragement certifi-

---

[12] According to a rough estimate of the cost of the main investment incentives, these costs, calculated as a percent of GNP, amounted to 2.2 in 1988, 2.1 in 1989, 1.8 in 1990, and 1.6 in 1991. The corresponding figures for the cost of export incentives are, respectively, 2.4, 2.3, 2.1, and 2.0 (Arslan 1993).

Table 10.1. Main elements of Turkey's incentive program

Instruments	Investment incentives	Export incentives
Tax incentives	Exemptions from customs Reductions in investment taxes Exemptions from taxes, duties, and credit charges Deferment of tax payments (Finance Fund) Exemptions from building and construction taxes Refunds of value-added tax (VAT) Additional employment incentives Exemptions from social security, compulsory savings, and contributions to housing fund Foreign-exchange allocations	Exemptions from customs Reductions in corporate income taxes Exemptions from financial transaction tax and VAT
Trade incentives		Foreign-exchange allocations Temporary import permits
Credit	Preferential credit (fund based)	Preferential credit (Eximbank)
Direct subsidy	Energy incentives Land allocations Investment subsidies	Energy subsidies Transportation premiums Rebates of export taxes

SOURCE: Various decrees published in official newspapers.

cates that detail the incentives and subsidies for which businesses may apply. In 1991, TUD and the responsibility for the administration of these certificates were transferred to the Treasury. The formal procedure involves business submission of forms detailing planned investment- and export-related activities; and at least in theory, the state makes a "case by case analysis of each investment application accompanied by a feasibility study and financial projection" (Ministry of Industry and Trade, 1991: 32).[13] Before 1980 state officials had routinely discriminated among applications from the vantage point of their fit within the priorities of five-year development plans. But in the 1980s and 1990s, as far as business was concerned, obtaining a certificate became almost automatic.[14]

Information with respect to the specific incentives and subsidies avail-

[13] Obtaining a certificate and thus access to incentives or subsidies entails, in the case of export incentives, undertaking a quantifiable export commitment or, in the case of domestic investors, commitments regarding employment levels, fixed investments, and so on.

[14] The lack of an initial screening of applicants suggests that an adverse selection process, (to borrow the language of economists) has been generated because certain applicants will be successful in their applications despite having too little commitment, preparation, or competence to undertake the proposed project.

able is published annually by TUD in two booklets—*Export Encouragement Procedures* and *Investment Encouragement Procedures*. Moreover, public opportunities exist for business input into the design of the industrial policy strategy. Before the publication of these documents, Treasury officials canvass the opinions of the chambers of Trade and Industry and various private actors.

In practice, however, the surface transparency of the incentive regime and public canvassing of business opinion mask a more arcane, particularistic, and hidden process. On the one hand, the basic parameters of the incentive regime, as laid out in the two documents we have mentioned, change frequently and in an often ad hoc way based on the publication of modifying decrees issued by the Council of Ministers. On the other hand, considerable ambiguity exists in the classifications and definitions of the benefits to which businesses are entitled.[15] Together, these motivate businesspersons to sharpen their skills in what Bhagwati (1982) calls "directly unproductive activities" as a means of ensuring that their particular needs are met. Firms routinely attempt political intervention on two levels. First, they attempt to influence the types and amounts of incentives and subsidies to which their certificate will provide access. This is particularly the case for contemplated export or investment activities of considerable magnitude. Second, and perhaps more important, firms exert political influence during the immediate stage following TUD's approval of a certificate, when various certificate holders vie with each other to obtain promised benefits, especially ones associated with access to cash grants or subsidized credits. This is a result of the fact that at various times some of the incentives and subsidies, may not be adequate to cover all existing claims on them (frequently the case with the Resource Utilization Fund).

This politicization of the incentive regime means that the costs of information collection and lobbying required to manipulate the incentive regime accord advantages to large conglomerate holdings as opposed to small and medium-sized firms, which cannot afford to hire personnel to work in Ankara. Moreover, the process undermines the overall coherency of industrial policy because business lobbying efforts do not contribute to the conceptualization of a long-term strategic vision for Turkish industrial development. Rather, lobbying remains fixed on the pursuit of par-

---

[15] What is the distinction between expansion and modernization investments, for instance? This is important because different benefits are attached to these classifications. Even the definition of these benefits, however, can be ambiguous. Thus, one benefit stipulates that with a completion investment a firm can import raw materials but not unprocessed materials without paying any custom duties. But as a Treasury official told us, "how clear is the distinction between 'unprocessed' and 'raw' materials? Does oil fall in the former or the latter category?"

ticular and narrow benefits at the implementation and disbursement stages of the industrial-policy process. The following example, reported by Bugra (1994: 152–53), illustrates the extent to which individual firms can manipulate these latter stages of the industrial-policy process for extremely narrow favors: "One of these cases had to do with the decrease from twenty-five to fifteen cents of the payments made to a particular fund by the exporters of dried figs. The decision for this change was taken at the end of the export season for this commodity, and the only person likely to benefit from it was a particular exporter who still had a certain amount of this export commodity to be shipped abroad. This exporter happened to be a close friend of the Minister of Finance, the future father-in-law of Tugut Ozal's son."

A final characteristic of the Turkish incentive regime, documented in our earlier research, is the general inability or unwillingness of economic bureaucrats or other state representatives to hold business recipients publicly accountable for their use of incentives and subsidies. It cannot be doubted that a business commits to undertake specific actions in exchange for access to encouragement certificates. Not only are firms required to fill out forms detailing actions they commit to undertake (such as volume of goods to be exported, new fixed investments to be undertaken, employment to be created, and so on), but they further sign a letter, endorsed by a notary public, agreeing to refund to the state any benefits received, plus interest and penalties, in the event they do not meet their public commitments. Nonetheless, our research found that bureaucrats in the Treasury and TUD generally do not attempt to monitor the performance of the vast majority of firms in receipt of incentive or export certificates.[16] Worse still, firms routinely renegotiate their contractual obligations with the state—for example, extending the life of the incentive or export certificate or increasing the number or level of benefits despite the lack of a bureaucratic monitoring process capable of determining whether such renegotiations are warranted on the basis of any economic criteria. There have been dramatic abuses of the incentive regime, such as those involving a fictitious hotel development in which firms were awarded investment certificates carrying access to direct subsidies from the Resource Utilization Fund when ground had not been broken for the proposed development. Although such cases appear to be rare, our interviews with business representatives and economic bureau-

---

[16] Monitoring of export incentives has been more successful than monitoring of investment incentives because the costs are much lower. As a high-ranking Treasury official noted during an interview, it is easier to monitor performance "by sitting in one's desk" because one can, with reasonable reliability, track business performance by obtaining the custom form proving that the commodity had been exported and a document from the central bank verifying that the counterpart in foreign exchange was received.

crats suggest that firms frequently take advantage of the state's lack of monitoring capacity in lesser ways. For example, firms regularly apply for an especially attractive investment certificate, claiming their investments will be made in an underdeveloped region, and then divert the investment to Istanbul or Ankara because there is likely to be no penalty for doing so.

BUREAUCRATIC INSULATION AND THE INCENTIVE REGIME

Our discussion has underscored the ineffectiveness of the incentive and subsidy regime, but we have not yet explained why this process developed and is allowed to continue. It is well known to economic bureaucrats that the incentive regime allows for considerable abuses on the part of certain businesses, yet this knowledge has not led to significant reforms. Why? To answer this question we first turn to an examination of the institutional character of the economic bureaucracy. Our argument is that there is a lack of insulation from pork-barrel and rent-seeking pressures in the TUD section of the Turkish economic bureaucracy, which helps explain the ineffectiveness of incentive policies. In general, the lack of insulation in the TUD is symptomatic of more widespread problems affecting the Turkish civil service today.

Of course, such problems are not unique to Turkey. Indeed, Turkey may be better positioned to deal with them than some other developing nations, for the Ottoman legacy of strong central political authority stood out as a rare example of a modernizing country with a distinct state tradition (Hale 1981). Furthermore, during periods of administrative modernization in the nineteenth century and economic modernization in the first half of the twentieth century, high-level bureaucrats formed a distinct status group that perceived themselves as the "sole formulator and the guardian of the long-term interest of the community" (Heper 1989: 461).[17]

Nonetheless, the independence, generalist backgrounds, and lingering elitist attitudes of top bureaucrats brought them into long-term conflict with the political elite. Consequently, from 1950 (following the transition to a multiparty democracy) until 1980, various governments, with differing degrees of success, attempted to transform bureaucrats into more loyal servants of politicians (Bugra 1994; Heper 1989). At the same time,

---

[17] Empirical studies conducted during the 1960s and 1970s (that is, during the heyday of protectionist industrial policy) invariably pointed to the fact that the bureaucratic elite in Turkey aspired to a substantive role in the development of the nation as opposed to being content with a Western–style technocratic role (Heper 1976; Bozkurt 1980).

the political elite, irrespective of party affiliation, deeply distrusted a spontaneous and pluralistic development of interest-group associations in the country. Thus, only limited legitimacy was accorded to pluralistic forms of interest representation, and professional associations were considered appendages of the state rather than autonomous bodies articulating the preferences of members (Bianchi 1984).

Consequently, even after the transition to a multiparty democracy, the political elite made most of the critical decisions concerning the economy, "virtually without consulting the traditional civil bureaucracy, the Parliament and the political parties as well as interest groups" (Heper 1991: 173). Because both voluntary associations and public professional organizations were prohibited from engaging in politics (*politics* being defined vaguely), state-imposed distrust of pluralist interest intermediation generated particularistic and clientelistic relations between the political elite and business interests (Kalaycioglu 1991). From the point of view of the political elite, these particularistic relations were expedient because they turned businesspeople into individuals and hence made them more vulnerable to government discretionism. That is, if businesspersons strayed from their preordained role of carrying out activities as dictated by government, they could be punished by selective measures aimed at them (Heper 1991). Indeed, governments acted on this threat by lowering the tariff for goods produced by a nonfavored business group, passing retroactive laws that had a devastating effect on a particular business activity, or not honoring a contract concluded with a businessperson who fell out of favor (Bugra 1994).

Why did businesspersons, despite these vulnerabilities, not cease individual-level contacts and instead attempt to exercise influence over the government through a professional association? The short answer is that those businesspersons who were powerful enough to strike individual relations with top politicians and bureaucrats benefited from these relations as well (Kalaycioglu 1991). The problem, however, is that, even though individual businesspersons often benefited from such rent seeking, it hindered the creation of a competitive and growth-conducive business environment not only because of the opportunity costs of rent seeking, such as foregone innovations, but also because the extent of particularism in state-business relations paralyzed the economic bureaucracy. An interviewee told Ayse Bugra (1994: 164):

He who explains his case to the Prime Minister or the Minister concerned solves his problem. You go to Isin Celebi [one of the ministers responsible for the economy], you cry on his shoulder and he says "O.K., I'll find you the necessary funds." When the Central Bank says that the funds are not available, the Minister orders the transfer of funds from one budget to the other. This leads to interferences at all levels of the bureaucratic process. And, of course, you are very happy because your problem is solved. You tell others what a nice, understanding person the Minister is, and how nicely he has solved your problem. But the institutions cannot function under these circumstances, the State Planning Organization cannot function, the Treasury and the Central Bank cannot function. Institutionalization becomes impossible.

Bureaucratic insulation in Turkey was not just hampered by the extent of particularism and clientelism in state-business relations; in addition, politicians increasingly influenced bureaucratic recruitment and promotion patterns (Heper 1985). This rendered bureaucrats overly sensitive to signals emanating from the political realm. As a former top bureaucrat, now a high-level executive in the private sector, told us, sensitivity to political signals correlates with the nature of the agency in question and the educational background of the incumbents. For example, an agency such as the central bank is somewhat less subject to political interference, save for pressures from the Treasury, because it is not generally a source of rent creation (although some subsidized credit is disbursed) and its high-level staff are technical specialists. In contrast, in an agency that is potentially a source of rent creation, such as the TUD, where most incumbents are generalists by background and can be fired by politicians or transferred to less desirable jobs, it is not realistic to expect bureaucrats to enjoy much insulation from political pressures. Opportunities for graft and rent seeking are built-in features of any incentive and subsidy system; but to the extent that civil servants enjoy legal guarantees against arbitrary political influence, they are more likely to withstand pressures from politicians to use the incentive and subsidy system to reward political allies and punish foes. From this vantage point, the decision (after the about-turn to a market-friendly economic policy in 1980) to centralize the administration of the incentive and subsidy regime within the State Planning Organization was apt. The meritocratic basis of recruitment in this agency, combined with the relatively high educational background of its personnel, made the SPO a highly competent agency that was relatively well protected against nonlegal political interference.

The insulation of the SPO from political pressures during the 1980s, however, was severely compromised by the recruitment of contract personnel into the agency through a separate process that bypassed the normal written and oral exams. More specifically, with Act 3046 in 1984, it was made possible to bypass restrictions of Public Personnel Law No. 657 regarding the hiring and laying off of state personnel and, more politically, to determine salaries by routing reviews through the Council of Ministers. After the passage of this legal act, in the administrative corps overall, "the conversion of managers to contract status has proceeded fairly rapidly: in 1984 there were 674 such administrators, in 1985 3,491, and in 1986 26,578 or about 10 percent of the administrative corps" (Waterbury 1988: 16). In the SPO, on the other hand, the percentage of contract personnel was much higher. Of the total 520 nonadministrative personnel (including assistant experts, experts, midlevel managers, and top managers), only 281 (about 54 percent) were recruited from the regular channels through written and oral exams; the rest were contract personnel. Most significant, of the 157 civil servants who were employed in the bureaus of the SPO that dealt with the implementation of the incentive and subsidy regime (the TUD), fully 69 percent were recruited on contract status.

One should not overstate the difference between contract personnel and other bureaucrats; irrespective of legal status, all top bureaucrats are vulnerable to political pressures. When asked about these pressures, all six of our interviewees who occupy director or vice president positions in the Treasury (all were involved in the administration of the incentive regime) acknowledged their existence. Even in the case of noncontract personnel, pressures from above to cater to particular interests carry weight because politicians can threaten to downgrade their status or exile them to less developed regions. When asked to what extent politicians affect their careers as opposed to the extent to which experience, competence, and expertise play roles, these bureaucrats repeated to us what was found in a similar, albeit more comprehensive, survey conducted twenty years ago—that subjective factors such as good personality and good relationships with important individuals were as important as expertise (Heper et al. 1980). In contrast, in Korea, which is renowned for the competency of its economic bureaucracy, politicians' ability to affect bureaucratic careers is limited, and expertise emerges as the most important criterion in career paths (Schneider 1993a).[18]

In an agency that is par excellence a source of rent creation, such as the TUD, the lack of insulation occasioned by the presence of contract personnel with considerable job insecurity renders the agency particularly vulnerable to political pressures. These pressures, as we have already discussed, often take the form of requests to grant certain incentives and

---

[18] If one discusses the general effects of administrative reforms in the 1980s, as opposed to focusing principally on how these reforms affected the incentive and subsidy regime, it is possible to discern positive aspects. One rationale behind these changes was actually to expand the application of meritocratic principles by bypassing existing salary limitations in order to draw top talent into public service. Another rationale was to create a cadre of reform-minded bureaucrats as a means to overcome a rigid and statist bureaucratic culture perceived to be hostile to contemplated market-oriented reforms.

subsidies to favored businesspersons or not to monitor and enforce penalties in the case of business noncompliance with mutually agreed-upon goals. From this angle, it becomes possible to understand why TUD officials do not aggressively collect data on, or otherwise monitor, the performance of businesses in relation to the actualization of investment or export commitments—data that could subsequently help these officials to enforce the incentive or export contracts. It is less the absence of administrative capacity than the incentive structure within which state officials are situated that is responsible for the reluctance to impose performance standards in line with the contracts. Thus, when asked to account for bureaucratic failure to monitor business performance, a high-level official in the TUD stated that such follow-up is like playing Russian roulette (author interview, 1994):

> If I tell my people to collect data on the actualization of investments, then what do I do with the data? Once I have the documentation on the implementation of incentives, then I have to do something with it. But this will pose a true dilemma for me. If I don't do anything about the situation, then I am violating the legal system which stipulates that I should punish the violators. But if I take steps to punish the violators, then this is like playing with fire. They are powerful individuals who have access to top politicians and they will find a way, sooner or later, to unseat me. So I would rather not collect data in order not to disturb anybody.

INDUSTRY POLICY NETWORKS AND THE INCENTIVE REGIME

We have discussed how the lack of insulation of Turkish economic bureaucrats from political pressures undermines the effectiveness of economic policy while the absence of strong private-sector associations able to articulate policy preferences has fostered a situation in which economic bureaucrats are overly sensitive to the preferences of well-positioned economic actors. We now turn to a fuller examination of state-business relations, examining the nature of the policy networks connecting economic actors with bureaucrats in two industries—autos and ready-wear clothing. We find that the rent-oriented network that characterizes the auto industry severely hampers policy effectiveness. In contrast, in the ready-wear clothing industry, a growth-oriented network developed in the mid-1980s that enhanced the effectiveness of incentive and subsidy policy by allowing for the decentralization of screening, monitoring, and disciplinary functions away from the TUD and into collective associations representing the industry.

Rent-Oriented Networks and the Auto Industry

Earlier we characterized as rent-oriented those networks that have a two-way communications flow and various established norms but a level of transparency low enough for some network members to develop particularistic and rent-oriented ties. The nature of state-business ties in the auto industry approximates these rent-seeking features. One organizational feature of the industry is that a formal business association exists—the Association of Automotive Manufacturers (OSD). Historically, the major role of the OSD, which was established in 1974, has been efforts to fix prices on intermediate goods needed for the industry. More recently, the organization has been crippled by a rivalry between old members, who control a captive domestic market, and new entrants such as Sabanci (with Toyota), Dogus (with GM), and potential new entrants (such as Hyundai, Honda, and Mazda) with export ambitions. Under these circumstances it becomes difficult for OSD to formulate any serious, positive, and long-term vision for the future of the industry. Instead, it has campaigned for high tariffs and a cap on imports (about one-fourth of the passenger vehicles are now imported) and lobbies for ending the issuance of licenses to multinationals (even those with domestic partners) to manufacture passenger vehicles domestically.

Auto industry leaders prefer to bypass the OSD in their dealings with the state, particularly when they think the stakes are high. This is not surprising because the auto industry, which is highly concentrated, has only a small number of active firms (all of which are multisectoral conglomerate holdings). These firms have had the incentive to, and been historically successful in, generating close, clientelistic ties with state policy-makers. Both the Turkish state and the large, influential firms of the auto industry enjoy certain benefits from such relations. Thus, it is not surprising that the top shareholders and managers of the two holdings that control the OSD—KOC Holding and Oyak-Renault—do not generally assume official positions in the organization. According to OSD's current general manager, an ex-academician, this fact thwarts the organization's efforts to convince decision makers that the organization, as opposed to individual auto manufacturers, should be treated as the main interlocutor of the state (author interview, 1994).[19]

The more significant interaction patterns between auto industry

---

[19] When we conducted our interviews in May and June 1994, a shrinkage in the absorption capacity of the internal market had plunged the auto industry in Turkey into a crisis. The general manager of OSD had invited a high-level official in Treasury to Istanbul, where OSD is located, to inform him about the crisis and lobby for the protection of the national industry. He also invited the head of a major car manufacturer, a member of OSD, to meet with the high-level bureaucrat. Neither invitation was accepted.

leaders and government decision makers are through informal networks. Based on a questionnaire we distributed, we can offer some generalizations about these networks in both the auto and ready-wear clothing industries. The Treasury is the bureaucratic agency that is contacted most frequently by business leaders in both industries. These contacts, however, occur more frequently and more informally in the auto industry. In our interviews with high-ranking bureaucrats in charge of industrial subsidies, they admitted that these contacts are frequent and acknowledged that they occur most regularly at the firm-level as opposed to through the intermediation of a business association. In fact, 80 percent of these bureaucrats, when asked to rank the most frequent level of contact with business, selected the "firm level" option first as opposed to other options representing more institutionalized levels of contact. Hence, in Turkey, particularistic state-business relations prevail.

This situation has implications concerning the nature of the information exchanged in these networks and the forms of trust and reciprocity that undergird them. When policy networks involve relations struck between individual firms and particular policymakers, the emergence of a broad policy consensus among bureaucratic, business, and political leaders regarding long-term growth-oriented goals often become less likely. This is because the emergence of such goals entails the collective involvement of business in the conceptualization stage of the incentive regime. Firm-level involvement in the auto and similar policy networks, however, is generally oriented toward individual manipulation at the implementation phase of the incentive delivery process. OSD generates much information concerning various aspects of the industry and regularly sends this information as well as commentary on the nature of auto industry policy to top bureaucrats. Nevertheless, because owners and top managers of the major auto firms do not consent to have this organization actually mediate their access to the government, bureaucratic officials do not perceive the information and policy recommendations to be of any great relevance. Instead, when information is needed about business policy preferences, state officials turn to heads of individual firms whom they know well. Given that state officials generally lack adequate capacity to collect data themselves and are often riddled by interagency rivalries that make accessing existing information difficult, this informal and nontransparent networking can impart an unwarranted legitimacy to auto makers' demands for protection and individual favoritism.

Longstanding relations among a handful of manufacturers in the auto and ready-wear clothing industries and top economic bureaucrats create a certain degree of trust based on reciprocal obligations. Our questionnaire revealed that auto executives, in contrast to executives in ready-wear clothing, hold a particularly positive evaluation of the responsiveness of bureaucrats to their concerns. This, of course, does not reveal the extent or full nature of reciprocity. Moreover, businesspersons in the auto industry do not solely contact top bureaucrats. Rather, when the issue at stake is important and communication with bureaucrats fails to address their concerns, they directly contact the minister in charge. A high-level official in a major auto company demonstrated the precision with which businesspersons network with various levels in the economic bureaucracy (author interview, 1994):

> It is important to know the level at which you should try to solve problems. We do not always want to contact the minister or the prime minister, even if these are friends. If we did this all the time, bureaucrats will become angry at us and, even if they comply with the minister's orders, may then obstruct us at the earliest opportunity. Instead, we start with the middle-level bureaucrat before we even talk to the top guy. If need arises to resolve things at a higher level, before contacting government members, we may call some congressmen whom we know well since there are many, both in the governing coalition and the opposition. Sometimes they are effective in solving our problems.

So what are the reciprocal obligations that underlie state-business relations in rent-seeking networks? Clearly, the principle of reciprocity at work does not include, as has been the case in Korea, the expectation that improved business performance is associated with continuing access to state subsidies (Amsden 1989). While this is a delicate subject, our confidential interviews revealed that in exchange for firms' desires for subsidies, political elites often ask for highly personalized services such as support for their political party or support for themselves or family members (which may take the direct form of payment or an indirect form such as employing a family member in the firm). Bureaucratic elites, in contrast, are generally content with the provision of information that they can incorporate into reports and rarely demand personalized favors. According to our interviews with businesspersons, this is partly to the subordinate position of the bureaucrat in the decision-making hierarchy (which, according to one businessperson, has become even more subordinate since the early 1970s) and partly due to the lingering effects of an elite educational system and bureaucratic tradition that instills strong notions of morality in bureaucrats.

There is little solace in the fact of a relative absence of sheer corruption, for the major structural characteristic of the policy network linking decision makers to businesspersons in the auto industry is the absence of transparency. This means that the major firms do not know the full extent of the subsidies that other firms receive nor how these rival firms became eligible for them. Therefore, they often presume that the success of their rival in securing subsidies is related to rent-seeking skills rather than economic performance. Decision makers in the auto industry do not pay too much attention to the specifics of any particular year's incentive regime, although this is published in a quite transparent document, because it has little bearing on many of the major outcomes of interest to them. Large conglomerates shy away from becoming involved in the initial conceptualization stages of decision-making processes concerning the incentive regime, which would likely be a waste of time and might even bind them to rules they might later desire to change. Instead, they attempt to manipulate policy at the later implementation stage.

The lack of transparency is both a cause and a consequence of the rent-oriented network in the auto industry because the uncertain environment in which business groups operate encourages them to seek privileged connections with top decision makers. To the extent that business in the auto and other industries is literally dependent on hundreds of government decisions that affect prices, costs of inputs, access to preferential credits, and so on, there are real and significant incentives for firms to seek allies in the state as an insurance mechanism. At the same time, however, a vicious circle is created because the resulting frequency of personal contacts among businesspersons and top politicians leads to arbitrary interventions by politicians into bureaucratic affairs, thereby causing ad hoc changes in the everyday implementation of the incentive program, sometimes at a dizzying speed. Consequently, any successful rent-seeking effort on the part of one business actor may easily lead to efforts by rivals to accomplish the same or to better the effort through their own rent seeking. While it is possible to score partial victories, the nature of the competition generated is unable to deal with industry-level collective problems such as restructuring to take advantage of changing world market conditions, even though the resolution of such collective problems would be in the interest of all major parties. In the end, given the absence of transparency among network members, the major players in the auto industry assume that their rivals have managed to obtain maximum benefits with minimum performance obligations. And this assumption gives them every reason to bad-mouth their rivals and engage in costly and inefficient rent seeking.[20]

---

[20] An anecdote reveals the severity of the situation. Despite numerous attempts, one of the authors of this chapter failed to obtain an appointment with a high-level manager of ToyotaSA. Finally an intermediary was found, and the firm official agreed to be interviewed. In the interview, the author was told that the meeting had been held up because, despite his credentials, which included a World Bank connection, he could have been a spy for a rival business holding; besides, ToyotaSA officials had had bad experiences with people who represented themselves as World Bank consultants, so they were now extremely cautious.

Growth-Oriented Network and Private-Sector Economic Governance in Ready-Wear Clothing

The case of ready-wear clothing is exceptional because the growth-oriented policy network in question was created from scratch in a relatively short time. During the import substitution years, the myriad of small-scale manufacturers in the industry that competed in the domestic market had no a collective organization to advance common goals. Given their small scale, they did not have the requisite political and economic clout to be able to enjoy the benefits of personalized contacts with decision makers, unlike the major firms in the auto industry. The situation did not automatically improve with the about-turn in development strategy after 1980; the most attractive rents attached to exporting—the export-tax rebates—were skimmed off by large export houses affiliated with various holdings. Moreover, the European Economic Community (EEC) and U.S. quotas affecting the industry were monopolized by large manufacturers (Onis 1992).

The Turkish Clothing Manufacturers' Association (TGSD), which was founded in 1976 by small-scale industrialists, became active in the 1980s in pursuit of a fairer system to distribute quotas that would not discriminate against small businesspersons. In October 1986, ninety-six members of TGSD formed what has now become the largest export house in the country, the GSD (Ready-Wear Manufacturers' Foreign Trade–Joint Stock Company). The GSD was established with the purpose of enabling small businesspersons to benefit from the incentive regime, which individually they could not have accessed (Öniş 1992). Even after the end of the lucrative export-tax rebates, the GSD continued to flourish by increasing exports. In contrast, many holding-affiliated export houses foundered after considerable abuse of the export-tax rebate system led to international pressures from the EEC and the World Bank, forcing the government to abolish the rebates in 1988 (Ilkin 1991). Specifically, members of GSD exported $690 million worth of ready-wear clothing in 1992— one-fifth of total clothing and textile exports—as opposed to a meager $218 million in 1987, the first year of the organization's existence (GSD 1993). This growth is not due to an increase in membership because GSD froze membership at one hundred.[21] Nor may it be attributed to increases in subsidies: Not only did the export-tax rebate program end but other export subsidies have also diminished during the life of the organization. Hence, organizational practices and the policy network associated with them seem to have made a positive difference in the performance of the industry.

---

[21] The reason for this number is that the Turkish Company Law stipulates that, when membership exceeds one hundred, the company has to float shares in the stock market.

Our main finding is that the growth-oriented network in ready-wear clothing enabled participants to reap the benefits of cooperation without forsaking the advantages of competition. Cooperation enabled these small business actors, who were unable to compete effectively with large holdings in lobbying and other efforts to manipulate the implementation of incentive and subsidy policy, to become influential at the initial conceptualization stage of incentive policy for their industry. In addition, thanks to cooperation, small-scale industrialists were able to derive tangible benefits, such as access to export quotas, preferential credits, information about market conditions and the macroenvironment, and so on. In the meantime, potential abuse of cooperation (such as free riding) was limited and a competitive environment maintained. First, access to incentives, which was mediated by GSD leadership, was linked to performance, in contrast to the usual operation of the Turkish incentive regime. Second, thanks to the existence of transparent and credible rules governing the distribution of incentives, uncertainties regarding the distribution of future growth were reduced and business energies could be channeled toward competition in exports rather than into efforts to lobby state officials. Finally, members were not allowed to free-ride by receiving information given to others, not only because they knew that in this case they would be put out of the information circle and lose advantages associated with it but also because certain organizational arrangements (explained later in the chapter) made it very difficult to do so.

How did all this happen? Success depended, at least initially, on wise choices by leading ready-wear industry entrepreneurs. For example, unlike members of the OSD, these entrepreneurs directly took part in the affairs of the TGSD; and after the GSD was formed as an export house, they delegated authority to a professional manager who had been a high-level officer in the Export Promotion and Research Center of the Undersecretariat of Foreign Trade. This manager's actions subsequently allowed for the institutionalization of a certain principle of reciprocity between the state and the private beneficiaries of the incentive regime. Reciprocity was based on mutual obligations because the state sanctioned the TGSD, conferred some benefits to members of the GSD, and allowed these organizations to participate in the decision-making process in exchange for their willingness to monitor and discipline those members who abused the incentive system. As such, it became possible to institutionalize the initial organizational choices over time.

How has successful monitoring occurred? We did not find a case of any member who was put out of the circle due to abuse, and certainly the discovery and documentation of such a case would have been helpful in building credibility for our argument. But does the lack of such an example imply the absence of monitoring or disciplinary capacity on the part of industry associations? Not necessarily, if monitoring and discipline have become self-enforcing over time, as we believe. In the first place, it is important to be clear that members derive real benefits from membership in the TGSD and the privileged export club, the GSD; thus, loss of these benefits would be costly. One benefit is that small businesspersons need a collective association to gain access to decision makers, and the archives of GSD contain letters that have been sent to those decision makers, including top bureaucrats and government ministers, with suggestions to reform the incentive system for the ready-wear clothing industry. These suggestions, many of which later became state policy, were not geared to particularistic concerns. Rather, they generally reflected certain collective aims associated with a vision for the long-term transformation and restructuring of the industry. Another benefit of membership is that GSD is very powerful in the quasi-public organization that distributes quotas for the United States and the EEC. (This organization is called ITKIB, the Exporter's Union for Ready-Wear and Textile Manufacturers.) Membership in GSD also provides access to preferential Eximbank credits for small exporters, many of whom would not otherwise be eligible for them because of their limited size.[22] GSD also addresses liquidity problems of members and provides working capital. The latter is a crucial service in a country where, due to certain rigidities and distortions in the financial markets, small businesses in industry rarely gain access to banking services. Another collective good generated by the GSD is information concerning market conditions and the macro environment— information formerly, but no longer, provided by the SPO. Moreover, useful information regarding government policy is generated through contacts between GSD leaders and economic decision makers. Finally, GSD provides basic import articles, such as cotton yarn, for members at prices lower than they can afford on their own.

Given the type of benefits derived from membership in the ready-wear clothing associations, it becomes easier to understand why flagrant abuse does not occur. Member firms are in a lasting relationship and at the same time belong to a powerful club that has frozen membership; a firm that cheats can be replaced by another, for many are waiting at the door. Maintaining a good public image has always been very important to ready-wear associations, legitimizing the fact that the industry greatly benefits from incentive certificates. A member that harms this image can be ostracized. Hence, peer pressure partly explains continuing good performance and internalization of monitoring functions. At the same time, the leadership has direct instruments to induce growth-oriented behavior. Specifically, it

---

[22] At the time of this study there was an export requirement of $45 million per year to gain access to these credits.

mediates between the TUD and individual businesspersons and links rewards to good performance in the form of escalating access to incentives for superior exporters.

Certain organizational features of these associations has made abuse by members unlikely. For one thing, because decisions are made collectively by often-changing boards of directors who are entrepreneurs themselves, those who inflate their achievements would have had a hard time convincing their peers, who are equally knowledgeable about conditions in the industry. Moreover, unlike the case of the auto industry, a certain trust has been created among GSD members because they know that GSD leadership has access to correct information concerning the export performance of their peers, information then used as a yardstick to allocate benefits, and that they can have access to this information as well. They also know that their peers have access to the same information. In other words, the information flow is open and transparent among network members. Of course, not everything is transparent. For example, no firm would want to share information with rivals concerning the identity of its foreign customers even though such information has to be given to the GSD leadership in order to make monitoring possible.

With respect to specific export markets, the leadership of the ready-wear clothing industry associations has acknowledged in interviews that free ridership in information poses a serious potential problem. In a nation such as Korea, the trust necessary for a continued two-way flow of information has been created over the years thanks to repeated interactions between the parties, the willingness of businesspersons to relegate decision-making authority to their professional association, and the insulation of top bureaucrats from political and social pressures. In Turkey, however, as the professional manager of the GSD acknowledged, trust had to be created from scratch (author interviews, 1994). The organization had to construct a system in which members could believe that giving crucial information was a safe practice, and no members, including those on the board, were empowered to free-ride on this information. Such a system was constructed by emulating the practice of the McKinsey Management Consultant Company: no single employee would have access to classified files of more than a handful of member companies; at the same time, employee morale and loyalty to the company would be kept high by attractive salaries, good working conditions, and promotion opportunities based on merit. To complement such Weberian elements, the organization adopted transparency, solidarity, efficiency, and respectability as operational principles to guide relationships among members and between the association and the state. (These principles are also laid out in the annual reports.) Our interviews with several entrepreneur-members and employees of this association, as well as with the state officials who have dealt with them, confirmed that everyday practices reflect these principles.

Can this success in export performance continue without generous subsidies? As we have indicated, the breakthrough in export performance for GSD members came after some state benefits were rescinded. Moreover, based on the questionnaire we distributed, we believe that GSD members are much less sanguine about the usefulness of subsidies than auto industry officials are. It is interesting, however, that most of these entrepreneurs do not question the general logic of incentives, which they think may be useful for the development of manufacturing. This is symptomatic of the lingering effect of an étatist ideology among businesspersons (even when they do not seek subsidies for their own industry). It is not possible to say how long this attitude, which is a legacy of the past, will continue. But the fact that certain beneficiaries of the incentive regime perceive that the subsidies to their industry are not particularly useful or necessary is contrary to the conventional wisdom that easy access to rents will always translate into a protectionist attitude for the infinite prolongation of these rents.

CONCLUSION

This chapter has drawn attention to certain consequences of sectoral business networks for industrial policy and growth without necessarily presuming an identity of preferences between business and state actors. Our findings are at odds with the deeply embedded neoliberal expression of skepticism regarding the capacity of business associations and institutionalized state-business consultative mechanisms to address collective-action dilemmas and deliver public goods. Hence, we agree with other contributors to this book, such as Doner and Ramsey and Schneider, who highlight important sectoral governance and general economic functions fulfilled by systematic consultation mechanisms between these two powerful sets of actors. Nevertheless, we also find a certain truth in Olson's (1982) notion that public-private interactions may degenerate into distributive coalitions aimed at securing rents at the expense of the public purse. Our challenge has been to specify institutional conditions under which state-business policy networks may promote sectoral policies conducive to overall efficiency as opposed to dragging down growth. Needless to say, our inquiry is preliminary, and our generalizations need to be tested further before they can guide policy-making.

Based on an empirical study of interaction patterns between businesspeople and public officials in the Turkish ready-wear clothing and auto industries, we developed a binary typology related to the nature of the networks. We characterized as growth-oriented those networks in which there exists not only abundant information concerning the performance standards according to which industrial subsidies are allocated but also mechanisms to link rewards to compliance with stated standards of performance. From this vantage point, the process of deciding the allocation of subsidies and the actual allocation patterns are transparent in a reciprocal sense: One network member (for example, a given firm) knows that it can learn about the level of access to subsidies of a rival firm; at the same time, it is also aware that the rival firm can find out about its own level of access to subsidies. This form of transparency breeds a certain degree of trust among network members because firms believe that the highest rewards go to the ones with an impressive, measurable track record. At the same time, such reciprocal transparency makes it easier to identify rent seekers who desire rewards without the commensurate performance record. Consequently, because membership in an exclusive community (network) brings it own rewards, potential rent seekers are deterred from seeking personalized and particularistic relations with decision makers on the grounds that, even if were they to strike it rich today, they risk getting thrown out of the privileged circle and thereby losing benefits over the long haul.

Not all networks have to be transparent in order to become growth-oriented. For instance, Karl Fields in this book highlights the importance of informal contacts between the highest-ranking state officials and top business leaders in the economic decision-making process in South Korea and Taiwan. Certainly, economic policy-making in "Korea, Inc." is not as transparent as it is in the ready-wear clothing industry in Turkey, given that chaebols neither know what subsidies their competitors are receiving nor how they are using them. Why does this lack of transparency not lead to an increase in rent seeking as it does in the Turkish auto industry? Our hunch is that, because Korea (unlike Turkey) is endowed with an elite bureaucratic corps that approximates Weberian characteristics, business members of the network (chaebol) rest assured that the bureaucracy will not use its discretionism to bend rules to favor some parties in exchange for kickbacks. In other words, because the existing rules of subsidy allocation hinge on developmental criteria, they are credible, and all members of the network can be assured of subsidies without engaging in wasteful lobbying efforts. A Weberian bureaucracy creates an environment conducive to economic development because the perception of its existence generates disincentives for private actors to preempt their competitors by bribing officials. Instead, incentives are generated to compete in the bureaucratic contests over incentives and subsidies or in the (external) marketplace.

Most countries, including Turkey, do not have a meritocratic bureaucratic corps endowed with a developmental mission, nor do existing political conditions allow us much hope for the formation of a Weberian official class in the near future. Under these circumstances, transparency becomes an important characteristic in order for sectoral state-business networks to enhance international competitiveness in a particular industry rather than degenerate into distributional coalitions. Unfortunately, growth-oriented sectoral networks in political environments characterized by weak states are rare. According to Eduardo Silva in Chapter 6, non-transparent rent-seeking networks are commonplace in Venezuela given the relative lack of business associations and the abundance of clientelistic relationships among top business and government leaders. His findings about the consequences of such networks on economic development are similar to ours. He notes that particularistic relations encourage fragmentation in the private sector and that the system "ceased to be even moderately functional for investment and production once oil revenues were no longer sufficient to drive the Venezuelan economy."

But do such clientelistic networks always place binding institutional constraints in the way of successful economic performance? Are there historical conditions under which, even in the context of a weak state and fragmented business community, systematic consultative mechanisms can be developed that enhance information flows, build credibility for policy commitments, and foster trust among state policy-makers and the business community? These are not easy questions to answer. According to our findings in the ready-wear clothing industry, small businesspersons had incentives to work with business associations and were eager to develop transparency in relations with the state given that they lacked the economic and political clout to strike the personal-level connections with bureaucrats and politicians that big business enjoyed. Thus, the Turkish case suggests that growth-oriented networks may be most likely to develop in competitive industries with smaller producers while more concentrated industries with larger producers are likely to generate rent-oriented networks. Nevertheless, a functional need for collective representation need not translate into an actual representative body because, as Olson (1965) reminds us, competition among small businesspersons makes organization difficult; and given the myriad of players involved and the often public nature of collective goods, it becomes difficult to exclude those who do not participate in a successful organization from enjoying its benefits. The collective associations for ready-wear clothing, such as the GSD, did not fall prey to these traps.

Perhaps cases structurally analogous to Turkey's GSD are not as uncommon as it may seem. Some contributors to this book mention other examples. Schneider, for instance, highlights the importance of systematic consultation between business and the state in the growth of the auto sector in Brazil. A comparison can be made to Turkey in the sense that Brazilian state-business relations are disembedded and there is no autonomous peak business association that brings together firms from different sectors. Similarly, Thorp and Durand draw attention to the success of the coffee sector in Colombia. Interestingly, the Colombian Coffee Federation succeeded in a manner similar to the Turkish GSD, organizing small producers and spearheading the effort to brave international markets without ceding control of production to international capital. But the macro policy environment in Colombia has been more predictable than that in Turkey. Thus, even if the bureaucracy did not approximate the Weberian ideal, it was sufficiently insulated from powerful private interests to be able to implement unpopular policies.

In Third World countries where states commonly lack the autonomy and capacity to undertake effective industrial and other economic restructuring policies, the successful self-organization of business, especially when coupled with institutionalized consultative mechanisms with the state, holds the potential to increase the predictability of policy-making and enhance the overall credibility of economic policy. In turn, this makes it possible to enlist the support of business associations in the monitoring and disciplinary enforcement necessary for success. The chapters in this book go some way toward buttressing this conclusion while emphasizing that a few sectoral success stories can be found amid the common pattern of nontransparent and clientelistic state-business relations at the macrolevel. Given the preponderance of rent-seeking business associations in developing countries, a significant challenge remains to specify the conditions under which such associations can evolve in a new direction and undertake more growth-oriented functions not handled—or mishandled—by weak states.

References

Akrasanee, Narongchai, David Dapice, and Frank Flatters. 1991. *Thailand's Export-Led Growth: Retrospect and Prospect*. Policy Study no. 3. Bangkok: Thailand Development Research Institute.

Alchian, A. A., and H. Demsetz. 1973. "The Property Rights Paradigm." *Journal of Economic History* 33 (March), 16–27.

Alduncin Abitia, Enrique. 1989. *Expectativas económicas de los líderes empresariales* [Economic expectations of business leaders]. Mexico City: Banco Nacional de México.

Alesina, Alberto. 1994. "Political Models of Macroeconomic Policy and Fiscal Reforms." In *Voting for Reform*, ed. Stephan Haggard and Steven Webb. New York: Oxford University Press.

Alexeev, Michael, and Jim Leitzel. 1991. "Collusion and Rent-Seeking." *Public Choice* 69, 241–52.

Alvarez, Michael R., Geoffrey Garrett, and Peter Lange. 1991. "Government Partnership, Labor Organization, and Macroeconomic Performance." *American Political Science Review* 85 (June), 539–56.

Amsden, Alice. 1989. *Asia's Next Giant: South Korea and Late Industrialization*. New York: Oxford University Press.

———. 1991. "Big Business and Urban Congestion in Taiwan: The Origins of Small Enterprise and Regionally Decentralized Industry (Respectively)." *World Development* 19 (September), 1121–35.

Amsden, Alice, and Takashi Hikino. 1994. "Project Execution Capability, Organizational Know-How, and Conglomerate Corporate Growth in Late Industrialization." *Industrial and Corporate Change* 3, no. 1, 111–49.

Anchordoguy, Marie. 1988. "Mastering the Market: Japanese Government Targeting of the Computer Industry." *International Organization* 42 (Summer), 509–43.

Anderson, Charles. 1977. "Political Design and the Representation of Interests." *Comparative Political Studies* 10 (April), 127–52.

Andrews, David. 1994. "Capital Mobility and State Autonomy: Toward a Structural Theory of International Monetary Relations." *International Studies Quarterly* 38 (June), 193–218.

Angell, Alan, and Carol Graham. 1995. "Can Social Sector Reform Make Adjustment Sustainable and Equitable? Lessons from Chile and Venezuela." *Journal of Latin American Studies* 27, no. 1, 189–219.

Ansoff, H. Igor. 1986. *Corporate Strategy*. London: Sidgewick & Jackson.

Anthony, Myrvin, and Andrew Hallett. 1992. "How Successfully Do We Measure Capital Flight?" *Journal of Development Studies* 28 (April), 538–56.

Arango, M., 1982. *Bonanza de precios y transformaciones en la industria cafetera: Antioquia, 1975–80*. Medellín: C. Valencia.

Arbix, Glauco Antônio Truzzi. 1995. "Uma aposta no futuro." Ph.D. diss., Universidade de São Paulo.

Arellano, José Pablo. 1981. "Elementos para el análisis de la reforma previsional chilena" [Elements for analysis of the forecast Chilean (social security) reform]. *Colección Estudios Cieplan*, no. 6, 5–44.

Arnold, Walter. 1989. "Bureaucratic Politics, State Capacity, and Taiwan's Automobile Industrial Policy." *Modern China* 15 (April), 178–214.

Arrow, Kenneth. 1974. *The Limits of Organization*. New York: Norton.

Arslan, I. 1993. "A Review of Turkish Incentive Systems." Washington, D.C.: World Bank, December 10.

Arthur, Brian W. 1990. "Positive Feedbacks in the Economy." *Scientific American*, February, 92–99.

Balassa, B. 1978. "Export Incentives and Export Performance in Developing Countries." *Weltwirtschaftliches Archiv* 114, 1.

———. 1981. "The Process of Industrial Development and Alternative Development Strategies." In *The Newly Industrializing Countries in the World Economy*, ed. Bela A. Balassa. New York: Pergamon.

Banco Central de Chile. 1992a. *Boletín mensual* [Monthly bulletin], March. Santiago.

———. 1992b. *Informe económico y financiero al 31 de mayo de 1992* [Economic and financial report to May 31, 1992]. Santiago: Gerencia de División de Estudios.

Banco de México. Various years. *Indicadores económicos* [Economic indicators].

Baptista, Asdrúbal. 1993. *Bases cuantitativas de la economía venezolana, 1830–1989* [Quantitative bases of the Venezuelan economy]. Caracas: María de la Mase.

Barros, José Roberto Mendonça de, and Gesner Oliveira. 1992. "Condicionantes e obstáculos à abertura comercial" [Contingencies and obstacles to commercial opening]. *Revista Brasileira de Comércio Exterior* 8 (April–June), 56–59.

Bartell, Ernest, and Leigh Payne. 1994. *Business and Democracy in Latin America*. Pittsburgh: University of Pittsburgh Press.

Barzelay, Michael. 1986. *The Politicized Market Economy*. Berkeley: University of California Press.

Bates, Robert H. 1987. "Contra Contractarianism: Some Reflections on the New Institutionalism." *Politics and Society* 16 (September), 387–401.

———. Forthcoming. *Politics, Trade, and Development: Domestic Politics and International Trade in Coffee*. Princeton: Princeton University Press.

Bates, Robert H., and Anne O. Krueger, eds. 1993a. "Generalizations Arising from the Country Studies." In *Political and Economic Interactions in Economic Policy Reform*, ed. Robert H, Bates and Anne O, Krueger. Oxford: Blackwell.

———. 1993b. *Political and Economic Interactions in Economic Policy Reform*. Oxford: Blackwell.

Becker, David. 1983. *The New Bourgeoisie and the Limits of Dependency*. Princeton: Princeton University Press.

Becker, Gary. 1983. "A Theory of Competition among Pressure Groups for Political Influence." *Quarterly Journal of Economics* 98 (August), 371–400.

Bennett, Douglas, and Kenneth Sharpe. 1985. *Transnational Corporations versus the State.* Princeton: Princeton University Press.

Berle, Adolph, Jr., and Gardiner C. Means. 1967. *The Modern Corporation and Private Property.* New York: Harcourt Brace & World.

Berry, Jeffrey. 1989. "Subgovernments, Issue Networks, and Political Conflict." In *Remaking American Politics,* ed. Richard Harris and Sidney Milkis. Boulder: Westview.

Beyer, R. 1947. "The Colombian Coffee Industry: Origins and Major Trends, 1740–1940." Ph.D diss., University of Minnesota.

Bhagwati, Jagdish N. 1982. "Directly Unproductive, Profit-Seeking (DUP) Activities." *Journal of Political Economy* 90 (October), 988–1002.

Bianchi, R. 1984. *Interest Groups and Political Development in Turkey.* Princeton: Princeton University Press.

Biddle, Jesse, and Vedat Milor. 1995. "Institutional Influences on Economic Policy in Turkey: A Three Industry Comparison." Occasional Paper no. 3. Washington, D.C.: Private Sector Development Department, World Bank.

Biggs, Tyler. 1991. "Heterogeneous Firms and Efficient Financial Intermediation in Taiwan." In *Markets in Countries: Parallel, Fragmented and Black,* ed. Michael Roemer and Christine Jones. San Francisco: ICS Press.

Biggs, Tyler, and Brian D. Levy. 1991. "Strategic Interventions and the Political Economy of Industrial Policy in Developing Countries." In *Reforming Economic Systems in Developing Countries,* ed. Dwight H. Perkins and Michael Roemer. Cambridge: Harvard University Press.

Blank, David Eugene. 1973. *Politics in Venezuela.* Boston: Little, Brown.

Bolton, P. 1990. "Renegotiation and the Dynamics of Contract Design." *European Economic Review* 34, 303–10.

Bowman, John R. 1989. *Capitalist Collective Action.* New York: Cambridge University Press.

Boylan, Delia. 1996. "Taxation and Transition: The Politics of the 1990 Chilean Tax Reform." *Latin American Research Review* 31, no. 1, 7–32.

Bozkurt, O. 1980. *Functionaries: A Sociological Perspective in Turkish Public Bureaucracy.* Ankara: Turkey and Middle East Public Policy Research Institute, University of Ankara.

Bresser Pereira, Luiz Carlos. 1974. *Empresários e administradores no Brasil.* São Paulo: Brasilense.

——. 1989. "Da crise fiscal à redução da dívida." In *Dívida externa,* ed. Luiz Carlos Bresser Pereira. São Paulo: Brasilense.

——. 1992. *A crise do estado.* São Paulo: Nobel.

——. 1993. "Economic Reforms and Economic Growth." In *Economic Reforms in New Democracies,* ed. Luiz Carlos Bresser Pereira, José María Maravall, and Adam Przeworski. Cambridge: Cambridge University Press.

Brimble, Peter. 1994. "Industrial Development and Productivity Change in Thailand." Ph.D. diss., Department of Economics, Johns Hopkins University.

Brimble, Peter, and Chatri Sripaipan. 1994. *Science and Technology Issues in Thailand's Industrial Sector: The Key to the Future.* Bangkok: For the Asian Development Bank.

Brock, Philip L., ed. 1992. *If Texas Were Chile: A Primer on Banking Reform.* San Francisco: ICS Press.

Brown, Ian. 1988. *The Elite and the Economy in Siam, c. 1890–1920*. Singapore: Oxford University Press.

Brunetti, Aymo, and Beatrice Weder. 1994. "Political Credibility and Economic Growth in Less Developed Countries." *Constitutional Political Economy* 5, no. 1, 23–43.

Bualek, Panee. 1986. *Wikhraw naithun thanakan panith khong Thai phaw saw, 2475–2516* [Analysis of Thai commercial banking capitalists, 2475–2516] Bangkok: Social Science Research Institute, Chulalongkorn University.

Buchanan, James M., R. Tollison, and G. Tullock, eds. 1980. *Toward a Theory of the Rent-Seeking Society*. College Station: Texas A&M University Press.

Buğra, A. 1994. *State and Business in Modern Turkey*. Albany: State University of New York Press.

Calder, Kent. 1989. "Elites in an Equalizing Role." *Comparative Politics* 21 (July), 379–404.

———. 1993. *Strategic Capitalism: Private Business and Public Purpose in Japanese Industrial Finance*. Princeton: Princeton University Press.

Camp, Roderic Ai. 1989. *Entrepreneurs and Politics in Twentieth-Century Mexico*. New York: Oxford University Press.

Campero, Guillermo. 1984. *Los gremios empresariales en el período 1973–1983* [Business organizations in the period 1973–1983]. Santiago de Chile: ILET.

———. 1991. "Entrepreneurs under the Military Regime." In *The Struggle for Democracy in Chile, 1982–1990*, ed. Paul W. Drake and Iván Jaksic. Lincoln: University of Nebraska Press.

Campero, Guillermo, and José A. Valenzuela. 1984. *El movimiento sindical en el régimen militar chileno, 1973–1981* [The union movement during the Chilean military government, 1973–1981]. Santiago de Chile: ILET.

Campos, Ed. 1993. "Insulation Mechanisms and Public Sector–Private Sector Relations." Part 1 of *The Institutional Foundations of High-Speed Growth in the High-Performing Asian Economies*. Washington, D.C.: World Bank.

Cardoso, Eliana. 1991. "Deficit Finance and Monetary Dynamics in Brazil and Mexico." *Journal of Development Economics* 37 (November), 173–97.

Cardoso, Fernando Henrique, and Enzo Faletto. 1979. *Dependency and Development in Latin America*. Berkeley: University of California Press.

Carnoy, Martin. 1984. *The State and Political Theory*. Princeton: Princeton University Press.

Centeno, Miguel Angel. 1994. *Democracy within Reason*. University Park: Pennsylvania State University Press.

Centro de Estudios del Desarrollo. 1985. *Concertación social y democracia* [Social pacts and democracy]. Santiago: CED.

Chang, Chan-Sup. 1988. "*Chaebol*: The South Korean Conglomerates." *Business Horizons* 31 (March–April), 51–57.

Chang, Ha-Joon. [1990?] "Interpreting the Korean Experience: Heaven or Hell?" University of Cambridge Research Paper 42.

Chelliah, Raja. 1971. "Trends in Taxation in Developing Countries." *IMF Staff Papers*, July.

Cheng, Tun-jen. 1990. "Political Regimes and Developmental Strategies: South Korea and Taiwan." In *Manufacturing Miracles: Paths of Industrialization in Latin America and East Asia*, ed. Gary Gereffi and Donald Wyman. Princeton: Princeton University Press.

———. 1993. "Guarding the Commanding Heights: The State as Banker in Taiwan." In *The Politics of Finance in Developing Countries*, ed. Stephan Haggard, Chung H. Lee, and Sylvia Maxfield. Ithaca: Cornell University Press.

Chenvidyakarn, Montri. 1979. "Political and Economic Influence: A Studies of Associations in Thailand." Ph.D. diss., University of Chicago.

Cho, Mun-boo. 1992. "Analyzing State Structure: Japan and South Korea in Comparative Perspective." *Pacific Focus* 7 (Fall), 161–74.

Choi, Byung-Sun. 1993. "Financial Policy and Big Business in Korea: The Perils of Financial Regulation." In *The Politics of Finance in Developing Countries*, ed. Stephan Haggard, Chung H. Lee, and Sylvia Maxfield. Ithaca: Cornell University Press.

Choi, Jang-Jip. 1983. "Interest Conflict and Political Control in South Korea: The Labor Unions in Manufacturing Industries, 1961–1980." Ph.D. diss., University of Chicago.

Choonhavan, Kraisak. 1984. "The Growth of Domestic Capital and Thai Industrialization." *Journal of Contemporary Asia* 14, 135–46.

Christensen, Scott R. 1991. "The Politics of Democratization in Thailand: State and Society Since 1932." Unpublished background paper. Bangkok: Thailand Development Research Institute.

——. 1992. *Between the Farmer and the State: Towards a Policy Analysis of the Role of Agribusiness in Thai Agriculture.* Bangkok: Thailand Development Research Institute.

——. 1993. "Coalitions and Collective Choice: The Politics of Institutional Change in Thai Agriculture." Ph.D. diss., University of Wisconsin—Madison.

——. 1994. "Muddling toward a Miracle: Thailand and East Asian Growth." *TDRI Quarterly Review* 9 (June), 13–20.

Christensen, Scott R., and Areeya Boon-long. 1993. "Institutional Problems in Water Allocation: Challenges for New Legislation." *TDRI Quarterly Review* 8 (September), 3–8.

Christensen, Scott R., David Dollar, Amar Siamwalla, and Pakorn Vichyanond. 1993. "The Lessons of East Asia: Thailand: The Institutional and Political Underpinnings of Growth." Washington, D.C.: World Bank.

Christensen, Scott R., Amar Siamwalla, and Pakorn Vichyanond. 1992. "Institutional and Political Bases of Growth-Inducing Policies in Thailand." Draft prepared for "Legacies and Lessons," the World Bank project on the East Asian development experience. Bangkok: Thailand Development Research Institute.

Chu, Yun-han. 1989. "State Structure and Economic Adjustment in the East Asian Newly Industrializing Countries." *International Organization* 43 (Autumn), 647–62.

——. 1994a. "The Realignment of Business-Government Relations and Regime Transition in Taiwan." In *Business and Government in Industrializing Asia*, ed. Andrew MacIntyre. Ithaca: Cornell University Press.

——. 1994b. "The State and the Development of the Automobile Industry in South Korea and Taiwan." In *The Role of the State in Taiwan's Development*, ed. Joel D. Aberbach. Armonk, N.Y.: M. E. Sharpe.

Clifford, Mark L. 1994. *Troubled Tigers: Businessmen, Bureaucrats and Generals in South Korea.* Armonk, N.Y.: M. E. Sharpe.

Cline, William. 1991. "Mexico: Economic Reform and Development Strategy." *Exim Review* (Tokyo) (Fall), 1–44.

CNI (Confederação Nacional da Indústria). 1990. "Competitividade e estratégia industrial." Rio de Janeiro.

——. 1991, 1992. "Abertura comercial e estratégia tecnológica." Rio de Janeiro.

Cohen, Benjamin. 1996. "Phoenix Risen." *World Politics* 48 (January), 268–96.

Cohen, Joshua, and Joel Rogers. 1992. "Secondary Associations and Democratic Governance." *Politics and Society* 20 (December), 393–472.

Colander, David C., ed. 1984. *Neoclassical Political Economy: The Analysis of Rent-Seeking and DUP Activities*. Cambridge, Mass.: Ballinger.

Colclough, Christopher, and James Manor, eds. 1991. *States or Markets: Neoliberalism and the Development Policy Debate*. New York: Oxford University Press.

Cole, Allan B. 1967. "Political Roles of Taiwanese Entrepreneurs." *Asian Survey* 7 (September), 645–54.

Cole, David, and Princeton Lyman. 1971. *Korean Development*. Cambridge: Harvard University Press.

Coleman, James. 1988. "Social Capital and the Creation of Human Capital." *American Journal of Sociology* 94 (supplement), S95–S120.

———. 1990. *Foundations of Social Theory*. Cambridge: Harvard University Press.

Coles, J. 1993. "Reforming Agriculture: The Venezuelan Experience." Mimeo. Caracas.

Collier, Ruth Behrens, and David Collier. 1991. *Shaping the Political Arena*. Princeton: Princeton University Press.

Confederación de la Producción y Comercio. 1983. "Recuperación económica: Análisis y proposiciones" [Economic recovery: Analysis and policy recommendations]. Santiago de Chile, July.

Corden, W. M. 1967. "The Exchange Rate System and the Taxation of Trade." In *Thailand: Social and Economic Studies in Development*, ed. T. H. Silcock. Singapore: Donald Moore.

Córdoba, José. 1991. "Diez lecciones de la reforma económica en México" [Ten lessons of economic reform in Mexico]. *Nexos* 158 (February), 31–48.

Cukierman, Alex. 1980. "The Effects of Uncertainty on Investment under Risk Neutrality with Endogenous Information." *Journal of Political Economy* 88, no. 3, 462–75.

Cukierman, Alex, and Allan Meltzer. 1986. "A Positive Theory of Discretionary Policy, the Cost of Democratic Government and the Benefits of a Constitution." *Economic Inquiry* 24 (July), 367–88.

Cumings, Bruce. 1984. "The Origins and Development of the Northeast Asian Political Economy." *International Organization* 38 (Winter), 1–40.

———. 1987. "The Origins and Development of the Northeast Asian Political Economy: Industrial Sectors, Product Cycles and Political Consequences." In *The Political Economy of the New Asian Industrialism*, ed. Frederic Deyo. Ithaca: Cornell University Press.

Cushman, Jennifer W. 1993. *Fields from the Sea: Chinese Junk Trade with Siam during the Late Eighteenth and Early Nineteenth Centuries*. Ithaca: Cornell University Southeast Asia Program.

Dahse, Fernando. 1979. *El mapa de la extrema riqueza* [The map of extreme wealth]. Santiago: Aconcagua.

de la Cuadra, Sergio, and Salvador Valdés. 1992. "Myths and Facts about Instability in Financial Liberalization in Chile: 1974–1983." In *If Texas Were Chile*, ed. Philip L. Brock. San Francisco: ICS Press.

Derossi, Flavia. 1971. *The Mexican Entrepreneur*. Paris: Organization for Economic Cooperation and Development.

Destler, I. M. *Anti-Protection: Changing Forces in United States Trade Politics*. Washington, D.C.: Institute for International Economics.

Deyo, Frederic. 1984. "Export Manufacturing and Labor." In *Labor in the Capitalist World-Economy*, ed. Charles Bergquist. Beverly Hills, Calif.: Sage.

———. 1989. *Beneath the Miracle: Labor Subordination in the New Asian Industrialization.* Berkeley: University of California Press.

———, ed. 1987. *The Political Economy of the New Asian Industrialism.* Ithaca: Cornell University Press.

Deyo, Frederic, Richard Doner, and Karl Fields. 1993. "Industrial Governance in East and Southeast Asia." Paper presented at the Social Science Research Council Workshop on Industrial Governance, New York City, September.

Diniz, Eli. 1995. "Reformas económicas y democracia en el Brasil" [Economic reforms and democracy in Brazil]. *Revista Mexicana de Sociología* 57 (October–December), 61–94.

Dinsmoor, James. 1990. "Brazil." Washington, D.C.: Interamerican Development Bank.

Domhoff, G. William. 1970. *The Higher Circles.* New York: Vintage.

———. 1978. *The Powers That Be.* New York: Vintage.

Doner, Richard F. 1991. *Driving a Bargain: Automobile Industrialization and Japanese Firms in Southeast Asia.* Berkeley: University of California Press.

———. 1992. "Limits of State Strength: Toward an Institutionalist View of Economic Development." *World Politics* 44 (April), 398–431.

Doner, Richard F., and Anek Laothamatas. 1994. "The Political Economy of Structural Adjustment in Thailand." In *Voting for Reform: Political Liberalization, Democracy and Economic Adjustment*, ed. Stephan Haggard and Steven B. Webb. Oxford: Oxford University Press.

Doner, Richard F., and Ansil Ramsay. 1993. "Postimperialism and Development in Thailand." *World Development* 21, no. 5, 691–704.

Doner, Richard F., and Ben Ross Schneider. 1994. "Can Business Associations Contribute to Development and Democracy? An Apology with a Framework for Analysis in Developing Countries." Unpublished paper.

Doner, Richard F., and Daniel Unger. 1993. "The Politics of Finance in Thai Economic Development." In *The Politics of Finance in Developing Countries*, ed. Stephan Haggard, Chung H. Lee, and Sylvia Maxfield. Ithaca: Cornell University Press.

Dore, Ronald. 1983. "Goodwill and the Spirit of Market Capitalism." *British Journal of Sociology* 34 (December), 459–82.

Dornbusch, Rudiger. 1990. "Comment." In *Latin American Adjustment*, ed. John Williamson. Washington, D.C.: Institute for International Economics.

Dreifuss, René Armand. 1989. *O jogo da direita na nova república* [The play of the right in the new republic]. Petrópolis: Vozes.

Durand, F. 1982. *La década frustrada: Los industriales y el poder, 1970–80* [The unsuccessful decade: Industrialists and power, 1970–80]. Lima: DESCO and Centro de Estudios y Promoción de Desarrollo.

———. 1994. *Business and Politics in Peru: The State and the National Bourgeoisie.* Boulder: Westview.

Eckert, Carter J. 1990–91. "The South Korean Bourgeoisie: A Class in Search of Hegemony." *Journal of Korean Studies* 7 (November), 115–48.

Edwards, Sebastian, and Alejandra Cox-Edwards. 1987. *Monetarism and Liberalization: The Chilean Experiment.* Cambridge: Ballinger.

Eisenstadt, S. N., and Louis Roniger. 1980. "Patron-Client Relations As a Model of Structuring Social Exchange." *Comparative Studies in Society and History* 22 (January), 42–77.

Encaoua, David, and Alexis Jacquemin. 1982. "Organizational Efficiency and Monopoly Power." *European Economic Review* 19 (September), 25–51.

Ernst, Dieter, and David O'Connor. 1992. *Competing in the Electronics Industry: The Experience of Newly Industrializing Countries.* OECD Development Centre Study. Paris: OECD.

Escobar, Gustavo. 1984. "El laberinto de la economía" [The economic labyrinth]. In *El caso de Venezuela: Una ilusión de armonía* [The case of Venezuela: An illusion of harmony], ed. Moisés Naím and Ramón Piñango, Caracas: IESA.

Esping-Andersen, Gosta. 1990. *The Three Worlds of Welfare Capitalism.* Princeton: Princeton University Press.

Evans, Peter. 1979. *Dependent Development: The Alliance of Multinational, State, and Local Capital in Brazil.* Princeton: Princeton University Press.

——. 1982. "Reinventing the Bourgeoisie: State Entrepreneurship and Class Formation in Dependent Capitalist Development." *American Journal of Sociology* 88 (supplement), S210–47.

——. 1986. "A Generalized Linkage Approach to Recent Industrial Development in Brazil: The Case of the Petrochemical Industry, 1967–1979." In *Development, Democracy and the Art of Trespassing: Essays in Honor of Albert Hirschman,* ed. Alejandro Foxley, Guillermo O'Donnell, and Michael McPherson. Notre Dame: University of Notre Dame Press.

——. 1987. "Class, State, and Dependence in East Asia: Lessons for Latin Americanists." In *The Political Economy of the New Asian Industrialism,* ed. Frederic C. Deyo. Ithaca: Cornell University Press.

——. 1989. "Predatory, Developmental and Other Apparatuses: A Comparative Political Economy Perspective on the Third World State." *Sociological Forum* 4 (December), 561–86.

——. 1992. "The State as Problem and Solution: Predation, Embedded Autonomy and Structural Change." In *The Politics of Economic Adjustment,* ed. Stephan Haggard and Robert Kaufman. Princeton: Princeton University Press.

——. 1995. *Embedded Autonomy: States and Industrial Transformation.* Princeton: Princeton University Press.

Evans, Peter, and James Rauch. 1995. "Bureaucratic Structures and Economic Performance in Less Developed Countries." University of California, Berkeley/San Diego. Mimeo.

Evans, Peter, Dietrich Rueschemeyer, and Theda Skocpol. 1985. *Bringing the State Back In.* New York: Cambridge University Press.

Evans, Peter, and John D. Stephens. 1988. "Studying Development Since the Sixties: The Emergence of a New Comparative Political Economy." *Theory and Society* 17, 713–45.

Evers, H. D., and T. H. Silcock. 1967. "Elites and Selection." In *Thailand: Social and Economic Studies in Development,* ed. T. H. Silcock. Durham, N.C.: Duke University Press.

Fairclough, Gordon. 1993. "Missing Class." *Far Eastern Economic Review,* February 4, 25–26.

——. 1996. "Too Much Interest? Missteps Shake Confidence in Thai Central Bank." *Far Eastern Economic Review,* March 21, 61–62.

Fama, E. 1980. "Agency Problems and the Theory of the Firm." *Journal of Political Economy* 88, 288–305.

Fazenda, Ministério da. 1994. "Avaliação das câmaras setoriais." Brasilia. Mimeo.

Ferguson, Thomas. 1984. "From Normalcy to New Deal." *Industrial Organization* 38 (Winter), 41–94.

———. 1995. *The Golden Rule.* Chicago: University of Chicago Press.

Ffrench-Davis, Ricardo. 1981. "Orígen y destino de las exportaciones chilenas, 1865–1980" [Origin and destination of Chilean exports, 1865–1980]. *Notas Técnicas Cieplan,* no. 31, 1–56.

———. 1989. "El conflicto entre la deuda y el crecimiento en Chile: Tendencias y perspectivas" [The conflict between debt and growth in chile: Trends and prospects]. *Colección Estudios Cieplan,* no. 26, 61–89.

Fields, Karl J. 1989. "Trading Companies in South Korea and Taiwan: Two Policy Approaches." *Asian Survey* 29 (November), 1073–89.

———. 1995. *Enterprise and the State in Korea and Taiwan.* Ithaca: Cornell University Press.

Flamm, Kenneth. 1987. *Targeting the Computer.* Washington, D.C.: Brookings Institution.

———. 1988. *Creating the Computer.* Washington, D.C.: Brookings Institution.

Fleming, M. 1962. "Domestic Financial Policies under Fixed and Floating Exchange Rates." IMF Staff Papers 9. Washington, D.C.: IMF.

Fligstein, Neil. 1990. *The Transformation of Corporate Control.* Cambridge: Harvard University Press.

Fontaine, Arturo. 1988. *Los economistas y el presidente Pinochet* [The economists and President Pinochet]. Santiago: Zig-Zag.

Fox, Julia. 1992. "The Nexus between the State and the *Chaebol*: Bringing Class Back In." Paper presented at the Annual Meeting of the Association for Asian Studies, Washington, D.C., April 1992.

Foxley, Alejandro. 1983. *Latin American Experiments in Neoconservative Economics.* Berkeley: University of California Press.

Francés, Antonio. 1988. "Abundancia, confusión y cambio: El ambiente en que se desenvuelven las empresas y sus gerentes en Venezuela" [Abundance, confusion and change: The environment in which enterprises and their managers develop in Venezuela]. In *Las empresas venezolanas: Su gerencia* [Venezuelan enterprises: Their management], ed. Moisés Naím Caracas: IESA.

Frieden, Jeffry A. 1989. "Winners and Losers in the Latin American Debt Crisis: The Political Implications." In *Debt and Democracy in Latin America,* ed. Barbara Stallings and Robert Kaufman. Boulder: Westview.

———. 1991. *Debt Development, and Democracy: Modern Political Economy and Latin America, 1965–1985.* Princeton: Princeton University Press.

Friedland, Jonathan. 1989. "Seeds of Empire." *Far Eastern Economic Review,* April 20, 46–47.

Friedman, David. 1988. *The Misunderstood Miracle.* Ithaca: Cornell University Press.

Fukuyama, Francis. 1995. *Trust.* New York: Free Press.

Gabriel Valdés, Juan. 1989. *La escuela de los Chicago: Operación Chile* [The Chicago school: Operation Chile]. Buenos Aires: Zeta.

Galletta, Paulo. 1988. "A Exaustão do setor público e a desestatização." *Economia em Perspectiva,* no. 50 (September), 1–3.

Gambetta, Diego, ed. 1988. *Trust: Making and Breaking Cooperative Relations.* Cambridge, Mass.: B. Blackwell.

Garrett, Geoffrey, and Peter Lange. 1991. "Political Responses to Interdependence: What's 'Left' for the Left?" *International Organization* 45 (Autumn), 539–64.

Garrido N., Celso, ed. 1988. *Empresarios y estado en América Latina* [Business and the State in Latin America]. Mexico City: CIDE et al.

GATT. 1991. *Trade Policy Review Mechanism: Thailand.* Geneva: GATT Secretariat.

Geddes, Barbara. 1986. *Economic Development As a Collective Action Problem: Individual Interests and Innovation in Brazil.* Ann Arbor, Mich.: University Microfilms.

——. 1990. "Building State Autonomy in Brazil, 1930–1964." *Comparative Politics* 22, no. 2, 217–36.

Gereffi, Gary. 1995. "Industrial Upgrading, State Policies, and Organizational Innovation in East Asia." Paper prepared for the Association for Asian Studies meeting, Washington, D.C., April 6–9.

Gerlach, Michael L. 1992. *Alliance Capitalism.* Berkeley: University of California Press.

Gil Yepes, Antonio. 1981. *The Challenge of Venezuelan Democracy.* New Brunswick: Transaction.

Gold, Thomas B. 1981. "Dependent Development in Taiwan." Ph.D. diss., Harvard University.

——. 1986. *State and Society in the Taiwan Miracle.* Armonk, N.Y.: M. E. Sharpe.

Goodman, John, and Louis Pauly. 1993. "The Obsolescence of Capital Controls? Economic Management in an Age of Global Markets." *World Politics* 46 (October), 50–82.

Gourevitch, Peter. 1986. *Politics in Hard Times.* Ithaca: Cornell Unversity Press.

Granovetter, Mark. 1985. "Economic Action and Social Structure: The Problem of Embeddedness." *American Journal of Sociology* 91 (November), 481–510.

——. 1994. "Business Groups." In *The Handbook of Economic Sociology,* ed. Neil Smelser and Richard Swedberg. Princeton: Princeton University Press.

Grant, Wyn, and Wolfgang Streeck. 1985 "Large Firms and the Representation of Business Interests in the UK and West German Construction Industry." In *Organized Interests and the State,* ed. Alan Cawson. London: Sage.

GSD. 1993. *Activity Report* Jannary 1–December 31 [in Turkish].

Gülfidan, Sebnem. 1993. *Big Business and the State in Turkey: The Case of TUSIAD.* Istanbul: Bogazici University Press.

Haggard, Stephan. 1990. *Pathways from the Periphery.* Ithaca: Cornell University Press.

——. 1994. "Business, Politics and Policy in East and Southeast Asia." In *Business and Government in Industrializing Asia,* ed. Andrew MacIntyre. Ithaca: Cornell University Press.

——. 1995. "Democratic Institutions, Economic Policy, and Development." Unpublished paper.

Haggard, Stephan, and Robert Kaufman, eds. 1992. *The Politics of Economic Adjustment.* Princeton: Princeton University Press.

——. 1995. *The Political Economy of Democratic Transitions.* Princeton: Princeton University Press.

Haggard, Stephan, Chung Lee, and Sylvia Maxfield. 1993. *The Politics of Finance in Developing Countries.* Ithaca: Cornell University Press.

Haggard, Stephan, and Sylvia Maxfield. 1993. "Political Explanations of Financial Policy in Developing Countries." In *The Politics of Finance in Developing Countries,* ed. Stephan Haggard, Chung Lee, and Sylvia Maxfield. Ithaca: Cornell University Press.

——. 1996. "The Political Economy of Financial Internationalization in the Developing World." *International Organization* 50, no. 1, 35.

Haggard, Stephan, and Chung-In Moon. 1986. "Industrial Change and State Power." Paper presented at the Annual Meeting of the American Political Science Association, Washington D.C., August 27–31.

———. 1990. "Institutions and Economic Policy: Theory and a Korean Case Study." *World Politics* 42 (January), 210–37.

Haggard, Stephan, and Steven Webb, eds. 1994. *Voting for Reform.* New York: Oxford University Press.

Hagopian, Francis. 1986. "The Politics of Oligarchy: the Persistence of Traditional Elites in Contemporary Brazil." Ph.D. diss., Massachusetts Institute of Technology.

———. 1994. "Traditional Politics against State Transformation in Brazil." In *State Power and Social Forces: Domination and Transformation,* ed. Joel Migdal, Atul Kohli, and Vivienne Shue. New York: Cambridge University Press.

Hale, W. 1981. *The Political and Economic Development of Modern Turkey.* London: Croom Helm.

Hamilton, Clive. 1986. *Capitalist Industrialization in Korea.* Boulder: Westview.

Hamilton, Gary G., Marco Orru, and Nicole Woolsey Biggart. 1987. "Enterprise Groups in East Asia: An Organizational Analysis." *Shoken Keizai* [Financial economic review] 161 (September) 78–106.

Hamilton, Gary G., and Tony Waters. 1995. "Chinese Capitalism in Thailand: Embedded Networks and Industrial Structure." In *Corporate Links and Foreign Direct Investment in Asia and the Pacific,* ed. K. Y. Chen and Peter Drysdale. Pymble, Australia: HarperEducational.

Hamilton, Gary G., William Zeile, and Wan-Jin Kim. 1988. "The Network Structures of East Asian Economies." Program in East Asian Culture and Development, Working Paper Series, no. 8. Institute of Governmental Affairs, University of California, Davis.

Hardin, Russell. 1993. "The Street-Level Epistemology of Trust." *Politics and Society* 21 (December), 505–29.

Hart, Jeffrey. 1992. *Rival Capitalists: International Competitiveness in the United States, Japan, and Western Europe.* Ithaca: Cornell University Press.

Hastings, Laura. 1993. "Regulatory Revenge." In *The Politics of Finance in Developing Countries,* ed. Stephan Haggard, Chung Lee, and Sylvia Maxfield. Ithaca: Cornell University Press.

Hausmann, R. 1990. *Shocks externos y ajuste macroeconómico.* Caracas: Banco Central de Venezuela.

Heinz, John, Edward Laumann, Robert Nelson, and Robert Salisbury. 1993. *The Hollow Core: Private Interests in National Policy Making.* Cambridge: Harvard University Press.

Heper, M. 1976. "The Recalcitrance of the Turkish Public Bureaucracy to Bourgeois Politics: A Multi-Factor Political Stratification Analysis." *Middle East Journal* 30 (Autumn).

———. 1985. *The State Tradition in Turkey.* London: Eothen.

———. 1989. "Motherland Party Governments and Bureaucracy in Turkey, 1983–1988." *Governance* 2 (October).

———. 1991. "Interest Group Politics in Post-1980 Turkey: Lingering Monism." In *Strong State and Economic Interest Groups: The Post-1980 Turkish Experience,* ed. M. Heper. Berlin. New York: Walter de Gruyter.

Heper, M., et al. 1980. "The Role of Bureaucracy and Regime Types." *Administration and Society* 12 (August), 137–57.

Heredia, Blanca. 1996. "Contested State: The Politics of Trade Liberalization in Mexico." Ph.D. diss., Columbia University.

Herschberg, Eric. Forthcoming. "Market-Oriented Development Strategies and State-Society Relations in New Democracies: Lessons from Contemporary Chile and

Spain." In *The New Politics of Inequality in Latin America*, ed. Douglas Chalmers, Scott B. Martin, and Kerianne Piester. New York: Oxford University Press.

Hewison, Kevin. 1987. "National Interests and Economic Downturn: Thailand." In *Southeast Asia in the 1980s: The Politics of Economic Crisis*, ed. Richard Robinson, Kevin Hewison, and Richard Higgott. Boston: Allen & Unwin.

———. 1989. *Bankers and Bureaucrats: Capital and the Role of the State in Thailand*. New Haven: Yale University, Southeast Asian Studies.

Hillier, Brian, and James M. Malcomson. 1984. "Dynamic Inconsistency, Rational Expectations, and Optimal Government Policy." *Econometrica* 52 (November), 1437–51.

Hirschman, Albert O. 1970. *Exit, Voice, and Loyalty*. Cambridge: Harvard University Press.

———. 1971. *A Bias for Hope*. New Haven: Yale University Press.

———. 1977. "A Generalized Linkage Approach to Development, with Special Reference to Staples." *Economic Development and Cultural Change* 25 (supplement), 67–97.

———. 1978. "Exit, Voice, and the State." *World Politics* 31 (October), 90–107.

Hirst, Paul, and Jonathan Zeitlin. 1991. "Flexible Specialization Versus Post-Fordism: Theory, Evidence and Policy Implications." *Economy and Society* 20 (February), 1–56.

Hollingsworth, J. Rogers, and Leon Lindberg. 1985. "The Governance of the American Economy: The Role of Markets, Clans, Hierachies and Associative Behavior." In *Private Interest Government: Beyond Market and State*, ed. Wolfgang Streeck and Philippe C. Schmitter. Beverly Hills, Calif.: Sage.

Hollingsworth, J. Rogers, Philippe Schmitter, and Wolfgang Streeck, eds. 1994. *Governing Capitalist Economies*. New York: Oxford University Press.

Hong, Lysa. 1984. *Thailand in the Nineteenth Century: Evolution of the Economy and Society* Singapore: Institute of Southeast Asian Studies.

Hsiao, Michael Hsin-huang. 1993. "The Political Economy of State-Business Relations in Taiwan. *Acta Oeconomica* 45, nos. 1–2, 145–72.

Hurtado, Carlos. 1988. *De Balmaceda a Pinochet: Cien años de desarrollo y subdesarrollo en Chile, y una disgresión al futuro* [From Balmaceda to Pinochet: One hundred years of development and underdevelopment in Chile and a digression on the future]. Santiago: Logo.

Hutchcroft, Paul D. 1993. "Selective Squander: The Politics of Preferential Credit Allocation in the Philippines." In *The Politics of Finance in Developing Countries*, ed. Stephan Haggard, Chung Lee, and Sylvia Maxfield. Ithaca: Cornell University Press.

———. 1996. "Corruption's Obstructions: Assessing the Impact of Rents, Corruption, and Clientelism on Capitalist Development in the Philippines." Paper presented at the annual meetings of the Association for Asian Studies, Honolulu.

IDB [Inter-American Development Bank]. 1992. *Economic and Social Progress in Latin America*. Washington, D.C.

IESP [Instituto de Estudos do Setor Público]. 1993. "Indicadores IESP," December.

Ilkin, S. 1991. "Exporters: Favored Dependency?" In *Strong State and Economic Interest Groups: The Post-1980 Turkish Experience*, ed. M. Heper. Berlin/New York: Walter de Gruyter.

Ingram, James C. 1971. *Economic Growth in Thailand, 1850–1970*. Stanford: Stanford University Press.

Interamerican Development Bank. 1993. *Towards Effective Social Policy in Venezuela*. Pilot Mission on Socioeconomic Reform of the Interamerican Development Bank, September.

Jensen, M., and W. Meckling. 1976. "Theory of the Firm: Managerial Behavior, Agency Costs and Ownership Structure." *Journal of Financial Economics* 3, 306–60.

Johnson, Chalmers A. 1974. "The Reemployment of Retired Government Bureaucrats in Japanese Big Business." *Asian Survey* 14 (November), 953–65.

——. 1982. *MITI and the Japanese Miracle*. Stanford: Stanford University Press.

——. 1987. "Political Institutions and Economic Performance: The Government-Business Relationship in Japan, South Korea and Taiwan." In *The Political Economy of the New Asian Industrialism*, ed. Frederic Deyo. Ithaca: Cornell University Press.

Johnson, Stephen. 1993. "Promises, Promises." *Manager*, September, 27–32.

Jones, LeRoy. 1980. *Jae-Bul and the Concentration of Economic Power in Korean Development*. Consultant Paper Series no. 12. Seoul: Korea Development Institute.

——. 1987 [1980]. "Jaebul and the Concentration of Economic Power in Korean Development." In *Macroeconomic Policy and Industrial Development Issues*, ed. Il Sakong. Seoul: Korean Development Institution.

Jones, LeRoy, and Il Sakong. 1980. *Government, Business, and Entrepreneurship in Economic Development: The Korean Case*. Cambridge: Harvard University Press.

Jung, Ku-hyun. 1988. "Business-Government Relations in the Growth of Korean Business Groups." *Korean Social Science Journal* 14 (April), 77–82.

Junguito, R., ed. 1978. *Economía cafetera colombiana*. Bogotá: Fedesarrollo and Fondo Cultural.

Junguito, R., and Pizano, D., eds. 1993. *El comercio exterior y la política internacional del café*. Bogotá: Fondo Cultural Cafetero and Fedesarrollo.

Kahler, Miles. 1992. "External Influence, Conditionality, and the Politics of Adjustment." In *The Politics of Economic Adjustment*, ed. Stephan Haggard and Robert Kaufman. Princeton: Princeton University Press.

Kalaycioğlu, E. 1991. "Commercial Groups: Love-Hate Relationship with the State." In *Strong State and Economic Interest Groups: The Post-1980 Turkish Experience*, ed. M. Heper. Berlin/New York: Walter de Gruyter.

Kandori, M. 1992. "Social Norms and Community Enforcement." *Review of Economic Studies* 59, 63–80.

Kang, David. 1995. "South Korea and Taiwanese Development and the New Institutional Economics." *International Organization* 49 (Summer), 555–87.

Kaosa-ard, Mingsarn Santikarn. 1992. "Manufacturing Growth: A Blessing for All?" In *Thailand's Economic Structure: Toward's Balanced Development?* Bangkok: Thailand Development Research Institute.

Katzenstein, Peter J. 1978. "Introduction." In *Between Power and Plenty*, ed. Peter J. Katzenstein. Madison: University of Wisconsin Press.

——. 1984. *Corporatism and Change: Austria, Switzerland, and the Politics of Industry*. Ithaca: Cornell University Press.

——. 1985a. "Small Nations in an Open International Economy: The Converging Balance of State and Society in Switzerland and Austria." In *Bringing the State Back In*, ed. Peter Evans, Dietrich Rueschemeyer, and Theda Skocpol. Cambridge: Cambridge University Press.

——. 1985b. *Small States in World Markets*. Ithaca: Cornell University Press.

Kaufman, Robert, Carlos Bazdresch, and Blanca Heredia. 1994. "Mexico: Radical Reform in a Dominant Party System." In *Voting for Reform*, ed. Stephan Haggard and Steven Webb. New York: Oxford University Press.

Kim, Chuk-Kyo. 1985. "Industrial Growth and Productivity Trends in Korea." In *Essays in Memory of Sang Chul Suh*. Seoul: Korea University Press.

Kim, Dong Ki, and Chon W. Kim. 1989. "Korean Value Systems and Managerial Practices." In *Korean Managerial Dynamics*, ed. Kae H. Chung and Hak Chong Lee. New York: Praeger.

Kim, Eun Mee. 1988. "From Dominance to Symbiosis: State and Chaebol in Korea." *Pacific Focus* 3 (Fall), 105–21.

Kim, Hyuk-Rae. 1992. "State and Economic Organization: Divergent Organizational Paths of Industrialization in East Asia." Ph.D. diss., University of Washington.

Kim, Jungsae. 1975. "Recent Trends in the Government's Management of the Economy." In *Korean Politics in Transition*, ed. Edward Wright. Seattle: University of Washington.

Kim, Kwang Suh, and Michael Roemer. 1980. *Growth and Structural Transformation*. Cambridge: Harvard University Press.

Kim, Kyong-Dong. 1976. "Political Factors in the Formation of the Entrepreneurial Elite in South Korea." *Asian Survey* 16 (May), 465–77.

Kim, Sookon. 1982. "Employment, Wages and Manpower Policies in Korea." Working Paper Series no. 82-04. Seoul: Korea Development Institute.

Kingstone, Peter. 1994. "Shaping Business Interests." Ph.D. diss., University of California, Berkeley.

Kirk, Donald. 1994. *Korean Dynasty: Hyundai and Chung Ju Yung*. Armonk, N.Y.: M. E. Sharpe.

Kitschelt, Herbert. 1991. "Industrial Governance Structures, Innovation Strategies, and the Case of Japan." *International Organization* 45 (Autumn), 453–93.

——. 1994. "Austrian and Swedish Social Democrats in Crisis." *Comparative Political Studies* 27 (April), 3–39.

Korea Exchange Bank. 1980. *Monthly Review*, November and December.

KOTRA [Korean Traders Association]. 1992. *Major Statistics of Korean Economy, 1992*. Seoul.

Krueger, Anne O. 1974. The Political Economy of the Rent-Seeking Society." *American Economic Review* 64 (June), 291–303.

——. 1980. "Trade Policy as an Input to Development." *American Economic Review* 70, no. 2, 288–92.

Krugman, Paul R., ed. 1986. *Strategic Trade Policy and the New International Economics*. Cambridge: MIT Press.

——. 1990. *Rethinking International Trade*. Cambridge: MIT Press.

Kuo, Cheng-Tian. 1990. "Economic Regimes and National Performance in the World Economy: Taiwan and the Philippines." Ph.D. diss., University of Chicago.

——. 1994. "Private Governance in Taiwan." Paper presented at the annual meetings of the Midwest Political Science Association, Chicago.

Kurzer, Paulette. 1993. *Business and Banking: Political Change and Economic Integration in Western Europe*. Ithaca: Cornell University Press.

Lal, D. 1983. *The Poverty of Development Economics*. London: IEA.

Landa, Janet T. 1991. "Culture and Entrepreneurship in Less-Developed Countries: Ethnic Trading Networks As Economic Organizations." In *The Culture of Entrepreneurship*, ed. Brigitte Berger. San Francisco: ICS Press.

Laothamatas, Anek. 1992. *Business Associations and the New Political Economy of Thailand: From Bureaucratic Polity to Liberal Corporatism*. Boulder: Westview.

——. 1994. "From Clientelism to Partnership: Business-Government Relations in Thailand." In *Business and Government in Industrializing Asia*, ed. Andrew MacIntyre. Ithaca: Cornell University Press.

Lee, Chung H. 1992. "The Government, Financial System and Large Private Enterprises in the Economic Development of South Korea." *World Development* 20, 187–97.

Leff, Nathaniel H. 1964. "Economic Development through Bureaucratic Corruption." *American Behavioral Scientist*, November, 9–14.

———. 1968. *Economic Policy-Making and Development in Brazil, 1947–1964*. New York: Wiley.

———. 1978. "Industrial Organization and Entrepreneurship in the Developing Countries." *Economic Development and Cultural Change* 26 (July), 661–75.

———. 1979. "Entrepreneurship and Economic Development: The Problem Revisited." *Journal of Economic Literature* 17, 46–64.

———. 1986. "Trust, Envy, and the Political Economy of Industrial Development: Economic Groups in Developing Countries." Unpublished paper, Columbia University.

Lemarchand, René. 1979. "The Politics of Penury in Rural Zaire: The View from Bandundu." In *Zaire: The Political Economy of Underdevelopment*, ed. Guy Gran. New York: Praeger.

Leonard, David K. 1977. *Reaching the Peasant Farmer: Organization Theory and Practice in Kenya*. Chicago: University of Chicago Press.

Lerman, Arthur J. 1977. "National Elite and Local Politicians in Taiwan." *American Political Science Review* 71 (December), 1406–22.

Li, K. T. 1988. *Economic Transformation of Taiwan*. London: Shepheard-Walwyn.

Lindblom, Charles. 1984. "The Market As Prison." In *The Political Economy*, ed. T. Ferguson and J. Rogers. Armonk, N.Y.: M. E. Sharpe.

Liu, Alan P. L. 1987. *Phoenix and the Lame Lion: Modernization in Taiwan and Mainland China, 1950–1980*. Stanford: Hoover Institution Press.

Lodge, George. 1989. "Roles and Relationships of Business and Government." *Business in the Contemporary World*, Winter, 93–108.

Lohmann, Susanne, and Sharyn O'Halloran. 1994. "Divided Government and U.S. Trade Policy: Theory and Evidence." *International Organization* 48 (Autumn), 595–633.

Lorenz, Edward. 1993. "Flexible Production Systems and the Social Construction of Trust." *Politics and Society* 21 (September), 307–25.

Loriaux, Michael. 1991. *France after Hegemony: International Change and Financial Reform*. Ithaca: Cornell University Press.

Loveman, Brian. 1991. "¿Misión cumplida? Civil-Military Relations and the Chilean Political Transition." *Journal of Interamerican Studies and World Affairs* 33, no. 3, 35–74.

Lustig, Nora. 1992. *Mexico*. Washington, D.C.: Brookings Institution.

Lyman, Princeton. 1975. "Economic Development in South Korea." In *Korean Politics in Transition*, ed. Edward Wright. Seattle: University of Washington Press.

MacIntyre, Andrew, ed. 1994. *Business and Government in Industrialising Asia*. Ithaca: Cornell University Press.

Mackie, J. A. C. 1992. "Changing Patterns of Chinese Big Business in Southeast Asia." In *Southeast Asian Capitalists*, ed. Ruth McVey. Ithaca: Cornell University Southeast Asia Program.

Mahon, James. 1994. "Capital Flight and the Triumph of Liberal Economics in Latin America." Williams College. Mimeo.

Malpica, C. 1968. *Los dueños del Perú*. 3d ed. Lima: Ensayos Sociales.

Mansbridge, Jane. 1992. "A Deliberative Perspective on Neocorporatism." *Politics and Society* 20 (December), 493–505.

Martin, Juan M. F. 1988. "Interaction between the Public and Private Sectors and the Overall Efficiency of the Economy." *CEPAL Review* 36 (December), 101–16.

Martz, John D., and David J. Myers, eds. 1977. *Venezuela: The Democratic Experience.* New York: Praeger.

Mason, Edward, et al. 1980. *The Economic and Social Modernization of the Republic of Korea.* Cambridge: Harvard University Press.

Mason, Edward S., Mahn Je Kim, Dwight H. Perkins, Kwang Suk Kim, and David C. Cole. 1981. *Studies in the Modernization of the Republic of Korea: 1979–81.* Cambridge: Harvard University Press.

Maxfield, Sylvia. 1989. "National Business, Debt-Led Growth and Political Transition in Latin America." In *Debt and Democracy in Latin America,* ed. Barbara Stallings and Robert Kaufman. Boulder: Westview.

——. 1990. *Governing Capital.* Ithaca: Cornell University Press.

——. 1994, 1995. "The Politics of Central Banking in Developing Countries." Unpublished manuscript, Yale University.

Maxfield, Sylvia, and James Nolt. 1990. "Protectionism and the Internationalization of U.S. Capital." *International Studies Quarterly* 34, 49–81.

McVey, Ruth. 1992. "The Materialization of the Southeast Asian Entrepreneur." In *Southeast Asian Capitalists,* ed. Ruth McVey. Ithaca: Cornell University Southeast Asia Program.

Meaney, Constance Squires. 1994. "State Policy and the Development of Taiwan's Semiconductor Industry." In *The Role of the State in Taiwan's Development,* ed. Joel D. Aberbach. Armonk, N.Y.: M. E. Sharpe.

Metroeconomía. 1993. "Mensajes para ejecutivos." [Messages for executives]. February.

Mills, C. Wright. 1956. *The Power Elite.* London: Oxford University Press.

Milner, Helen V. 1988. *Resisting Protectionism.* Princeton: Princeton University Press.

Ministry of Industry and Trade. 1991. *Turkey: Economic and Industrial Report.* Ankara: Ministry of Industry and Trade.

Miyamoto, Matao. 1988. "The Development of Business Associations in Prewar Japan." In *Trade Associations in Business History,* ed. Hiroaki Yamazaki and M. Miyamoto. Tokyo: University of Tokyo Press.

Mizala, Alejandra. 1985. "Liberalización financiera y quiebra de empresas industriales: Chile, 1977–82" [Financial liberalization and bankruptry of industrial firms: Chile, 1977–82]. *Notas Técnicas Cieplan* 67 (January), 1–40.

Mody, Ashoka. 1990. "Institutions and Dynamic Comparative Advantage: The Electronics Industry in South Korea and Taiwan." *Cambridge Journal of Economics* 14, 291–314.

Moe, Terry M. 1980. *The Organization of Interests.* Chicago: University of Chicago Press.

——. 1984. "The New Economics of Organization." *American Journal of Political Science* 28 (November), 739–77.

Moncada, S. 1995. "Entrepreneurs and Governments in Venezuela, 1944–1958." D.Phil. thesis, University of Oxford.

Moon, Chung-In. 1994. "Changing Patterns of Business-Government Relations in South Korea." In *Business and Government in Industrializing Asia,* ed. Andrew Macintyre. Ithaca: Cornell University Press.

Moon, Chung-In, and Rashemi Prasad. 1993. "Beyond the Developmental State: Institutions, Networks and Politics." Paper presented at the meeting of the American Political Science Association, Washington.

Moran, Theodore H. 1974. *Multinational Corporations and the Politics of Dependence.* Princeton: Princeton University Press.

Morawetz, David. 1981. *Why the Emperor's New Clothes Are Not Made in Colombia.* New York: Oxford University Press.

Morell, David L. 1974. "Power and Parliament in Thailand: The Futile Challenge." Ph.D. diss., Woodrow Wilson School, Princeton University.

Mueller, Dennis. 1989. *Public Choice II.* Cambridge: Cambridge University Press.

Mundell, R. 1963. "Capital Mobility and Stabilization Policy under Fixed and Flexible Exchange Rates." *Canadian Journal of Economics and Political Science* 29 (November), 475–85.

———. 1968. *International Economics.* New York: Macmillan.

Muscat, Robert J. 1990. *Thailand and the United States: Development, Security, and Foreign Aid.* New York: Columbia University Press.

———. 1994. *The Fifth Tiger: A Study of Thai Development Policy.* Armonk, N.Y.: M. E. Sharpe.

Naím, Moisés. 1984. "La empresa privada en Venezuela: ¿Qué pasa cuando se crece en medio de la riqueza y la confusión?" [Private enterprise in Venezuela: What happens when it grows amid wealth and confusion?]. In *El caso de Venezuela: Una ilusión de armonía* [The case of Venezuela: An illusion of harmony], ed. Moisés Naím and Ramón Piñango. Carases: IESA.

———. 1988. "El crecimiento de las empresas privadas venezolanas: Mucha diversificación, poca organización" [The growth of Venezuelan private firms: Much diversification, little organization]. In *Las empresas venezolanas: Su gerencia.* [Venezuelan companies: Their management], ed. Moisés Naím. Caracas: IESA.

———. 1993. "The Launching of Radical Policy Changes, 1989–1991." In *Venezuela in the Wake of Radical Reforms,* ed. Joseph Tulchin with Gary Blan. Boulder: Lynne Rienner.

Nelson, Douglas. 1989. "Endogenous Tariff Theory." *American Journal of Political Science* 32 (August), 796–837.

Nelson, Joan, ed. 1990. *Economic Crisis and Policy Choice.* Princeton: Princeton University Press.

———. 1994. "Labor and Business in Dual Transitions." In *Intricate Links,* ed. Joan Nelson. Washington, D.C.: ODC.

Noble, Gregory W. 1987. "Contending Forces in Taiwan's Economic Policymaking: The Case of Hua Tung Heavy Trucks." *Asian Survey* 27 (June), 683–704.

Nordlinger, Eric A. 1981. *On the Autonomy of the Democratic State.* Cambridge: Harvard University Press.

North, D. C. 1990. *Institutions, Institutional Change and Economic Performance.* Cambridge: Cambridge University Press.

North, D. C., and Barry W. Weingast. 1989. "The Evolution of Institutions Governing Public Choice in 17th-Century England." *Journal of Economic History* 49, 803–32.

Numazaki, Ichiro. 1991. "The Role of Personal Networks in the Making of Taiwan's *Guanxiqiye* (Related Enterprises)." In *Business Networks and Economic Development in East and Southeast Asia,* ed. Gary Hamilton. Hong Kong: Center for Chinese Studies, University of Hong Kong.

O'Brien, Philip. 1983. *The Pinochet Decade.* London: Latin American Bureau.

Ocampo, J. A., and E. Reveiz. 1979. "Bonanza cafetera y economía concertada" [Coffee bonanza and planned economy]. *Desarrollo y Sociedad* 2 (July), 231–55.

327

Ockey, James Sorin. 1992. "Business Leaders, Gangsters and the Middle Class: Societal Groups and Civilian Rule in Thailand." Ph.D. diss., Cornell University.

O'Donnell, Guillermo. 1978. "Reflections on the Patterns of Change in the Bureaucratic- Authoritarian State." *Latin American Research Review* 13, 3–38.

———. 1979. "Tensions in the Bureaucratic-Authoritarian State and the Question of Democracy." In *The New Authoritarianism in Latin America*, ed. David Collier. Princeton. Princeton University Press.

Offe, Claus, and Helmut Wiesenthal. 1980. "Two Logics of Collective Action." *Political Power and Social Theory* 1, 67–115.

Ogle, George. 1981. "South Korea." In *International Handbook of Industrial Relations*, ed. Albert Blum. Westport, Conn.: Greenwood.

Okimoto, Daniel I. 1989. *Between MITI and the Market: Japanese Industrial Policy for High Technology.* Stanford: Stanford University Press.

Oks, Daniel, and Sweder van Wijnbergen. 1993. "Mexico in the International Financial System." In *Mobilising International Investment for Latin America*, ed. Colin Bradford. Paris: OECD.

Olson, Mancur, Jr. 1965. *The Logic of Collective Action.* Cambridge: Harvard University Press.

———. 1982. *The Rise and Decline of Nations.* New Haven: Yale University Press.

———. 1993. "Dictatorship, Democracy, and Development." *American Political Science Review* 87 (September), 567–76.

Öncü, A. 1980. "Chambers of Industry in Turkey: An Inquiry into State-Industry Relations As a Distributive Domain." In *The Political Economy of Income Distribution in Turkey*, ed. E. Ozbodun and A. Ulusan. New York: Holmes and Meier.

Öniş, Ziya. 1991. "The Logic of the Developmental State." *Comparative Politics* 24, no. 1, 109–26.

———. 1992. "Organization of Export-Oriented Industrialization: The Turkish Foreign Trade Companies in Comparative Perspective." In *The Economics and Politics of Turkish Liberalization*, ed. T. Nas and M. Odekan. Bethlehem, Penn.: Lehigh University Press.

Öniş, Ziya, and Steven B. Webb. 1994. "Turkey: Democratization and Adjustment from Above." In *Voting for Reform: Democracy, Political Liberalization, and Economic Adjustment*, ed. Stephan Haggard and Steven B. Webb. New York: Oxford University Press.

Oshima, Harry. 1971. "Labor-Force 'Explosion' and the Labor-Intensive Sector in Asian Growth." *Economic Development and Cultural Change* 19 (January), 161–83.

Ostrom, Elinor. 1990. *Governing the Commons.* Cambridge: Cambridge University Press.

Paige, Jeffrey. 1987. "Coffee and Politics in Central America." In *Crises in the Caribbean Basin*, ed. Richard Tardanico. Beverly Hills, Calif.: Sage, 141–89.

Palacios, M. 1979. *El café en Colombia, 1850–1970: Una historia económica, social y política.* Bogotá: Presencia.

Pang, Chien-kuo. 1992. *The State and Economic Transformation: The Taiwan Case.* New York: Garland.

Park, Chong-Hee. 1962. *Our Nation's Path: Ideology for Social Reconstruction.* Seoul: Dong-A.

Park, Moon Kyu. 1987. "Interest Representation in South Korea: The Limits of Corporatist Control." *Asian Survey* 27 (August), 903–17.

Pastor, Manuel. 1990. "Capital Flight from Latin America." *World Development* 18 (January), 1–18.

Payne, Leigh. 1994. *Brazilian Industrialists and Democratic Change.* Baltimore: Johns Hopkins University Press.

Perrow, Charles. 1990. "Economic Theories of Organization." In *Structures of Capital*, ed. S. Zukin and P. DiMaggio. Cambridge: Cambridge University Press.

Pfefferman, Guy, and Andrea Madarassy. 1992. "Trends in Private Investment in Developing Countries." Discussion Paper 16, International Finance Corporation, Washington, D.C.

Pindyck, Robert. 1993. "A Note on Competitive Investment under Uncertainty." *American Economic Review* 83 (March), 273–77.

Polanyi, Karl. 1944. *The Great Transformation*. Boston: Beacon.

———. 1957. *Trade and Market in the Early Empires*. Glencoe, Ill.: Free Press.

Poulantzas, Nicos. 1973. *Political Power and Social Classes*. London: NLB and Sheed & Ward.

Powell, Walter, and Laurel Smith-Doerr. 1994. "Networks and Economic Life." In *The Handbook of Economic Sociology*, ed. Neil Smelser and Richard Swedberg. Princeton: Princeton University Press.

Przeworski, Adam. 1985. *Capitalism and Social Democracy*. New York: Cambridge University Press.

Przeworski, Adam, and Michael Wallerstein. 1988. "Structural Dependence of the State on Capital." *American Political Science Review* 82 (March), 11–29.

Puga, Cristina. 1994. "La Participación empresarial en la negociación del TLC" [Business participation in the NAFTA negotiations]. Paper presented at the CLACSO conference "Empresarios y Estado," Mexico City, September.

Putnam, Robert D. 1993a. *Making Democracy Work: Civic Traditions in Modern Italy*. Princeton: Princeton University Press.

———. 1993b. "The Prosperous Community." *American Prospect* 13 (Spring), 35–42.

Raczynski, Dagmar. 1983. "Reformas al sector salud: Diálogos y debates" [Reforms in the health sector: Dialogues and debates]. *Colección Estudios Cieplan* 10, 5–44.

Ramos, Joseph. 1986. *Neoconservative Economics in the Southern Cone*. Baltimore: Johns Hopkins University Press.

Ramsay, Ansil. 1987. "The Political Economy of Sugar in Thailand." *Pacific Affairs* 60 (Summer), 248–70.

Ranis, Gustav. 1973. "Industrial Sector Labor Absorption." *Economic Development and Cultural Change* 21 (April), 387–408.

Reisen, Helmut. 1993. "Financial Opening and Capital Flows." In *Mobilising International Investment for Latin America*, ed. Colin Bradford. Paris: OECD.

Reynolds, Clark. 1992. "The Political Economy of Interdependence in the Americas." *Asian Journal of Economics and Social Studies* 11, no. 1, 1–39.

Rivera Ríos, Miguel Angel. 1992. *El nuevo capitalismo mexicano*. Mexico City: Era.

Rock, Michael. 1995. "Thai Industrial Policy: How Irrelevant Was It to Export Success?" *Journal of International Development* 7, no. 5, 745–57.

Rodrik, Dani. 1989. "Promises, Promises: Credible Policy Reform via Signalling." *Economic Journal* 99 (September), 756–72.

———. 1991. "Policy Uncertainty and Private Investment in Developing Countries." *Journal of Development Economics* 36 (October), 229–42.

———. 1994. "The Rush to Free Trade in the Developing World." In *Voting for Reform*, ed. Stephan Haggard and Steven Webb. New York: Oxford University Press.

Rodrik, Dani, and R. Zeckhauser. 1988. "The Dilemma of Government Responsiveness." *Journal of Policy Analysis and Management* 7 (Fall), 601–20.

Rogowski, Ronald. 1988. "Structure, Growth, and Power." In *Toward a Political Economy of Development*, ed. Robert H. Bates. Berkeley: University of California Press.

REFERENCES

——. 1989. *Commerce and Coalitions: How Trade Affects Domestic Political Alignments.* Princeton: Princeton University Press.

Romer, Paul. 1994. "The Origins of Endogenous Growth." *Journal of Economic Perspectives* 8 (Winter), 3–22.

Ros, Jaime. 1987. "Mexico from the Oil Boom to the Debt Crisis." In *Latin American Debt and the Adjustment Crisis,* ed. Rosemary Thorp and Laurence Whitehead. London: Macmillan.

Rosenbluth, Frances. 1989. *Financial Politics in Contemporary Japan.* Ithaca: Cornell University Press.

Roxborough, Ian. 1992. "Inflation and Social Pacts in Brazil and Mexico." *Journal of Latin American Studies* 24, 639–64.

Rozas, Patricio, and Gustavo Marín. 1989. *El mapa de la extrema riqueza: 10 años después la* [The map of extreme wealth: Ten years later]. Santiago: América.

Rueschemeyer, Dietrich, and Peter Evans. 1985. "The State and Economic Transformation: Toward an Analysis of the Conditions Underlying Effective Intervention." In *Bringing the State Back In,* ed. Peter B. Evans, Dietrich Rueschemeyer, and Theda Skocpol. New York: Cambridge University Press.

Rueschemeyer, Dietrich, Evelyne Huber Stephens, and John D. Stephens. 1992. *Capitalist Development and Democracy.* Chicago: University of Chicago Press.

Ruiz-Tagle, Jaime. 1985. *El sindicalismo chileno después del plan laboral* [The union movement in Chile after labor sector reform]. Santiago: PET.

Sabel, Charles. 1992. "Studied Trust." In *Industrial Districts and Local Economic Regeneration,* ed. F. Pyke and W. Sengenberger. Geneva: ILO.

——. 1994. "Learning by Monitoring: The Institutions of Economic Development." In *The Handbook of Economic Sociology,* ed. Neil Smelser and Richard Swedberg. Princeton: Princeton University Press.

Salgado, René. 1987. "Economic Pressure Groups and Policy-Making in Venezuela: The Case of FEDECAMARAS Reconsidered." *Latin American Research Review* 22, no. 3, 91–105.

Samuels, Richard J. 1987. *The Business of the Japanese State: Energy Markets in Comparative and Historical Perspective.* Ithaca: Cornell University Press.

Saxenian, Annalee. 1994. *Regional Networks.* Cambridge: Harvard University Press.

Schmitter, Philippe C. 1971. *Interest Conflict and Political Change in Brazil.* Stanford: Stanford University Press.

——. 1974. "Still the Century of Corporatism?" *Review of Politics* 36 (January), 85–121.

——. 1988. "Sectors in Modern Capitalism: Modes of Governance and Variation in Performance." Paper presented at the Conference on Markets, Institutions, and Corporations: Labour Relations and Economic Performance, Venice, October 20–22.

Schmitz, Hubert, and Bernard Musyck. 1994. "Industrial Districts in Europe: Policy Lessons for Developing Countries?" *World Development* 22, no. 6, 889–910.

Schneiberg, Marc, and J. Rogers Hollingsworth. 1991. "Can Transaction Cost Economics Explain Trade Associations?" In *Political Choice,* ed. Roland Czada and Adrienne Windhoff-Héritier. Boulder: Westview.

Schneider, Ben R. 1989. "Partly for Sale." *Journal of Interamerican Studies and World Affairs* 30 (Winter), 89–116.

——. 1991a. "Brazil under Collor." *World Policy Journal* 8 (Spring), 321–47.

——. 1991b. *Politics within the State: Elite Bureaucrats and Industrial Policy in Authoritarian Brazil.* Pittsburgh: University of Pittsburgh Press.

——. 1993a. "The Career Connection: A Comparative Analysis of Bureaucratic Preferences and Insulation." *Comparative Politics* 25, no. 3, 331–50.

——. 1993b. "The Elusive Embrace: Synergy between Business and the State in Developing Countries." Paper presented at the workshop "The Role of Collaboration between Business and the State in Rapid Growth on the Periphery," Princeton University, October 8–9.

——. 1996. "The Material Bases of Technocracy: Investor Confidence and Neoliberalism in Latin America." In *Technocrats and the Politics of Expertise in Latin America*, ed. Miguel Centeno and Patricio Silva. Amsterdam: Amsterdam University Press.

——. Forthcoming. "Brazil's Disarticulated Bourgeoisie." In *Whither Brazil after Collor?* ed. Keith Rosenn. Miami: North-South Center.

Schvarzer, Jorge. 1994. "Grandes grupos económicos en la Argentina" [Large economic groups in Argentina]. Paper presented at the CLACSO conference "Empresarios y Estado," Mexico City, September.

Schwartz, Herman. 1994. "Small States in Big Trouble." *World Politics* 46 (July), 527–55.

SEAMICO. 1993. "Thailand's Economy at a Glance." Bangkok: SEAMICO Business Information and Research.

Shafer, D. Michael. 1994. *Winners and Losers: How Sectors Shape the Developmental Prospects of States*. Ithaca: Cornell University Press.

——. Forthcoming. *Sectors, States, and Social Forces: Toward a New Comparative Political Economy of Development*. Ithaca: Cornell University Press.

Shapiro, Helen. 1994. *Engines of Growth: The State and International Auto Companies in Brazil*. New York: Cambridge University Press.

Shapiro, Helen, and L. Taylor. 1990. "The State and Industrial Strategy." *World Development* 18 (June), 861–79.

Shieh, Gwo-Shyong. 1992. *"Boss" Island: The Subcontracting Network and Micro-Entrepreneurship in Taiwan's Development*. New York: Peter Lang.

Shin, Roy W. 1991. "The Role of Industrial Policy Agents: A Study of Korean Intermediate Organization As a Policy Network." *Pacific Focus* 6 (Fall), 49–64.

Shleifer, Andrei, and Robert W. Vishny. 1993. "Corruption." *Quarterly Journal of Economics* 108 (August), 599–617.

Siamwalla, Amar. 1975. "Stability, Growth and Distribution in the Thai Economy." In *Finance, Trade and Economic Development in Thailand*, ed. Prateep Sondysuvan. Bangkok: Sompong Press.

Silcock, T. H., ed. 1967. *Thailand: Social and Economic Studies in Development*. Durham, N.C.: Duke University Press.

Silva, Eduardo. 1993. "Capitalist Coalitions, the State, and Neoliberal Economic Restructuring in Chile, 1973–88." *World Politics* 45, no. 4, 526–59.

——. 1996. *The State and Capital in Chile: Technocrats, Business Elites and Market Economics*. Boulder: Westview.

——. Forthcoming. *Capitalist Coalitions and the State in the Neoliberal Transformation of Chile, 1973–1990*. Boulder: Westview.

Silva, Patricio. 1991. "Technocrats and Politics in Chile: From the Chicago Boys to the Cieplan Monks." *Journal of Latin American Studies* 23, no. 2, 385–410.

Skinner, G. William. 1957a. "Chinese Assimilation and Thai Politics." *Journal of Asian Studies* 16 (February), 237–50. Reprinted in *Southeast Asia: The Politics of National Integration*, ed. John T. McAlister. New York: Random House, 1973.

——. 1957b. *Chinese Society in Thailand: An Analytical History*. Ithaca: Cornell University Press.

———. 1958. *Leadership and Power in the Chinese Community of Thailand.* Ithaca: Cornell University Press.

Skocpol, Theda. 1985. "Bringing the State Back In." In *Bringing the State Back In,* ed. Peter B. Evans, Dietrich Rueschemeyer, and Theda Skocpol. New York: Cambridge University Press.

Smith, William; Carlos Acuña, and Eduardo Gamarra, eds. 1994. *Democracy, Markets, and Structural Reform in Latin America.* New Brunswick, N.J.: Transaction.

Smitka, Michael J. 1991. *Competitive Ties: Subcontracting in the Japanese Automotive Industry.* New York: Columbia University Press.

Sola, Lourdes. 1991. "Heterodox Shock in Brazil." *Journal of Latin American Studies* 23 (February), 163–95.

Soskice, David. 1991. "The Institutional Infrastructure for International Competitiveness." In *Economics for the New Europe,* ed. Anthony B. Atkinson and Renato Brunetta. International Economic Assn., vol. 104. Hampshire: Macmillan.

Sricharatchanya, Paisal. 1988. "The Jewels in the Crown." *Far Eastern Economic Review,* June 30, 60–62.

Stallings, Barbara. 1992. "International Influence on Economic Policy." In *The Politics of Economic Adjustment,* ed. Stephan Haggard and Robert Kaufman. Princeton: Princeton University Press.

Stallings, Barbara, and Philip Brock. 1993. "The Political Economy of Economic Adjustment: Chile, 1973–90." In *Political and Economic Interactions in Economic Policy Reform,* ed. Robert H. Bates and Anne O. Krueger. Oxford: Blackwell.

Stallings, Barbara, and Robert Kaufman, eds. 1989. *Debt and Democracy in Latin America.* Boulder: Westview.

Steers, Richard, Yoo Keun Shin, and Gerardo Ungson. 1989. *The Chaebol.* New York: Harper & Row.

Stewart, Douglas B., and Yiannis P. Venieris. 1985. "Sociopolitical Instability and the Behavior of Savings in Less-Developed Countries." *Review of Economics and Statistics* 67 (November), 557–63.

Stiglitz, Joseph E. 1993. "Some Lessons from the Asian Miracle." World Bank, mimeo.

Story, Dale. 1982. "Trade Politics in the Third World: A Case Study of the Mexican GATT Decision." *International Organization* 36 (Autumn), 767–94.

Streeck, Wolfgang. 1991. "Interest Heterogeneity and Organizing Capacity: Two Class Logics of Collective Action?" In *Political Choice,* ed. Roland Czada and Adrienne Windhoff-Héritier. Boulder: Westview.

Streeck, Wolfgang, and Philippe C. Schmitter. 1985. "Community, Market, State—And Associations?" In *Private Interest Governance,* ed. Wolfgang Streeck and Philippe C. Schmitter. London: Sage.

Suehiro, Akira. 1985. *Capital Accumulation and Industrial Development in Thailand.* Bangkok: Chulalongkorn University, Social Research Institute.

———. 1992. "Capitalist Development in Postwar Thailand: Commercial Bankers, Industrial Elite, and Agribusiness Groups." In *Southeast Asian Capitalists,* ed. Ruth McVey. Ithaca: Cornell University Southeast Asia Program.

Suh, Sang-Mok. N. d. "Development Strategies." Seoul: Korea Development Institute.

———. 1979. "The Patterns of Poverty in Korea." Working Paper no. 79-03. Seoul: Korea Development Institute.

Suh, Tai-Suk. 1975. "Import Substitution and Economic Development in Korea." Working Paper no. 75-19. Seoul: Korea Development Institute.

———. 1981. "Effects of Export Incentives on Korean Export Growth, 1953–79." Working Paper no. 81-07. Seoul: Korea Development Institute.

Suphachalasai, Suphat. 1992. "The Structure of the Textile Industry and Government Policy in Thailand." Bangkok: Thailand Devlopment Research Institute, Year-End Conference.

Sweeney, John. 1989. "Crisis de dirigencia" [Leadership crisis]. *Veneconomía* 6, no. 7, 1–3.

Taira, Koji, and Teiichi Wada. 1987. "Business-Government Relations in Modern Japan." In *Intercorporate Relations*, ed. Mark Mizruchi and Michael Schwartz. Cambridge: Cambridge University Press.

Tarre Briceño, Gustavo. 1993. "Opposition in Times of Change." In *Venezuela in the Wake of Radical Reforms*, ed. Joseph Tulchin. Boulder: Lynne Rienner.

Taub, Richard P. 1969. *Bureaucrats under Stress: Administrators and Administration in an Indian State*. Berkeley: University of California Press.

Taylor, Michael. 1990. "Cooperation and Rationality." In *The Limits of Rationality*, ed. Karen Cook and Margaret Levi. Chicago: University of Chicago Press.

Teitelboim, Berta. 1987. *Serie de indicadores económico sociales, 1960–1986* [Economic and Social indicators, 1960–1986]. Santiago: Programa de Economía y Trabajo.

Thanamai, Patcharee. 1985. "Patterns of Industrial Policymaking in Thailand: Japanese Multinationals and Domestic Actors in the Automobile and Electrical Appliance Industries." Ph.D. diss., University of Wisconsin, Madison.

Thorp, Rosemary. 1974. "The Klein Correspondence." Oxford University, mimeo.

———. 1991. *Economic Management and Economic Development in Peru and Colombia*. Pittsburgh: University of Pittsburgh Press.

Thorp, Rosemary, and Geoffrey Bertram. 1978. *Peru, 1890–1977: Growth and Policy in an Export Economy*. New York: Columbia University Press.

Thorp, Rosemary, and C. Londoño. 1984. "The Effect of the Great Depression on the Economies of Peru and Colombia." In *Latin America in the 1930s: The Role of the Periphery in World Crisis*, ed. Rosemary Thorp. New York: St. Martin's Press.

Toledo Neto, Celso de Campos. 1994. "Avaliação dos acordos setoriais automobilísticos." Master's thesis, Fundação Getúlio Vargas, São Paulo.

Tollison, Robert, and Roger Congleton, eds. 1995. *The Economic Analysis of Rent Seeking*. Aldershot, U.K.: Elgar.

Toro Hardy, José. 1992. *Venezuela, 55 años de política económica, 936–1991: Una utopía keynesiana* [Venezuela, 55 years of political economy, 1936–1991: A Keynesian utopia]. Caracas: Panapo.

United Nations Economic Commission for Latin America. 1966. *Economies of Scale in the Cotton Spinnning and Weaving Industry*, E/CN, 12/748.

United Nations Industrial Development Organization. 1969. *Industrialization of Developing Countries: Prospects and Problems, Textile Industry*. UNIDO Monograph on Industrial Development, no. 7, II.B.39. Vienna.

Useem, Michael. 1984. *The Inner Circle: Large Corporations and the Rise of Business Political Activity in the U.S. and U.K.* New York: Oxford University Press.

Vacs, Aldo. 1994. "Convergence and Dissension." In *Latin American Political Economy in the Age of Neoliberal Reform*, ed. William Smith, Carlos Acuña, and Eduardo Gamarra.

Valdés Ugalde, Francisco. 1994. "From Bank Nationalization to State Reform." In *The*

Politics of Economic Restructuring, ed. Maria Cook, Kevin Middlebrook, and Juan Molinar Horcasitas. San Diego: Center for U.S.-Mexican Studies.

Valenzuela, Arturo. 1991. "The Military in Power: The Consolidation of One-Man Rule." In *The Struggle for Democracy in Chile, 1982–1990,* ed. Paul W. Drake and Iván Jaksi. Lincoln: University of Nebraska Press.

Vásquez, E. 1995. "The Role, Origins and Strategies of Business Groups in Peru." D.Phil. thesis, Oxford University.

Verdier, Daniel. 1994. *Democracy and International Trade.* Princeton: Princeton University Press.

Vergara, Pilar. 1994. "Market Economy, Social Welfare, and Democratic Consolidation in Chile." In *Democracy, Markets, and Structural Reform in Latin America,* ed. William C. Smith, Carlos H. Acuña, and Eduardo A. Gamarra, New Brunswick, Transaction.

Wade, Robert. 1990. *Governing the Market: Economic Theory and the Role of Government in East Asian Industrialism.* Princeton: Princeton University Press.

———. 1992. "East Asia's Economic Success." *World Politics* 44 (January), 270–320.

Waller, Gordon. 1994. "Winds of Change." *Far Eastern Economic Review,* April 28, 64–66.

Wallerstein, Michael, and Adam Przeworski. 1995. "Capital Taxation with Open Borders." *Review of International Political Economy* 2, no. 3.

Warr, Peter G. 1993. *Thailand's Economic Miracle.* Thailand Information Papers. Canberra: Australian National University, National Thai Studies Center.

Waterbury, John. 1988. "Coalition-Building, Export-Led Growth and the Public Sector in Turkey." Paper prepared for "Dynamics of a Mixed Economy: The Turkish Case," at the annual meeting of the Middle East Studies Association, Los Angeles, November 2–6.

———. 1992. "The Heart of the Matter?" In *The Politics of Economic Adjustment,* ed. Stephan Haggard and Robert Kaufman. Princeton: Princeton University Press.

Weber, Max. 1968 [1904–11]. *Economy and Society.* Ed. Guenter Roth and Claus Wittich. New York: Bedminster Press.

Westphal, Larry. 1982. "The Private Sector as 'Principal Engine' of Development." *Finance and Development* 19, no. 2, 34–38.

Weyland, Kurt. 1992. "The Dispersion of Business Influence in Brazil's New Democracy." Unpublished paper, Vanderbilt University.

Whang, In-Joung. 1985. "The Role of Government in Economic Development in Korea during the Sixties and Seventies." In *Industrialization and Rural Change.* Seoul: Korea Development Institute.

Whitehead, Laurence. 1987. "The Adjustment Process in Chile: A Comparative Perspective." In *Latin American Debt and the Adjustment Crisis,* ed. Rosemary Thorp and Laurence Whitehead. Pittsburgh: University of Pittsburgh Press.

Williamson, John. 1990. *The Progress of Policy Reform in Latin America.* Washington, D. C: Institute for International Economics.

Williamson, John, and Stephan Haggard. 1994. "The Political Conditions for Economic Reform." In *The Political Economy of Policy Reform,* ed. John Williamson. Washington, D.C.: Institute for International Economics.

Williamson, Oliver. 1993. "Calculativeness, Trust, and Economic Organization." *Journal of Law and Economics* 36 (April), 453–502.

Wilson, David. 1962. *Politics in Thailand.* Ithaca: Cornell University Press.

Winters, Jeffrey. 1994. "Power and the Control of Capital." *World Politics* 46 (April), 419–52.

——. 1996. *Power in Motion: Capital Mobility and the Indonesian State*. Ithaca: Cornell University Press.

Wise, Carol. 1993a. "State Policy and Social Conflict in Peru." Claremont McKenna College, mimeo.

——. 1993b. "Trading Outward." Paper presented at the conference "The Collaboration between Business and the State in Rapid Growth," Princeton University, October.

Woo, Jung-en. 1991. *Race to the Swift: State and Finance in Korean Industrialization*. New York: Columbia University Press.

World Bank [IBRD]. 1987. *Korea: Managing the Industrial Transition*, vol. 1. Washington, D.C.

——. 1990. *Thailand Financial Study*, vol. 1. Report no. 8403-TH. Washington, D.C.

——. 1991. *World Development Report, 1991: The Challenge of Development*. New York: Oxford University Press.

——. 1993a. *The East Asian Miracle: Economic Growth and Public Policy*. A World Bank Policy Research Report. New York: Oxford University Press.

——. 1993b. *World Development Report, 1993*. New York: Oxford University Press.

——. 1994. *World Development Report, 1994*. New York: Oxford University Press.

Wriston, Walter B. 1992. *The Twilight of Sovereignty*. New York: Scribner's.

Yamazaki, Hiroaki, and M. Miyamoto, eds. 1988. *Trade Associations in Business History*. Tokyo: University of Tokyo Press.

Yoo, Sangjin, and Sang M. Lee. 1987. "Management Style and Practice of Korean Chaebols." *Californian Management Review* 29 (Summer), 95–110.

Zeitlin, Maurice, and Richard E. Ratcliff. 1988. *Landlords and Capitalists: The Dominant Class of Chile*. Princeton: Princeton University Press.

Zysman, John. 1983. *Governments, Markets, and Growth: Financial Systems and the Politics of Industrial Change*. Ithaca: Cornell University Press.

Index

337

Sylvia Maxfield is Associate Professor of Political Science at Yale University.

Ben Ross Schneider is Associate Professor of Political Science at the Center for International and Comparative Studies, Northwestern University.

Cornell Studies in Political Economy

EDITED BY PETER J. KATZENSTEIN